Global Development and Poverty Reduction

INTERNATIONAL INSTITUTIONS AND GLOBAL GOVERNANCE

Series Editors: John-ren Chen, *Professor of Economic Theory and Econometrics, Department of Economic Theory, Policy and History, Director of the Centre for the Study of International Institutions, University of Innsbruck, Austria* and David Sapsford, *Sir Edward Gonner Professor of Applied Economics, University of Liverpool, UK*

Titles in the series include:

Global Development and Poverty Reduction

The Challenge for International Institutions

Edited by

John-ren Chen

Professor of Economic Theory and Econometrics, Department of Economic Theory, Policy and History and Director of the Centre for the Study of International Institutions, University of Innsbruck, Austria

David Sapsford

Sir Edward Gonner Professor of Applied Economics and Head, Economics Division, University of Liverpool, UK

INTERNATIONAL INSTITUTIONS AND GLOBAL GOVERNANCE

Edward Elgar
Cheltenham, UK • Northampton, MA, USA

Published by
Edward Elgar Publishing Limited
Glensanda House
Montpellier Parade
Cheltenham
Glos GL50 1UA
UK

Edward Elgar Publishing, Inc.
136 West Street
Suite 202
Northampton
Massachusetts 01060
USA

A catalogue record for this book
is available from the British Library

Library of Congress Cataloguing in Publication Data

Global development and poverty reduction: the challenge for international
    institutions/edited by John-ren Chen and David Sapsford.
        p.   cm.
    Includes bibliographical references and index.
    1. Poverty—international cooperation. 2. Economic assistance.
    3. International agencies. 4. International economic relations.
    5. Globalization—Economic aspects. I. Chen, John-ren. II. Sapsford,
    David. III. Series.
    HC79.P6G66   2005
    338.91—dc22

                                                            2004062632

ISBN 1 84542 248 1

Typeset by Manton Typesetters, Louth, Lincolnshire, UK.
Printed and bound in Great Britain by MPG Books Ltd, Bodmin, Cornwall.

Contents

Contributors

Professor Syed M. Ahsan, Department of Economics, Concordia University, Canada.

Professor V.N. Balasubramanyam, Professor of Development Economics, Department of Economics, Lancaster University, UK.

Professor John-ren Chen, Professor of Economic Theory and Econometrics, Department of Economic Theory, Policy and History and Director of the Centre for the Study of International Institutions, University of Innsbruck, Austria.

Doctor Teofilo C. Daquila, Southeast Asian Studies Programme, National University of Singapore, Singapore.

Doctor Mirjana Dragičević, Faculty of Economics, University of Zagreb, Croatia.

Doctor Andreas Exenberger, Department of Economic Theory, Policy and History, University of Innsbruck, Austria.

Professor Kwan S. Kim, Professor of Economics and Policy Studies, Kellogg Institute for International Studies, University of Notre Dame, IN, USA.

Professor Sanjaya Lall, Queen Elizabeth House, Department of International Development, University of Oxford, UK.

Doctor Klaus Liebscher, Governor of the Austrian Central Bank – Oesterreichische Nationalbank, Austria.

Doctor Hakan Mihci, Department of Economics, Hacettepe University, Ankara, Turkey.

Doctor Sevinç Mihci, Department of Economics, Hacettepe University, Ankara, Turkey.

Ms Melania Nica, Department of Economics, Concordia University, Canada.

Doctor Stephan Pfaffenzeller, Lecturer in Economics, University of Liverpool, UK.

Professor Kunibert Raffer, Department of Economics, University of Vienna, Austria.

Professor David Sapsford, Sir Edward Gonner Professor of Applied Economics, Head, Economics Division, Management School, University of Liverpool, UK.

Professor Karl Socher, Emeritus Professor of Political Economy, Centre for the Study of International Institutions, University of Innsbruck, Austria.

Professor Alois Wenig, Faculty of Economics, Martin-Luther-Universität Halle Wittenberg, Germany.

Preface

At the beginning of the third millennium, underdevelopment and poverty continue to remain critical problems on a global scale. The purpose of this volume is to explore the various ways in which the institutions of the global economy might rise to the challenges posed by the twin goals of increasing the pace of global development and alleviating poverty.

The expert authors provide a much-needed analysis of the successes and failures of international institutions in achieving these aims, while at the same time providing important insights into the potential future paths that they might follow. Amongst other themes, the contributors investigate the design of international institutions for raising the standard of living in the developing world in order to achieve global development and stability. They also study particular institutions such as the IMF and the WTO to assess their effect on the growth performance of developing nations. In additional chapters, the authors study institutions and regional issues such as privatization and poverty in Russia, the Asian Financial Crisis and the role of the IMF, and the development crisis in sub-Saharan Africa.

This book offers a rigorous examination and informed discussion of the potential role of international institutions in the quest to alleviate poverty. Academics and professionals working in the fields of development studies, international economics and business management will welcome this stimulating book. It will also appeal to decision-makers involved in the formulation of trade, monetary and development policy.

We are indebted to the Oesterreichische Nationalbank (Austrian Central Bank) for the financial assistance to set up the Centre for the Study of International Institutions (CSI). We are very grateful to the Österreichische Forschungsgemeinschaft (Austrian Research Association) who supported our annual conference and the publication of this book. Also, we want to express our appreciation to the Tiroler Sparkasse Bank for sponsoring the Böhm-Bawerk Lecture.

Last but not least we are very much indebted to members of the Advisory Boards of the CSI, especially our friends Christian Smekal and Karl Socher (both at the University of Innsbruck), to Richard Hule and Herbert Stocker (University of Innsbruck), Hans Pichler (Economic University Vienna), John Toye (Oxford University) and Christian Keuschnigg (University of St Gallen) for their referee support to edit this book, and finally to Gudrun Eder (CSI, University of Innsbruck) as well as Helga Landauer for making the conference such a successful event.

John-ren Chen
Innsbruck

Introduction

Karl Socher

When the international institutions were created at the Bretton Woods conference at the end of World War II, the most important aims had been to help reconstruction after the war and to create a framework for economic stability, development and growth. Growth and development are necessary (but not sufficient) conditions for reducing poverty, so this aim had already been included in the goals of Bretton Woods institutions at their foundation. However, the aim of reducing poverty had not originally played the central role in the process of developing the strategies of the international institutions because it was believed that, included in the aim of reconstruction and development, economic growth in these war-torn and underdeveloped countries would be a basis to diminish both poverty and also the difference in per capita income between the poor and the rich countries. But in reality these aims have not been reached sufficiently. Therefore the issue of poverty reduction has risen to become a primary goal of international institutions.

The aim of the third CSI conference was to discuss the controversial questions raised by critical economists in academia and non-governmental organizations (NGOs) about the effective strategies for fighting poverty.

The contributions in this book are organized in three parts as follows:

1. The first part deals with general issues about the role of international institutions in economic growth and raising the standard of living in developing countries;
2. The second part looks into the role of particular international institutions in poverty reduction;
3. The third part deals with the role of international institutions in economic development and poverty reduction in the following regions: Eastern Europe, Russia, South-East Asia and the Sub-Sahara.

PART I: GENERAL ISSUES: INTERNATIONAL
INSTITUTIONS AND POVERTY

Chapter 1: Economic Development and Povery Reduction in the Developing World

In his first contribution John-ren Chen deals with the general problems of developing countries. Empirical evidence has shown that the performance of economic development has been better in countries which have integrated into the global economy, for instance, the Tiger states. International institutions have helped to liberalize cross-border trade in goods and services (GATT), to provide a sound global payments system and to create global capital markets (International Monetary Fund and World Bank). The provision of these global public goods, however, has been far from efficient. The liberalization of services is going on very slowly, and the international financial architecture is still vulnerable. Free trade in general is welfare-improving. However, the basic assumptions of neo-classical trade theory do not always exist in the real world: for instance, a lot of markets are not perfect, there is long-term unemployment, most adjustment processes such as transition problems are far from smooth, and the necessary compensation of the losers by the winners to justify the welfare gains of free trade (the compensation principle applied by neo-classical international economics to argue the superiority of free trade over autarky) is lacking in most cases. The volatility of primary commodities together with the deteriorating terms of trade is not solved, and crises are not only caused by external factors but partly by government failures or market failures.

Governments of sovereign states are mainly responsible for economic development. The international institutions can only carry out assistant functions to support governments of sovereign states to improve allocation of resources, to create and to reform the institutions, such as the rule of law for property rights and contract laws for the functioning of the market and the provisions for public goods, internalization of externalities and dealing with other market failures. However, there is no 'one-size-fits-all' development policy for the developing countries. Each country needs an individual therapy of development policy.

In the last section of his contribution the author deals with export processing zones – a development policy measure – as effective experiments for developing countries as well as transition countries to learn about the working of a market system.

Chapter 2: Raising the Standard of Living

In this chapter John-ren Chen comes to the conclusion that international institutions have to play a much more important role in raising the standard of living because there are still famines, poverty, denial of human rights, civil war, infectious diseases and so on.

He defines the standard of living as including not only the GDP per capita but also non-pecuniary circumstances for well-being, such as the length of life expectancy, health, education, human rights and political participation. To raise this standard of living, international institutions exist which specialize in fulfilling particular functions with respect to these indicators of the standard of living. These functions are complementary to each other. Therefore a higher efficiency of the measures of these institutions can be reached by a better coordination of international institutions. John-ren Chen then discusses the possibility of increasing the efficiency of measures of international institutions in the field of economic and non-economic factors by more efficient markets and providing global public goods:

- one of the most important economic factors would be the abolition of protectionism in agriculture. In an Appendix he proves the Singer thesis, that is, that protectionist measures deteriorate the terms of trade for the developing countries;
- security and peacekeeping by the UN;
- economic stability in goods and financial markets by GATT/WTO and IMF;
- production and use of knowledge, especially about good governance;
- humanitarian assistance: for instance, in famine relief by international emergency food reserves, or protection of human rights, for instance, by the creation of international courts;
- global health (avoidance of contagious diseases); and
- political stability and democracy as measures for avoiding crises, corruption and famine.

John-ren Chen closes with the statement that the task of the study of international institutions is especially to show what role they could fulfil and how this role is to be played in the development of the developing world.

Chapter 3: Growth and Stability as Challenges

The governor of the Austrian Nationalbank and governor in the IMF for Austria, Klaus Liebscher, describes the different elements of the strategy of international institutions to reduce poverty: the UN Millenium Development

Goals with their eight key areas, the partnership for development of the international conference on Financing for Development (Monterrey 2002) and the efforts of the IMF and WB with the Poverty Reduction Strategy and special measures for debt relief for the Highly Indebted Poor Countries. With these strategies, the IMF approach to low-income countries changed by launching the Poverty Reduction and Growth Facility, making poverty reduction a key objective. These initiatives of the Fund have become an integral part of the efforts of other international institutions such as the World Bank. These new approaches include more collaboration with the governments of the poor countries in designing the strategies for their better governance and best practices by donor countries under the guidance of the OECD Development Aid Committee (DAC).

A main part of the paper deals with the importance of financial stability for the reduction of poverty. Poor countries, and especially the poor part of their population, are hit more than developed countries by financial crises. Some progress has been achieved by international cooperation and international institutions to overcome crises and also to prevent future crises. Cooperation between the Fed and the ECB prevented a major crisis after September 11. The Financial Stability Forum was created in 1999 and the IMF is devoting an increasing amount of resources to crisis prevention. There has been a shift in the strategy of crisis prevention by the IMF. Mistakes had been made at the time of the Asian crises – mistakes in the assessment of sovereign debts, and hasty capital liberalization before a good supervision of banks and capital markets existed – and the role of flexible exchange rates as a measure of shock absorption has been neglected. Today, the Financial Sector Assessment Program together with the World Bank draws up profiles of the strength and weaknesses of the financial sector of a country. Standards for better statistics, transparency rules and supervisory standards are promoted by this programme. But one initiative which was started by the IMF has still not been realized: the author pleads for an international treaty which would facilitate the orderly resolution of sovereign debt crises. He ends optimistically: there will still be overshooting and its correction in the financial markets in the future, but this should become rarer and less severe by means of these measures.

Chapter 4: Industrialization

In the Böhm-Bawerk Lecture Sanjaya Lall deals with the problems of industrializing the poor countries in the globalized world based on his work for UNIDO's *Industrial Development Report*. He sees a cumulative and structural process of a growing wedge between a few successful countries and a large number of others. The cause lies in the problems of unevenly distributed immobile assets, which are necessary for developing, attracting the basis for developing: skills, work discipline, technological competence, supplier clusters, infrastructure and administrative capabilities. Developing countries as a group are doing well in the important arena of manufacturing exports and even – unexpected in theory – in high-technology exports! However, on the regional and on the country level there is a high concentration on a few successful countries, for instance, the East Asian nations on the one hand and Sub-Saharan Africa on the other, or Mexico in the Latin Americas. Also, contrary to neo-liberal theories, the author finds much evidence that government intervention has existed in the successful countries: selective interventions in most markets to guide resource allocations, for instance, FDIs, developing national capabilities, such as skills and R&D, and take-over of new technologies. Up to now, there has been the autonomous way, developing R&D and drawing-in of foreign technology, and the alternative, using FDI and transnational companies in the labour extensive products sector. For the future, however, there may be many 'roads to heaven' for the poor countries, and the same successful strategies may not necessarily be repeated. The developing countries need new, focused and intelligent strategies which have to be industry-specific, so that the strategy of the key players in each value chain becomes important for the integration of the global value chains.

Chapter 5: Ability, Failures and Proposals for Reforms

In a similar way to other contributors, Andreas Exenberger defines development as including economic as well as political and social elements. The role of international institutions is analysed according to the theory of Douglass North, who stresses the importance of adaptation of their rules, because it is necessary to adapt the institutions for changing conditions. By using the formulation of four different levels of social analysis by Oliver Williamson he distinguishes the level of the institutional environment (the constitutions and bureaucracy) and of the governance of this given framework for their implementation.

The empirical failure of the institutions in the last 40 years is analysed by a cluster analysis for the different elements of economic, social and political development. This analysis shows the break between the 'Northern' and the 'Southern' clusters, but no cluster for all dimensions. He distinguishes four groups: the advanced, the well developing, the developing and the non-developing countries (one-fifth of the total). The role of international institutions has been small or negligible in the examples of an extra-ordinary development – such as in China – and important in the countries of non-development. This is the starting point for his proposals for reforms:

- the UN should act as a governing body for the coordination to avoid transaction costs and duplication or even contradictions between the different institutions;
- more democracy: not only 'one vote–one state' but also double majorities (vote weight for population size);
- a change of rules for more participation of the whole community of states and NGOs;
- more precise definition of tasks (for example, what constitutes a market failure), and more transparency for reducing uncertainty and transaction costs;
- criteria for good governance, and independent tribunals with retaliations and reparation payments;
- some criteria should be handled as flexibly as possible, and incentives for improvements in human development should be added;
- stabilization of export revenues and relief for debt burdens; and
- more aid, even with a moderate form of global taxation.

The author is aware of the fact that these proposals are paradigmatic and therefore will take time. What is needed desperately is more legitimacy of the organizations and a clear distinction between the groups of countries. The non-developing countries do not need credits. The 'Washington consensus' is inadequate for their needs: they need grants and help. The developing group needs supervised credits and assistance. There should be a clear distinction between the agencies dealing with the different groups guided by an overall framework. However – in the sense of Williamson – it is not the organizations that are to blame for the bad performance of development, but the underlying institutions, which may have been appropriate for the post-war period, but which now have to be changed. A global discussion about this reform is necessary.

Chapter 6: IMF Lending and Freedom Effects

In their chapter Sevinç and Hakan Mihci test empirically whether the volume of IMF credits and loans and economic and political freedom have a positive influence on growth and therefore development. In their model they test these two relations for 34 countries.

The result for the IMF credits and loans is the same as in many other previous studies: there is a negative relation between the volume of credits and loans and growth performance. This can be explained by the demand-restrictive influence of IMF-adjustment programmes, which compensated the positive influence of credits and loans on investment. However, the authors admit that it may be possible in the long run that the effect of higher investment on productivity yields a positive effect on growth.

The effect of economic freedom is found to be positive for growth, consistent with other previous studies. It is more important in middle-income countries. As an explanation for this fact they offer the thesis that improvements of economic freedom become effective only above some threshold level.

The result of the test of the influence of political freedom on growth is inconsistent with other studies: the authors do not find a positive impact. An explanation for this inconsistency may be that the panel of countries in their test includes only those countries which repeatedly got credits and loans from the IMF.

The authors conclude that the IMF does not seem to be playing a role in the improvement of the welfare levels of developing countries by means of providing loans and credits. This conclusion may be challenged with the argument that the Fund today has other tasks which may be more important for developing countries than credits and loans.

PART II: PARTICULAR INTERNATIONAL INSTITUTIONS AND POVERTY

Chapter 7: WTO Membership

After a review of the literature about the economic benefits of joining the WTO David Sapsford, V.N. Balasubramanyam and Stephan Pfaffenzeller develop an analytical framework for an evaluation. They apply this framework for an estimation of the possible benefits and costs of joining the WTO for Taiwan, which became a member in 2002. The analytical framework suggests that an increase in trade flows is neither a necessary nor a sufficient condition for a benefit in terms of growth. If the competitive advantages persist, Taiwan will experience a decline in heavy industry and the service sector, but gain in the non-heavy manufacturing sector. However, it cannot be assumed, as in the standard trade models, that the comparative advantages do not change by entering the WTO. And even when there is not a large benefit in terms of improved real incomes, the membership gives the participating countries an orderly rule-based process offering certainty and transparency for trade.

Chapter 8: Critical Views on World Bank and IMF

Kunibert Raffer describes very critically the long historical process of developing the goal and the instruments for poverty reduction of the World Bank and the IMF, with many examples of ineffective and contra-productive measures.

It is clear that the goal of poverty reduction was not the original aim of the IMF and not the primary aim of the World Bank at their foundation. Gradually, however, this aim was becoming the prime goal of both institutions. Even the organizations themselves, for instance, the IMF, have admitted that there were many failures made to achieve this aim (see, for example, the contribution by Governor Klaus Liebscher in Chapter 3). But the two organizations have learnt a great deal. Also, there are still many suggestions (including those made in this book) to improve the efficiency of the institutions. In spite of this, Kunibert Raffer comes to the conclusion that both organizations are 'either unlikely to be really interested in fighting poverty or incapable of doing so'.

To give only one example of his arguments: he accuses the World Bank of having changed its strategy of evaluating projects from an economic cost–benefit method to a more subjective assessment in an attempt to immunize against accountability. However, the former cost–benefit analysis had even been criticized by economists, because more 'soft' criteria – for instance, social factors, democracy and gender questions – should be included which are more difficult to measure than economic factors.

He explains the divergence between the declaration of 'poverty reduction' and the activity to be a marketing device in a Parkinsonian survival strategy of the two organizations. 'If poverty reduction were indeed as dear a goal to the international community as various declarations … this important issue must not be left to the Bretton Woods institutions.' When he demands more grants and debt reductions – a demand which today comes from many countries – he leaves open the question as to whether the two existing institutions could be used for administering these measures. It is also left open as to whether the new function of these institutions as a 'think tank' or a 'knowledge bank' should be retained or not.

Chapter 9: Poverty in the Transformation Path

Mirjana Dragičević shows, in a similar way to former chapters, the failures made by international organizations in advising the transformation process, using the example of Croatia. The same failures had been made as in the transformation process of other countries: privatization too quickly, before a competition and regulatory framework was created; no awareness of the sequencing of the measures and of creating necessary institutions. These failures, together with the effects of the war, created a dramatic drop in the national income, but high rents for the elite and poverty for the masses. In a second stage in the transition some advice came from international institutions for building institutions. However, because they came from outside, the government was not open to a participatory process and raised barriers to change.

One may object that the international organizations did not have experience with a transformation process: they had not been created for this difficult task. Even economic theory did not offer prescriptions for an optimal transformation. Only in the last few years, have theory and international organizations learnt from their failures. These remarks are also applicable to the two following chapters, which deal with the role of international institutions in transformation regions.

PART III: INTERNATIONAL INSTITUTIONS AND REGIONAL ISSUES

Chapter 10: Transformation Regions

Syed Ahsan and Melania Nica examine the growth and poverty development in 18 countries in transformation between 1987 and 2000, and the influence of institutions (the 'institutional capital') on these two aspects. Their main findings are that institutions have a very important role in explaining growth, and that growth may be dampened by a rising inequality. The latter finding is different to the results of other studies, which assert the importance of growth for reducing poverty. The authors find that only early in the transition phase, up to 1995, did growth have an influence on poverty, together with the initial inequality.

The conclusions of their empirical research for policy reforms are that there is a need for:

- distribution-friendly growth;
- sustainable public transfer schemes, such as social insurance;
- efficient worker training incentives for skill acquisitions;
- the promotion of self-employment; and that
- public authorities should encourage initiatives by NGOs for local provision of educational and health services.

Chapter 11: Russian Privatization

Alois Wenig discusses the Russian privatization process, which had brought poverty to the masses and tremendous wealth to the few managers who were able to gain ownership of the state enterprises. It was not the intention of the privatization law, but the managers profited from the fast liberalization of foreign payments and a corporate law which did not give enough rights to the shareholders to control the company. The managers could therefore strip the assets of the company, transfer the wealth abroad, and buy the shares from the workers and the public at very low prices.

Wenig does not discuss the influence of international institutions, but it is known that they were in favour of a quick privatization with a 'shock-therapy' because it was believed that a gradual approach would not succeed: according to Wenig, there would have been permanent struggles over the 'right' direction. Wenig's opinion fits into the hypothesis that a newly created democracy is not capable of a gradual transformation, which could have avoided the hardships of the 'big bang'.

Chapter 12: Role of the IMF in the South-East Asian Crisis

Teofilo Daquila describes the Asian crisis of 1997/98 and then asks whether the IMF fulfilled its role in this crisis. As is well known and well documented today, the IMF made many mistakes: it had insisted on keeping the exchange rate fixed, liberalized capital flows too quickly, gave credits for bailing-out and replenished foreign currency reserves. The conditions of the credits were a restrictive fiscal policy – a cure which had been the right one for countries with high budget deficits, but not for the East-Asian countries. Malaysia, which weathered the crisis better than Indonesia because it did not follow the prescriptions of the IMF, introduced capital controls and an expansionary monetary policy.

Most of the author's five proposals for better management of future crises have already been accepted by the IMF: rethinking the exchange rate; improving regulatory standards; bailing-in the private sector; and (not lifting) capital controls (too fast). Only the proposal for the creation of an international lender of last resort is still under discussion.

Chapter 13: Development Crisis in Sub-Saharan Africa

Kwan Kim states that the African crisis has been caused as much or perhaps more by the internal factors related largely to poor governance by often corrupt African governments; however, the focus of his chapter is on the external factors. Africa has been more affected by the changing global environment than other countries. Not content with the role of the international institutions and their neo-liberal paradigms, the author's proposals for the role of international institutions begin with abolishing agricultural protectionism and subsidies. The institutions have to play a more active role in developing a competitive export sector. The second task is debt relief. Third, more aid should be given, concentrated on education and health. Finally, the international institutions should promote region-based economic cooperation. The author ends with the example of the East Asian countries, which were in a similar economic condition 40 years ago to Africa today. Therefore, he concludes that African recovery 'is not impossible'.

PART I

General issues: international institutions and poverty

1. The role of international institutions in economic development and poverty reduction in the developing world

John-ren Chen

I INTRODUCTION

In the current global community the per capita income of its approximately 200 countries is distributed very unequally, the per capita income of the richest country being more than 100 times that of the poorest country given in official exchange rates. Most countries of the globe are less developed countries (LDCs) and developing countries (DCs) with low per capita income. In this chapter the DCs and the LDCs are called 'the developing world' (DW) and the rest are called 'the industrialized world' (IW). More than half of the world population is living in countries with an annual per capita income of less than $700. More than five decades since the end of World War II politicians and social and economic scientists have expended much effort in proposing measures for improving economic development and reducing poverty, but without much success, especially in the LDCs. The global community is still confronted by serious poverty in the DW and unequal income distribution between the members of the IW and DW. More seriously, about two decades after the implementation of the Washington Consensus, about 1.2 billion people (or approximately 20 per cent of the world population) around the world are living on less than a dollar a day with more than 50 per cent of the global population living on less than two dollars a day. Therefore the need for economic development and poverty reduction in the DW, especially in the LDW, has lost none of its urgency over the past half-century. In this period experiences of DW have shown very different pictures. There are successful stories such as the 'Asian miracles'. But there are also countries whose economies remain in a low-level equilibrium trap without having achieved any economic progress for decades. Over the same period the mainstream economic policy changed from Keynesian interventionism to the 'Washington Consensus' which is a conglomerate of trade liberalization, privatization, deregulation and observance of the fiscal and monetary fundamentals.

International institutions such as the GATT (since 1995 the WTO), the IMF and the World Bank started to implement the globalization of economic activities by liberalizing cross-border trade, capital movement and investment in the 1980s. Following the collapse of the socialistic regimes in Eastern Europe the process of globalization has been extended to the transition countries. This change of paradigm has had important implications for development policy (of a DC) and global poverty reduction.

Over the very long period since the beginning of industrialization the picture of the distribution of per capita income between the countries in the IW and DW has not really changed, although some countries in the DW have caught up and become members of the IW. The different performances in the economic development therefore provide very interesting empirical material for the study of development economics. Both successful and failing experiences of the national development policy can give us very valuable input for the design of national economic development policy. Successful experiences of the outward-looking policy in several emerging market countries, especially the so-called 'Asian Tigers', have shown the relevance of international economic activities for good performance of economic development in the DW.

Eighty years of fiasco of the socialistic development policy in the former Soviet Union and the Eastern European socialist countries have been followed by implementing market economy in these countries and carrying out outward looking development policy. Economic development is a process of changing the economic structure to improve allocation of domestic resources (natural resources as well as capital and human resources, such as labour and human capital) in order to increase productivity of the economy under consideration. Higher productivity means higher rewards and higher material welfare for the owner of the factor, especially for labour. The main focus of development policy is how to carry out the optimal allocation of domestic resources, especially in the long run. Thus development policy in the first place is domestic policy in which the internal political economy has to play a dominant role. But this does not mean that international economic activities and international political economy are not important for development policy. On the contrary, they have to play a significant role in development policy, especially in the current globalizing world economy. Integration of a national economy in the global world economy can contribute mainly to improving allocation of its domestic resources and thus the process of economic development.

When we mention that development policy is in the first place a domestic policy we mean, first, that the national government is responsible for the performance of its national economic development with the goal to improve the standard of living of domestic inhabitants; and second, that the role of international institutions in development and poverty reduction of countries in the DW should be supporting development of the national economy through aid, providing global public goods (such as global security, global economic stability, knowledge and global environment) and enforcing international cooperation.

Summarizing the above discussion, the study of modern development economics should be a synthesis of the traditional development economics and international economics, and the policy of national economic development has to be designed within a context of special consideration of the role of international institutions. This chapter seeks to identify new challenges and also proposes new focuses for the study of modern development economics and poverty reduction under consideration in the global context. First, globalization has been a trend of the current world economy. Globalization will provide the DW with a chance to gain access to the worldwide global market, but it also means higher risks for the DW because of the weaknesses in its economic systems (such as bottlenecks and failing infrastructure) whose resolution is necessary for a well functioning market-oriented economy. While the chance of access to the global market may enhance economic development and improve welfare, the higher risk means that the economy will become more vulnerable. Therefore both opportunities chance and the risks of globalization have to be considered in designing an economic policy for sustainable development in the DW.

Second, perfect markets are efficient. But markets are only perfect if a series of necessary conditions or prerequisites are met; for instance, a system of rules and laws (property rights, contract law and so on). Such systems have the character of public goods and are not typically adequately provided resulting, for example, in a suboptimal infrastructure in the DW. Therefore, in order to make markets efficient for economic development in the DW, missing public goods have to be provided. They may be either regional or global public goods. Two kinds of public goods are needed for economic development in the DW: hardware public goods and software public goods. The infrastructure belongs to the first, while a system of laws and rules as well as a sound financial system, a social security system, the ability to enter the global market, the marketing know-how and the use of trade barriers, can be classified as software public goods. The list of inadequately provided public goods in the DW includes both hardware and software public goods. Additionally, there are many market failures because of externalities, asymmetric information or moral hazard and so on. How to provide the lacking public goods for a well functioning market system in the DW and how to correct these market failures are essential issues for modern development economics.

Third, global economic stability, which has been identified as a global public good, has been essential for the development of the world economy, especially for sustainable development and successful poverty reduction in individual DW states. Knowledge, especially in economics, is fundamental for designing a well functioning policy of economic development in the DW. Knowledge is a public good and, even more, as pointed out by Stiglitz (2000, p. 9), a global public good. A central part of the logic of global collective action is the provision of global public goods by the international institutions (see Chen, 2003, p. 7). The study of international institutions should therefore be an essential element of modern development economics.

In this chapter a main topic of discussion is the role of international institutions in development and poverty reduction of the countries in the DW. The phrase 'Asian Miracles' has been used in a World Bank publication to describe the economic performance of the East and Southeast Asian countries. Their outward looking development policy has been identified as a reason for their economic success and was recommended for low-income countries in the DW. A globally free trade regime and a sound international payment system have been seen as essential for the success of the outward looking development policy. International institutions, such as the GATT, have provided a system of rules to set up a global market for free trade. International institutions, such as the IMF and the Basle Accord, have played an essential role in promoting a sound international payment system. Thus international institutions like the FAO and the World Bank can play a very important role in economic development and poverty reduction in the DW.

International institutions can efficiently provide international public goods needed for economic development in the DW. An important question about the role of international institutions in economic development in the DW is which global and regional public goods have to be provided for successful development policy. Are the existing international institutions able to provide these public goods? Or will new international institutions have to be initiated?

This chapter is organized as follows. In sections II to IV we will discuss in detail the challenges faced by modern development economics, international economics as well as economics of international institutions. In section V the role of international institutions in the development of a national economy will be discussed. In section VI a popular development measure, the setting up of an export processing zone (or special economic zone), will be discussed. In the last section a short summary will be given.

II   A WORLD COMMUNITY WITH UNEQUALLY DEVELOPED MEMBERS

Winners and Losers from Globalization: Between and Within Countries

Globalization does not only produce winners but also losers, both between countries and within them. According to a World Bank Policy Research Report (2002), globalization has mostly reduced inequality between countries. During the 1990s, the group of the DW grew 5 per cent per capita on average compared to 2 per cent for the IW. Between 1993 and 1998, the number of absolute poor declined by 120 million according to the World Bank report. (ibid., p. 2). Within countries, following the Stolper–Samuelson theorem, owners of relatively rich (poor) endowment factors will be winners (losers) from globalization. Even that globalization has not affected the inequality on average.

The unequal income distribution between countries reflects the similarly unequal factor endowments between them. According to the theory of comparative advantage, international trade will improve resource allocation and therefore also have a positive effect on the material well-being of the global community in general. This essential proposition of international trade theory gives the fundamental reasoning for free trade and thus for economic globalization.

Following the fundamental welfare improvement proposition of free trade in the neoclassical international trade theory, 'Free trade could in general improve (or in limiting case not deteriorate) welfare of the global community and the trading countries in the sense that through free trade every individual could be made better off (or in the limiting case, no worse off) ... Free trade – given the usual assumptions – necessarily makes available to the community as a whole a greater physical real income in the form of more of all commodities and ... shall result in more of every commodity for every class of the community' (Viner, 1937, p. 533).

Since trade regulations will cause higher transaction costs they will reduce the welfare-improving effect of free trade. There are at least three critical points with respect to the assumptions necessary to prove the welfare-improving effect of free trade in neoclassical trade theory. First, the proposition of neoclassical trade theory on the welfare effect of free trade is based on the assumption of perfect markets, that is, there is no market failure, and markets clear, which implies full employment. But in reality there is either asymmetric or imperfect information, and there are other market failures (due to non-perfect markets) including market power of buyers or suppliers, externalities and incomplete markets, and, in many cases, markets do not clear, hence the problem of unemployment in lots of countries.

Second, for the applicability of this proposition of neoclassical trade theory, it is necessary that the compensation principle be applied. In this case those who would be worse off through free trade (for instance according to the Stolper–Samuelson theorem) could receive a payment to compensate their loss. If the compensation principle could be perfectly implemented then nobody would be made worse off by free trade. But in reality the compensation principle is not only difficult to implement but it entails cost. Therefore, in general, there are not only winners but also losers from globalization, at least in the short run.

Third, in theory, trade equilibrium can be immediately and smoothly realized without distortions. There are many indications that the realization of trade equilibrium is not quite smooth and also not immediate. There are market failures. Labour markets in many countries (in both the DW and in the IW) do not clear; that is, unemployment has been a long-run phenomenon, not just a short-run consequence of the adjustment process in the labour market. The world market prices of raw commodities have been highly volatile and suffered a long-term deterioration against industrial products. Neither supranational compensation schemes for temporary export losses of the member in the DW nor national compensation policies have worked well enough to justify the general welfare improvement proposition of globalization provided by neoclassical international trade theory. Thus there are losers from free trade who are discontented and therefore fear globalization.

Low-income countries, however, have usually been confronted with a surplus labour problem; not all markets are perfect, there are incomplete markets and the adjustment process to new equilibrium is not always smooth and quick (see Toye, 1999). Countries and individuals who suffer from globalization have rarely been compensated for the losses completely (see Winters, 1999, p. 62).

Therefore how to counter the problems of inefficient resource allocation caused by market failures, how to solve the problem of (hidden) unemployment and how to compensate the loser from trade liberalization can be seen as new challenges to the study of international political economy and economic globalization. The very difference in properties between individual states in the DW is a serious challenge to the study of modern development economics and design of useful development policy for a country in the DW, the problem of implementing the compensation principle and the problem how to arrive smoothly at a new trade equilibrium.

High Price Volatility, the Prebisch–Singer Thesis and the Need for Supranational Multilateral Compensation Schemes for Losers in the DW

The high price volatility of primary commodities and the long-term deterioration of terms of trade against primary commodities (the Prebisch–Singer thesis) have been two intensively discussed topics in development economics. Keynes, in 1942, went so far as to describe the problem of the volatility of world market prices of primary products as 'one of the greatest evils in international trade' (see Singer, 1996, p.1). Many attempts were made to reduce the price volatility of primary commodities. Keynes and several great economists in his time proposed commodity money as a measure to stabilize fluctuation of commodity price. One of the most discussed policies in the economics of international commodity markets has been the devising of international commodity agreements aimed at keeping the prices of commodities within a pre-agreed range. This approach reached its zenith with the agreement at UNCTAD IV in Nairobi, in 1976, on an Integrated Programme on Commodities (see Toye, 1998, p. 349). The world market of primary products has been characterized by high price volatility, but international economic policy has been less successful in stabilizing this price fluctuation. Markets are a suitable instrument neither for preventing crisis nor for arriving at a more equal income distribution between members of the global community. Furthermore markets will not implement the compensation principle automatically by taking from the winners and giving to the losers from trade liberalization, or by compensating temporary export losses of a low-income DC. The need for a useful approach to reduce the volatility of world market prices of primary products has not lost its actuality and should still be considered as a main issue of international trade policy and development economics. This topic is especially significant for the development policy of the less developed countries, since primary commodities remain the most important source of their export revenues.

A Challenge to the Modern International Political Economy

Traditional development economics has paid much attention to the role of factor accumulation and the question of how to support industrialization by policy measures, such as investment stimulation and export subsidies. Attention has also been paid to the problem of international cooperation to improve resource allocation for economic development, but less attention has been given to the problem of crisis in the DW, such as (a) how to prevent crises, (b) how to find a way out of a crisis, (c) how to return to normal development, and (d) how to compensate the loss from a crisis. Recently the DW has been confronted by several crises which in turn have set back development for several years and seriously exacerbated the poverty problems. Therefore the study of crisis prevention and crisis solution has become an important issue of modern development studies.

Crises have usually been caused either by internal market failure or by failures of domestic government as well by external disturbances. In many cases markets can correct government failures and regulation can be used to correct failures of domestic markets. How to combine markets and regulation for a crisis prevention system by implanting a system of transparent regulatory laws or rules for functioning markets is therefore a fundamental issue for the study of theory and policy of modern development economics.

In a globalizing world economy each individual state has to arrange international cooperation to control cross-border economic activities which have played an increasingly important role in recent economic development of the DW. International cooperation has usually brought a win–win situation for every player, either to enforce international trade or to prevent an international crisis and to avoid the contagion effect of a crisis. International institutions have contributed significantly to enforce international cooperation. The study of international institutions in order to intensify international cooperation is therefore a new challenge for modern development economics.

III INDIVIDUAL DEVELOPMENT POLICY INSTEAD OF THE 'ONE-SIZE-FITS-ALL' POLICY

All states in the DW share some general properties which have been considered in development economics, but there are also at least as many special properties of the individual members within the DW, because of their political system, cultural background, and social and economic structure. Also the endowment of resources between the countries in the DW is very different. Therefore, to propose a well functioning development policy, both the common and the special properties as well as the resource endowment of an individual state have to be considered. This implies that development policies should provide individual therapy which fits the particular state in the DW instead of a 'one-size-fits-all-therapy', if the policy recommendations are really going to work.

We do not deny the universal truth of basic economic theorems, such as mathematical theorems which are true in Europe as in Japan, the USA, Russia and Africa. A globally true mathematical theorem can be applied in many different disciplines, such as in physics and economics. The results of such applications are in general different in meaning and interpretation between diverse disciplines. There is a similarity between applying a mathematical theorem for the study of science and using an economic proposition for the design of development policy for the economy of a state in the DW. Therefore well functioning development policies for individual national economies resulting from application of some basic economic propositions will be very different, such as the conclusions resulting in diverse disciplines from applying a mathematical theorem. The laws in economics which deal with problems of scarcity may also be universally true and applicable. As the British economist John Maynard Keynes, in mining the special character of the theory of economics, points out:

> The Theory of Economics does not furnish a body of settled conclusions immediately applicable to policy. It is a method rather than a doctrine, an apparatus of the mind, a technique of thinking, which helps its possessor to draw correct conclusions.

The very difference in properties between individual states in the DW is a serious challenge to the study of modern development economics and the design of a useful development policy for a country in the DW. At the end of the World War II the European countries and Japan were poor, their production facilities having been destroyed during the war, and most members of the current DW were colonies. They shared some similarities, such as low per capita income, shortage of foreign exchange and capital shortage. There were only a very few 'rich' countries in the world. But, soon after the end of the war, the Western European countries and Japan industrialized and their per capita income became closer to that of the USA. Without doubt foreign aid such as the Marshall Plan provided from the USA to Western European countries and Japan was an important factor in the successful reconstruction of Europe and Japan. Models of development aid were therefore proposed to promote development in the DW without achieving similar effects, since obviously most countries in the DW have not achieved similarly good performance in their economic development. The income gap relative to the USA has not become smaller, but bigger. A comparison between the economic development of the Western European and the former colonies is interesting. Though they share similar phenomena of initially being poor, there are lots of differences.

The West European countries lost their production facilities in manufacturing because of destruction during the war, but they still kept their know-how to run a business. This means that they still had the relevant human capital (that is, people who know how to run an industry). The former colonies had not accumulated such know-how and special skills to run businesses, nor had they had experience of accumulating industrial capital. This difference matters to the performance of economic development in the DW. This can be seen as a proof of the failure of the belief that a 'one-size-fits all' therapy can in general work to solve problems in the DW. Development issues are complicated. Individual therapy is needed for each developing country.

The better performance of economic development in the market-oriented countries than in the former socialistic countries in the period of the Cold War (after World War II) has clearly demonstrated that the market economic system has provided a better system for economic development than the socialistic planning system. This in turn implies the superiority of the market as a tool for resource allocation. The collapse of the former socialistic economies in the Eastern European countries has induced a transition process from socialistic planning to new market economies. Recent experiences of the transition countries show that the transition process has not always been smooth. In most cases transition begins with a short-run setback to economic activities and a reduction in per capita income as well as national income. Several years later, in many countries, per capita income is still lower than at the beginning of the process: the gap between rich and poor has become bigger, and poverty has increased.

Perfect markets are an efficient institution to rule resource allocation, but markets are only able to work efficiently if the necessary prerequisites – both software, such as a regime of rules and laws, and hardware, such as infrastructure – exist. During a long period of experiences with the functioning markets the ICs have already implemented a set of necessary prerequisites for a well functioning market system, both hardware and software. But this is in general not the case in the transition countries and the DW. In these countries, especially in the latter, most of these prerequisites have to be implemented. Transaction costs are high, and many markets are imperfect: in other words, market failures prevail. Since both software and hardware systems usually have the properties of a public good, their provision by private agents is not efficient and in general they will be underprovided.

Low per capita income does not only mean poor material well-being but also high risk and vulnerability of the economy. It is a fact that the DW has more often been confronted by currency crisis, financial crisis and economic crisis than the high-income countries in the recent history of the world economy. A crisis can cause a halt or setback in its economic development. Therefore crisis prevention should be considered an important element in development policy, at least as important as the stimulation of economic development. The recent Asian crisis has given us empirical evidence of the significance of crisis prevention for economic development and poverty reduction in the DW. A crisis can cause the collapse of an economy and set back its development for years.

Economic theory generally assumes symmetry between upward and downward movements of economic development, but, in reality, we can find very strong indications of asymmetric development between the upward and downward movement of economic variables. Recently economists have paid more attention to these asymmetries. Phenomena such as irreversibility and hysteresis in economic life, together with their implications, have been discussed.

To sum up: the variety of societal properties, political systems, cultures, education systems, geographical situations, economic structures and their dynamics makes development economics much more complex than other disciplines in economics. The challenge to design appropriate policies taking into account these complexities will be crucial for the future success of the DW.

IV   COUNTRIES IN THE DW: ECONOMIES WITH MANY BOTTLENECKS

In comparison with industrialized countries (ICs) economies in the DW are characterized by many bottlenecks, such as capital shortage, disguised unemployment (dual economy), shortage of foreign exchange, insufficient knowledge about international markets, insufficient capacity in foreign languages, the low literacy of people, insufficient infrastructure, the lack of sound financial systems, the insufficient property right system, the failing law system, the failing social security system, the lack of a sound administration system (corruption) and an insufficient irrigation system. This list of bottlenecks can be easily extended. The preponderance of agriculture in the DW is a reason for the strong influence of random factors on income fluctuations and surplus labour (unemployment or disguised unemployment).

Capital markets in developing economies are in general incomplete, shallow and far from perfect because of the problem of asymmetric information between the borrower and the lender. The latter problem is more serious in a state of the DW because it is more difficult to get credit information. In a market-oriented economy the capital market plays a vital role for sustainable development. In this type of economy individuals who save are usually different from those who invest. Enabling investors to gain capital for financing investments is essential for development, therefore a well functioning capital market is important.

Because of these bottlenecks in the DW the benefit of integration in the global resource allocation system for a country in the DW will be very significant. The experiences of the emerging market countries in the last three decades (and China in the last two decades) have given us very clear evidence. But, with participation in international economic activities in the world markets, many emerging market economies have also been confronted by several financial, currency and debt crises in the last decades. More serious crises have caused contagion effects to other nations.

Therefore the steps taken in opening up the economy should be carefully considered. Foreign trade belongs to the most important ones and it should be the first international activity to be carried out by a country in the DW. Even in this case experience such as how to make foreign trade, marketing know-how about foreign markets, and so on is needed. Countries in the DW generally do not have such capacity. For example, in the 1960s Taiwan needed Japanese trading houses to carry out exports, since Taiwanese enterprises did not have the capacity to conduct export business by themselves (see Chen, 1998, pp. 151–3).

Not only the restrictive export capacity of a national economy in the DW but also the protectionism of the IW against main export products of the DW are a hindrance for the low-income countries to participate fairly in the benefits of globalization. The negative effects of protection in the IW against imports from the DW are much more serious because of low demand, supply and low income elasticity for this group of products. The high volatility of the world market price of primary commodities (the main export of the DW) and strong fluctuation of export revenues have been given as reasons for multilateral support schemes for countries in the DW. The Prebisch–Singer thesis of long-term deterioration of terms of trade against the DW can be seen as empirical evidence.

These bottlenecks indicate that many markets in the DW are not perfect. This is also a reason why countries in the DW have limited access to credits on the usual conditions. International credit is urgently needed to solve the problem of capital shortage. Low income means also low savings. In addition, because of the small size, the capital markets in the DW are much more easily manipulated by an attack by a single big speculator. According to Stiglitz (2002, pp. 30–31), Ethiopia's entire banking system is somewhat smaller than that of Bethesda, Maryland, a suburb of Washington with a population of 55 277.

Foreign direct investment (FDI) is, after foreign trade, the second most important international economic activity in the DW. But with a few exceptions the incoming foreign investment in a DC is limited. The imperfect markets, externalities and insufficient provision of public goods are serious problems in the DW. In a market-oriented economy goods and services are usually produced by private agents, such as private enterprises or other private producers. Public goods can also be provided by private agents. But the provision of public goods by private agents is in general not efficient. An efficient provision of public goods can be realized either by the state or by private producers with public support to compensate the social benefits induced by the respective public goods. For consumers most public goods have a complementary character for private goods and services. For producers most public goods have a positive effect on entrance productivity in producing private goods and services. Therefore sufficient provision of public goods is a central issue of development policy.

Even the provision of domestic public goods is an important constituent of development policy in the respective country; international institutions can make an important contribution. The role of international institutions in economic development will be discussed in the following section.

V   THE ROLE OF INTERNATIONAL INSTITUTIONS IN ECONOMIC DEVELOPMENT AND POVERTY REDUCTION OF THE COUNTRIES IN THE DW

Both developed and developing economies around the world are becoming more integrated. We are now living in a world of almost global markets for merchandise and capital with about 200 sovereign states, lots of global players, such as multinational enterprises and non-governmental organizations, but without a global government. In this globalizing world with rapidly growing cross-border economic activities there is an increasing need for global governance to rule international activities. There is also an urgent need for sovereign members to carry out international coordination and cooperation as well as to provide international public goods to increase efficiency of global resource allocation, especially for countries which are integrated in the global markets. In this global situation international institutions can play a very important role for global governance, since they significantly increase the efficiency of international coordination, cooperation and provision of international public goods.

It is not necessary to mention the significant role of international cooperation in economic development for countries in the DW. In a sovereign country access to domestic markets is restricted to its citizens as natural persons and persons in law. For access to foreign markets and realization of the advantages from international exchange of goods, factors, technology and know-how are often only possible through international cooperation between sovereign nations. International cooperation can be bilateral or multilateral. Several areas of international cooperation are particularly important for economic development: trade in goods and services, the international payment system, foreign direct and portfolio investment, transfer of technology and protection of property rights, migration (brain-drain) and so on. These agreements have properties of international public goods which can be more efficiently provided by international institutions.

Economists have identified three waves of globalization since 1870. The first wave took place from 1870 to 1914. International flows of goods, capital and labour increased rapidly. Also global per capita income rose at an unprecedented rate. The period between World War I and World War II, with beggar-thy-neighbour protectionism, caused a giant step backward in global economic globalization, with a sharp reduction in the trade–income ratio compared with the level of 1870. Also the growth of per capita income fell by around a third, and the number of poor people continued to rise.

The second wave of globalization took place in the period from 1950 to 1980. Economic integration during this period was concentrated among the members of the OECD (especially Europe, North America and Japan). A series of negotiations to liberalize multilateral trade under the auspices of the GATT have been mainly responsible for the enormous increase in cross-border trade in goods between these areas and also the surging ahead with an unprecedented growth rate. In the period of the second wave the world was separated into a group of market-oriented capitalistic countries, a group of central planning socialistic countries and a group of countries in the DW. The countries in the two groups of less integrated areas have grown less strongly than the more integrated members of the OECD. But, among the countries in the DW, some of the so-called 'emerging market economies' have implemented outward looking policies and enabled enormous growth both of trade and of income – especially the four Asian Tiger countries. One very important lesson from the empirical studies about world economic development in this second wave of globalization might be the superior economic performance of countries which have participated in the economic integration. Nevertheless international institutions have strongly contributed to liberalization of the cross-border economic activities and thus to the global economic integration in this period. The GATT, the IMF and the World Bank are among the international institutions which have made the most important contribution to the second wave of globalization. The tariff rate of the IC against the imports of the members of the GATT was rapidly reduced. Also regulations against international flows of capital among the OECD members were removed at the end of this period.

For a well functioning world economy after the World War II, the British economist John Maynard Keynes at Cambridge designed a three-pillar system for a world economic order. Three international institutions or organizations were conceived by Keynes: the International Trade Organization (ITO), the International Monetary Fund (IMF) and the World Bank (WB). The latter two are still called the Bretton Woods Institutions. The ITO, despite successful negotiations in Havana, was not ratified by the USA. The bad start of the ITO meant that it was later successfully replaced by the GATT, with its eight trade negotiation rounds. After the successful end of the Uruguay Round the World Trade Organization (WTO) was founded in 1995. The trade of manufactured products has been liberalized within the GATT negotiations. The trade restrictions within the Multi Textile Agreement were liberalized in the Uruguay Round. But trade in agricultural products, which are important export goods from the DW, is still seriously protected by the countries in the DW.

The IMF was designed as an international institution to solve short-run balance of payments problems for a world of fixed exchange rates. The Keynesian plan for a system of fixed but correctable exchange rates regimes between the currencies of the world had to pave the way for a liberal world trade system. This system collapsed in 1972. The implementation of flexible exchange regimes between the main currencies has changed the main activities of the IMF significantly. The IMF changed from its original function of protecting a system of fixed exchange rates to areas such as development, crisis management and transition of economic systems. According to the budget of the IMF, the largest share (more than 40 per cent) has been spent to provide a global public good, knowledge.

The World Bank, as one of the three pillars for a world economic system after World War II designed by Keynes, should provide development funds needed by the members in the DW to support their economic development. Both the World Bank and the IMF have played an important role in providing knowledge, especially for designing policy of economic development.

The third wave of modern globalization started around 1980. The Washington Consensus has provided important impetus by giving a new theoretical reasoning for globalization. International institutions, especially the GATT and now the WTO and both the Bretton-Woods institutions, have been the main forces pushing the new wave of globalization. Privatization, liberalization and deregulation have been enforced worldwide in most countries and have made a significant contribution to the new wave of globalization which is characterized by the broad participation of almost all countries on the globe, with a very few exceptions, especially since the collapse of the former socialistic countries in Eastern Europe. Countries such as Brazil, China, Hungary, India and Mexico that strongly increased their participation in global trade and investment have enjoyed unprecedented high growth rates both in trade and in income, as have other countries in the DW which have now participated in the global markets.

Not only the technical progress in transport, communication and information but also the successful close of the Uruguay Round negotiation under the auspices of the GATT and the setting up of the WTO have contributed significantly to the new wave of globalization.

Summarizing the discussion above, international institutions have played a vital role in the globalization of the world economy and also in the successful development of the countries in the DW. Other international institutions include UNCTAD, UNDP, ILO, FAO and the Regional Development Banks. The development story of the above international institutions has shown that the provision of global public goods in coordination with the existing international institutions to meet the needs of the countries in the DW is far from efficient, let alone optimal.

There are several categories of international regional or global public goods identified in economic literature (see Chen, 2003). The broad category, 'international economic stability' can be subdivided into a global liberal trade system, a sound international payment system (a sound currency market), stability of international commodities, a functioning international capital market, and so on.

At the Doha Ministers Conference the WTO decided to liberalize agricultural trade with special treatment of the DW. The failing Ministers Conference of the Doha Round (2003) in Mexico has shown clearly the further need for liberalization of trade in goods, especially for the benefit of the countries in the DW, but also the liberalization of trade in services, which has a major share of value added (about 70 per cent in most of the IC countries) has to be carried out in the near future under the auspices of the more recent General Agreement on Trade in Services (the GATS). As services have been considered as non-tradable and the volume of trade in services is still very low, a liberalization of trade in services will enhance their cross-border trade significantly.

The current international financial architecture is far from free of vulnerability. The currencies of countries in the DW are still the object of speculative attacks. Therefore provision of a sound international payment system is still an important part of the effort of international institutions to support development and poverty reduction of the countries in the DW. Several international institutions, the Bretton Woods Institutions and the Basle Accord have made efforts to set up a sound international payment system.

Kaul et al. (1999) mention three key weaknesses in the current arrangements for providing global public goods:

(1) The jurisdictional gap;
(2) The participation gap; and
(3) The incentive gap.

How to fill in these gaps is a main issue in the further study of international institutions and development economics.

VI EXPORT PROCESSING ZONES: A SMALL-SCALE MARKET ECONOMY SYSTEM EXPERIMENT IN COUNTRIES IN THE DW

Most DCs are agricultural economies with a high share of employment and value-added in the agricultural sector. Agricultural production has a seasonal character, depends on an indispensable factor (land) and is influenced by several random factors. Therefore agricultural production can fluctuate strongly and causes high volatility. Because the land is fixed in a country, and owing to its low productivity, a DC with a dominant agricultural sector is confronted by low income, highly volatile export revenue, as well as high volatility of income, often combined with hunger, especially in cases of natural catastrophes. Influenced by the seasons, labour requirements fluctuate very strongly. For planting and harvesting, a high volume of labour is needed for an usually short period of time. But in the rest period only limited input of labour is necessary. In addition, agricultural products have a low elasticity of demand, low income elasticity and their world market is seriously influenced by the protectionism of the ICs. History shows us that industrialization provides a necessary step for the economic development of a DC. In contrast to agriculture, production in industry is a controllable process and almost seasonally independent. The influence of random factors is almost negligible. Furthermore the manufacturing process can usually be divided into several stages, such as raw material, intermediate and final product. Division of labour can be intensively applied. Thus industrial production is in several aspects superior to that of agriculture.

While land plays only a subordinate role, capital is indispensable for industrial production. Capital is accumulated by investment. Because of low saving in a low-income DC, investment is also very limited. Therefore countrywide industrialization can only be carried out slowly. To attract foreign investment, infrastructure has to be set up. But this in turn is limited by low domestic saving. Therefore an export processing zone can be a device used in this case to improve industrialization in a DC.

Export processing zones have been implemented in more than a hundred countries, especially in DCs, since the 1960s. Recently a similar idea has been successfully applied in ICs, developing High Tech Clusters and Science Parks, such as Silicon Valley, and the Science Park in Sing-tsu. The successful history of the export processing zone experiments (the Special Economic Zones) in Viet Nam and in China has provided additional empirical evidence for the relevance of export processing zones as a measure for development policy. An export processing zone is an experiment with a market economic system on a small scale. For a DC, an export processing zone is relevant in the light of at least four aspects (see Chen, 1997).

First, a DC has in general a shortage of capital and foreign exchange. An export processing zone provides an environment for attracting foreign capital. The product of the export processing zone is mainly for export and therefore helps to solve the shortage of foreign exchange. Second, the export processing zone provides an environment for the transfer of technology. Third, an export processing zone also provides jobs and helps to solve the problem of surplus labour in a DC. Fourth, the export processing zone provides the possibility for a DC to learn how to run a business in a market economic system. Last, but not least, because of its small scale, a DC does not need a big infrastructure investment for building an export processing zone. Therefore it is possible for almost every individual DC to experiment with export processing zones.

In the development literature export processing zones have been discussed with respect to their aggregated welfare gain in the context of a static macroeconomic model for small open economies under consideration of tax revenues of the host country. In this case there is either an aggregated gain or loss induced by the export processing zone. It is not possible to use compensation to realize a general welfare gain of the host country of the export processing zone. Therefore, to study its development implications, the export processing zone has to be integrated in a model of development economics. In a paper on the 'optimal export processing zone' in a dynamic dual economic model, Chen (1995) proposed an optimal export processing zone which is dependent on the individual development of a DC and the structure of the dual economy. Within this model the problem of compensation can also be discussed. But because of the labour surplus in a DC the export processing zone will increase employment in the modern sector with an increase of labour productivity. Therefore there might not be a serious problem of compensation between the winners and the losers resulting from the export processing zone.

International institutions, such as the WTO, can play an important role in the success of export processing zones by providing free access of the producer in the zone to the world market. International institutions which provide a stable international payment system can improve the performance of the firms in the zone.

VII SUMMARY

Globalization is a chance and also a risk for a developing country. It provides a chance to gain access to the global market, but there is also a risk because of bottlenecks and failing infrastructure for a well functioning market system which, therefore, makes a developing economy more vulnerable.

The theoretical foundation for a welfare-improving globalization is provided in international economics, especially neoclassical international trade theory, under the basic assumptions of full employment and perfect markets as well as a smooth adjustment process from one equilibrium under autarky to another under free trade. But these requirements are usually not fulfilled. In addition, the compensation principle is necessary to demonstrate the welfare improvement from free trade. But in reality the implementation of compensation is much less than perfect. Therefore the losers are not compensated by the winners from globalization. A challenge for international economics is to find a more suitable theory.

A policy of economic development is in the first place a domestic policy and the internal political economy has to play a dominant role. This, nevertheless, does not deny the vital role of the international political economy in the economic development of countries in the DW.

Individual countries of low per capita income are very different. A 'one-size-fits-all' approach to providing developing countries with development policy is not possible. Individual therapy is necessary for successful development policy. This is a challenge to development economics because of the widespread difference between developing countries.

Three waves of modern globalization since 1870 have demonstrated the better performance of economies that have been integrated in the global markets. Countries that have participated in each wave of globalization have achieved unprecedented rates of growth in trade and income. International cooperation, and especially international institutions, have contributed significantly to the implementation of globalization. International institutions have helped to carry out international cooperation efficiently and also to provide international public goods. Both local and international public goods are needed for sustainable development of countries in the DW. This is a new challenge for the study of international institutions.

Export processing zones provide a possibility for a developing country as well as a transition country to learn and to experiment with ways to run a business in a market economic system on a small scale.

REFERENCES

Chen, John-ren (1995), 'Optimal Export Processing Zone', *Internationale Ökonomik*, Universität Innsbruck.
Chen, John-ren (1997), 'Was kann man aus den Erfahrungen der Tiger-Länder lernen?', in Paul Trappe (ed.), *Beiträge zu Transformationsprozessen und Strukturanpassungsprogrammen*, in Social Strategies, vol. 28, Basle: Social Strategies Publishers Co-operative Society, pp. 129–48.
Chen, John-ren (1998), 'Liberalization, Privatization and the Pace of Economic De-

velopment in Taiwan', in John-ren Chen and David Sapsford (eds), *Development Economics and Policy*, Basingstoke: Macmillan, pp. 146–71.

Chen, John-ren (2003), 'Global Market, Nation Sovereignty and International Institutions', in John-ren Chen (ed.), *The Role of International Institutions in Globalization*, Cheltenham, UK and Northampton, MA, USA: Edward Elgar.

Kaul, I., I. Grunberg and M.A. Stern (1999), 'Introduction', in I. Kaul, I. Grunberg and M.A. Stern (eds), *Global Public Goods, International Cooperation in the 21st Century*, UNDP, Oxford: Oxford University Press, pp. xix–xxxviii.

Singer, H.W. (1996), 'Commodity stabilization: the rounded whole policy', mimeo, Institute of Development Studies, Brighton.

Stiglitz, J.E. (2000), 'Globalization and the logic of collective action: re-examining the Bretton Woods institutions', www.wider.edu/publications/1998-1999-5-1/1998-1999-5-9.pdf.

Stiglitz, J.E. (2002), *Globalization and Its Discontents*, New York and London: W.W. Norton.

Toye, J. (1998), 'Supra-national compensation schemes for temporary export losses: a critique', in: D. Sapsford and J.R. Chen (eds), *Development Economics and Policy*, Macmillan, pp. 349–73.

Toye, J. (1999), 'The sequencing of structural adjustment programmes: what are the issues?', UNCTD/UNDP Occasional Paper.

Viner, J. (1937), *Studies in the Theory of International Trade*, Harper & Row, pp. 533–4.

Winters, L.A. (1999), 'Trade and poverty: is there a connection?', in World Trade Organization (ed.), *Special Studies 5: Trade, Income Disparity and Poverty*, pp. 43–69.

The World Bank (2002), *Globalization, Growth, and Poverty – Building an Inclusive World Economy*, A World Bank Policy Research Report, Oxford University Press.

2. Designing the role of international institutions in raising the standard of living in the developing world

John-ren Chen

I INTRODUCTION: THE LEVEL OF LIVING AND THE STANDARD OF LIVING

Modern development economics deals with special economic problems of backward countries to find out the reasons for economic underdevelopment and to propose policy measures to strengthen their economic progress and to improve their social welfare. The concept of the standard of living has increasingly approached the economists' idea of welfare in development economics. Early in the post-World War II period, a narrower concept of the standard of living, that is, the level of living, which was typically conceived in purely material terms and used real GDP per capita as the primary measure, was widely used in development economics as a measure of social welfare.

The standard of living depends on a wide variety of both pecuniary and non-pecuniary circumstances as well as both the material and non-material terms to include the most important issues: what people want out of life. Many indicators have been considered as sources of well-being, such as the level of living (GDP per capita), length of life (life expectancy at birth), education, human rights and so on. Hadley Cantril (1965), a social psychologist, has used the level of living, family, health, values, job, social and international issues, status quo and political issues as indicators to represent the social well-being of countries. Cantril published the results of an incentive survey about these indicators (see Easterlin, 2000, p. 9, Table 1). In his paper, Easterlin, following Cantril, uses these indicators of the standard of living as measures of social well-being and studies the development of the worldwide standard of living in both the developed and developing areas and several major regions of the world since 1800. One of the interesting findings in the empirical study of Easterlin is the different speed of improvement in diverse indicators of the standard of living, such as that the rate of improvement in life expectancy, like that in GDP per capita. This is much more rapid nowadays than it was in earlier times (ibid., p. 12). Global health as a global public good provided by international institutions such as the WHO has mainly contributed to the improvement in life expectancy in the DW.

Development policy has in the first place to improve allocation efficiency of the domestically owned resources in global markets to raise the standard of living. For this purpose both goods in the usual sense and public goods (regional as well as global) have to be provided. There are cross-border externalities, there are global common resources, there is competition over global capital and so on. International cooperation can therefore improve economic progress of individual countries. International institutions have proved to be efficient in enforcing international cooperation and enforcing compliance with international agreements.

This chapter will study the role of international institutions (IIs) and how to support the DW in raising social well-being. In doing so it will apply the standard of living indicators published by Easterlin and study how to design IIs to influence positively the indicators of the standard of living in the DW. This approach is of special interest for the aim of IIs to improve well-being in the DW, since there are a variety of IIs. Every II is designed to fulfil particular functions with respect to an indicator of the standard of living. These functions as well as these indicators are related or, more precisely complementary to each other. The coordination of these IIs can therefore improve their performance to raise the standard of living in the DW because of the synergy effect, especially those institutions whose functions are complementary. How to coordinate the IIs to achieve an optimal synergy effect must therefore be a crucial issue for the aim of IIs to raise the standard of living in the DW.

In this chapter, 'II' implies a set of rules without drawing a distinction between institutions and regimes. This definition comes from Simmons and Martin (2002, p. 8). The distinctions between international institutions and international organizations are of secondary importance, since most of the arguments here apply to both. The chapter is organized as follows.

After this Introduction the world improvement in the standard of living and its determinants will be discussed, in sections II and III, respectively. In section IV the designing of international institutions to enforce industrialization in the DW will be considered. International institutions are seen as the provider of global public goods (GPG) to support the development efforts of the countries in the DW, such as knowledge for development policy, for raising development funds, for setting up fair rules for cross-boarder trade in goods and services, and so on, but not as the active driver of economic development in the DW.

In section V the role of international institutions in providing a safety network for protecting short-term famine problems is considered. Section VI will discuss the role of international institutions in setting up a stable international payment system and a sound global financial architecture. In Section VII the new role of UNCTAD and the New International Economic Order as well as the Integrated Programme on Commodities for raising the standard of living in the DW will be discussed. In Section VIII the role of three international institutions, the WHO, the International Labor Organization (ILO) and the Food and Agricultural Organization (FAO) for raising the standard of living in the DW will be considered. In Section IX I will discuss whether international institutions should play a complementary or an initiative role in economic development and in reducing poverty in the DW. In Section X a brief summary of the discussions in this paper will be given. Finally, in the Appendix the effects of protection against import of agricultural products in the industrialized world (IW) will be studied with a simple theoretical model and a proposal for a two-step programme to liberalize the global market for agricultural products is presented.

II WORLD ECONOMIC DEVELOPMENT AND THE STANDARD OF LIVING

Countries in the DW are backward agrarian countries with an overwhelming majority of their population employed in the agricultural sector, especially in the naturally agricultural sector. Empirical studies show that an agrarian economy has usually produced low GDP per capita and the higher the share of the 'naturally agricultural sector (NAS)' the lower the GDP per capita. A DC has usually high NAS and an LDC has a higher share of NAS than a DC.

Empirical study in development economics has shown that the growth of GDP per capita has been accompanied by industrialization, that is, with the increase in employment share of the industrial sector (and with a steadily decreasing share of agricultural labour) and growing labour productivity both in the industrial as well as in the agricultural sector. Therefore, the main effort to raise the level of living and to reduce poverty in the DW must involve industrialization in the DW. By 'industrialization' I mean not only growth of the manufacturing sector, but also expanding application of an industrial production approach in the agriculture and services sectors.

Usually an increase in labour productivity in the industrial sector will increase the national wage rate and the share of industrial labour. This is made possible either by increasing productivity of agricultural labour through increasing use of mechanical tools and fertilizer, or by increasing the price of agricultural products. It is true that successful industrialization can only be realized by the DW's own efforts. International institutions can only play a complementary role, to support but not to initiate, or to carry out, industrialization in the DW.

According to Easterlin (2000) the worldwide level of living standards has improved in the era following World War II and in almost every IC it is possible to identify a turning point which is usually called the 'industrial revolution' of the country. Subsequently living standards begin to advance at an unprecedented rate, and agricultural productivity begins to grow much faster thanks to the mechanical revolution and invention of machines such as the reaper, the binder, the thresher and the combine. Many other machines and tools were part of the mechanical revolution, for instance harnessing the internal combustion engine to create the tractor. The demand for labour in agriculture after the mechanical revolution fell enormously. The direct labour input used to produce a ton of grain in the United States is estimated to have declined by 70 per cent in the nineteenth century. Consequently, after the industrial revolution, the transfer of labour from agriculture to non-agricultural pursuits was more likely limited by the rate of growth of non-agricultural employment than by the labour requirements of agriculture (see Johnson, 2000, p. 6). An increase in labour productivity is a necessary condition for raising living standards. Furthermore the use of chemical fertilizers and insecticide has contributed significantly to the fast growth in agricultural yield. The stabilization of agricultural productivity is of crucial importance for the standard of living.

Thus modern development economics should answer questions such as how to increase the agricultural yield and agricultural income and how to foster industrialization of the backward agrarian countries. An essential problem in improving living standards in the agrarian DW is the need to increase agricultural income. This problem raises two important issues for the debate about economic development in the DW: increasing agricultural productivity and stabilizing the price of primary commodities. While agricultural productivity is a necessary condition for increasing agricultural income, it is not also a sufficient one. In a global market economy, agricultural income depends on the terms of trade between agricultural products and manufacturing products. International institutions, for instance the Food and Agriculture Organization (FAO), have made many contributions, such as dissemination of new seeds (miracle wheat, miracle rice), and new methods of production to increase agricultural yield in the DW. But this is only one side of the coin. Hans Singer (1950) has studied the long-term development of the terms of trade between primary commodities and manufacturing products and has come to his thesis of the long-term deterioration of terms of trade against the primary products. The Singer thesis is meanwhile an empirical observation and clearly shows that an increase in yield does not necessarily mean also an increase in income, which depends both on the yield and on the price of agricultural products.

In its report on 'Globalization, Growth, and Poverty' the World Bank (2002) uses the subtitle 'Building an Inclusive World Economy' and reaches an important conclusion: that globalization reduces poverty, but not everywhere. The protectionism of the ICs against the importing of agricultural products has had a negative influence on the price received by their producers in the DW (see the Appendix). Furthermore a naturally agricultural economy faces many handicaps, such as low and fluctuating yields, highly volatile prices on the world market, low elasticity and low income elasticity of demand. Thus the highly volatile world market price of the primary commodities and the strong fluctuation in export revenue of the countries in the DW have deteriorated the economic development in the DW and need to be stabilized in order to improve economic performance and reduce poverty among members of the DW in an integrating global economy.

An integration of the DW in the global economy shows that the global community needs international institutions (IIs) to provide global public goods and to improve international cooperation. In view of the well-known problem of the underprovision of public goods by individual states IIs can provide these global public goods efficiently. Among these goods global economic stability might be the most important for improving economic development and poverty reduction in the DW. IIs, for instance the WTO, can play an important role in liberalizing trade also in agricultural products, the main export and source of export revenue of countries in the DW. In doing so, the terms of trade for exports of members of the DW can be improved and thus raise their standard of living.

The yields of a natural agriculture (NA) fluctuate strongly because of its dependence on a series of natural random factors, such as weather – sunshine, rain, temperature, wind – as well as the seasonal character of its production.In comparison to an NA the production in an industrialized agriculture (IA) is protected through installation of equipment to counter the natural random influences, such as glass houses against snow, low temperatures and storms, and irrigation systems to combat the dry season. Such equipment enables a much more stable yield for IA production than that of NA production, since production depends neither on seasonal nor on naturally random influences.

As a consequence the export revenue of individual countries in the DW has been very volatile, owing to fluctuation in yield or the volatility of the world market price, or both. Global economic stability has long been identified as a global public good. IIs have therefore been designed to provide this global public good.[1] Several multiple compensation schemes have been implemented to meet the problems caused by the short-run fall in export revenues in the DW. In the 1980s, international institutions, especially the United Nations Conference on Trade and Development (UNCTAD), passed a resolution for a

New World Economic Order in which an Integrated Programme on Commodities (the IPC) was proposed to stabilize the price of commodities. However, the IPC has failed to stabilize the world market price of commodities. How to stabilize commodity prices and the export revenues of the DW has remained a fundamental problem in development economics.

Knowledge such as a mathematical theorem and the laws of economics is universally true. Economics deals with the problem of scarcity and proposes a set of laws. Development economics provides knowledge, especially for the design of development policy to improve resource allocation and to raise the standard of living in the DW. IIs such as the IMF and the World Bank are important providers of knowledge in development economics and policy. Like the application of mathematical theorems to solve problems, the application of economics laws in development policy has to consider special properties of the country in the DW under consideration.

To improve progress in economic development of the DW the experience of the ICs as pioneers has been very useful. 'Knowledge' resulting from the study of economic development is a global public good (see Chen, 2003, p. 7). IIs can therefore play an important role in the economic development of the DW by providing such global public goods. Theoretical and empirical study of development economics has provided a series of fundamental theorems as well as a set of stylized facts which should be considered for proposing development policy. Among them, without claiming any causality, it appears that industrialization has been accompanied by both increase in and stabilization of income and, in its turn, also reduction in poverty (see, for examples, Kuznets, 1966).

Applying the indicators reported in an intensive survey by Cantril and used by Easterlin (2000) in his studies of the development of the standard of living in major areas (both more developed and less developed) of the world since 1800, the less developed areas are classified as China, India, Rest of Asia, Latin America, Northern Africa and Sub-Saharan Africa. The major areas of the world show huge differences in regard to the development of diverse indicators under consideration.[2]

There are credible reasons to assume a high interdependence between real GDP per capita (as an indicator for the level of living) and many other dimensions of the standard of living, even without a clear causal relationship between these indicators. The DW has a much lower level of living as well as a much lower standard of living than the rich ICs. Additionally, economic development is usually not smooth. There are business cycles, financial crises, currency crises, famine and so on. Thus a developing economy is prone to diseases and can be set back by a crisis. The economic, political and social crises in a developing country can cause very severe damages for a developing economy. The provision of public goods is an important determinant of the standard of living. IIs, as important providers of global public goods, such as global economic stability, and as enforcers of international cooperation and compliance with international agreements, can play an important role in raising the standard of living in the DW.

III NON-ECONOMIC DETERMINANTS OF THE STANDARD OF LIVING

In this section non-economic determinants of the standard of living in the DW and the role of IIs will be discussed. Life expectancy, health and health status, fertility, mortality, school enrolment and literacy, human rights and political democracy are the most important non-economic indicators of the standard of living. There are both economic and non-economic determinants of these indicators. Famine has been one of the most important.

Famine

Famine is a complex problem. It has been not only an economic problem of poverty, but also a problem of failing political democracy and social conflicts. Therefore, to find a solution to famine, not only economic, but political and social aspects have to be considered. Humanitarian assistance is identified as a global public good (GPG) and can be efficiently provided by global IIs. But famine relief can only mitigate famine, not resolve the problem of its causes. Poverty reduction, political democracy and conflict resolution will provide the fundamental long-run solution to the famine problem. IIs can make an important contribution to solving the famine problem, but, because of the complex nature of the problem, coordination of the IIs is essential for efficient tackling of the famine problem in the DW.

Poverty, famine and volatile income are strongly related. Almost all famines occurred in the natural agricultural economies with a major share of agricultural labour (over 80 per cent) but not in an IC with a very low share of agricultural labour (under 5 per cent). Famine has never occurred in a rich IC, but it has remained one of the worst evils in the poor DW. ICs which produce with less than 5 per cent of labour a food surplus for domestic demand, have been able to build up food storage to prevent any short-term famine. In contrast, the DW, with a high proportion of agricultural labour, has not been able to produce enough food for domestic need, let alone building up food storage to prevent short-term famine. Famine can be of a short-term character, as a result of natural catastrophes, or of a long-term character because of poverty. Industrialization is a necessary step to solve the problem of famine due to poverty. International institutions can also play an important role in industrialization of the DW. This was discussed in the first chapter of this book.

Food reserves have to be provided to protect against short-term famine; for instance, the International Emergency Food Reserve can play an important role in reduction of short-term famine in the DW.

In the underdeveloped world, famine has been not only a short-term but, more seriously, also a long-term phenomenon. People at a very low level of living, or living in poverty, are not free from famine, with a standard of living which does not include dignity. Poverty has different faces, famine being the ugliest. According to the report of the FAO, 'The State of Food Insecurity in the World 2002', in the period from 1998 to 2000 worldwide there were about 840 million underfed, about 799 million of them (or 95 per cent) living in the DW.

Approximately 80 per cent of the people under famine have lived in the conflict zones of the world. In the 1990s, for instance, famine distress occurred in the Congo (in about 70 per cent of the population), North Korea (34 per cent), Burundi and Afghanistan (70 per cent), Angola (50 per cent).

According to Sen (2000) famine has never occurred in a democratic country.

Political Stability

Political stability, especially peace, has been a necessary condition for sustainable development. In recent history, especially since World War II, international institutions have made very important contributions to solve civil wars and international conflicts, and have kept the peace in the conflict areas, such as, Korea, Cyprus, Golan, Kosovo and Liberia. International institutions have also contributed to help the refugees from the conflict areas. Thus international institutions have to play an important role in providing necessary conditions for a sustainable development, such as setting up a democratic system, a legal system, a market economic order and an administrative system.

Political Democracy

Political democracy has been considered as a measure for the standard of living. A democratic system gives people a greater sense of freedom. Human rights are much better protected in a democratic than in a dictatorial country. The transparency and the legal security provide an important component of the standard of living. Additionally, good governance has been common in a democratic system and corruption (bad governance) a common phenomenon of dictatorial systems. The political system of the ICs is one of pluralistic democracy, while all dictatorial and totalitarian political systems exist in the countries of the DW.

Corruption is a serious problem of bad governance which is, in its turn, a general phenomenon shared by dictatorial political systems. Democratization should therefore be considered as a process of improving both non-material welfare and the material standard of living in the DW. Corruption has been a serious problem in a lot of countries in the DW. Inefficient administration is the inevitable result. An implementation of good governance in the DW is therefore important for executing developing policy. International institutions have to play an active role, maybe not only a passive one, in protecting human rights and improving governance. Recently an international institution, the 'New Partnership for Africa's Development (NEPAD)', was launched by 12 African countries to monitor each other's governance in order to attract development aid and private foreign investments.

Health

Health and life expectancy are essential issues in raising the standard of living. International institutions such as the WHO have played an important role in improving health, in reduction of infectious diseases and in preventing the transmission of contagious diseases. The extermination of some serious contagious diseases worldwide has been the main achievement of the international institutions in the health sector, especially the WHO.

IIs have to play a crucial role in disseminating medical knowledge, to prevent the international dissemination of infectious diseases and so on. Recently the role of the WHO, to prevent and to eradicate infectious disease, such as SARS in some Asian countries, has realized very impressive results. In a very short period the international spread of SARS has been stopped. The progress in information, communication and transportation technology causes the globalization, not only of economic activities, but also of contagious diseases. The rapid spread of a contagious disease can only be stopped by global international cooperation. Therefore IIs in the health sector should be open to all members of the global community.

To summarize the discussion in this section, there are non-economic determinants of several components of the standard of living. Since the rate of progress in improving diverse components of the standard of living varies and since several IIs which have been set up for their own special functions are involved, a plan to coordinate their activities can improve the efficiency of IIs, especially in fulfilling their function and effectiveness to raise the standard of living in the DW.

IV   THE CHALLENGE TO REFORM INTERNATIONAL INSTITUTIONS

The following basic principles are applied to design the role of international institutions in raising the standard of living in the DW:

a.   Most current economies of the world, both in IW and DW, are mainly based on the functioning markets. Private agents are the main actors in a market economy.
b.   The state can also play an important complementary role, such as by providing public goods, by correcting market failure or by enforcing economic activity of the private actors. Thereby government of a sovereign state is made responsible for the success of its development policy and for the performance of its economy.
c.   Integration of a national economy in the global world market can improve efficiency in resource allocation of both the national economy under consideration and the global economy. Integrating an additional national market in the global market will generally not deteriorate the efficiency of national and global resource allocation.
d.   Liberalization of trade in goods and services to the countries in the DW is necessary to integrate them in the global markets of goods and services. IIs, as important providers of global public goods, can play an important role in supporting the national government in its efforts to raise the standard of living of the countries in the DW; and coordination of IIs can improve the synergy effect of diverse IIs in the above role.

Government, as the policy maker, has to play an appropriate role in economic development and assume the main responsibility for the performance of the national economic development. According to the first basic principle mentioned above, the main economic function of government is not as an actor to carry out economic activities in the market; it has to correct market failure and establish laws and regulations to improve efficiency in resource allocation and economic development, and to raise the standard of living.

In his keynote address to the Annual World Bank Conference on Development Economics (ABCDE) in 1998, Joseph E. Stiglitz discusses the role of government in economic development. Government has to play an important role in economic development, but the main actors should be the private agents who act on the market as the centre of their activities. Economists have long recognized the need for selective interventions in the marketplace to remedy well-identified problems such as externalities (see Stiglitz, 1998, p. 12). In addition to the six important roles he delineates for the government in general he adds a special role of the government in developing economies to take note of the particular problems facing developing and transition economies, in which more markets are lacking. The markets that do exist may function less effectively, and information problems are more severe than in industrial countries. Therefore, in the DW, governments have to help create markets, especially financial markets. They have to establish and enforce laws and regulations to make financial markets more stable and increase competition.

Development policy is a policy of a sovereign nation, but this does not mean that international economic relations are irrelevant for development policy. To the contrary, the success stories of the emerging market economies and the growing activity of transnational enterprises have shown the essential role of international economic relations in the development policy. The growth of international economic relations has increased interdependence of the development policies of the sovereign countries. The current global community consists of about 200 sovereign governments. International economic relations are thus a very complex issue. There are countries with very wide gaps in the level of per capita income; there are very different economic structures between ICs and the DW; there are divergent interests of the individual countries; there are different market sizes of individual countries. And, last but not least, there are different degrees of market power between the individual countries. As a public actor and as a player in the international political economy, government has implemented policy measures to improve development of its economy, such as trade policy to encourage exports, to regulate the import of goods and services, as well as to enforce foreign direct investment. Such measures can cause trade distortion.

International cooperation can in general provide favourable conditions for international economic activities of all participants, especially of countries in the DW. IIs can improve self enforcing of or compliance with international agreements. For instance, the GATT and now the WTO have set up rules and regimes to liberalize cross-border trade in goods and services and provide a framework for international negotiations and conflict resolution.

In his comments on the contributions to the Innsbruck Conference, Joe Wilmshurst (1998, p. 507) proposes two main roles of the IIs in promoting economic development in the DW: (a) provision of a framework for global economic and social relationships, an orderly system which is conducive to world development; and (b) provision of international aid: this means transfer of resources from rich to poor countries. To play these roles he suggests that the IIs should complement the activities of the private sector, in some cases correcting market failure. But they should not compete with, or crowd out, private activities. Dirigisme should be avoided.[3]

Through provision of the global public goods (GPG) such as global security, global economic stability, knowledge, global environment, humanitarian assistance and global health, especially the eradication of contagious diseases (see Chen, 2003a, p. 7) IIs can play an important role in supporting the DW in raising the standard of living of its members. In addition to the GPGs given above there are at least three which are related to the indicators used by Easterlin to define the standard of living: international conventions, human rights and political democracy. The international convention has to be designed and developed. The design and development of international conventions can be classified as knowledge. While human rights are declared as a global concern, the relevance of political democracy to well-being is suggested because democratic systems give people a greater sense of freedom to influence the course of public events and realize their individual human potential.

Countries in the DW, as latecomers in the global community, can share with the countries in the developed world the benefits of the GPGs provided by IIs. To propose a design for the roles of IIs to raise the standard of living in the DW the following issues have to be considered:

1. Provision of global economic stability with (a) a rule-based global trading system, open, especially, for the goods and services of the DW, with a principle of non-discrimination against any member; (b) a rule-based system for international movement of factors, such as labour, human capital, especially for the transfer of resources from IW to DW (financial capital and FDI) and of technology; (c) a sound international financial system with multilateral schemes for compensation of temporary loss in export revenue and balance of payment difficulty of the DW.
2. Provision and dissemination of knowledge, especially to the DW.
3. Global security.
4. Global humanitarian assistance such as from an international food emergency reserve programme for global famine relief.
5. Global environment.
6. Global health.
7. Human rights and political democracy.
8. Relations and cooperation between regional and global IIs.

To summarize the above discussion in this section Table 2.1 can be used to identify the kind of GPGs and their contribution to the components of the standard of living.

The study of the role of international institutions in the economic development of the DW has also to do with the issue of the intensity of that role. In this sense the following categories of intensity for the international institutions can be classified: (a) low intensity: to provide a framework for international negotiations and to carry out international coordination and international cooperation for regional and global governance, (b) to provide

Table 2.1   Design of international institutions for raising the standard of living in the developing world

GPG	LL	LE	HS	F&M	S&L	PD	HR
GS	*	*					*
GES	**						
K	**				*		
GE		*	*	*			
HA	*	*		*			
GH		*	**	**			
HD						**	**

Notes:
LL = level of living; LE = life expectancy; HS = health status; F&M = fertility and mortality; S&L = school enrolment and literacy; PD = political democracy; HR = human rights; and GPG = global public goods.
GS = global security; GES = global economic stability; K = knowledge; GE = global environment; HA = humanitarian assistance; GH = global health; HD = human dignity.
* means that the GPG has positive influence on the component of the standard of living under consideration and ** means very crucial positive influence.

GPG, (c) to settle international conflicts, and (d) high intensity: regional integration.

Usually regional institutions, such as high-intensity regional integration like the European Union, play their role in economic development with high intensity, and the Association of Southeast Asian Nations (ASEAN) and Asian and Pacific Economic Cooperation (APEC) play a lower level of regional integration, with the North American Free Trade Agreement (NAFTA) playing a level of regional integration in between. These regional organizations are usually classified as 'club goods', since non-members can be excluded from the use of such goods.

Among the global institutions the General Agreement on Tariffs and Trade (GATT) and now the WTO have increased the degree of intensity from an informal forum of international trade negotiation to a formal global international organization, and from a forum of international negotiation to a global international institution with the function of conflict settlement. Among the general kind of IIs the United Nations provides a higher intensity to maintain global security and protect human dignity. According to a report by Frey (1996), there were about 350 international institutions in 1997. How to design the functions of these IIs and how to coordinate them to raise the standard of living is therefore a crucial topic for the study of international institutions.

In his comments (cited above), Wilmshurst proposes a very reserved and passive standpoint for the role of international institutions in raising the standard of living in the DW. Therefore the question, 'Should international institutions only be assigned a complementary role to raise the standard of living in the DW, or should they also play a much more active role?', is also a crucial topic for the study of the role of IIs in raising the standard of living in the DW.

IIs are to be seen neither as a form of global central authority, nor as a failed attempt at world government, nor as a precursor of world government. Consequently IIs usually have only a minimal influence to force states to do anything they do not want to do. IIs acquire authority and power as the result of acts of delegation by their member states. Therefore a delegation of the sovereign nation states IIs might also be able to play a more active role to raise the standard of living, especially as regards the protection of human dignity, as the human rights have been adopted by the General Assembly in the United Nations Declaration and more recently in the United Nations Millennium Declaration in September 2000. Furthermore IIs also have to play an active role in providing GPGs, such as global security, global environment, humanitarian assistance and global health.

In playing this role in economic development the magic word for the IIs may be 'participation'. In development theory 'participation' has been used in several different senses. In this chapter, 'participation' is used in the sense of integration of the states in the DW, either as supplier or as buyer, in the global market of goods, services and factors to improve efficiency of resource allocation by joining in international economic activities and, in doing so, also to share the benefits of GPGs. Thus the question, 'How to attract states in the DW to participate in global resource allocation' is a further crucial topic for the study of the role of IIs in raising the standard of living in the countries of the DW.

A market is an institution for carrying out transactions. Perfect competitive markets are efficient, but in the real world not all markets are perfect. Therefore regulations and interventions of the state are needed to correct market failure and externalities, especially with respect to international markets. Sovereign states have carried out many kinds of protection against the importing of goods and services from foreign countries, especially agricultural goods and textile products.

International economics has provided a set of theoretical propositions and empirical findings which maintain welfare gains and optimal resource allocation under a global free trade regime. To reach a global free trade environment a global free trade regime has to be set up. The GATT and now the WTO (and the GATS since 1995) provide a worldwide set of rules and regimes to set up a global liberal trading system. But the global trade regime has remained far from free. The liberalization of trade in services (more than 60 per cent of the

GDP in the ICs), trade-related investments and agricultural products has to be further negotiated. Among these, agricultural products are important export goods of the DW. Import protection against agricultural products excludes the participation of the DW in the global market and therefore impedes its economic development (see the Appendix).

International institutions can therefore play an important role in the development of global, national, regional and local economy, but urgent questions remain concerning improvement of the standard of living in the DW: 'How to remove the barriers against participation of the states of the DW in trade in goods and services in the global market?' and 'How to enable the states of the DW to participate in the activity of providing and using GPGs?' A proposal for a two-step programme to liberalize the global market for agricultural products is presented in the Appendix.

V INTERNATIONAL INSTITUTIONS AND GLOBAL ECONOMIC STABILITY

Theory of international economics has provided a set of propositions to present the welfare-improving effect of free international trade and international movement of capital and factors. Recent empirical studies of the emerging economies have provided a series of results about the better performance of outward-looking development policy in comparison to that of inward-looking policy. The successful economic development of four Asian Tigers in the 1970s and the emerging countries in the 1980s has provided very impressive examples of the outward-looking development policy.

Recent history of economic development in the DW has shown some significant contributions of international transfer of technology and foreign direct investment (FDI) to economic development in the DW. The recent economic development in China following the reforms of the 1980s after the failure of three decades of socialistic inward-looking development policy is an impressive example of the success of outward-looking development policy and of the important development of the push effect of FDI. The liberalization of cross-border trade or the openness of the national markets, especially for the export products of the DW, is nevertheless a necessary condition for the success of an outward-looking development policy. The liberalization of the international capital market and FDI are also at most a necessary but never a sufficient condition for the success of economic development and raising the standard of living in the DW.

The WTO has a history of successful liberalization of international trade in goods since the 1950s. Over the last five decades the liberalization of trade in goods can be shown in the significantly reduced tariffs on the import of industrial products within the member countries from the prohibitive levels at the beginning of the GATT negotiations to free imports at the instigation of the WTO in 1995. Not only has there been a reduction of import tariffs on industrial products, but also a lot of trade-restrictive non-tariff measures have been liberalized. This successful trade liberalization has nevertheless contributed mainly to the growth of the ICs in this period. A series of newly industrialized countries have also shared the benefits of the trade liberalization in this period.

The success of trade liberalization has not extended or not arrived to the same degree of liberalization as the main export products of the DW. The trade in textile products has to be liberalized. The negotiation to liberalize the trade-restrictive barrier as well as the trade distorting measures of the ICs against agricultural products in September 2003 in Cancún failed.

The protective policy of the EU and the USA against the import of agricultural products has been criticized as a main reason against the integration of the DW in the global market of goods and has imposed handicaps on its economic development, since agricultural products and raw commodities are the main export goods and the main source of foreign exchange revenues of the DW.

Trade distorting measures, such as price support measures and export subsidies for agricultural products used in the EU and in the USA, have impeded the participation of the DW in the global market. As the members of the WTO agreed to negotiate on liberalizing international trade in agricultural products in the Ministers Conference in September 2003 in Cancún, the EU proposed to change its Common Agricultural Policy (CAP) to implement trade-neutral measures instead of the trade-distorting measures of the agricultural sector. Support price and export subsidies should be replaced by measures which do not cause market as well as trade distortion.

The measures such as support price, tariffs against the importing of agricultural products and the export subsidy for surplus agricultural products in the EU and the United States have a negative influence on the terms of trade to the detriment of the agricultural products of the DW. Furthermore a special import tariff system of the European Community which absorbs completely the difference between the support price in the EC and the world market price according to a study on the influence of economic policy on price volatility (see Chen, 1996, 1999), may increase the volatility of the world market prices for agricultural products, but stabilize the price in the EC at the support price.

Since an increase in the volatility of price has in turn a negative influence on the supply of agricultural products in the DW, the protectionism in the EU and the United States against imports of agricultural products has had an additional depressive effect on the main export products and thus on the economic development of the DW. The above discussion shows that a liberalization of the cross-border trade in agricultural products is urgently required. Since the states in the DW are mainly agricultural economies and agricultural products are part of the main exports of these countries, to remove the barriers to the states in the DW participating in the global market, the WTO has to play its role in liberalization of trade in agricultural products more effectively (see the Appendix).

In relation to the role of the WTO in liberalizing cross-border trade in goods and services, countries in the DW have often been confronted by the problem of shortage in foreign exchanges. Therefore improvement in participation of the DW in international capital and financial flows can support the economic performance of a country in the DW. But the domestic financial market is shallow and is open to attack from foreign participants, especially from the so-called 'institutional investors'. The WTO, the Bretton Woods institutions and recently the Basle Accord together can play an important role in providing global economic stability with a rule-based trading system to liberalize access to the global market for the countries in the DW.

The Mexican, Asian and, recently, Argentinian financial crises have demonstrated the weakness of the developing economies. A crisis usually sets back economic development severely. Therefore, for a sustainable and a resistant economic development of the countries in the DW, the GPG 'global economic stability' is urgently needed.

Topics such as 'the need for a global lender of last resort' and 'the need for a set of rules for sovereign insolvency' have been crucial to the recent study of the designing of IIs to raise the standard of living in the DW.

VI KNOWLEDGE, TRANSFER OF RESOURCES, COMPENSATION SCHEMES AND A SOUND INTERNATIONAL FINANCIAL SYSTEM

The DW is poor, with low income and low saving and therefore financing industrialization calls for resource transfer from the rest of the world. The DW usually has a small share of the world market of goods and services, especially so in a monocultural country of the DW with a very limited but highly volatile revenue of foreign exchange. A multilateral compensation scheme against the sudden shortfall in export revenue has proved to be crucial for a sustainable industrialization of the DW. International institutions such as the IMF, founded as institutions that provide emergency credit to countries which have found themselves in difficulties, can therefore play a crucial role in the sustainable industrialization of the DW, since a sudden shortfall in export revenue can cause irreparable damage, such as insolvency, to an individual producer and, for a national economy, the collapse of a branch of industry.

The IMF, from its origins as the guardian of the Bretton Woods adjustable exchange rate system and financier of temporary current account deficits to its present primary roles as development financier and crisis manager for the emerging world, has played a crucial role in supporting the DW against the backdrop of major shocks since the 1970s following the collapse of the peg exchange rate system, such as the oil shocks of the 1970s, the debt crisis of the 1980s, the collapse of the Soviet Union in the late 1980s and the emerging market financial crisis in Mexico, East Asia and, recently, Argentina. Though there have been many critics of the crisis management programme of the IMF, especially of its one-size-fits-all programme of the Fund, the effectiveness of the crisis management measures and its conditions for giving credit to the crisis countries, it is important, nonetheless, to mention the necessity of such an international institution to fulfil the crucial function of multilateral compensation mechanism against the sudden shortfall of export revenue or major shocks.

The DW has an urgent need of foreign capital, not only for covering the financial gap resulting from any short-term fall in export revenue, but, more importantly, also to get long-term capital for the financing of economic development. The DW has been caught by the so-called 'vicious cycle of poverty' due to the situation where a low income will result in low saving, which in turn causes low investment and thus low income. There are two main sources for the DW to accede to the global financial market: either through the channel of public development aid or via foreign direct investment. Though FDI has provided an important source of capital for the DW, considerable effort has to be invested in encouraging FDI. The DW has not been able to find enough FDI. As a Bretton Woods institution, the World Bank was founded, according to the idea of Keynes, to help the DW to accede to the global capital market at a reasonable interest rate.

In the DW there has been either no financial market or a market with very little depth. In this situation the market can be easily manipulated by a single big actor or a small group of actors. Therefore a liberalization of the financial sector in the DW can improve resource allocation but will also cause financial turmoil, as in a lot of financial crises in the emerging market countries.

VII   UNCTAD: WHAT IS LEFT OUT OF THE NEW INTERNATIONAL ECONOMIC ORDER AND THE INTEGRATED PROGRAMME ON COMMODITIES?

In the 1980s the global community spent much effort within the UNCTAD in setting up a new world economic order to provide a development-friendly global economic environment for the DW and to realize significant poverty reduction, especially in the least developed countries. In 1976 the UNCTAD passed the New International Economic Order (NIEO) with the Integrated Programme on Commodities (IPC) to correct the Prebisch–Singer Effect and to stabilize the very volatile world market commodity price. Implementation of buffer stock measures with the financial support of the Bretton Woods institutions has failed to stabilize the volatile world market price of raw commodities. The long-term deterioration of the terms of trade for raw commodities, the main export products of the DW, has not been stopped. A large number of studies have tried to provide evidence that the liberalization of the industrialized world (IW) towards the import of agricultural products and raw commodities would significantly correct the Prebisch–Singer Effect and make an important contribution to improve the development situation of the DW (see the Appendix at the end of this chapter).

Since the implementation of the NIEO, the situation of the DW, with the exception of the most south and eastern Asian countries, has not really changed. The least DW, especially the Sub-Saharan African area, has not been able to make any progress either in its economic development or poverty reduction, not to mention achieving a higher growth rate to catch up with the IW.

What is wrong with the NIEO and with the IPC? Soon after the resolution of the UNCTAD in 1976 a change of paradigm in the philosophy of economic policy in general, and development policy in particular, occurred. Since the 1980s the Washington Consensus has been the dominant philosophy in economic policy instead of Keynesian interventionism. The main contents of the Washington Consensus can in short be described as privatization, liberalization, deregulation and observance of financial and monetary fundamentals (see Singer, 1998, p.114). The collapse of the Soviet Bloc has given the Washington Consensus a big push in its implementation. The world seems to be convinced by the superiority of the free market economic system over the planned economic system. In many south and eastern Asian countries trade liberalization, privatization, deregulation and the policy of attracting inflows of FDI have been believed to be responsible for the successful performance of economic development in these countries. In comparison with the least developed countries and with the bad performance in economic development in the Sub-Saharan area, the integration of the south and eastern Asian countries in the world economy is believed to be the most important reason for the success of these countries in economic development. There is no doubt that the change of paradigm in economic policy, that is, the economic opening and integration of the Chinese economy into the world economy has been the main reason for the good performance of Chinese economic development since 1979.

The recent globalization of the world economy and the implementation of the main contents of the Washington Consensus have removed the NIEO and the IPC from the UNCTAD. Since then the publication of the World FDI Report has become its main activity. In their paper, Sapsford and Balasubramanyam (2003) have outlined the case for a multilateral accord on FDI under the aegis of the WTO (rather than the UNCTAD). For them, one principal conclusion worth emphasizing is that such an accord should be centred on the development objectives of developing countries and it should not be an instrument for facilitating increased flows of FDI. The main role of the accord should be one of monitoring and coordinating existing policies with the proviso that it should have the principles of non-discrimination, national treatment and transparency as its building blocks (see Sapsford and Balasubramanyam, 2003, p. 56).

VIII   WHO, ILO AND FAO: THE NEED FOR NEW DESIGN?

Health, life expectancy, value, level of living, and so on are the main components of the standard of living, therefore the role of international institutions such as the WHO, the ILO, and the FAO for raising the standard of living in the DW has to be considered briefly within the challenge of reforms in this section:

The WHO and Provision of Global Health Services to the DW

As health is an important component of (the standard of living the global institution, the WHO, has contributed mainly to the provision of the global health services as GPG since the foundation of the precursor of the WHO at the end of the nineteenth century. In the recent era of globalization the WHO has to play a more important role in raising the standard of living in the DW and in maintaining a healthy community for the world population. Three main aims have been identified for the global health services, namely the prevention of infectious diseases, international health information, and communication systems and health knowledge (see Chen, 2004).

The most important issue in designing the role of the WHO for raising the standard of living in the DW is to recognize the importance of technology in achieving the first aim of the global health services – prevention against the infectious diseases – and the strong interdependence of countries in the global community. Due to the weakest linkage property of the technology of provision for health services' prevention against infectious diseases, the global level of prevention against infectious diseases depends on the weakest level of the countries in our global community. By means of modern transportation and communication technologies the emergence of an infectious disease in any place on our planet can reach any other country within a few days. Therefore the WHO has to support raising the level of preventing infectious diseases in the least DW, where the level of the provision of such global health services probably remains at its lowest.

The ILO and International Norms of Labour

Labour standards in the DW have been criticized, especially because of the employment of children as workers there. The education and employment of children are a trade-off between short-term income and the long-term welfare of the individual and the state as a whole. Labour standards have been a main international concern for a long time. The precursor of the ILO was founded to set up international norms and standards of labour and to improve the employment situation. The ILO belongs to one of the oldest IOs. During its long history the world labour situation has changed. Since the collapse of the Soviet Bloc there are now two categories of member countries in the ILO, namely the group of the IW and the group of the DW. Among the more than 170 member countries a large majority of the members belong to the DW. The two different categories of members have caused controversies which affect the activities of the ILO. The many countries in the DW have been confronted with the following problems:

1. trade unions in the DW have not been well organized to represent the interests of labour;
2. human rights have not been sufficiently protected in the DW; and
3. the ratio of illiteracy is high – even very high – and the level of education is low in many countries in the DW.

The ILO therefore has to take note of these issues in its activity programme and in this way to support the DW in raising the standard of living there.

The FAO and the World Food Programme to Solve Hunger in the DW

Hunger is a serious problem for humankind. In the long historical period of the agricultural economy, most effort was directed towards increasing the food supply, but humankind was not able to overcome the hunger problem. In the current world economy, the IW has been able to produce sufficient food not only to satisfy its own demand but also to export to the rest of the world. However, many countries in the DW have not been able to provide enough food for their own needs, even though the majority of their resources have been used in the agricultural sector.

The hunger problem has been caused not only because of low agricultural productivity but also because of the failure to set up a well-functioning system of food distribution. Therefore there are both problems of agricultural technology and food distribution.

The market has placed the main role of food distribution in the IW. The market needs a supporting framework such as infrastructure, transportation and communication systems, an adequate legal framework and so on, in order to fulfil the food distribution function well. However, in many countries of the DW such a supporting framework for the market does not exist or at least not sufficiently. Therefore in these countries the food market has been incomplete and does not work well to fulfil the food distribution function.

The seasonally dependent character of food production means that a crucial necessity to avoid hunger is the building up of food stocks. The modern technology of food storage can not only maintain the good quality of food stocks for a long time but also achieve this for reasonable costs. However, in a lot of countries of the DW such technology of food storage has not been available, or is available only in a very limited capacity. Therefore the improvement of the food distribution function of the market and food storage technology, as well as increasing the volume of food stocks in the countries of the DW should be a crucial role of the FAO.

IX COMPLEMENTARY AND SYNERGIC EFFECTS OF INTERNATIONAL INSTITUTIONS: HOW SHOULD INTERNATIONAL INSTITUTIONS COORDINATE THEIR ROLES IN RAISING THE STANDARD OF LIVING IN THE DW?

According to Bruno Frey (1996), there were, worldwide, more than 350 international institutions in 1997. There are political, economic, military, social, scientific, labor, agricultural, educational and environmental international institutions, as well as international courts and so on. The different functions designed for the current IIs also mean that different but related global public goods are provided by them (see Chen, 2003). It is therefore meaningful to discuss how to coordinate IIs to achieve higher synergy effects. Should international institutions use conditionality when giving development funds to the DW and take more influence on the development policy of the DW, such as the Bretton Woods Institutes used to do when giving credit to countries which suffered a financial crisis. Implementation of the programme proposed among the conditions is required. There have been a lot of critical comments about the conditions imposed by the Bretton Woods institutions.

In talking about raising the standard of living there are economic aspects of raising the living standard, such as encouraging economic growth, and also social and political aspects, such as family circumstances, school enrolment and literacy, as well as political democracy and good governance. With respect to the social and political aspects, such as peacekeeping and good governance, international institutions might have to play a much more active role. As human rights are declared as a universal value, international institutions have to set up rules to protect them. To implement such rules, international institutions have to play a more active role. The recent creation of international courts may be a first step to setting up a sanction system against the violation of human rights.

X SUMMARY

The concept of the standard of living has increasingly approached the economists' idea of welfare in development economics. The standard of living depends on a wide variety of both pecuniary and non-pecuniary circumstances including the most important issues that people want out of life. In this chapter we discuss the role of international institutions in raising the standard of living in the DW. A nation state is mainly responsible for its economic development. But a favourable global framework can play a very important role in supporting the development of the economies in the DW. We believe therefore that international institutions can, in efficiently providing GPG and ruling cross-border externalities, play a very crucial role in supporting the development of the economies in the DW. We will emphasize that the nation state has to take over an active role in its economic development. International institutions can play a crucial role in supporting economic development in the DW but cannot take over the active role of the national government.

Since the end of World War II some changes in the policy of economic development with respect to the role of government and international institutions have taken place. In the period immediately after the war the 'Keynesian Consensus' proposed appropriate regulation and intervention of public hands in the markets.

The Keynesian Consensus ended in the early 1970s. In a race of the so-called 'system competition' a new world economic order, with an Integrated

Programme on Commodities as an important component to stabilize commodity prices on the world market, and multilateral compensation schemes was proposed by the UNCTAD with financial support from the Bretton Woods institutions for the Integrated Programme on Commodities in the 1970s. An almost total change of scene occurred in the 1980s as the Washington Consensus, with privatization, deregulation, liberalization and observance of the fiscal and monetary fundamentals as the main contents was declared. Since the Washington Consensus the cross-border trade in goods has been liberalized through negotiations within the GATT. The collapse of the peg exchange rate system in the 1970s changed the role of the Bretton Woods institutions, especially the IMF. The role of international institutions in economic development in the DW has been changed, along with the change of scene in economics in general and development economics in particular.

Irrespective of these changes in economics and development economics, the global economy has still been characterized by a very unequal development between members. As the study of Easterlin (2000) very clearly shows, the development of the standard and level of living has a very broad distribution between the very poor and very rich countries. There have still been famines, poverty, denial of human rights, civil war, infectious diseases and so on. International institutions have to play in the context of globalization a much more important role in development of the DW. The study of international institutions has to show especially what role and how it is to be played in the development of the DW.

NOTES

1. John Maynard Keynes was very concerned about the high volatility of commodity prices. He proposed initially a world currency based on a bundle of 30 primary commodities to stabilize their average prices automatically. In his proposal for an Economic Order after World War II, he suggested a three-pillar system consisting of three international institutions, an International Trade Organization (ITO) to set up a liberal global trade system with commodity price stabilization as its major function; an IMF to establish a stable convertible global monetary regime with fixed exchange rate regimes; and a World Bank to transfer financial resource from the ICs to the DW with a reasonable interest rate (see Singer, 1998, p. 107).
2. 'It is true that, in regard to all of the indicators above, Western Europe and its offshoots are the leaders and, at the other extreme, the newly emergent nations of Sub-Saharan Africa are the laggards. The distribution of the level of living (using the GDP per capita) shows a considerable gap between the rich ICs and the poor DW. This pattern of geographical diffusion is largely responsible for the current cross-national association among these indicators proclaimed by regression analysts' (Easterlin, 2000, p. 24).
3. What role can international institutions play in raising living standards, especially in the DW? Six papers on the role of international agencies in economic development of the DW were presented to the Innsbruck Conference in honour of Sir Hans Singer's 85th birthday. The six contributions to the Innsbruck Conference concern the role of international agencies which are in general formal international organizations, such as the United Nations

and its suborganizations, FAO, UNCTAD and ILO, as well as the Bretton Woods institutions, the IMF and the World Bank. Besides these formal international governmental organizations and non-government organizations, there is a lot of informal international cooperation and sets of international rules which have played an essential role in global development.

BIBLIOGRAPHY

Cantril, Hadley (1965), *The Pattern of Human Concerns*, Rutgers University Press.
Carlsnaes, W., T. Risse and B. Simmons (2000), *Handbook of International Relations*, Sage.
Chen, John-ren (1996), 'Influences of economic policy on the price fluctuation of commodity price', working paper, University of Innsbruck.
Chen, John-ren (1998), 'Stabilization of economic fluctuation and commodity price by a commodity-based currency', in S. Sharma (ed.), *John Maynard Keynes: Keynesianism into the Twenty-First Century*, Edward Elgar, pp. 194–214.
Chen, John-ren (1999), 'The sources of trend and fluctuation of commodity prices', *Journal of International Development*, 871–92.
Chen, John-ren (2003), 'Global market, national sovereignty and international institutions', in John-ren Chen (ed.), *The Role of International Institutions in Globalization: The Challenges of Reform*, Edward Elgar, pp. 1–18.
Chen, John-ren (2004), 'International institutions and global governance in the era of globalization', paper presented at the Asian-European Conference on Globalization and its Impacts, October, in Taichung, Taiwan.
Chen, John-ren (2005), 'The role of international institutions in economic development and poverty reduction in the developing world', in John-ren Chen (ed.), *Global Development and Poverty Reduction: The Challenge for International Institutions*, Edward Elgar, Chapter 1, this volume, pp. 1–22.
Easterlin, R.A. (2000), 'The worldwide standard of living since 1800', *Journal of Economic Perspectives*, **14**, 7–26.
Johnson, D.G. (2000), 'Population, food and knowledge', *American Economic Review*, **90**(1), 1–14.
Frey, B. (1996), 'The public choice of international organizations', in D.C. Mueller (ed.), *Perspectives on Public Choice: A Handbook*, Cambridge University Press, pp. 106–23.
Kuznets, S. (1966), *Modern Economic Growth: Rate, Structure and Spread*, Yale University Press.
Kuznets, S. (1971), *Economic Growth of Nations: Total Output and Production Structure*, Harvard University Press.
Sapsford, D. and V.N. Balasubramanyam (2003), 'The WTO system and foreign debt investment: a policy challenge', in John-ren Chen (ed.), *The Role of International Institutions in Globalization: The Challenges of Reform*, Edward Elgar, pp. 44–57.
Sen, Amartya K. (2000), *Development as Freedom*, Alfred A. Knopf.
Simmons, B. and L. Martin (2002), 'International organizations and institutions', in W. Carlsnaes, T. Risse and Simmons, B. (eds), *Handbook of International Relations*, Sage.
Singer, H.W. (1950), 'The distribution gains between investing and borrowing countries', *American Economic Review*, **10**, 423–85.

Singer, H.W. (1998), 'How relevant is Keynesianism today for understanding problems of development', in S. Sharma (ed.), *John Maynard Keynes: Keynesianism into the Twenty-First Century*, Edward Elgar, pp. 104–15.

Stiglitz, J.E. (1998), 'The role of government in economic development', in M. Bruno and B. Pleskovic (eds), *Annual World Bank Conference on Development Economics*, World Bank.

Toye, John (1998), 'Supra-national compensation schemes for temporary export losses: a critique', in D. Sapsford and John-ren Chen (eds), *Development Economics and Policy*, Macmillan, pp. 349–74.

Wilmshurst, J. (1998), 'The role of the international agencies: an assessment', in D. Sapsford and John-ren Chen (eds), *Development Economics and Policy*, Macmillan, pp. 507–9.

World Bank (2002), *Globalization, Growth and Poverty: Building an Inclusive World Economy*, World Bank and Oxford University Press.

APPENDIX

To show the effects of the support price and the export subsidy, and the negotiation for liberalization of trade in agricultural products, we apply the following simple partial equilibrium world market approach model with two countries: IW and DW.

Assumption 1: the demand for the agricultural product (AP) is a differentiable function of its price with a negative coefficient; for example, f and F represent the demand curve of IW and DW (see Figure 2A.1).

Assumption 2: the supply of the AP is a differentiable function of its price with a positive differential coefficient; for example, g and G represent the supply curve of IW and DW (see Figure 2A.1).

Assumption 3: the DW market price, that is, the equilibrium price on the DW market which is a free market without regulation, is lower than the price for a producer in the IW under consideration. For simplification of representation, the country under consideration is an IC which carries out price-regulating measures in the agricultural sector to increase the income of farmers and protect against imports.

Two cases of regulation for the agricultural product can be classified.

First, IW buyers' price is equal to the producer's price, which is equal to the support price in the country under consideration and the IW supply surplus is removed by a subsidy to export the IW supply surplus. The point A in Figure 2A.1 represents the DW equilibrium in this case.

Second, IW buyers pay the DW market price, while the producers get the support price. The domestic surplus demand is removed via international trade, by import from or export to foreign markets with neither an export subsidy nor an import tariff.

In a proposal for a new negotiation round concerning liberalization of trade in agricultural products, the first step involves removing the export subsidy and import tariff. If the first step is implemented, the equilibrium of the DW market can be represented by the equilibrium (point B in Figure 2A.1) where the demand and supply function of DW is represented by F and G respectively.

The equilibrium price on the DW market, which is also the price of the agricultural product for the rest of the world, is P_w (see Figure 2A.1). Thus, $P_w > P_0$, i.e. the export subsidy of IW has a negative effect on the AP price in the DW.

The following comparative static properties can be easily derived (see Figure 2A.2). For a given P_w:

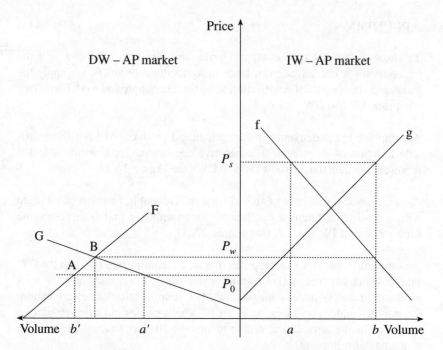

Note: $\overline{a'b'} = \overline{ab}$; $\overline{a'b'}$: import of DW; $P_s - P_0$: export subsidy of IW; $\overline{ab}$: export of IW.

Figure 2A.1   Joint effects of support price, import tariff and export subsidy of IW on the DW

1. There is an IW balanced trade in AP for a given support price P_S^0 in the second case
2. For a higher support price than P_S^0 IW will get an AP supply surplus which is represented by $\overline{ab}$ (Figure 2A.2)
3. IW will get a positive demand for AP import if the SP is lower than P_S^0 (Figure 2A.2). The import demand is represented by $\overline{ca}$.

The second step involves removing the trade distortion support price for the farmers. In this case the world market is liberalized.

The properties of comparative static analysis are qualitative, the same as those given for the first step. Since $P_s > P^*$, therefore $P^* > Pw$; thus the trade-distorted support price for the IW farmers has an inhibiting effect on economic development in the DW. Removal of domestic support price for the IW farmer will integrate the DW in the global market and improve its economic development (see Figure 2A.3).

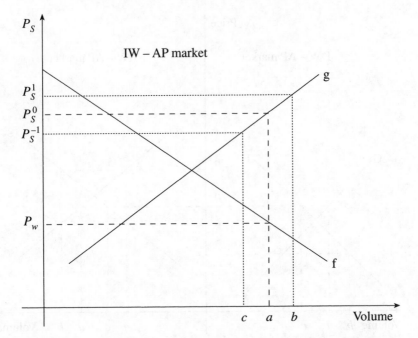

Note: P_S^0: support price for balanced AP trade in IW; P_S^1: support price for excess supply of AP in IW; P_S^{-1}: support price for excess demand of AP in IW.

Figure 2A.2   Implications of support price for domestic market development

The impeding effects of the trade-distorted regulative measures such as support price, import tariff and export subsidy on the development of the DW can be shown by the difference between P^* and P_0.

The free world market price at equilibrium is given by P^* (Figure 2A.3). Thus $P^* > P_w > P_0$.

This shows the negative terms of trade effect or the Singer effect of the trade distortion regulative measures against the DW (see Figure 2A.3).

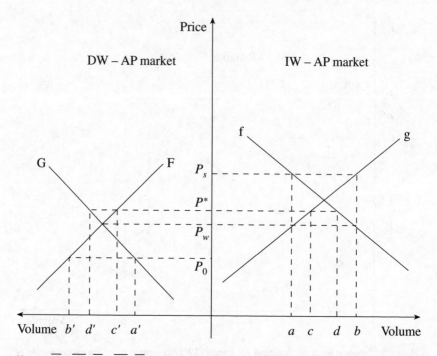

Note: $\overline{ab} = \overline{a'b'}$; $\overline{cd} = \overline{c'd'}$; $\underline{cd} =$ import of IW in case of liberal AP market; $c'd'$: export of DW in case of liberal AP market; $\overline{ab}$: export of IW in case of import tariff and export subsidy of IW; $a'b'$: import of DW in case of import tariff and export subsidy of IW.

Figure 2A.3   Effects of liberalization and deregulation of the agricultural sector on the world market

3. Global development and stability: the challenge for international institutions

Klaus Liebscher

The organizers of a conference have presented me with a formidable challenge. The topic I am to cover is vast, and it is a challenge to delineate the essentials without neglecting the overall picture. As the governor of the International Monetary Fund (IMF) for the republic of Austria, my deliberations will focus on the role that the IMF in particular plays in fostering global development and stability. This does not imply that other organizations or agencies are less relevant or minor. However the IMF has the task of providing the global public good of a stable international financial and monetary system, without which nation states around the world would not enjoy economic growth and rising standards of living.

The main challenge international institutions face today is how to provide the best framework for the governance of globalization so that this process becomes a 'win–win' situation, in which all economies ultimately benefit through productivity and growth effects. This means that a level playing field should govern the international division of labour and the integration of national economies via trade in goods and services to minimize unfair cross-border competition. This also means that there have to be rules which regulate corporate and foreign direct investment as well as financial flows. In the political arena, the United Nations (UN) attempts to deliver global public goods, while the World Bank, the World Trade Organization, the International Labour Organization, the Bank for International Settlements (BIS) and the International Monetary Fund are charged with delivering these goods in the economic arena.

The market appears to be the best coordinating mechanism between free agents, but there is also no doubt that market forces alone are not sufficient. That is why we need an international regulatory framework for the global community, with recognized and clear rules and with effective institutions. This framework also has to ensure that global public goods such as international financial and monetary stability, a clean environment and free trade are defined and provided, even if this requires nation states to give up part of their sovereignty.

There is no intention here to imply that international institutions must endeavour to impose a global harmonization of economic and social models. The market economy has many different facets and competition is healthy for the world economy. International institutions help preserve such social and cultural differences by making all countries stakeholders in the global polity. The 1930s have shown that, without multilateral cooperation, the lack of national self-responsibility and of international cooperation can have dramatic and devastating effects.

A recent World Bank study[1] gives clear evidence that opening markets and integrating them into the world economy has contributed to enormous economic progress for many developing countries over the past 20 years. Countries such as Brazil, China, India and Mexico have doubled their ratio of trade to income. Many of these countries have moved up the value chain from mere raw material exports to intermediate and even to finished products and services. The average annual per capita economic growth increased from 1 per cent in the 1960s to 5 per cent in the 1990s. Real per capita income in China has increased more than fivefold since 1978. Hence, on average, the global income distribution has improved rather than deteriorated.[2] Life expectancy, too, has improved: for example, in China, it has increased by nearly 30 years.[3] However some countries, especially countries in Africa which have not been integrated into the global economy and have not been exposed to globalization, have been left behind.

Dramatic and distressing poverty is still widespread. Undoubtedly one of the major challenges the international community as well as international institutions face is the eradication of poverty. According to a World Bank classification, nearly 1.2 billion people continue to live in absolute poverty, with incomes of less than one US dollar a day. In many countries, durable economic and social progress remains elusive. In most of these countries, trade has decreased and, on average, economic growth has not kept pace with population growth. The situation in Africa is particularly dramatic because it is aggravated by the AIDS pandemic. The fight against global poverty is therefore the greatest challenge for stability and security in the twenty-first century.

In its fight against poverty the international community is following a strategy based on three interrelated elements. First, the UN has set a specific objective with the Millennium Development Goals (MDGs) which have identified eight key areas, including, for example, the halving of absolute poverty or the reduction of child mortality by two-thirds by 2015. Second, the International Conference on Financing for Development held in Monterrey, Mexico in 2002 called for a partnership for development. Industrialized countries offered more comprehensive support while developing countries agreed to make greater efforts with respect to good governance and ensuring a better investment climate. Third, the World Bank and the IMF have formulated the HIPC (Highly Indebted Poor Countries) and PRSP (Poverty Reduction Strategy Papers) processes as operational vehicles to achieve the MDGs. Both these initiatives are encouraging developing countries to develop their own long-term poverty reduction plans in the form of Poverty Reduction Strategy Papers.

Experience[4] over the past decades has shown that IMF programmes in particular are more successful if these programmes are 'owned' by the government and if the support is based on a broad consultation process including government and civil society, who set the priorities for development.

Almost simultaneously with the genesis of the enhanced HIPC, a further basic change in the Fund's approach to low-income countries occurred. A review of the Enhanced Structural Adjustment Facility (ESAF), led the Fund to reframe substantially its role in the low-income countries by launching the PRSP and PRGF (Poverty Reduction and Growth Facility) approaches, making poverty reduction, growth and a participatory process that enhances ownership the key objectives and modalities for programmes supported by the Fund's concessional lending. While the PRGF relates strictly to the Fund's role, the HIPC and the PRSP are initiatives that guide all cooperation with developing countries, not only that of the Fund, but also that of the World Bank and, increasingly, the entire community of donors.

The Fund's role in the developing countries is increasingly becoming an essential and integral part of the efforts of the whole international community to advance development. The HIPC and PRSP are clear examples of such integration and of the coordination of development efforts. They are also novel, given that heavily indebted poor countries must design poverty-reducing strategies in collaboration with their parliaments, subnational entities, business and trade union organizations, and civil organizations representing the poorest members of society. It is evident that much more progress is needed in coordinating multilateral and bilateral support more closely with the poverty reduction strategies and in reducing the administrative burden linked to aid. Better governance in the poorest countries, and the pursuit of best practices by donor countries under the guidance of the OECD's Development Aid Committee (DAC) could help to reduce these administrative burdens.

Finally patience and perseverance are needed. Effective poverty reduction requires that the recipient countries receive consistent support from donor countries, international financial institutions (IFIs) and UN organizations to help them pursue the right policies unswervingly for very long periods.

If we follow through with the elements I have outlined, developing countries stand a reasonable chance of eradicating poverty. Constantly starting new initiatives to fight poverty, probably a sign that the involved parties are not willing to live up to their responsibilities, is likely to be counter productive. Poverty will only be eradicated by economic growth, which also depends on integrating, in particular, African countries into the world economy and offering them fair and equitable access to markets in developed countries. Trade is one of the best forms of self-help. Therefore it was very disappointing that the multilateral trade talks in Cancún failed. However, at the annual meetings of the IMF and the World Bank in Dubai, there was a general consensus that the parties have to return to the negotiation table as soon as possible.

Next to the fight against poverty, the strengthening of the international financial architecture is a major challenge. Since the Asian crisis, the international financial system has undergone significant reform. An important outcome of this has been the relative resilience of international financial markets to a series of shocks over a period of three years. Owing to the decisive intervention and cooperation of the Federal Reserve System and the Eurosystem, September 11 did not produce a major financial crisis, the synchronized economic slowdown of major industrial countries has not led to any major stress in the financial system, and the financial meltdown in Argentina did not entail any significant contagion, except on Uruguay, which proves that financial market agents may be pricing risk better and have become more discriminating without falling into irrational herding behaviour.

Particular progress has been made on three fronts. First, international dialogue has been broadened and has been made more inclusive. The committees of the BIS as well as the creation of the G-20 have enabled emerging market countries (EMCs) as well as developing countries to get involved in the discussion on how to strengthen the international financial system. Second, the establishment of the Financial Stability Forum in 1999, which brings together high-ranking G-7 officials and market participants, has been an important step taken to identify gaps and weaknesses in the international financial system. Third, the IMF, with its near universal membership, is devoting an increasing amount of resources to crisis prevention. The main element that the IMF has at its disposal is bilateral and multilateral surveillance work, with which it regularly examines economic developments and policies at the national and international level.

One can also identify a shift in the crisis prevention strategy the IMF employs. Indeed mistakes were made in assessing vulnerabilities up to the time of the Asian crises. But now the IMF is concentrating on identifying vulnerabilities such as excessive sovereign debt or balance sheet mismatches. Also its stance on capital account liberalization has changed. Now the IMF advocates that member countries should first have the institutional capacity and a relatively strong financial sector with good supervision before taking this major step of liberalization. IMF members are advised to move to flexible exchange rates as a shock absorber as well as to implement fiscal policies that permit cyclical behaviour in the case of a crisis. One important initiative is the Financial Sector Assessment Programs (FSAP) which are conducted together with the World Bank. An FSAP draws up profiles of the strengths and weaknesses of the financial sector of a country. This initiative is geared not only towards EMCs or developing countries, but also towards industrial countries. Austria, for example, is currently conducting an FSAP.

Another key area is economic and financial standards and codes, which are formulated in collaboration with public and private sector institutions. The aim of such standards is to promote meaningful comparable statistics, transparency rules for fiscal and monetary policies and supervisory standards for the banking, securities and insurance sectors. The idea behind this is to facilitate the integration of countries into the global economy. Will all of these initiatives prevent financial crises from occurring? Overshooting and correction will always be part of financial markets. This means that, in an open and dynamic market economy, there are limits to our capacity to anticipate and prevent crises. With skilful and prudent economic, monetary and financial policies, however, crises should be rarer and less severe.

An important initiative which the IMF started to discuss in 2001 proposed the establishment of an international bankruptcy procedure for unsustainable sovereign debt. However the time may not yet have been right to establish such a comprehensive framework for the restructuring of sovereign debt. Nevertheless public and academic awareness has been raised; the debate has helped prompt many EMCs to introduce Collective Action Clauses (CACs) in their sovereign bond contracts, as the EU, Canada and Switzerland have done. Also this awareness has induced the Paris Club to change its debt restructuring procedures for insolvent countries. Nevertheless, I am still firmly convinced that we need an international treaty which would facilitate the orderly resolution of sovereign debt crises.

Very often, the strong track record that the IMF as well as the World Bank have established in transition countries appears to be overlooked. At the beginning of the 1990s, all of those countries, apart from Slovenia, had some form of IMF involvement via a fully fledged IMF programme or technical assistance. The IMF, together with the World Bank and the country authorities concerned, have worked hard to stabilize the economies of those countries, devise economic policies and build up modern institutions. The Bretton Woods institutions have thus successfully contributed to transforming these economies into today's very successful market economies. We have also contributed to this effort by setting up, together with the IMF, the Joint Vienna Institute, which has trained many officials from these countries.

Their successful work in that area has also helped pave the way for the inclusion of many of these countries into the European Union, while for other transition economies the EU represents an anchor of stability. The Bretton Woods institutions, supported by the EU, will help them to graduate successfully from the status of transition economies to that of modern market economies.

I have tried to deal with some of the challenges that international institutions face today. At the present moment, there is a certain tendency in some parts of the world to turn back the hands of time. I believe that, instead, we must look ahead and work to find global solutions to global problems, solutions that are both practical and garner sufficient support. While they are not without flaws, international institutions contribute to making the global economy more stable and to promoting economic growth.

NOTES

1. Subsequent references to the World Bank refer to 'Globalization, Growth and Poverty', *A World Bank Policy Research Report*, World Bank and Oxford University Press, 2002.
2. Xavier Sala-i-Martin, 'The Disturbing "Rise" of Global Income Inequality', NBER Working Paper 8904, April 2002.
3. Angus Maddison, *The World Economy: A Millennial Perspective*, OECD, 2001.
4. James Boughton, 'Who's in Charge? Ownership and Conditionality in IMF-Supported Programs', IMF Working Paper WP/03/191.

4.   Global development and industrialization

Sanjaya Lall

INTRODUCTION

Globalization is perhaps the most pervasive and powerful influence on industrialization today. As the embodiment of technological progress and more open markets, it offers enormous productive benefits to developing countries. Indeed the current advocacy of 'openness' is premised on such productive potential. That the potential is real is not in doubt. What is in doubt is how developing countries can best exploit it. One strand of globalization advocacy argues that this is best done by neoliberal policies, a withdrawal of the state from all economic activity apart from the fundamental provision of law and order and basic public goods. In a more moderate version, this strand admits a larger role for the government, but a 'market-friendly' one where it does not influence the allocation of resources at the activity level (it does not, in the jargon, 'exercise selectivity'). The underlying assumptions of both approaches are that markets are efficient and governments inefficient and that technology flows across countries most rapidly and effectively (in terms of its absorption and use) via free market channels.

Neither assumption is justified. There is a large literature on this subject that will not be reviewed here. The purpose of this chapter is to describe the recent evolution of the industrial economy in the developing world and show that, while globalization is catalysing rapid growth in some countries it is also driving a growing wedge between the (relatively few) successful countries and the (large mass of) others. The wedge is not a temporary one, a 'J-curve' that will reverse itself if countries persist in liberalizing and globalizing. On the contrary, it is cumulative and structural, and is likely to carry on growing unless strong policy measures are undertaken to reverse it.

This chapter is based on work by the present author (in collaboration with Manuel Albaladejo) for the United Nations Industrial Development Organization in the context of its new Industrial Development Report 2003/2003 (UNIDO, 2002). This 'flagship' report presented a new scoreboard of industrial performance and capabilities, benchmarking 87 countries at all stages of

development. The full report is available on the Internet at www.unido.org/
idr.

FEATURES OF CURRENT GLOBALIZATION

The word 'globalization' has many different meanings and manifestations.
Here it is taken to refer only to the aspects relevant to industrialization in the
developing world.

Economic distance is shrinking rapidly because of technical progress in
information processing, transport and communications. The impact of this
is that the 'natural protection' countries have enjoyed through history has
been sharply reduced: international competition now appears far more
quickly and intensely. In combination with trade liberalization (see below),
this changes completely the setting in which developing countries can build
up new industries. At the same time, it opens up new market opportunities.
With some well-known exceptions, markets in developed countries are
more open than before, and shrinking distance allows exporters to reach
international markets more efficiently. It also allows importers in developing countries to gain access to foreign products, services and technologies
more cheaply and consumers to collect information at very low cost. There
are clearly mixed implications for employment: larger exports promote it
while intensified competition can lower it unless local enterprises can raise
their efficiency.

There is rapid technical change in all activities, forcing enterprises in all
countries, regardless of the level of development, to adopt new technologies
to be viable (new 'technologies' include not just products and processes but
also new methods of organizing firms, managing inter-firm relations and
supply chains, linking to innovation and so on). Analysts talk of a new
'revolution' or 'paradigm shift' in technology, so widespread and dramatic
are its effects on economic life. This revolution calls for new skills, production structures, infrastructure and institutions, in particular those related to
emerging information and communication technologies (ICTs). In this setting, the ability to generate and sustain employment depends on the ability of
countries and firms to gain access promptly to, efficiently use and then keep
up with new technologies. This needs, in turn, new sets of skills, organizational relations and infrastructure.

Every country, regardless of its level of development, has to engage in
constant technological effort. Industrial leaders have to invest in technology
generation; followers have to invest in absorbing and adapting technologies,
which is also difficult and demanding. The pace, complexity and skill needs
of technology make participation increasingly demanding but they also allow

countries to specialize more narrowly in particular processes and functions within globalized production systems.

Technical change affects all activities, but it benefits some more than others. There are enormous structural changes under way, with innovation-based manufacturing activities gaining at the expense of others. In particular, primary products and resource-based manufactures are losing shares to other activities, while high-technology products are gaining at the expense of all others.

Patterns of competitive advantage are changing as exports grow in response to two forces: innovation and relocation (of activities, processes or functions to lower cost areas). Both are seen in most industries, but their importance differs by technology and physical characteristics. Some products (like pharmaceuticals) grow rapidly mainly because of innovation; there is little relocation to take advantage of low wages. Some (like electronics) benefit from both innovation and relocation: they have low-technology assembly processes that can be placed in poor countries. Some (like apparel) are driven primarily by relocation. Some (like motor cars) undergo some relocation, but their technological complexity and 'weight' (critical components are, unlike electronics, heavy in relation to their value) mean that distances have to be small (NAFTA is a good example). Exports in which neither innovation nor relocation is relevant tend to grow slowly. Clearly these differences are important, as a major driver of employment in a globalizing world is the relocation of export-oriented activities to poorer countries. However note also that the process of relocation is very dynamic, and new forms are appearing constantly. In the service area, in particular, there is a veritable surge of functions like data entry, call centres and so on being sent to low-wage countries.

Productive resources – goods, inputs, capital, technology and high-level skills – move around the globe more easily and rapidly. A great deal of mobility does not involve ownership, but in general it does: hence the role of transnational companies (TNCs) with affiliates under their control is growing. New organizational techniques and ICTs allow TNCs to grow larger and spread their activities efficiently across greater distances. Their growth is accompanied by a growing trend to internalize more tightly the most valuable technologies, so that entering these activities necessarily involves entry by TNCs. Employment generation in such activities thus needs the attraction of FDI by developing countries and the targeting of particular activities and investors that promise the most rapid export and employment growth. At the same time, competitive pressures force them to specialize more narrowly and hive off non-core activities and functions to other firms. The process is very dynamic and yields some unexpected results. An excellent example is the use of contract manufacturers by leading electronics firms: many firms are moving to innovation and marketing, leaving all production, procurement and logistic functions to unrelated firms. It also opens up new opportunities for external suppliers and subcontractors with the capabilities needed to meet the needs of technology-intensive TNCs.

However FDI in the developing world remains highly concentrated, and is growing more so over time. The share of the leading five and ten recipients of FDI in the developing world has grown, while declining in the world as a whole.

International industrial value chains are more tightly coordinated than before, both within firms (by TNCs[1]) and externally (by contractual or informal relationships[2]). As noted, functions and processes are being subdivided and located across the globe to take advantage of fine differences in costs, logistics, markets and innovation.[3] The process is cumulative and path-dependent, with first movers building up greater advantages based on learning and agglomeration.

Locations that have been able to plug into dynamic value chains have seen large, sustained increases in employment. A large part has been in relatively low-skill assembly activities, but, in the high-technology end, such as electronics, activities have tended to 'stick' rather than move on as wages rise. It is low-technology activities like clothing that have been relatively footloose. However only a few countries have become part of global supply chains to a significant extent, even in low-technology activities (and here one of the main drivers, the Multi-Fibre Arrangement, has expired). There are large numbers of low-wage countries that have been effectively marginalized.

The changing nature of global value chains also means that strategies to benefit from globalization have to change. The more autonomous strategies that countries pursued 30 or 40 years ago are less feasible and more risky. This does not mean that local capabilities cease to matter – quite the contrary. Moreover entering into global sourcing activities also needs assiduous identification and attraction of the international players involved.

The determinants of competitive advantage (for export-oriented and other activities) are changing. Mobile resources increasingly need strong complementary immobile resources in host economies, and these are far more than primary resources or cheap unskilled labour; they also need sophisticated strategies of attraction, FDI targeting and leveraging to maximize their benefits for local capability development. Technological competence, skills, work discipline and trainability, competitive supplier clusters, strong support institutions, good infrastructure and well-honed administrative capabilities are the new tools of comparative advantage. In sum, developing countries that are able to develop these immobile assets are the ones best placed to generate employment growth. However the evidence suggests that such immobile assets are unevenly distributed over the developing world, and are growing more so as globalization proceeds and first movers get onto a virtuous circle of growth and development of more advanced capabilities. However even a number of first movers face severe challenges in sustaining employment growth, while the 'outsiders' are in danger of continued marginalization from the mainsprings of growth.

Global value chains, particularly integrated production systems, cannot spread evenly over developing countries because of inherent technological features. Many advanced activities have strong economies of scale and agglomeration, and so tend to concentrate in the few locations that can provide the minimum critical mass of skills, suppliers, services and institutions they need. There is therefore unlikely to be continuous 'cascading' of production facilities as wages rise: on the contrary, there may be large discontinuities in the relocation process. Once established in particular developing countries, TNCs are likely to 'stick' for long periods, at least until wage and congestion costs rise to uneconomic levels or the supply of relevant skills runs out.[4] The main drivers of recent export growth in medium to high technology industries – electronics and motor cars – are therefore unlikely to reproduce their benefits in new developing regions. Other production systems may arise, of course, but whether they provide the same dynamism as seen in the past two decades remains to be seen. In the low-technology area, the main activity, clothing and apparel, may carry on spreading to new locations, but the factor that drove its relocation earlier, the Multi-Fibre Arrangement, will end in 2005 and the future is unclear thereafter. There is a risk that much of the industry will relocate to Asia, from which quota restrictions drove it out.

TECHNOLOGICAL PATTERNS OF TRADE

Rapid technological progress is causing significant long-term shifts in the structure of industrial activity. As noted above, activities with higher 'technological intensity' (those with higher than average expenditures on R&D) are growing faster than other activities. While every activity makes use of new technologies, differences in innovative potential, the speed of application of new innovations and different rates of demand expansion affect relative growth rates. The data in Table 4.1 show that high-technology activities the world over are expanding in both production and trade much faster than other manufacturing activities; moreover trade is growing faster than production, indicating the 'globalization' of all economies.

Not only do technology-intensive industrial activities lead in dynamism, they also generally offer greater learning potential and greater spillover benefits for other activities. Such activities have become the most active field for international investment. This has important implications for developing coun-

Table 4.1   Rates of growth of high technology and other manufacturing, 1985–97 (per cent)

	All production	All exports	High-tech production	High-tech exports
68 countries	2.7	7.3	5.9	10.8
China	11.70	20.50	14.90	30.20
Korea	10.20	10.60	15.40	18.70
Singapore	8.00	15.00	13.10	21.70
Taiwan	4.70	12.00	11.60	18.90
Hong Kong	–0.20	13.50	3.50	18.10
United States	2.90	8.80	4.70	10.10
Germany	2.20	4.10	3.80	5.80
UK	1.70	6.30	3.30	8.00
Japan	1.70	2.40	5.20	4.40
France	1.20	5.80	3.60	10.80

Source: National Science Foundation (1999).

tries. First is the 'market positioning' argument. A country that wants to locate its production and exports in the fastest-growing markets has to move into technology-intensive activities and upgrade its technology structure. Second, countries that want to deepen technological development and gain from the spillover effects of learning in lead sectors again have to focus on technology-intensive activities. Third, those that wish to share in the most dynamic segments of world trade – the international production systems of transnational companies – have to build the capabilities for technology-intensive activities. They can enter the assembly stage, but later have to upgrade, moving into deeper manufacturing, design, development and regional service activities.

Now consider (Table 4.2) detailed technological breakdown of exports, divided between primary and manufactures, with the latter subdivided into four categories: resource-based; low-technology (such as textiles, clothing, footwear and simple engineering products); medium-technology (industrial machinery, cars, chemicals, and so on); and high-technology (with ICT shown as a subcategory). The medium-technology group is the largest – the heartland of heavy industry – but the high-technology group, with only 18 products at the 3-digit SITC (Standard International Trade Classification) level, is driving world trade and may soon be the single largest category.

Table 4.2 shows growth rates for the period 1985–2000. Primary products grew the slowest, and nearly halved their share of total exports. Resource-based manufactures followed. Low and medium-technology manufactures

Table 4.2   Structure of world exports, 1985–2000 ($ million and %)

Products	1985	2000	Annual growth rate (%)	Distribution 1985 (%)	Distribution 2000 (%)
All sectors	1 703 582 494	5 534 008 649	8.17	100	100
Primary products	394 190 554	684 751 141	3.75	23.1	12.4
Manufactures	1 252 573 675	4 620 266 770	9.09	73.5	83.5
Resource-based	330 863 869	863 503 545	6.60	19.4	15.6
Low technology	241 796 065	862 998 972	8.85	14.2	15.6
Medium technology	485 784 011	1 639 871 870	8.45	28.5	29.6
High technology	198 029 682	1 269 587 194	13.19	11.6	22.9
(of which, ICT)	90 151 843	773 119 244	15.40	5.3	14.0

Source: Based on UNCTAD (2002).

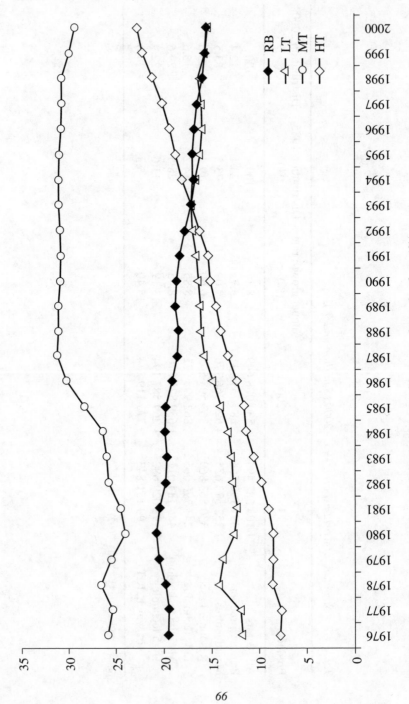

Figure 4.1 Shares of manufactured products in world exports by technology (%)

grew at more or less the same rate, and both slightly raised their market shares (in a more detailed calculation, not shown here, MT products grew faster than LT after 1995). The fastest-growing group was high-technology products. At the start of the period, in 1985, the 18 high-technology products comprised about 10 per cent of total world trade; by 1998, they accounted for nearly a quarter. At current rates, these few products (at the 3-digit SITC, rev 2, classification used here, there are 45 primary products, 65 RB, 44 LT and 58 MT products) will soon account for the largest share of exports. Of the 20 fastest growing products in world trade (with export values of $5 billion or more) in 1990–2000, the five leaders are all high-technology products. Of these, four are electronic or electrical products and one is pharmaceuticals.

In terms of market shares, primary products have been losing ground steadily since 1976. Within manufactured products, RB products have lost shares since the early 1980s, LT since 1993 and MT since 1998 (Figure 4.1). The only group to steadily raise its market share is HT. While these results may not capture real long-term trends, they do suggest that the conclusion drawn earlier about the dynamism of technology-intensive products is well-founded.

COMPETITIVENESS OF DEVELOPING COUNTRIES

Developing countries as a group are doing well in this export scene. To start with, their total manufactured exports are growing faster than those of developed countries. This is to be expected, since they started from a lower base. However the technological patterns of their growth are interesting, and somewhat unexpected. Developing countries grew more slowly than developed countries in primary products and resource-based manufactures (Figure 4.2), presumably because of the faster application of new technology or because of trade barriers and subsidies in the industrial world. Within other manufactures, their relative lead over industrial countries rose with technology levels.

At first sight, this is counterintuitive: theory leads us to expect that developing countries would grow fastest relative to developed countries in low technology, less in medium technology, and least in high technology, products. The data show the reverse. Moreover, it is not just rates of growth that show this trend (caused by the small initial base in high-tech exports); the values involved are also very large. High-technology exports are now the largest single component of developing country manufactured exports. In 2000, at $445 billion, they were $60 billion larger than developing country primary exports, $210 billion larger than resource-based manufactured exports, $39 billion larger than low technology exports and $140 billion larger than medium technology exports.

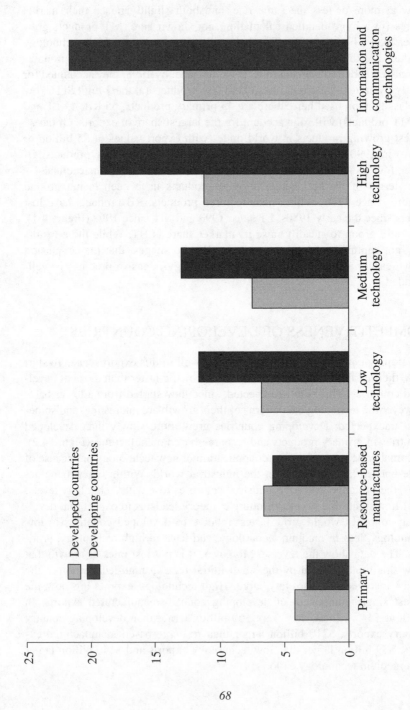

Figure 4.2 Annual growth rates of exports by developed and developing countries, 1985–2000 (per cent)

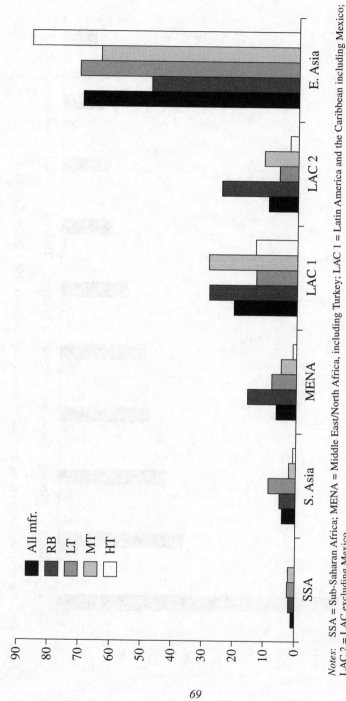

Notes: SSA = Sub-Saharan Africa; MENA = Middle East/North Africa, including Turkey; LAC 1 = Latin America and the Caribbean including Mexico; LAC 2 = LAC excluding Mexico.

Figure 4.3 Regional shares of developing country manufactures exports, 1998

69

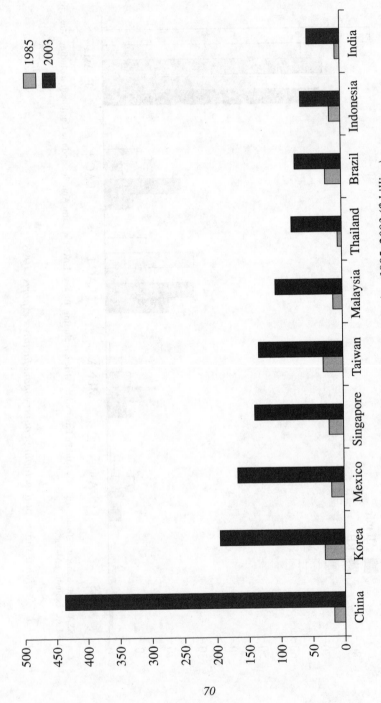

Figure 4.4   Manufactured exports by ten leading developing countries, 1985–2003 ($ billion)

This pattern suggests that developing countries are doing very well under globalization, raising their competitiveness overall and also moving rapidly into dynamic technology-based exports. Unfortunately this is only partially true. Export dynamism and success in technology-intensive exports are highly concentrated, both by region and by country. Moreover the local depth and 'rooting' of high-technology activity vary greatly among the successful exporters; those with shallow roots may find it difficult to sustain their recent growth of competitive production. Consider first the concentration at the regional level (Figure 4.3).

East Asia now accounts for about 70 per cent of total manufactured exports, and about 85 per cent of high-technology exports. What is more, its dominance has increased in practically all categories since 1985. At the other end, Sub-Saharan Africa (even including South Africa, which accounts for over 40 per cent of industrial production and even more of manufactured exports) is very weak, and is losing its small shares over time. Its virtual absence in high-technology exports is one sign of its marginalization in the dynamics of world trade. South Asia does well in low-technology products, basically clothing, but greatly underperforms other categories (this excludes Indian exports of software, which are not captured by these data).

Latin America and the Caribbean (LAC) are shown twice: LAC 1 includes Mexico and LAC 2 excludes it. The reason for this distinction is the massive effect on exports of NAFTA, which has given Mexico privileged access to the US and Canadian markets. Without this large trade 'distortion', LAC 2 does rather poorly in dynamic products in world trade – surprising in view of the size and industrial traditions of Brazil, Argentina and Chile. In Mexico, by contrast, assembly activity in maquiladoras aimed at the US market is driving medium-technology exports like cars and high-technology exports like electronics.

Now take concentration at the country level. Figure 4.4 shows the ten largest developing world exporters of manufactures in 1985 and 2003. These countries now account for over 80 per cent of developing country exports and their dominance has been rising over time. Levels of concentration rise by technology levels, being highest for technology-intensive products (the Appendix shows their exports by technology groups for 1985 and 2000). Thus liberalization and globalization are leading to higher rather than lower barriers to entry for new competitors in advanced activities.

THE COMPETITIVE PERFORMANCE (CIP) INDEX

This section considers the UNIDO (2002) CIP index, which focuses on the national ability to produce manufactures competitively. This is clearly relevant to the analysis of globalization and its role in industrial performance (the impact on employment has to be taken as an unobserved outcome). Since no single indicator can capture all dimensions of competitive production, the performance index is constructed from four components on which data are available.

MVA

The base indicator of industrial performance is the (dollar) value of manufacturing value added (MVA) per capita in each country. MVA is deflated by population to account for country size.

Manufactured Exports

Manufactured exports per capita take account of the competitiveness of industrial activity. If all industrial production were fully and equally exposed to international competition, MVA would automatically capture the competitive element. However it is not. Trade and other policies limit exposure of domestic industry to international competition. So do 'natural' barriers to trade like high transport costs, access to natural resources, taste differences, legal and institutional variations and information gaps. Production for home markets (particularly in countries with large markets or with strong import substitution policies) faces less intense competition than production for export. The export measure helps to overcome part of this lacuna, indicating how competitive industrial activity is in one set of markets. This variable also captures another important aspect of industrial performance. It shows the ability of national industry to keep pace with technical change, at least in exported products: exports can be taken to demonstrate that producers are using competitive (that is, modern) technologies. This is important because the technology measures below do not capture technological upgrading within broad product groups; the export indicator partially offsets this inability.

Technological Structure of MVA

The share of medium- and high-technology activities in MVA (MHT) is the third component of CIP. The higher the MHT share (the more technologically complex the industrial structure) the better is competitive industrial performance taken to be. This is not just because industrial development generally entails moving up from low-technology and RB activities, but also because technology-intensive structures are structurally better for growth, development or competitiveness.[5] Because of the slow, incremental and path-dependent nature of learning, structural change is not automatic or easy; thus structures with more complex activities are considered 'better'. This is, of course, a simplification. Many LT and RB industries can have bursts of rapid growth. Individual activities within them can have high-technology segments. Industries can shift between the categories over time. All this granted, the technological complexity measure offers useful insights into the ability of countries to sustain growth.

Technological Structure of Manufactured Exports

Similar arguments on technological complexity apply to export structures, leading to the final component of CIP: the share of medium- and high-technology products (MHT) in manufactured exports. It is useful to consider export structures separately from MVA structures because in certain circumstances the two differ significantly. In the developing world, for instance, large import-substituting economies tend to have more complex MVA than export structures.

The values for each variable are standardized to range from zero (worst performers) to one (best performers). The final index is the average of the four standardized values. No weights are attached to any of the components, as there is no a priori case for giving different weights. However, the results are shown step-wise so that the effect on the rank of each component is clear.

The average value of the CIP index for each region is shown in Figure 4.5 (note that, since CIP is not a share, it can go up for every region). Industrial countries raise their performance and, not surprisingly, retain a significant lead over the rest of the world. In the developing world, East Asia with or without China (East Asia 1 and 2, respectively) are by far the best performers, in terms of both their absolute levels of the index and improvements over time. Latin America with Mexico (LAC 1) shows some improvement in performance but, without, (LAC 2) it stays almost stagnant.

Note two features of the CIP index. First, there is considerable stability in CIP ranks over 1985–98. The correlation coefficient between the two index values for the two years is 0.940, suggesting that performance reflects slow and incremental processes. Second, leaps in the rankings are nevertheless possible. Over the period, 22 countries change ranks by ten or more places. Countries near the top and bottom tend to be relatively stable, while those in the middle are more mobile.

The main cause of the large upward leaps between 1985 and 1998 is one form of globalization: increasing participation in integrated production networks. This raises the share of complex products in exports (and in MVA over a longer period) for several countries. In the top 40 countries, the largest improvements are in Ireland, Philippines, China, Thailand, Malaysia, Costa Rica and Hungary, with Mexico, Korea, Taiwan and Singapore close behind.

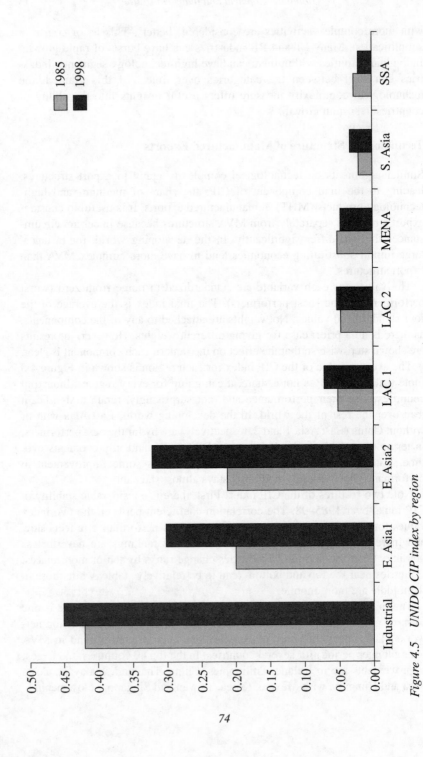

Figure 4.5   UNIDO CIP index by region

However there are different modes of participation in global networks. Two countries, Korea and Taiwan, have done so, not by significant increases in MNC presence in export activity, but by non-equity arrangements like OEM (original equipment manufacture), subcontracting to buyers and, of course, directly establishing export channels. This has entailed a massive development of technological and other capabilities on the part of local firms, sustained by extensive government intervention in all markets, including selective infant industry promotion.

The other successful countries have relied more heavily on FDI (see below), but with different substrategies. Singapore, for instance, has relied heavily on industrial policy to identify and attract hi-tech MNCs, build local skills and institutions and develop specialized infrastructure. As a result, it has moved to the top of the technological ladder, and is now concentrating on R&D and high-value service activities by MNCs.

Malaysia, Thailand, Indonesia and Philippines have been less proactive on FDI and the development of local skills and institutions (though they have used industrial policy in other ways). As a result they are much lower than Singapore on the technology spectrum. However they are now acutely conscious of the need to upgrade capabilities and supplier networks to retain a competitive edge as wages rise and cheaper competitors emerge. As shown later, their capabilities lag well behind those of Korea and Taiwan.

China is a case on its own, because of its size, industrial tradition, political background and ethnic linkages. It can combine elements from all the other successful strategies with its own set of policies to restructure and develop domestic enterprises, large and small (Nolan, 2001). While its base of skills and technological effort is low by international standards, it has enough to have caused a spectacular surge in exports across the technological spectrum. And it is building its capability base rapidly while bringing its 'surplus' human capacity into modern industrial activity, suggesting that the surge still has a considerable way to go.

None of these dynamic countries conforms to the 'ideal' model propagated by the Washington Consensus. The ones that have upgraded their capabilities most rapidly have broken practically every rule in the neoclassical book, using selective intervention in most markets to guide resource allocation, develop national capabilities and dynamize comparative advantage. It is their strategies that form the template on which other developing countries have to base their industrial strategies to build competitiveness today.

THE STRUCTURAL DRIVERS OF COMPETITIVENESS

Let us look now at the structural drivers of competitiveness. For benchmarking purposes, these were FDI, skills, domestic R&D, licensing and physical infrastructure (UNIDO, 2002). This is not, of course, a comprehensive 'explanation' of industrial performance, since it leaves out of account policies, institutions, governance and other factors that are difficult to quantify across a large number of countries. It does, nevertheless, provide a plausible picture of the structural factors in industrial success, and the 'drivers' correlate quite nicely with performance as measured above.

The first driver is directly relevant to our interest in globalization, foreign direct investment (FDI). Figure 4.6 shows FDI as a percentage of gross domestic investment in 1997 (but the picture is more or less the same over the longer term). Reliance on FDI differs sharply among the newly industrializing countries (NIEs), as noted, with very high reliance in Malaysia and Singapore in East Asia and in most of Latin America. There is low reliance in the Republic of Korea and Taipei, China, which deliberately restricted inward FDI to build up their innovative capabilities. This suggests a trade-off between deepening technological capabilities and relying on ready-made technology from TNCs.

One factor to note about Latin America, with the exception of Mexico and Costa Rica, is that much of recent FDI has gone not into export-oriented manufacturing but into resource-based activities and into services. This means that the region has not integrated into dynamic value chains, and its lag in electronics is particularly striking. With local firms unable to mount the effort to become competitive in hi-tech activities, this has given the region a low-growth export structure with low spillover and learning benefits. One major plank of future strategy to cope with globalization has to be to target export-oriented FDI in technology-intensive activities. But, given relatively high wages, this needs better human capital, to which we now turn.

There are sharp disparities in the base of skills that countries have to compete on in technology-based global markets. The figures are only a rough guide to skill formation, since they only deal with formal school and university enrolments, ignoring quality and other differences in the education provided. But these are the only comparable data available, and do show the main form of skill formation. The focus here is on high-level technical skills, as measured by tertiary enrolments in core technical subjects (pure science, mathematics, and computing and engineering) as a percentage of the population. Statistical analysis shows that this measure is the best variable for human capital in explaining export dynamism (Figure 4.7).

The most striking fact about the figure is the enormous lead established by the four mature Asian Tigers (Hong Kong, Republic of Korea, Taiwan and Singapore), far outpacing even the industrialized countries. They lead the

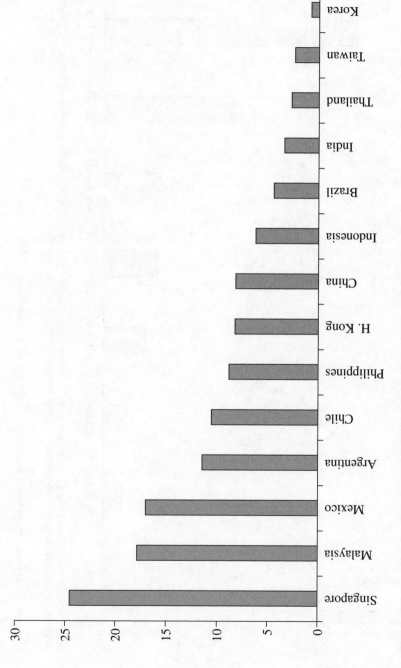

Figure 4.6   Foreign direct investment as % of gross domestic investment, 1997

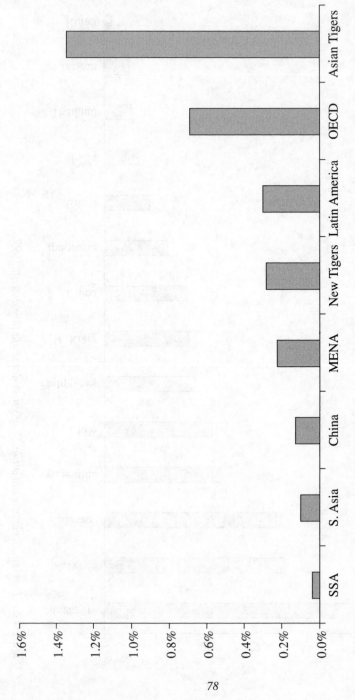

Notes: Asian Tigers = Hong Kong, China, Singapore, Korea, Taiwan; New Tigers = Malaysia, Philippines, Thailand, Indonesia; OECD = Organization for European Cooperation and development (industrialized countries); SSA = Sub-Saharan Africa.

Figure 4.7 Tertiary enrolments in technical subjects as % population, 1995

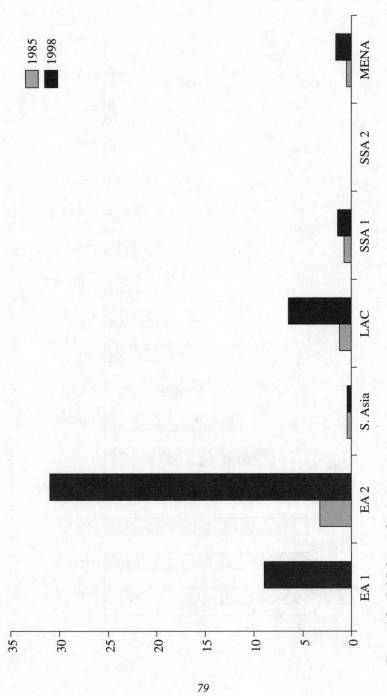

Figure 4.8 R&D by productive enterprises

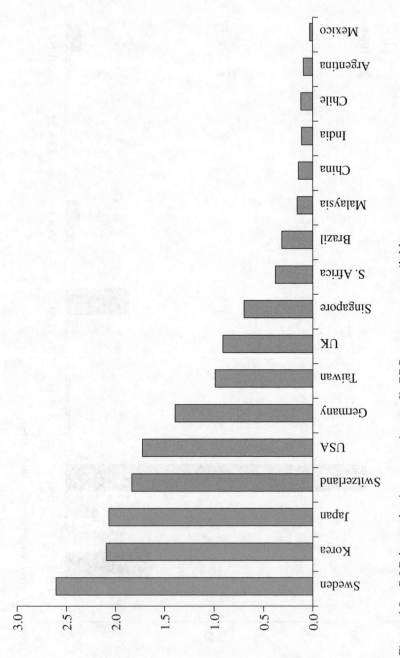

Figure 4.9   R&D by productive enterprises as % GDP, most recent available year

'New Tigers' (Malaysia, Philippines, Thailand and Indonesia) and the main industrial powers in Latin America (Argentina, Brazil and Mexico) by an even higher margin. Sub-Saharan Africa lags the most in skill creation, reinforcing the picture of marginalization.

Let us now look at R&D spending, taking not total R&D (which can be misleading for analysing industrial technological activity) but that financed by productive enterprises (Figures 4.8 and 4.9). The leaders in the world in this activity as a percentage of GDP are Japan and Korea, yet, only some 20 years ago, Korea was a typical developing country, with about 0.2 per cent of GNP going into research and development and 80 per cent of that coming from the public sector. Today total R&D is over 3 per cent of GDP, with over 80 per cent coming from the private sector.

These data show highly differentiated responses among developing countries. The three mature Tigers lead the rest, with other industrializing countries in Latin American and Asia lagging. While the New Tigers, Malaysia, the Philippines or Thailand, do well in technology-intensive exports, their capability base remains weak and shallow. The discrepancy between the technology intensity of their exports and skills and technological capabilities made up by MNC assembly activities has to be rectified if they are to maintain their performance. Otherwise technical change and the entry of rivals with stronger skill bases will lead dynamic activities to locate elsewhere.

China is in an intermediate position, with a combination of capabilities and strategies from each of the leading Tigers. Latin American countries come fairly low on the R&D scale in comparison to East Asia, but they do much better than other developing regions. At the national level, Brazil is the leader in Latin America, and ranks fourth in the developing world after Korea, Taiwan and Singapore.

There is no need to reproduce data on the other drivers (they are available in the UNIDO report). The picture for licensing is very similar, with East Asia leading the regions by far. In ICT infrastructure, however, Latin America compares well with East Asia.

R&D, FDI AND HIGH-TECH EXPORTS

It is interesting to explore the relationships between R&D, FDI and high-technology exports. Differences between these modes of acquiring technology show up more clearly here than they do in overall industrial performance. Moreover, given the role of high-tech exports in industrial performance, it is instructive to analyse its technological drivers separately.

Competitiveness in high-technology exports (particularly electronics) is due either to innovation within exporting countries or to the relocation of facilities by TNCs from innovating countries. It is possible to get an indication of these alternative drivers by comparing national R&D and FDI intensities with HT export performance. Table 4.3 shows two sets of relationships: R&D per unit of HT exports and R&D per unit of inward FDI.[6] The analysis is conducted for all the major exporters of HT products (with exports over $5 billion in 1998). The group includes nine developing countries: all are East Asian economies except for Indonesia and Mexico.

The table ranks countries by the value of R&D per unit of HT exports in 1998. It seems a reasonable presumption that countries with high R&D in

Table 4.3   Relationships between R&D and FDI in major HT exporters

Ranking		Country	R&D per unit of HT exports ($)		R&D per unit of inward FDI ($)		HT exports ($ b.)		Share of HT in total exports (%)	
1998	1985		1998	1985	1998	1985	1998	1985	1998	1985
1	3	Japan	0.937	0.635	100.40	62.42	114.9	36.6	29.6	20.8
2	2	USA	0.622	0.686	1.75	1.68	196.9	53.3	31.0	25.8
3	1	Germany	0.368	0.816	5.01	13.09	92.7	24.3	17.1	13.2
4	6	Switzerland	0.331	0.282	1.35	2.33	18.3	4.7	23.2	17.0
5	9	Sweden	0.283	0.231	0.71	3.33	20.4	4.1	24.7	13.4
6	8	France	0.266	0.245	0.76	1.67	65.1	14.3	21.6	14.6
7	18	S Korea	0.264	0.119	5.90	3.50	36.0	3.7	27.2	12.2
8	5	Austria	0.233	0.284	0.65	2.19	7.4	1.6	12.2	9.2
9	11	Denmark	0.225	0.228	0.57	5.50	7.6	1.8	16.0	10.9
10	10	Spain	0.213	0.229	0.28	0.20	10.2	1.5	9.3	6.0
11	15	Italy	0.210	0.141	1.45	0.97	24.5	7.5	10.1	9.5
12	4	Finland	0.200	0.342	1.45	2.95	10.5	0.8	24.4	5.7
13	7	Canada	0.177	0.278	0.52	0.98	23.8	6.2	11.1	7.1
14	19	Belgium	0.159	0.105	0.26	0.20	17.4	3.5	9.7	6.4
15	13	UK	0.134	0.167	0.49	0.72	76.3	17.9	28.2	17.6
16	12	Israel	0.113	0.211	0.67	2.76	6.6	1.1	28.3	17.0
17	14	Netherlands	0.098	0.164	0.34	0.78	40.8	6.9	24.3	10.2
18	17	Taiwan	0.068	0.131	1.50	1.37	38.6	4.7	35.0	15.4
19	26	China	0.033	0.000	0.03	0.00	33.5	0.3	18.2	1.2
20	21	Ireland	0.022	0.019	0.38	0.31	25.2	2.7	39.3	25.8
21	23	Singapore	0.010	0.008	0.07	0.02	62.3	4.7	56.7	20.4
22	16	Mexico	0.004	0.134	0.02	0.28	31.3	1.9	26.6	8.6
23	25	Malaysia	0.004	0.001	0.03	0.00	34.3	2.3	46.9	14.8
24	24	H Kong	0.002	0.003	0.00	0.00	6.0	2.4	24.5	14.2
25	20	Thailand	0.001	0.043	0.01	0.03	15.6	0.2	28.3	2.4
26	22	Philippines	0.000	0.014	0.01	0.07	19.0	0.3	64.3	5.8

Note: The table includes only countries with HT exports above $5 billion in 1998; rankings are based on R&D per unit of HT exports in 1998.

relation to HT exports and FDI have strong local technology bases. The top countries in the table comprise, not surprisingly, the major industrial and technological powers; these are also generally the main HT exporters by value. The bottom ones are developing countries specializing in assembly and testing operations. Clearly this method of distinguishing competitive strategies has some merit. There are interesting aspects in Table 4.3.

Japan is now the most 'autonomous' country in the world in terms of R&D per unit of HT exports. In 1985, however, Germany held this place, followed by the USA. Clearly TNC production systems have spread faster to Western countries than to Japan. The degree to which Japan relies on R&D rather than on FDI is strikingly illustrated by the figures for R&D per unit of FDI: in 1998, this figure for Japan ($100) is 20 times higher than in the next developed country, Germany ($5).

Among the other highly industrialized countries, the USA maintains a fairly stable profile in terms of both sets of ratios. Germany, by contrast, shows a sharp decrease in R&D per unit of both HT exports and FDI, indicating a rapid growth in the role of TNC systems. The UK, the fourth largest HT exporter in the world in 1998, has a surprisingly low R&D ratio, indicating its growing role as a base for the operations of foreign TNCs in electronics.

The lowest ranking country in the industrial world in R&D per unit of HT exports is Ireland, bearing out the dominant role of TNCs in building its competitiveness. In the developing world, the most 'autonomous' strategy is by Korea, which, after Japan, has the second highest value of R&D spending per unit of FDI in the world. Note, however, the enormous difference in the value of R&D between it and Japan: $5.9 compared to $100.4 in per capita terms. Next comes Taiwan, also with a relatively high value of R&D per unit of FDI, followed by China (with very low values of R&D per unit of FDI: only $0.03 in 1998).

The other countries in the list are all highly dependent on TNCs for their HT exports, though Singapore has a relatively strong R&D base compared to the others. Each of the four countries with an increase in the share of HT in total exports of over 20 percentage points (Singapore, Malaysia, Thailand and Philippines) is producing and selling within international integrated production systems.

DO THE 'DRIVERS' EXPLAIN INDUSTRIAL PERFORMANCE?

The CIP index and the various drivers of performance are shown for each of the main regions in Figure 4.10. That there is a positive relationship between

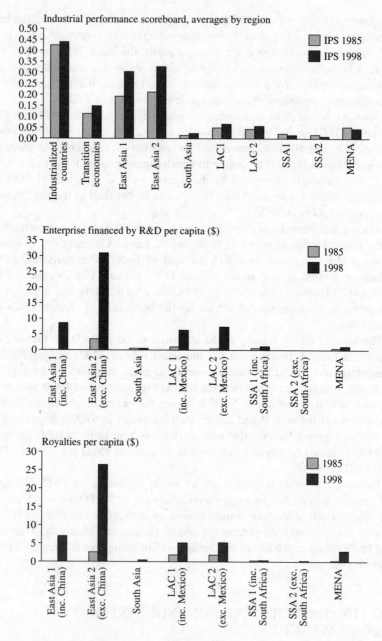

Industrial performance scoreboard, averages by region

Enterprise financed by R&D per capita ($)

Royalties per capita ($)

Source: UNIDO, 2002 report.

Figure 4.10   CIP index and drivers of performance, by region

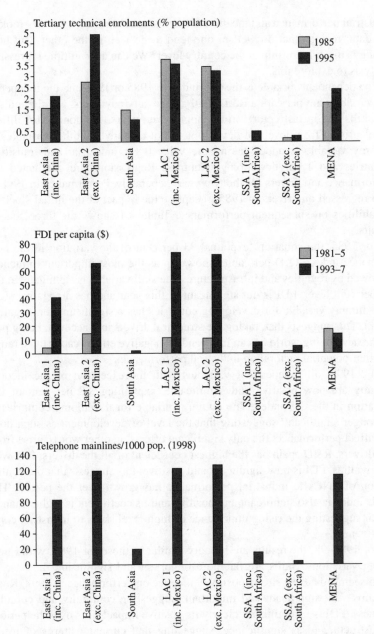

Tertiary technical enrolments (% population)

FDI per capita ($)

Telephone mainlines/1000 pop. (1998)

industrial performance and the drivers is apparent even from a cursory look at the data: regions that do well in one tend to do well in the other. But how strong is this relationship at the country level? We can use multiple regression analysis to explore this.

The dependent variable is the CIP index in 1985 or 1998 and the independent variables are per capita R&D, FDI and royalty payments, and the indices for skills and infrastructure, in the appropriate years.[7] To control for differences arising from levels of development not captured by other variables, a dummy variable is added taking the value 0 for industrial and transition countries and 1 for developing countries. Regressions are conducted for performance and drivers for the two years separately. Performance in 1998 is also regressed on drivers in 1985 to capture the impact of the initial stock of capabilities on subsequent performance. Table 4.4 shows the three sets of results.

For 1985, the equation 'explains' 93 per cent of the variation in the performance index. R&D per capita shows up as the most important influence, followed by royalties and infrastructure. The skill variable is significant at the 10 per cent level. FDI is not significant in this year and has a negative sign. The dummy variable for developing countries has a significant and negative effect. This suggests that, taking the structural drivers into account, being part of the developing world has an independent negative effect (capturing a range of other potential factors) on industrial performance.

For 1998, all independent variables with the exception of the income dummy are now positive and significant, 'explaining' 88 per cent of the variation in the CIP index. The dummy variable for developing countries is no longer significant, suggesting that the level of development as such does not affect performance: the only significant effects, in other words, arise from the drivers. R&D again has the highest coefficient of all the drivers, followed by royalties. FDI is now significant and positive; this suggests that the contribution of TNCs to industrial performance has grown over the period. The skills index is also significant and positive and its coefficient is higher than in 1985, suggesting the rising importance of high-level skills to industrial competitiveness.

For 1985–98, the results are broadly similar to those for 1985, with interesting variations. Skills are far more important and significant: the base in 1985 seems to have a strong positive influence on performance in 1998. R&D remains very significant and important, suggesting continuity and cumulativeness. FDI is insignificant; clearly its positive impact rises over the period. Infrastructure loses significance, suggesting that current patterns of infrastructure investment are more related to industrial performance. The dummy variable has a significant negative effect; being a developing country in 1985 held back industrial performance in 1998.

Table 4.4 Regression results for drivers of industrial performance on the CIP index

Dependent variable: CIP 1985 (75 countries)

Independent variables	Standardized coefficient	T statistic
Skills 85	0.090*	1.832
R&D 85	0.443***	9.300
FDI 85	–0.112	–1.575
Royalties 85	0.384***	5.228
Infrastructure 85	0.204**	2.240
Development dummy	–0.203***	–3.188
Adjusted R square = 0.928		

Dependent variable: CIP 1998 (85 countries)

Independent variables	Standardized coefficient	T statistic
Skills 98	0.130*	1.822
R&D 98	0.466 ***	8.846
FDI 98	0.183***	3.379
Royalties 98	0.253***	5.986
Infrastructure 98	0.196**	2.018
Development dummy	–0.024	–0.401
Adjusted R square = 0.881		

Dependent variable: CIP 1998 (75 countries)

Independent variables	Standardized coefficient	T statistic
Skills 85	0.261***	2.911
R&D 85	0.493***	5.270
FDI 85	0.074	0.651
Royalties 85	0.342**	2.902
Infrastructure 85	–0.125	–0.851
Development dummy	–0.299**	–2.922
Adjusted R square = 0.809		

Note: Significance: *** 1% level, ** 5% level, *10% level; all statistical tests for functionality, heteoscedasticity and collinearity are satisfied.

What does this mean in terms of industrial performance and its drivers? 'Technology' in the generic sense – local R&D as well as access to foreign technology via FDI and licensing – clearly has a powerful influence on industrial performance. Of the technology drivers, R&D is statistically the most important, in each year and over time. This highlights the need for domestic technological effort even at low levels of industrial development. While it is possible that the causation runs in both directions (that is, more industrialized countries invest more in R&D), theory does suggest that the one running from R&D to industrial performance is likely to be predominant. The capability literature shows that (formal and informal) technological effort is a critical input into competitive industrial performance in developing as much as in developed countries. Crude as the R&D measure admittedly is when it comes to informal technological effort, there is likely to be a real correlation between R&D and the intensity and quality of informal effort.

Licensing foreign technology is also significant in all the equations, but its coefficient falls over time perhaps indicating a diminishing role. FDI, by contrast, grows in significance over time. This corresponds with other evidence that the role of 'international production' is growing in the world economy, that technology transfer within TNCs is of rising importance and that TNC export activity is a very dynamic element in the industrial competitiveness of developing countries. Within such export activity, it captures the growth of international production systems. The significance of skills also grows, again entirely in line with the conventional wisdom on human capital, technology and competitiveness. It is, however, reassuring to see the finding confirmed for such a broad sample.

Infrastructure remains important in all periods. The unmeasured influences captured by the developing country dummy grow less important over time. Thus 'being a developing country' has a negative effect in 1985 but this effect vanishes by 1998, when structural drivers explain much of the variance in performance.

CONCLUSIONS

The strongest impression conveyed by this analysis is of growing diversity and divergence in manufacturing performance. A few developing countries have done very well in this fast-changing industrial scene, while others, a disturbingly large number, have done badly. This is, of course, hardly news. It is now well known that economic, and in particular industrial, performance is highly variable in the developing world. The tendency for inequalities to perpetuate themselves – cumulative causation and path dependence – is accepted as part of the hard reality of development and globalization. Early models of inevitable convergence, based on simple neoclassical growth models, have given way to more diffuse analyses that stress that endogenous structural, institutional and social factors may carry on driving economies apart.

This chapter shows how wide dispersion is in the industrial sector, how it has grown and how it reflects structural factors. Such factors are notoriously difficult to alter in the short to medium term and, because of cumulativeness, cannot be left to reverse themselves by further liberalization. Thus they raise strong policy implications. The international community and national governments together have to address the growing structural gaps that drive divergence, and they have to reverse or relax the stringent rules of the game that constrain the use of (previously successful) industrial policy. If they do not, there will be continued marginalization of many countries from the dynamics of industrial development.

The other important lesson is that there are 'many roads to heaven'. Successful developing countries have used widely differing strategies to build capabilities. Some, but relatively few, have succeeded with 'autonomous' strategies, drawing in foreign technology largely at arm's length while building strong technological and innovative capabilities in local firms. Others, a larger number, have gone some way by plugging into TNC production systems by becoming suppliers of labour-intensive products and components, without having strong domestic capabilities. Of these economies, a few have managed to combine their reliance on FDI with strong industrial policy, concentrating on the activities they wish to enter and the functions they wish to upgrade into. Others have tapped the potential of FDI by using passive policies, benefiting from sound economic management, pro-business attitudes, attractive locations and good luck. The less successful developing countries have not followed any of these strategies effectively.

The distinction between the autonomous and FDI-reliant strategies cannot, however, be pushed too far. Most countries have had mixed strategies. Strategies are also converging, partly from natural evolution and partly as a result of changing rules of the game. Autonomous countries are opening up to FDI to gain access to new and expensive technologies, while FDI-reliant countries are trying to build local R&D capabilities, often by inducing TNCs to upgrade technological activity. In a world increasingly bound in tight production, knowledge and trade networks it makes less and less sense to draw sharp distinctions between these traditional strategies. This does not, however, mean that strategies are not needed. Quite the contrary: as resources become more mobile, attracting the most valuable ones and rooting them becomes more difficult. Local capabilities become more important to link with international resources and leverage them, and building capabilities is a difficult strategic challenge.

The industrial world also shows similar strategic differences in reliance on R&D and FDI. These sometimes reflect deliberate policy (say, Japan as compared to Ireland). More often they show different patterns of historic evolution of industry and technology. For advanced economies, the difference between the two strategies is of little practical significance today. FDI and domestic R&D are for them largely complementary: technological leaders draw upon foreign firms to provide specialized forms of technology and foreign firms draw upon and feed into domestic innovation. Technological followers are integrated into larger systems; some establish independent areas of technological competence while others remain as production bases.

At first sight, the best strategy for latecomers without strong technological capabilities appears to be to battle their way into TNC production systems and let local capabilities develop slowly. This may not be true in the future. Industrial latecomers entering integrated production systems may find it difficult to sustain growth as wages rise, unless they raise their skill and technological bases. Insertion into TNC systems does not ensure that participants will upgrade their drivers, yet such upgrading is essential. Integrated production systems are also highly concentrated and the level of concentration rises with the sophistication of the technology. There are strong first-mover advantages and, while some systems will spread and new ones will evolve, it is unlikely that the South East Asian experience will be repeated in many other developing countries. Economies of scale may lead to a very small number of production and innovation sites in each region. Economies of clustering and agglomeration may lead these facilities to be sited in established locations with advanced capabilities and infrastructure. There is bound to be some 'trickle down' as the initial sites suffer rising costs and congestion, but this may take a long time and may not ultimately involve many other locations.

In general developing countries need new, focused and 'intelligent' strategies for linking to global markets, leveraging foreign technologies and skills and learning from their links. The value of strong linking and leveraging strategies is illustrated by the experience of the Asian NIEs; these can be adapted to the needs of the rest of the developing world. However strategy also has to be industry-specific. Each industrial value chain differs in its organizational, technological, logistical and institutional needs. As local value chains become integrated into global chains, the nature, structure and strategies of the key player in each become important.

NOTES

1. Thus some 30–40 per cent of the trade handled by TNCs is actually within the firm (between different affiliated companies) and is not transacted on open markets (UNCTAD, 1999).
2. There is a tendency for lead firms to rely on a smaller number of 'first tier' suppliers, which in turn deal with and coordinate second and third tier suppliers. The first tier suppliers are major TNCs in their own right.
3. In some low-technology activities like apparel, lead coordinators are international buyers rather than TNCs. The role of direct ownership (that is, of FDI) in coordinating globalized activities depends on the nature and pace of change of the technology and the availability of specialized suppliers; it is also changing rapidly over time as systems become more open.
4. This is in fact a real danger for countries without strong local industrial bases that have benefited greatly from TNC relocation. Examples are Malaysia, Thailand and the Philippines, where there is a strong challenge emerging from China, with lower wages, more low-level skilled labour, a large supply of technical manpower and a developed supplier base. See Lall (2001).
5. Technologically complex structures offer greater learning potential and lend themselves more to sustained productivity increase over time (because of the greater potential for applying new scientific knowledge). Many have stronger spillover benefits, especially those in 'hub' activities that disseminate technology across different activities. High-technology activities enjoy better growth prospects in production and trade, and are the areas frequented by dynamic international production systems.
6. The two ratios (for R&D per unit of high technology exports and R&D per unit of inward FDI) are strongly correlated, with a coefficient of 0.745 in 1998.
7. All the necessary econometric tests for collinearity, functionality and heteroscedasticity are satisfied. The potential problem raised by the high correlation between the capabilities does not affect the result.

REFERENCES

Lall, S. (2001), *Competitiveness, Technology and Skills*, Cheltenham, UK and Northampton, MA, USA: Edward Elgar.

Nolan, P. (2001), *China and the Global Business Revolution*, Basingstoke: Palgrave.

NSF (1999), *Science and Engineering Indicators 1999*, Washington, DC: National Science Foundation.

UNCTAD (1999), *World Investment Report 1999: Foreign Direct Investment and the Challenge of Development*, Geneva: UNCTAD.

UNCTAD (2002), *World Investment Report 2002: Transnational Corporations and Export Competitiveness*, Geneva: UNCTAD.

UNIDO (2002), *Industrial Development Report 2002/2003*, Vienna: UNIDO.

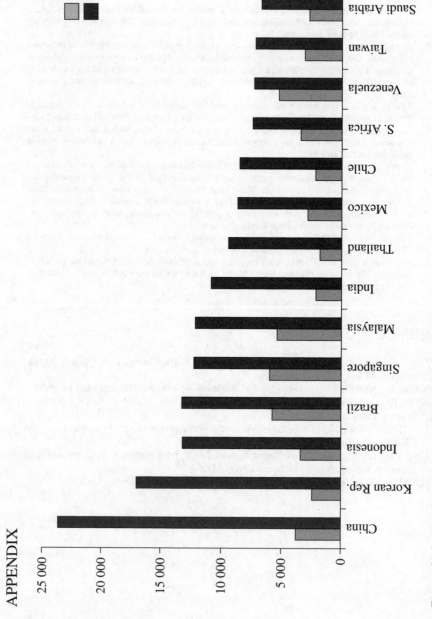

Figure 4A.1   Leading exporters of RB manufactures ($m)

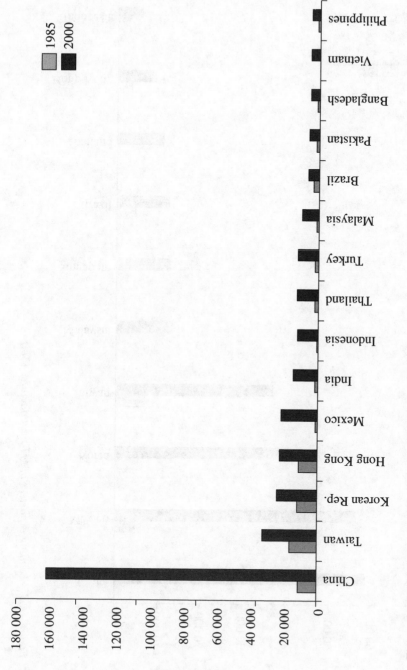

Figure 4A.2   Leading exporters of LT manufactures ($m)

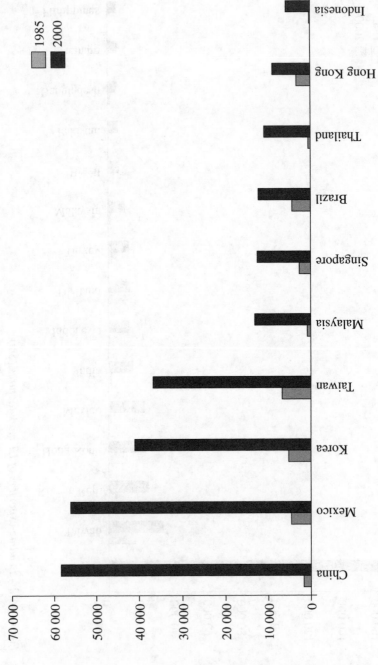

Figure 4A.3   Leading exporters of MT manufactures ($m)

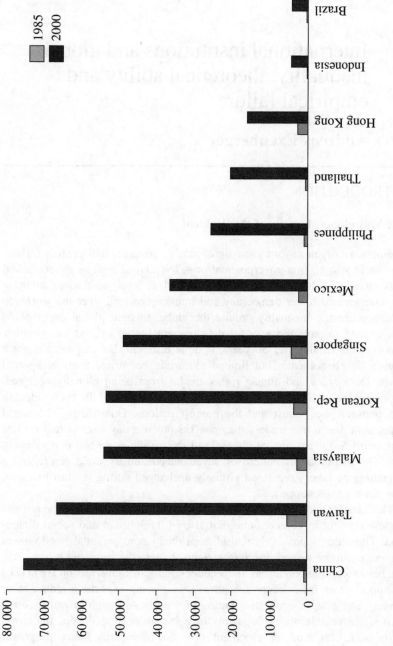

Figure 4A.4   Leading exporters of HT manufactures ($m)

5. International institutions and global inequality: theoretical ability and empirical failure

Andreas Exenberger

INTRODUCTION

The Multidimensionality of the Problem

International organizations grew significantly during the half-century follow-ing World War II: non-governmental ones (NGOs) as well as governmental ones (IGOs). A lot of hope was associated at least with some of these organizations to foster democracy and human rights all over the world, to reduce economic inequality around the globe, to fight global poverty and hunger, and to pave the way for development for all nations and peoples. However the result, after 50 years, is quite different. Development is not a worldwide phenomenon but limited to certain countries, areas and social strata. Democracy and human rights are far from being globally accepted. Economic inequality has grown, especially with respect to the ever-widening gap between the richest and the poorest nations. One-fifth of the world population has to live on less than one US dollar a day, almost half on less than two US dollars, and nearly 800 million people go to bed hungry every day. The dichotomous pattern of an advanced and dynamic centre and a stagnating periphery remained virtually unchanged during the last half-cen-tury. So what has happened?

This chapter addresses two important issues. First, it addresses the process of development in its economic, but also in its political and social dimen-sion. Thus 'development' is multidimensional: more personal freedom and democracy, more respect for human rights, better education and health serv-ice, better working conditions and a better environmental situation are at least as important as faster economic growth, increasing exports, a reduction of poverty and a more equal distribution of wealth. Although growth is often seen as the vehicle of development, there are not only spillovers, but also a lot of trade-offs. And 'development' does not necessarily mean 'progress', but simply 'change' in a somehow normative way of 'advancing towards better living conditions' (whatever might be considered as being 'better'). It is not achieved automatically, nor is it an irrevocable process. There can be setbacks and breaks in developmental processes, as well as virtual 'de-development' (in the sense of retrogression), which in fact is going on now in some parts of the world.

Poverty is a major part of this problem. The World Bank gives a good description of poverty that focuses on its multidimensionality: 'Poverty is hunger. Poverty is lack of shelter. Poverty is being sick and not being able to see a doctor. Poverty is not being able to go to school and not knowing how to read. Poverty is not having a job, is fear for the future, living one day at a time. Poverty is losing a child to illness brought about by unclean water. Poverty is powerlessness, lack of representation and freedom' (World Bank, 'Understanding Poverty'). Many countries have been lacking even the slightest progress in all of these fields for years. It is a serious challenge for all social scientists to look for ways to break the vicious circle of poverty, for poverty means hunger, illness, bad education and a lack of economic opportunities, which all reproduce poverty. Many countries and hundreds of millions of people all around the world are virtually trapped in this circle. The World Bank has been aware of this fact for at least 25 years. A report published in 1980 tells about the multidimensionality of (human) development, about the interdependence of poverty and growth (so that a cycle is formed that may be either vicious or virtuous), about the achievements made during 'three decades of poverty reduction' (before 1980), and about the fact that the poor have been facing less economic growth than the already rich (cf. World Bank, 1980).

The second issue addressed here is the specific role of international organizations in this process. Organizations are a sub-category of institutions with a higher degree of formalization and relatively transparent rules. This chapter will clearly focus on global intergovernmental organizations, particularly on the United Nations (UN), the International Monetary Fund (IMF), the World Bank and the World Trade Organization (WTO).

Institutions and Organizations

Two approaches to institutional economics guide this chapter. The first one is Douglass C. North's. He has well elaborated the connection between institutions and development and he also distinguishes formal from informal rules as well as the 'rules of the game' from 'choices within the rules' (cf. North, 1990). His starting point is simply that acquiring all the relevant information for one's decisions is impossible and acquiring some is not costless. A second crucial point for North is the question of property rights, in particular that the security of private property rights is an essential stimulus for innovation and therefore is a necessary condition of technical progress and development. Hence the main tasks of institutions (and organizations) are to reduce transaction costs and to give incentives. North adds that institutional change usually depends on the path taken and that, the longer an environment lasts, the costlier it is to leave, leading finally to a 'lock-in' situation and institutional stagnation. Institutional change is driven by changes in relative prices and the adaptation to these, either evolutionary or revolutionary, depending on the institutional framework. This seems to be one of the major problems: the global institutional environment has not adapted itself to the changes in relative prices over the last 50 years and the rules in global organizations do not allow for a smooth evolutionary process; as a consequence, the danger of revolutionary changes cannot be ruled out.

The second approach is Oliver Williamson's four levels of social analysis (cf. Williamson, 2000). From his point of view, four dimensions of the institutional setting have to be distinguished: 'embeddedness' in customs, tradition and religion (long-lasting, centuries), institutional 'environment', formal rules, constitutions, polity and bureaucracy (middle-lasting, decades), 'governance' of a given framework, which is the world of contracts and laws (short-lasting, years) and, finally, resource 'allocation' (day-to-day). Thus we are, for example, embedded in the enlightenment and the international system of nation-states; our institutional environment is the United Nations system guided by the UN Charter and the Universal Declaration of Human Rights. This system is in some areas governed by the IMF and the World Bank, using adjustment programmes which end up in everyday business, when projects are financed and bills are paid. Each higher level directly influences the levels below by defining their constraints, and each lower level gives feedback that may lead to changes in higher levels, which last longer, the higher the level. The most important levels for this chapter are the second and the third: the second ('environment') for guidelines of global (economic) politics, the third ('governance') for their implementation.

The Dimensions of Development

'Development' means opportunities that can be achieved by growing wealth, good health, more freedom and participation. This multidimensionality of development should lead to a discussion of three main dimensions: economic, social and political. Economic development performed quite well on the global scale from 1945 onwards. In the period 1950–73, advances were achieved at a historically unprecedented speed, when world GDP per capita grew by almost 3 per cent annually in purchasing power terms (cf. Maddison,

2002:129). Therefore this period is often referred to as the 'golden age', an era of (slow) global convergence due to the extraordinary performance by Japan, and Western Europe as well, and an acceptable growth performance in the rest of the world, especially due to overall GDP. This period following World War II has been recently referred to as a 'second wave' of globalization, with the first happening in the half-century before World War I (cf. Baldwin and Martin, 1999).

Three main features dominated this 'wave'. The first was the liberalization of the world economy, especially of world trade, which was of great overall importance. Worldwide mean tariffs fell from more than 40 per cent in 1948 to less than 7 per cent in 2000. The second feature was the reduction of communication costs (telephone, satellite, Internet), which was much more significant during this wave of globalization than the reduction in transportation costs. The third feature was the growing importance of international organizations built out of the ashes of World War II, a development which is often identified as a source of the growth process. But the growth story – although there have been some exceptions – did not continue: world GDP per capita grew by 1.33 per cent per year in 1973–98, which is almost the same rate as during the period 1870–1913, but considerably less than during the 'golden age'. The growth rates of all regions, with the exception of Asia (mainly due to China and Korea) decreased; and world GDP in 1973–98 grew by 3.0 per cent per year, compared to 4.9 per cent per year in 1950–73. Finally the story of convergence versus divergence is ambivalent: there is a clear convergence at the top end of the income ladder as well as at the bottom end (the 'twin-peaks' phenomenon), but general divergence has been growing (cf. Baldwin and Martin, 1999:10–11; Jones, 1997).

The second crucial dimension of development is the broad area of social development, consisting of life expectancy and the quality of life, of attacking poverty, of fulfilling basic needs, of improving education and school enrolment, and of achieving gender equality focused on empowerment (cf. Sen, 1999). The United Nations Development Programme (UNDP) especially has made valuable contributions in structuring the phenomenon and it defines 'human development' via the Human Development Index (HDI) as a combination of GDP per capita (purchasing power taken into account) as a measure of the quality of life, of life expectancy as a measure of the access to health care and therefore of physical well-being, and of a combination of school enrolment and literacy as a measure of the chances to improve one's living conditions, in particular the access to economical and social participation (cf. UNDP, 1990, 2003). In this field the 'growth' picture is clearer: almost all countries made great advances during the last half-century, although the negative impact of HIV/AIDS is strongly visible (especially in Africa), gender inequalities remain almost unchanged in large areas of the world, the reduction of poverty has been achieved mainly thanks to positive developments in China and India and their large populations, and social 'de-development' has been or is going on in transition economies in Eastern Europe and the former Soviet Union.

The third dimension of development is political development, meaning most of all two things: democratization and enforcement of the rule of law. The number of societies and countries considered as free has definitely increased over the last 50 years. One major break was the collapse of state socialism around the world from 1985 to 1992, which transformed the political systems of more than 20 countries, particularly in Eastern Europe and the former Soviet Union. These systems had been totalitarian or at least authoritarian single-party systems and became (although more or less paternalistic) multi-party systems. Some of them went a long way towards building up functioning democracies ready for access to the European Union within a single decade. While in the former communist world the breakdown of regimes resulted in democratization, in other areas of the globe the development was not that clear. Many authoritarian regimes came into power all over the world. Some countries were even torn apart by civil wars, sometimes long-lasting ones. Deficits in human rights and civil rights, not to speak of social rights, are even more serious. Despite the fact that the Universal Declaration of Human Rights is celebrating its 57th anniversary in 2005, it is not really recognized by many signatory countries and the annual reports of Amnesty International are full of violations of human rights, often very grave ones (cf., for example, Amnesty International, 2003). Other declarations (on labour rights, children's rights and women's rights) are even less significant, although often more than a hundred countries have signed these treaties (cf. UNDP, 2000:48–55).

Organization of the Chapter

This chapter deals with the ability international governmental organizations should have to strengthen global development, their failure in practice, and lessons that should be learned. It is organized as follows. The next section considers the theoretical ability of international organizations to foster global development; the third section deals with the obviousness of their failure (via a cluster analysis of 106 countries) and presents some facts showing that only parts of the world are developing and large parts are not; the fourth section offers some proposals on how to adapt the existing organizations to transform (theoretical) ability into (practical) power; concluding remarks close the chapter.

THEORETICAL ABILITY

The Most Important International Organizations

The UN system as a whole emerged from the disastrous experiences of the inter-war period and World War II. It was built in recognition of the necessity to organize intergovernmental politics more transparently and according to certain laws and guidelines, formulated in the Charter of the United Nations and the Universal Declaration of Human Rights (other declarations followed).

The United Nations, the most significant international governmental organization, consists of a lot of suborganizations. The principal organs of the UN are the Secretariat, the Security Council (15 members, ten of them rotating and five of them permanent and with veto power; it is by far the most important decision-making body of the UN), the General Assembly, the Trusteeship Council, the Economic and Social Forum, and the International Court of Justice. The United Nations system was one of the most important achievements of the twentieth century for the industrialized world. Besides the advantages discussed below, it especially helped to prevent wars between the major powers, although not completely. The system became fundamental for the foundation of powerful suborganizations (less 'powerful' are programmes and funds such as the UNDP, UNHCR or UNCTAD, functional and regional commissions, specialist agencies like ILO, FAO, UNESCO and WHO, and special entities like the United Nations University (UNU)).

In the sphere of development, the International Monetary Fund (IMF) and the World Bank Group are definitely outstanding. The IMF 'was established to promote international monetary cooperation, exchange stability, and orderly exchange arrangements; to foster economic growth and high levels of employment; and to provide temporary financial assistance to countries to help ease balance of payments adjustment' (IMF, 'About the IMF'). It became very important because it gave credit to countries with financial problems and therefore collected a lot of debtors depending on its financial resources (paid by member countries). But the IMF was not interested in development before the collapse of the Bretton Woods system during the 1970s, and development is not one of its original goals. The World Bank Group consists of the International Bank for Reconstruction and Development (IBRD), the International Development Association (IDA), the International Finance Corporation (IFC), the Multilateral Investment Guarantee Agency (MIGA) and the International Centre for Settlement of Investment Disputes (ICSID). Although it was founded initially to organize the reconstruction of Western Europe after World War II, it also took over developmental programmes during the 1970s. Currently the World Bank is the world's largest source of development assistance. It funds development programmes all over the world with primary (although not original) goals of reducing global poverty, lowering the debt burden and financing development.

These two organizations are usually meant when we talk about 'international financial institutions' (IFIs) and their common failures and problems. Both linked their assistance to adjustment programmes and stopped money if the requirements were not met. Hence they are accusers and judges at the same time – one of the major criticisms levelled against them (cf. Raffer, 2001). Another main source of criticism is that their programmes are too country-specific and not country-specific enough at the same time. This means that the IMF and World Bank for a long time have, on the one hand, given every country the same advice, while on the other hand not recognizing the spillovers from the same cure being offered for several countries that compete for the world market of a certain good and therefore treating every country as if it would be the only one assisted (cf. Stiglitz, 2002).

Another, much younger, organization is the World Trade Organization (WTO). It was founded in 1995 and defines itself as the only global international organization dealing with the rules of trade between nations. Furthermore the WTO is an international (economic) organization outside the UN system. Nevertheless there is a far longer history of multilateral regimes in trade policy. The General Agreement on Tariffs and Trade (GATT) for example allowed for a tremendous reduction in tariffs and non-tariff barriers of trade and a general liberalization of trade via the vehicle of trade 'rounds', starting as early as 1948.

Arguments and Benefits

Organizations (and institutions as well) and development are closely linked. Many of the existing international organizations even refer directly to development and developmental goals, although often a long time after their foundation. While, for example, UNCTAD and UNDP were even founded as organizations for development, and also the World Bank was an organization of reconstruction and development (although it took some time until the focus was shifted to developing countries) from the beginning, the IMF developed only slowly into an agency of development and the WTO took some years of work before discussing the Doha Development Agenda. Now it numbers assistance for developing countries and their preferential treatment among its goals, even though its primary goal remains liberalization of trade.

There are three main characteristics of international organizations like the ones discussed above: (1) they give binding norms for members and potential members, usually combined with some kind of sanctioning mechanisms; (2) they are intergovernmental and therefore transnational, as associations of different nations and as global organizations made of decision makers, workers and specialists from different nations; (3) they provide a more or less open forum for discussion and negotiation. These characteristics lead to the following implications: organizations lower transaction costs and therefore increase the efficiency of international economic relations; they help to avoid and resolve conflicts and equalize (to some degree) differences in political and military power; they allow for the correction of world market failures as well as the distortions coming from state interventionism; and finally they facilitate the discussion of transnational issues and help to build a global society.

The reduction of transaction costs is one of the benefits of institutions most often stressed by economists. Although (depending on the rules) decision making might be a long and difficult process and the results may not be satisfying, the difference between the institutional environment in the interwar period and that in the postwar period emphasizes the benefits. Multilateral negotiations are much easier and less costly than bilateral agreements leading to the same degree of coordination; common norms facilitate the whole process of decision making as well as the transactions themselves; uncertainty is reduced and planning is eased, as is contract enforcement; and misunderstandings because of implicit contracts become less of a problem. Also conflicts in all fields can be resolved more easily, more quickly and at less cost. Finally cooperation and technical assistance are enforced by organizations that provide a pool of specialists or at least ready access to these specialists by sharing the costs.

Organizations may even place some kind of 'safety net' at the disposal of certain members with serious problems (due to currency crises, economic breakdown or other external shocks) which can reduce uncertainty for all members. Thus organizations can be interpreted as providers of global public goods in certain areas, such as technical assistance, crisis management or a stable institutional environment in general. Organizations produce norms, councils and infrastructure that are useful for all members and, via feedbacks and spillovers, for non-members, too. Abilities and expertise can be pooled and the advantages of groups can be exploited. International organizations also allow for an international division of labour at the institutional level and they produce common knowledge, so the wheel does not have to be invented twice.

Owing to the three characteristics identified above, organizations are able to correct differences in power. Within organizations these differences are not completely eradicated, but they have been levelled. The information asymmetries are not fully removed, but the access to information is easier. Both parties gain from cooperation and conflict management and the arguments of all members have to be heard, which gives the best arguments a better chance of being recognized. Being the only interventionist power on a global scale, organizations principally are also able to correct for (global) market failures. If too many people are hit by, for example, the price uncertainties of the world market, an organization is capable of negotiating stabilization payments or currency regimes linked to commodity prices (on the world market). Furthermore organizations can provide rules, incentives and measures fostering technology transfer and education, fair trade and wealth, or the diffusion of political, social or environmental standards and therefore better living conditions. Usually none of this is provided effectively by the world market. International organizations are one channel of supply of this often demanded political management of world markets in particular and of globalization forces in general.

Organizations are able to correct another very special kind of market failure as well. Until now no fair competition of developmental concepts has existed, although the preconditions of development are different in all countries around the world. Most of the alternative approaches cannot be tested in practice owing to the power of the world market (and the resulting financial and economical pressure) or simply because of political pressure on the countries 'testing' them. But there is a need to challenge the developmental mainstream to investigate more and better options, especially in view of the needs of certain countries. The 'one-model-fits-all-countries' approach is definitely not appropriate, but there is a danger of following this approach in monolithic organizations. This can be avoided if organizations allow discussion of different approaches. The safety net that organizations could offer would allow countries to follow alternative approaches independently of the world market, if the organizations gave the necessary financial and institutional back-up. It would also be easier then to control for transnational spillovers of 'independent' developmental paths.

Being intergovernmental and transnational, organizations are capable of correcting market distortions coming from state interventionism: whether customs, non-tariff trade barriers, violations of internationally accepted political or social rights, excessive corruption or expropriations. International organizations are the only means to overcome this harmful aspect of the sovereignty of states through freely negotiated norms, which guarantees these corrections of 'state failures' global legitimacy. In general, international organizations play an increasingly important role in a globalizing world. They are the only way to deal with transnational problems like environmental problems, multilateral conflicts, general rules of international trade, the debt problem or global security. They are a unique chance to discuss a lot of these questions in the arena of a worldwide public and to allow the member countries to deal with transnational problems in a transnational way, so that the level of the solution is the same as the level of the problem.

Well-working international organizations may even contribute to the formation of a global society. They build up a public transnational interest, not necessarily due to the institutional setting, but even in contradiction to it or to the actions of a certain organization. The most famous and most recent example of this development is the World Social Forum (WSF) that was formed in 2001 in strict opposition to the inappropriate and ineffective policies of the IFIs as a direct reaction to the World Economic Forum (WEF).

Finally organizations form an environment that is favourable to the reaching of certain goals (such as global development, fair trading conditions or more political and personal freedom) provided that (1) they have to follow guidelines that are appropriate for reaching these goals and that (2) a relevant number of decision makers within the organizations have to follow these goals as well. If the environment is right, the governance structures will be right, and finally the resources will be allocated properly. One of the major elements that seems to be lacking is these guidelines, because there are conflicting ones implemented in the 'system' of international organizations, so the institutional environment is not stable. Another major problem that is readily avoided is decision makers who follow their private interest of profit maximizing instead of the public interest of the nations they represent. However this practice is easily countered by organizations which are able to visualize egocentric behaviour relatively easily.

EMPIRICAL FAILURE

The evidence of the failure of more than 50 years of developmental politics – and poverty reduction as well – in the international system and of more than 30 years of specific developmental efforts by the IMF and the World Bank is in fact disastrous with respect to many countries, especially those which are the targets of these organizations. For this reason, and to reaffirm the focus on poverty reduction renounced in the 1990s, the UN in 2000 published its Millennium Development Goals (MDG).[1] The half-way results of improvements in this 25-years agenda (1990–2015) are not really satisfying so far (cf. UNDP, 2003). A lot of further effort is necessary to enforce these goals. One way to go is a global compact, which could lead to a change of rules on the second level of social analysis, a change of the institutional environment. To quote the UNDP: 'But just as globalization has systematically benefited some of the world's regions, it has bypassed others as well as many groups within countries … Thus the need for a Millennial Development Compact: without it, poor countries will remain trapped in poverty, with low or negative economic growth' (UNDP, 2003:16f).

Economic Development

As has been said already, economic development performed very well on the global scale from 1945 onwards. The following tables present some data on GDP per capita in purchasing power terms (international 1990 dollars). Table 5.1 shows absolute values and Table 5.2 percentage changes for the world in general and seven regional sub-groups in particular.

These tables show how diverse economic development has been during this half-century. Although world growth declined fairly steadily, Western Europe and Asia (from a very low level) had growth rates above the world

Table 5.1   GDP per capita of world regions, 1950–98, international 1990 dollars

	1950	1960	1970	1980	1990	1998
World	2 114	2 781	3 748	4 521	5 154	5 709
Western Europe	4 594	6 930	10 297	13 226	15 988	17 921
Western offshoots	9 288	10 986	14 597	18 057	22 356	26 146
Eastern Europe	2 120	3 075	4 315	5 780	5 437	5 461
Former USSR	2 834	3 935	5 569	6 437	6 871	3 893
Latin America	2 554	3 167	4 016	5 413	5 055	5 795
Asia	713	1 032	1 536	2 036	2 781	3 565
Africa	852	1 024	1 311	1 484	1 385	1 368

Source: Maddison (2002:330).

Table 5.2   GDP per capita growth of world regions, 1950–98, international 1990 dollars, percentage change per year

	1950–60	1960–70	1970–80	1980–90	1990–98
World	2.78	3.03	1.89	1.32	1.29
Western Europe	4.20	4.04	2.53	1.91	1.44
Western offshoots	1.69	2.88	2.15	2.16	1.98
Eastern Europe	3.79	3.45	2.97	–0.61	0.06
Former USSR	3.34	3.53	1.46	0.65	–6.86
Latin America	2.17	2.40	3.03	–0.68	1.72
Asia	3.77	4.06	2.86	3.17	3.15
Africa	1.86	2.50	1.25	–0.69	–0.15

Source: Maddison (2002:330); own calculation.

average over the whole period, as the communist countries had until the 1970s and the Western offshoots (USA, Canada, Australia, New Zealand) from the 1970s on. All other regions (except for Latin America during the 1970s) faced growth rates below the average, most extremely Latin America and Eastern Europe during the 1980s, the former USSR during the 1990s and Africa from the 1980s on.

Hence a widening gap of intraregional divergence can be examined: while the difference between the richest and the poorest of these world regions even decreased in the 1950s, from 13 to 1 to 10.7 to 1, it increased from the 1960s on and especially in the 1980s and 1990s, from 11.4 (1970), 12.2 (1980), 16.1 (1990) to 19.1 (1998). Besides the large temporal difference between the periods before and after the first oil shock, several regional differences also occurred, especially during the second period. Economic performance differed remarkably from country to country, but also from region to region. While, for example, China reached its growth peak during the 1980s and 1990s, several countries in Sub-Saharan Africa never again reached the historical high in absolute value of GDP per capita they had already achieved in the 1960s. Divergence grew all over the world: while the top end of the GDP ladder realized growth rates above average, the bottom end even absolutely lost ground. On (arithmetic) average, 42 African countries in 1998 held only 77 per cent of their historical postwar maximum of GDP per capita; for only eight of them, this maximum was reached in 1998, but ten held less than 60 per cent, two even less than 40 per cent. Even in Asia the (arithmetic) average of 37 countries is not higher than 84 per cent, although mainly owing to

Table 5.3   Shares of world GDP, by world regions, 1950–98 (per cent)

	1950	1960	1970	1980	1990	1998
World GDP (international 1990 $ trillions)	5.34	8.45	13.80	20.03	27.08	33.73
World GDP (annual growth rate)	—	4.71	5.03	3.79	3.06	2.78
Western Europe	26.3	26.8	26.3	24.3	22.3	20.6
Western offshoots	30.6	27.5	25.6	24.4	24.6	25.1
Eastern Europe	3.5	3.6	3.4	3.4	2.4	2.0
Former USSR	9.6	10.0	9.8	8.5	7.3	3.4
Latin America	7.9	8.2	8.3	9.8	8.3	8.7
Asia	18.5	20.6	23.3	26.2	31.9	37.2
Africa	3.6	3.4	3.4	3.5	3.2	3.1

Source: Maddison (2002:329); own calculation.

excessive losses in GDP per capita by several oil-exporting countries during
the 1980s and 1990s (cf. Maddison, 2002, appendix C, own calculation).

The shares in world-GDP (Table 5.3), which rose sixfold from 1950 to
1998, also give clear evidence of the change in economic weights. While the
share of the (former) communist world dropped from 13.6 per cent (1960) to
5.4 per cent (1998), and the share of the West dropped by more than 12 per
cent, Asia doubled its weight to 37.2 per cent (1998). Africa stayed at the
marginal level of 3 per cent, although its population share grew to almost 13
per cent.

Social Development

At first, some numbers about the improvements in literacy and life expectancy, also used for the overall analysis following later, shall be presented in
regionally grouped aggregates (see Table 5.4).

Life expectancy has clearly improved during the last half-century. In 1950,
people in industrialized countries lived for 60 to 70 years, in 2000 usually for
around 80. The same is true of developing countries that improved a wide
range of life expectancy (of 30 to 60 years in 1950) by around 15 years on
average. This development held until recently, but during the 1990s some
countries, especially in Sub-Saharan Africa, suffered a setback in life expect-

*Table 5.4   Social indicators, by regional country groups (number of
countries in brackets)*

	Illiteracy*		Life expectancy		Illiteracy, women		Life expectancy, women	
	1975	1998	1975	1999	1975	1998	1975	1999
Western Europe (16)	—	—	72.8	77.8	—	—	76.1	80.8
Western offshoots (4)	—	—	72.7	77.9	—	—	76.3	80.7
Latin America (22)	25.6	14.3	62.5	69.9	28.7	15.6	64.8	73.0
Asia (29)	44.3	25.7	57.7	67.8	55.6	33.2	59.1	69.6
Africa (35)	64.2	39.8	48.6	52.0	74.4	48.1	50.3	53.2

Note: * Illiteracy rates of industrialized countries are not calculated, because these countries
do not collect and report actual illiteracy rates to the UN, for political reasons. Although there is
relevant functional illiteracy in all of these countries, they officially neglect the problem completely.

Source: UNDP (2000), World Bank (CD-ROM); own calculation.

ancy because of HIV/AIDS (in some countries the reduction was 10 years and more during the 1990s; see the appendix for some country data). Even worse, this disease mainly affects the economically most active population (people around 25 years of age) and is therefore a serious challenge for development.

Absolute poverty was even more resistant to reduction strategies. Following development strategies of the 1970s that focused on basic needs, poverty was the target, during the 1990s once more, of international organizations, but the absolute number of impoverished people did not decrease, remaining at 1.2 billion people living on less than one dollar a day. India and Sub-Saharan Africa are particularly hit by poverty; in some countries more than 90 per cent of the population have to live on less than two dollars a day. Directly connected with this is the problem of the distribution of goods that satisfy basic needs (food, shelter, security and so on). Food, water, housing, clothing, heating, lighting, health care, sanitary facilities, the absence of civil order and the presence of wars, not to speak of the lack of social safety nets and insurance, are closely connected. Therefore hunger and disease are global realities of the twenty-first century, although there would be enough food and enough medicine to cure both. The people in charge of the resources and the organizations obviously lack the will to restructure the distribution of these goods to meet the needs of all human beings around the globe.

The educational situation has indeed been improved, especially at primary level and for men. In absolute numbers, primary school enrolment has risen tenfold in Africa since 1950 and more than fivefold in the developing world in general. Literacy rates increased to almost 75 per cent in 2000 even in developing countries, and combined (primary and secondary) school enrolment rose to more than 60 per cent (cf. UNDP, 2002:149–52). Although a lot has been done already to achieve gender equality, inequality in this field is still a worldwide fact. Women are discriminated against in many respects and in almost all countries of the world. In some countries the life expectancy of women is even lower than that of men, while in the developed world the difference is around three years in favour of women. Estimates for the differences in earned income shares are around one-third (more only in very poor countries), while differences in the access to education have decreased most, except for some strongly patriarchal societies (ibid.:222–5).

Finally some general trends in human development (following the UNDP) should be presented (Table 5.5). Three main features can be seen: world development is (slowly) growing: 24 per cent of theoretically possible improvements have been made since 1975; the (former) communist countries have in fact been stagnating since 1975; and Africa is lagging far behind. This overall view can also be reproduced by comparing the countries which

Table 5.5   Trends in human development, HDI 1975–2000, arithmetic means

	1975	1980	1985	1990	1995	2000
World (number of countries)	100	112	123	135	139	173
World (mean)	0.593	0.630	0.642	0.664	0.675	0.692
World (maximum)	0.874	0.886	0.906	0.926	0.932	0.942
World (minimum)	0.232	0.253	0.246	0.256	0.262	0.275
Western Europe	0.832	0.846	0.860	0.880	0.901	0.919
Western offshoots	0.856	0.871	0.886	0.901	0.922	0.934
Eastern Europe and former USSR	0.766	0.762	0.777	0.789	0.768	0.776
Latin America	0.654	0.676	0.689	0.705	0.724	0.752
Asia	0.581	0.614	0.631	0.643	0.678	0.701
Africa	0.390	0.425	0.449	0.464	0.475	0.498

Source: UNDP (2002:153–6); own calculation.

improved their scores most and least. The absolute index value of 11 out of 18 former communist countries decreased during the 1990s; the same is true for nine out of 39 African countries; another nine enhanced their scores by less than 5 per cent. On the other hand, five countries (Indonesia, Tunisia, Egypt, China and Nepal) improved their scores from 1975 to 2000 by more than 0.2 points and 22 closed more than half of the remaining gap to the theoretical maximum of 1 (ibid.: 153–6; own calculation).

Political Development

As discussed above, 'progress' in political development is not completely clear, for various reasons. Although it is true that the breakdown of communism was a great leap towards freedom in most of the affected countries, and it is true that some kind of democratization is going on all over the world, there are also serious setbacks. Many countries are facing authoritarian regimes, violations of human rights (even in the North, but graver in the South), civil disorder, uncertainty of the rule of law, and long-lasting civil wars, while Western Europe saw some successful liberation movements during the 1970s (Spain, Portugal, Greece), and Africa and Asia faced decolonization during the 1940s, 1950s and 1960s – often to replace a repressive colonial regime with a repressive post-colonial one. The picture is quite ambivalent, despite multi-party elections spreading across the globe. Although elections of that type are not a sufficient condition for democracy, one can legitimately doubt whether they are a necessary one, because elections and parties do not save people from repression.

Nevertheless all these developments have led to more political freedom around the world. This can be seen by the growing relative number of demo-cratic governments and by the improving scores of political and civil rights of Freedom House. Although these scores are ideologically and technically questionable, they give on average an overview of the situation of the world and, at least during the late 1990s, they covered almost all countries of the world.

Table 5.6 shows that 'freedom' is improving worldwide on average, at least from 1985 onwards. The number or countries with average scores of political and civil freedom (arithmetical mean) from 1 to 1.5 (fully free) increased from 24 to 59 (31 per cent of all countries rated) while especially the number of countries with scores above average decreased from 88 to 72 (or from 60 to 38 per cent of all countries rated, which means growing convergence). Especially during the last years also the number of countries with a score of 7 (not free) decreased sharply.

Table 5.6   Scores of Freedom House, 1975–2000

Year	Number of countries rated	Arithmetic mean of score	Score 1–1.5	Score 2–4	Score 4.5–6.5	Score 7
1975	147	4.39	24	35	72	16
1980	161	4.26	22	48	74	17
1985	166	4.27	32	41	76	17
1990	167	4.04	40	41	66	20
1995	191	3.70	48	70	52	21
2000	192	3.51	59	61	59	13

Source: http://www.freedomhouse.org/research/freeworld/FHSCORES.xls; own calculation.

Overall Analysis: Clusters of Development

Owing to the extreme differences between developmental paths and the seri-ous break following the first oil price shock, we will focus on the developmental process during the 'period of problems', as it might be called, from 1975 on. While before this break development had been almost a global phenomenon, and the growth rates and social developments as well as political progress occurred in all continents, a sharp break and growing divergence can be observed afterwards. Furthermore world (economic) growth slowed down

significantly, whereas achievements in social development and political turno-
vers continued to happen, especially at the beginning of the 1990s.

Cluster analysis can help us to understand better the structure of the data.
We use average linkage between groups and (simple) Euclidean distances
(software SPSS) as well as 11 variables, grouped according to the three
dimensions of development and distinguishing between variables that measure status (in 1998/9) and variables that measure the direction and strength of
change (for data description and sources, consult the appendix). Economic
development is measured by GDP per capita in purchasing power in 1998, its
average growth in 1975–98 and the standard deviation of its growth rates in
1975–98; political development is measured by the average of the Freedom
House Index of 1993–8 and of its change from 1972–7 to 1993–8; finally
social development is measured by life expectancy at birth in 1998, the adult
illiteracy rate in 1999, a women's development index 1998/9 (which comprises the other social variables) and the changes of these variables from
1975 to 1998/9.

The GDP per capita variable was transformed into natural logarithms, and
all variables were normalized and weighted, so that all status and change
variables (whether composed of more than one indicator or not) accounted
for half of the measurement in each of the three distinguished dimensions of
development, these dimensions being equally weighted by one-third each. In
all, 106 countries could be incorporated in the analysis: 16 from Western
Europe, four Western offshoots (USA, Canada, Australia and New Zealand),
22 from Latin America, 28 from Asia and 36 from Africa. Unfortunately the
countries of Eastern Europe and the countries of the former USSR could not
reasonably be incorporated (owing to a lack of serious estimates of GDP
comparable to Maddison's data), along with most of the small countries of
the world. Hence the group of 'transformation countries', which would be
clearly visible in the data, is entirely missing. So a lot of gaps could be filled
that would help us to understand even better the controversial developmental
picture of recent decades.

The results (Table 5.7) indicate that quite useful solutions could be found
at the level of three or five, to a lesser extent also of seven, clusters (for
numerical details, consult the appendix). All country data are provided in the
appendix, sorted by the seven-cluster solution.

At the three-cluster level there are three groups: the 'special case' Gambia
(bad development in all dimensions, especially the political), a group of 27
'Northern' countries and a group of 78 'Southern' countries. At the five-
cluster level the picture is more diverse: the group of advanced countries is
split into a cluster AC1 with lower economic and social status (not political)
but serious progress in all fields (0.3 per cent more growth, less volatility of
the growth path, better political development, more improvement of life

Table 5.7 Arithmetical group means of cluster variables, five-cluster solution

Cluster	No. of countries	VEDS	VEDC1	VEDC2	VPDS	VPDC	VSDS1	VSDS2	VSDS3	VSDC1	VSDC2	VSDC3
AC1	21	16 813	2 324	2 643	1.3	0.876	2.84	76.81	0.782	5.61	4.25	0.002
AC2	6	18 506	2 035	5 216	1.6	0.028	1.67	78.65	0.773	5.90	2.93	-0.006
DC	40	3 921	0.821	4 743	5.3	-0.102	26.05	65.43	0.543	8.37	20.65	0.096
NC	38	2 167	0.193	5 589	3.6	0.433	34.37	56.12	0.501	4.82	19.80	0.004
Gambia	1	850	-0.832	11 591	6.4	-0.733	65.40	45.90	0.474	7.69	21.90	-0.103
Total	106	6 643	0.947	4 722	3.7	0.285	23.4	64.9	0.588	6.4	16.1	0.037

Source: own calculation.

113

expectancy and better conditions for women) and a cluster AC2 (where the opposite is true). The other group of 'developing' countries consists of a cluster DC with better social indicators and especially better changes in the field of social development and also higher economic status and change (but a worse situation in the political field), and a cluster NC, where the opposite obtains: poor economic growth, social improvements from a lower starting point, but some political developments and better political status. Thus the picture is still quite diverse, and it seems to be useful to turn to the seven-cluster solution to identify certain characteristics within these 'developmental' clusters.

AC1 and AC2 remain unchanged (as well as, obviously, Gambia). However a lot of change of strong analytical interest is going on in the DC and the NC clusters. The 'old' DC cluster forms two clusters: the first (DC1) has a relative low status of development in all respects (although in the political dimension much better than the NC cluster), but stronger changes going on; the second one (DC2) has a relatively high status of development, but the changes are slower (except for gender equality, where this cluster represents a quite high standard).

Even more interesting is the story of the 'old' NC cluster. It splits into a cluster of 21 countries caught in real 'de-development' (low status in all dimensions, negative developments in economy and in gender equality, slow development in public health, high volatility of the growth path and therefore high vulnerability) and a cluster of 17 well developing countries (WCs). The latter have the best economic growth performance of all clusters apart from the advanced countries and they have the highest status of political development as well, whereas only their social indicators lack optimal improvements.

Summing up, we can see from this analysis: (1) that there is a very sharp break between a group of 'Northern' countries (AC1 and AC2) and a group of 'Southern' countries (all other clusters); (2) that, furthermore, clusters of different speeds of development can be identified, particularly a cluster of countries with very serious problems in development; and (3) that development is a multidimensional phenomenon and no cluster represents a high standard in all dimensions. Especially the existence of an 'NC' cluster, lacking development in almost all respects, and composed of one-fifth of all countries in the sample, is a serious challenge to a half-century of international organizations actively attacking poverty and fostering development. Also the differences between countries and groups of countries, as well as the number of people concerned, should not be neglected. Therefore proposals to improve international organizations with respect to the needs of these people, in particular the poorest ones, and the differences within and between countries, represent a serious task.

Table 5.8 Arithmetical group means of cluster variables, seven-cluster solution

Cluster	No. of countries	VEDS	VEDC1	VEDC2	VPDS	VPDC	VSDS1	VSDS2	VSDS3	VSDC1	VSDC2	VSDC3
AC1	21	16 813	2 324	2 643	1.28	0.88	76.8	2.8	0.782	5.6	4.3	0.002
AC2	6	18 506	2 035	5 216	1.57	0.03	78.7	1.7	0.773	5.9	2.9	−0.006
WC	17	3 570	1 423	4 936	2.65	0.59	62.8	20.9	0.640	5.9	16.3	0.051
DC1	23	2 695	945	4 985	6.33	−0.09	62.0	29.1	0.459	8.6	24.6	0.075
DC2	17	5 581	652	4 416	3.92	−0.12	70.1	21.9	0.656	8.1	15.3	0.125
NC	21	1 031	−803	6 118	4.42	0.31	50.8	45.2	0.389	3.9	22.6	−0.035
Gambia	1	850	−832	11 591	6.40	−0.73	45.9	65.4	0.474	7.7	21.9	−0.103
Total	106	6 643	947	4 722	3.7	0.285	64.9	23.4	0.588	6.4	16.1	0.037

Source: own calculation.

115

PROPOSALS

Worldwide economic development is diverse, as has been shown in the previous section. Social conditions improved even more than the political ones, but there is still a lot of work to do and there are serious setbacks in certain areas (decreasing life expectancy in Africa, hunger, re-emergence of certain diseases due to bad sanitary and medical conditions, even growing gender inequality in certain regions, new authoritarian regimes, civil wars and failing states).

The evidence of explicit organizational failure in this field is thus obvious. Some 50 years of poverty-reduction strategies were on the one hand partially successful but on the other hand led to growing economic divergence, to an increasing number of sick and hungry people, and to civil disorder in parts of the world. This is true not only in the long run, but also for the last 30 years as well as for the last ten years of poverty-reduction strategies. And there is little hope that conditions will change in a positive way as long as the payments for debt services from the South to the North exceed by far the payments of development assistance from the North to the South.

This negative conclusion is especially valid in the case of the IFIs, though this is often completely neglected by them, and the criticism is manifold (cf. Cavanagh, 1994; Chossudovsky, 2001; Raffer and Singer, 2001; Stiglitz, 2002; Tetzlaff, 1996; Ziegler, 2003). Even frequently cited textbook examples of extraordinary development, of 'newly industrializing' (Korea, Taiwan, Hong Kong and Singapore and, to a much lesser extent, Thailand, Viet Nam and Indonesia), developed virtually without any assistance from these organizations. The same is true for China and its dual system of a 'planned market economy'. Conversely the countries most assisted by the IFIs (such as Argentina, Haiti, Panama, Uruguay, Guyana, Bangladesh, Sri Lanka, Madagascar, Uganda and Zambia) have a much worse record of development. This seems to be quite usual if it is taken into account that, since the 1970s, the IMF and the World Bank have been assisting countries in economic and, especially, financial trouble, but there are two important issues that should not be forgotten: crisis and trouble create jobs in these organizations and, because they are not held to account for their actions, crisis and trouble are not prevented but even enforced (cf. Raffer, 2001). And the overall economic costs of IMF programmes are often as high as the economic costs of the crisis managed, or even higher, so that the cure becomes worse than the disease (cf. Hutchinson, 2001).

Most of the intellectual criticisms (and the public protests as well) during the last years and decades have been aimed at the IMF, some also at the World Bank, while the WTO seems to be young enough to have avoided most criticism until recently. However the WTO is now heavily attacked by a somehow globalized 'civil society' for its policy focus on 'everywhere-and-everything-now liberalization' without any acknowledgment of possible spillovers. Therefore all three organizations definitely require reforms to fit the real needs of the people confronted by the outcomes of their policies – and their broad majority does not live in the North, but in the South.

Some Paradigmatic Remarks

To sum up the criticisms some proposals for reform should be presented in this section. What seems to be most important is the adaptation of the institutional framework to the levels of social analysis introduced by Oliver Williamson. A structure containing all international organizations has to be built, that defines overall norms, rules and polity, a structure that formulates binding guidelines for all international organizations to act as their roof. If certain conditions are met (to be elaborated in this section), the result will be a slim, efficient, transparent and transnational organization to define the institutional environment, containing also rules to clarify how rules are to be changed (for example, how to introduce new or different bodies of decision-making, how to change voting provisions, or how to exchange or clarify guidelines), but being close to the actual needs of the people at the same time. At a lower level special agencies should be formed to get the governance structures of the global institutional environment right and to organize everyday business, but should be fully responsible (with respect to the guidelines) for their actions.

At first, the General Assembly and the Secretariat of the United Nations can play the role of the roof-structure, the former being the democratic forum for discussing and defining the rules, the latter the organizational unit to enforce these rules and to care for a smooth operation of the whole system. This is, indeed, the same idea that guided the foundation of the United Nations system post World War II: one general organization defines rules and guidelines via its Charter and a 'Universal' Declaration of Human Rights, other organizations and special agencies follow them, for economic development, financial assistance, social questions, human rights, children, trade and many other issues. Some of these organizations were never actually founded, some never gained real importance, while in the developmental process especially the IMF and World Bank achieved an even higher prominence than the UN itself, finally defining their own guidelines. And the WTO stands entirely outside the whole UN system. Therefore reforms are desperately needed to establish the essential governing body that smoothly coordinates the policies of suborganizations in order to avoid transaction costs resulting from duplicate or even contradictory actions.

If this concept is to function, further conditions have to be met: what seems to be crucial is the democratization of all organizations. Although 'democracy' is a concept much advertised in international relations, it is not elaborated in practice, as can be shown best by the WTO's decision-making structure, which is 'consensual' precisely because of the fact that developing countries have the majority of votes in the formal decision-making bodies of the WTO. The same is true of the UN system and the central position of the Security Council with the veto power of its five permanent members and the very special (and somehow hegemonic) position of the United States in particular within the whole system (single veto power within the IMF, host of the headquarters, main financier). This is all too true of the IFIs. In fact a real 'democratization' of international organizations would mean changing the institutional paradigm of the era post World War II, which can only be achieved by a higher level being able to define binding norms, such as the structure outlined above. To be clear: one may legitimately doubt whether the principle of 'one-country-one-vote' is very democratic (it is democratic on the basis of the existing institution 'international system of states'), or whether it is rather unfair to give the Maldives the same power as India or Luxembourg as much as Angola. However this principle in some way levels the inequality of the real world, where the populous and rich nations dispose of considerably more power and resources than the small and poor. Nevertheless one should discuss some practice of double majority to make the system more realistic (and therefore gain support also in powerful countries) and to correct the economic inequalities of 'real' power. This is especially important to ensure the democratic legitimacy of the institutional framework, its acceptance by the elites and the people, and for gaining their support.

The main dilemma to be solved seems to be that the gains of negotiations have to exceed their unavoidable costs (due to the duration of decision making and discussion), which increase because of democratic procedures. Otherwise mutual negotiations will be stopped, bilateralism will triumph over multilateralism, and the institutional system will collapse. In order to avoid such problems, further conditions have to be met: democratization means the implementation of clear and binding norms and the real empowerment of the rule of law in international relations. It is of importance to note that this does not simply mean applying the laws already codified (such as the articles of the IMF or the World Bank and the UN Charter). While being a step forward, it would not be sufficient. What is required is new norms appropriate for the needs of the whole community of states, not to speak of peoples or – even more – people, that have to be newly negotiated by the members of the international community. This leads to another important step. The character of almost every international organization as a forum of discussion has to be taken seriously and has to be strengthened to raise transparency and commitment by the people affected by the outcomes of global politics. Besides the crucial need to use the advantages of the division of labour by organizing work in special bodies, commissions and working groups of selective countries, the proposals elaborated have to be discussed by all members to come up with the best solution possible. 'Green room' meetings (that is, those with a very restricted attendance) are the wrong way, as one of the most important tasks of international organizations is to correct differences in real power and to empower the formerly powerless.

Strongly connected with this aspect is another one. The power of the slowly emerging global civil society that often defines its common identity by opposing the politics of international governmental organizations has to be utilized in this process. The conflict between governmental and non-governmental organizations has to be taken seriously because it gives hints about the deficits of the whole institutional system. The criticism and the proposals by non-governmental organizations like the WSF, reflecting the opinion of a big group of people organized worldwide, should be taken as a chance to come closer to the needs of people all over the world and to gain support for specific policy measures and political legitimacy in general. Furthermore these needs are constantly changing, and these changes can be observed better by non-governmental organizations and the civil society. Therefore any international organization without their effective participation is inappropriate. The participation will help to strengthen the global civil society that is necessary for the legitimacy (in the sense of the acceptance or even support by a broad majority) of the whole system. Hence another change of paradigms is needed: the right mix of inter-governmentalism (which is efficient, but not appropriate, and which dominated the past decades institutionally), transnational political citizenship and democratic control (which is appropriate, but so far not efficient on a global scale) has to be found. Sanctioning power too is an element of this discussion and negotiation process as it is a logical outcome of it.

For a reduction of transaction costs and of uncertainty more transparency is needed, too, as well as a clear focus on assistance and cooperation: much more substantial than is actually implemented. The pooling of expertise, the advantages of the division of labour, the financing of technical assistance, the strengthening of technology transfer, and so on, have to be clearly formulated and implemented. Binding norms to avoid misunderstandings and serious interpretational differences are essential. Therefore definitions are required: what is a market failure, what is a distortion coming from state interventionism, what is a transnational problem, what do democracy and the rule of law mean (at least in minimum standards)? It is necessary to find a global compromise on questions like these that bind all countries to general norms: broadly defined, but substantial norms. Without a common understanding on major issues, discussions and negotiations, especially about sanctions, are fruitless. The best recent example is the 'War on Saddam': most of the people in the world (even in Islamic countries) have agreed that Saddam Hussein should be deprived of his power for being a brutal dictator; but the same people have largely disagreed about the precise reason why (and have therefore asked: why he alone?). And the concrete reasoning put forward by the USA and Great Britain (weapons of mass destruction, supporting terror) was not very convincing, in fact being based on an interpretation of so-called 'facts' that was obviously completely misleading.

Some Concrete Steps

These paradigmatic changes will definitely take time, but they have to be started. Initial steps are indicated by the following concrete proposals for reforms and changes in the institutional environment needed desperately, especially by NCs, but also by DCs and WCs. First, criteria of good governance and priorities in human development are necessary and have to be implemented globally. In this way the whole process of negotiating conditions for grants and assistance would be more transparent, and this would lead to greater confidence and better support in donor countries as well as receiving countries. This clearly means the definition of minimum standards and it cannot mean the oppression of certain forms of government, of democracy, or of a certain amount of social expenses.

Second, fair dispute settlement is required to prevent conflicts and wars, regionally as well as globally. Therefore independent fixed tribunals are to be installed on certain issues, following clear and stable rules, and enforcing these rules effectively. The WTO system provides a nucleus of dispute settlement of this kind, with two serious deficits. First, the tribunal is not really independent. It should consist, not mainly of members appointed by the parties involved, but of specialists appointed for the concrete cases. Second, and more important, the outcome of the process must have serious consequences which include collective retaliation and reparation payments that correct differences in real power.

Third, several criteria, (trade) preferences and institutional requirements (liberalization) should be handled as flexibly as possible – even more than in the WTO system. At least they should depend on the specific situation in the country and should follow the needs of the people there. This means that nobody should be forced to take actions that exceed his (or her) abilities (what this stands for is a question to be agreed on first), criteria and requirements have to be adapted flexibly to those abilities. Additionally preferences should be extended for countries with more developmental deficits than others, while requirements should be much stronger for advanced countries (ACs) than for well-developing countries (WCs), developing countries (DCs) and, especially, non-developing countries (NCs). A system of incentives for improvements in human development (particularly in its social and political dimension) should be added to this flexible scheme. NCs need more preferences, but also more freedom, flexibility, obligingness and incentives than DCs or WCs.

Fourth, the correct sequencing of all measures in the different spheres of development is indeed significant, therefore a collaboration of organizations and local authorities should be implemented as another 'paradigm' of development, as development means partnership and there is nothing like an 'overall theory' of 'the best way to develop'. In this process, North and South are both teachers and pupils at the same time.

Fifth, because export is a vehicle of growth and often the main or single source of revenue, and public debts are a main reason for budgetary problems in NCs (and DCs as well), export revenues of countries dependent on certain resources (especially primary ones) have to be stabilized and the debt burden has to be relieved (for example, by the instrument of the insolvency of states). This will also stabilize the production costs in industries using these resources and it gives creditors in the long run better chances of repayment of their credits and therefore stabilizes the international financial markets. This measure, best enacted by insurance, is closely linked to the liberalization of the markets for food and textiles in the industrialized countries to employ the possible gains of comparative advantage.

Finally, if there is a clear orientation of all organizations on developmental tasks, more money will be needed. Most of the ACs do not spend the often cited 0.7 per cent of their GDP on development assistance; in most cases it is considerably less. Obviously most of the countries are not willing to follow this goal voluntarily, so some kind of global taxation (in a very moderate form) is to be implemented, if – and only if – the conditions of transparency, legitimacy and credibility will be met by the global institutional environment. Otherwise it will not be possible to gain enough public support for this measure.

Some Final Reasoning

Thus steps for liberalization of markets in favour of developing countries, following their needs (as is even expressed in the UN Charter of 1945) have to be taken. These measures cost money, market shares, employment and revenues, so why should the elites in ACs (and in other countries as well) which guide the development of the institutional environment act in this way?

First of all, the measures mentioned above are paradigmatic and therefore their implementation will take a lot of time. It is a question, not of ten years to implement this institutional scheme, but of less than ten years to start this process. Taking the necessary steps is the only way to change the institutional system in such a way that it will fit the needs of the people within – let us say – a half-century. There are two main reasons for this necessity, the first being theoretical, the second very practical.

From a theoretical point of view reforms are required to make the institutional scheme consistent with the processes of social change, in its institutional dimension elaborated by North and represented by the levels of social analysis of Williamson. Organizations are not the right instrument to define the overall embeddedness of the system, as the shaping of customs, conventions and culture is a very informal process, which is reflected in organizations, but not guided by them. So what organizations have to manage are the three remaining levels: environment, governance and allocation. The way this is done has to be consistent with the ongoing changes in relative prices emphasized by North as a crucial feature in global economics as well as in history.[2] Apparently 'eternal' organizations are not able to reflect these changes readily and therefore steadily lose support, legitimacy and importance. If this radical change, reflected by – at the same time – a democratization of all organizations and the construction of a slim, but efficient overall structure, is not implemented, the outcome is clear: social change will reflect the changes in relative prices sooner or later, and the longer this process is (seemingly) slowed down, the greater and faster will be the actual change. Instead of a smooth evolutionary process of change, a revolutionary change will occur, being anything but smooth.

This leads to the very practical reason for reforms. The alternative to a managed reform and a transition into a more democratic institutional system which better reflects the needs of the people is simply growing inequality and therefore growing insecurity in the world. Conflicts (political as well as economic), migration, social clashes, rioting, political extremism, terrorism, wars (not regionally terminable and particularly dangerous because of the proliferation of weapons of mass destruction) and civil disorder in general will increase owing to growing inequality and economic contraction in some parts of the world and in some social strata. There is also a danger of political blockades as a reaction to these structures because of the lack of legitimacy of organizations (and political elites in general) in the eyes of many people and, sometimes, also elites. The failed WTO conferences of Seattle (1999) and Cancún (2003) are examples of these two types of failure by blockade. All this raises control costs and transaction costs very considerably; it complicates the decision-making process and it lowers the efficiency and profitability of ordinary business (while some businesses will always profit from disorder). Furthermore it turns the actions of international organizations into pure crisis management, only sometimes successful and without any creative and productive component, and therefore accelerates a vicious circle of legitimacy loss.

A serious problem for the whole process is the fact that some countries definitely believe that they will be able to avoid or to control the negative outcomes of the growing need for change and of the possible revolutionary changes (in North's sense) in the near future. This view is entirely misleading. Certainly, some regions will cope with their problems, but it is hardly possible to name these regions reliably in advance, while in general the global situation worsens. Hence the probability of getting into serious (economic and political) trouble is quite high, which leads us (another theoretical argument) to contract theory: as long as there is uncertainty about the future connected with a strong probability of negative consequences, it is efficient to avoid risky situations in advance and therefore to build up a stable institutional framework like the one outlined above.

Even the strongest and richest nation on earth, the United States, has not been able to avoid the negative outcomes of global politics. The 'War on Terrorism', declared after 9/11, does not help to make the world a safer place (the contrary is true, as can be seen daily in the news). It does not even help to make the United States a safer place (if the severe restrictions on civil rights are taken into account). What it does is increase costs, leading to the most excessive budget deficit in the history of the United States, which in the medium run will severely damage its economic competitiveness. This case is also a good example of how difficult and costly unilateral politics is today, because unilateral actions taken without considering opposing opinions result in 'collateral damage'. A lot of effort (by both sides) is necessary to rebuild confidence and the willingness to collaborate, which in fact is urgently needed in a world as interdependent as today's.

The path to follow is not an easy one. The political and economical elites of most countries are not nearly as affected by the negative consequences of their actions as is the majority of the people. Their interest in the short run is dominated by different attitudes towards global fairness, justice and even development, and will be far more inward-oriented than outward-oriented. So what dominates politics is national crisis management instead of international crisis prevention. This means that the political agenda has to be changed, a task for which, in democratic political systems, the electorate is fully responsible, because it is, at least in theory, possible to exchange the elites and to gain democratic majorities in favour of crisis prevention, implying institutional fair and just structures, which are therefore more efficient in the medium and the long run than the existing ones.

CONCLUSIONS

What is desperately needed is more legitimacy of organizations, a coming closer to the people represented by them. Furthermore a clear distinction is necessary between groups of countries and respect for their within-and-between differences, otherwise organizations will always remain far from the people and will lose support day by day. Although every single country is unique and therefore has to be treated 'individually', many countries have the same or at least similar problems. Therefore awareness of these differences and of the similarities is badly needed. In fact, NCs do not need credits, they need grants and help, while DCs need supervised credits and assistance binding both sides equally, and WCs and ACs need some 'technical' assistance and institutions for the smooth operation of business, because it is quite easy for them to acquire money on ordinary international financial markets. An appropriate step in reform would be a clear distinction between agencies dealing with ACs, WCs, DCs and NCs, guided by an overall framework, being aware of the spillovers of policy measures between countries and (regional and functional) country groups, and of the different dimensions of development, as well as organizations that focus on these different dimensions. This would be a big, but necessary step.

To change the institutional paradigm in the ways mentioned above (democracy, partnership, evenness, human development) means correcting a serious institutional failure of recent decades. It seems that the institutions of the era post World War II are not really appropriate for the needs of the majority of the world's population. Thus organizations are not to blame for the whole mess; institutions are to blame as well. An institution like the 'Washington Consensus' seems to be completely misleading and inadequate for the needs especially of the NCs. More generally, the global institutional framework of 'trade liberalization', unaware of criticism, of variable conditions and of the different dimensions of the developmental process, that has been in power for the whole period since World War II, has to be discussed. What seems to be one step in the right direction is to read the principles of the institutional system as they were formulated in 1945 once more, and to take them seriously. These principles have not changed since then, but they are read in a different way today. A global discussion about what is good or bad for all of us is necessary to correct for misinterpretations.

So far – and maybe for the first time in history – it is in our hands to ensure our very future, a future of peace, freedom and wealth all over the world, or a future of inequality and at least partial disorder. Changes will come and there are two ways to react: either change or being changed, either to some degree control the direction of change or simply to adapt to it. Thus, while institutions and organizations fail to fulfil the needs of the people, scientists as well as policy makers and citizens in countries with the power of global decision making share the responsibility for changing them. Many steps in the right direction are needed and every single one can be useful. So let us make a start.

NOTES

1. These eight goals, general goals for all international organizations somehow linked to the UN system, are (1) eradicate (!) extreme poverty and hunger; (2) achieve universal primary education; (3) promot gender equality and empower women; (4) reduce child mortality; (5) improve maternal health; (6) combat HIV/AIDS, malaria and other diseases; (7) ensure environmental sustainability; (8) evolve a global partnership for development. Cf. UN, 'UN Millennium Developmental Goals'.
2. What is meant by theses changes in relative prices is, for instance, the change in the distribution of GDP between labour and capital, or the price of raw materials relative to capital goods or certain services.

BIBLIOGRAPHY

Amnesty International (2003), *Amnesty International Report 2003*, London: Amnesty International Publications (see also http://web.amnesty.org/report2003/index-eng).

Arrighi, Giovanni, Robert P. Korzeniewicz, David Consiglio and Timothy P. Moran (1996), 'Modeling zones of the world-economy: a polynomial regression analysis (1964–1994)', Fernand Braudel Center working paper, August.

Baldwin, Richard E. and Philippe Martin (1999), 'Two waves of globalization: superficial similarities, fundamental differences' in Horst Siebert (ed.), *Globalization and Labour*, Tübingen: Mohr Siebeck, pp. 3–58.

Bordo, Michael D. and Harold James (2000), 'The International Monetary Fund: its present role in historical perspective', NBER working paper 7724, June.

Cavanagh, John (1994), *Beyond Bretton Woods. Alternatives to the Global Economic Order*, London: Pluto Press.

Chossudovsky, Michel (2001), *The Globalization of Poverty. Impacts of IMF and World Bank Reforms*, London: Zed Books.

Crafts, Nicholas (2000), 'Globalization and growth in the twentieth century', International Monetary Fund, working paper 00/44, March.

Exenberger, Andreas (1997), *Geldmaschinen oder Blutsauger? Die Rolle von Exportverarbeitungszonen im Entwicklungsprozess*, Innsbruck: Diplomarbeit.

Exenberger, Andreas (2002), *Außenseiter im Weltsystem. Die Sonderwege von Kuba, Libyen und Iran im Vergleich*, Frankfurt/M. and Vienna: Brandes & Apsel, Südwind.

Freedom House (website): http://www.freedomhouse.org/; for details, see text.

Furubotn, Eirik G. and Rudolf Richter (2000), *Institutions and Economic Theory. The Contribution of the New Institutional Economics*, Ann Arbor: University of Michigan Press.

Höller, Evelyn (2001), *The Role of International Institutions in the Asian Financial Crisis. The Case of South Korea*, Innsbruck: Diplomarbeit.

Hutchinson, Michael M. (2001), 'A cure worse than the desease? Currency crisis and the output costs of IMF-supported stabilization programmes', NBER working paper 8305, May.

IMF ('About the IMF'): http://www.imf.org/external/about.htm.

IMF (website): http://www.imf.org.

Jones, Charles I. (1997), 'On the evolution of world income distribution', *Journal of Economic Perspectives*, **11** (3), 3–19, Summer.

Krueger, Anne O. (1997), 'Whither the World Bank and the IMF?', NBER working paper 6327, December.

Maddison, Angus (1995), *Monitoring the World Economy 1820–1992*, Paris: OECD.

Maddison, Angus (2002), *The World Economy. A Millennial Perspective*, Paris: OECD.

North, Douglass C. (1990), *Institutions, Institutional Change, and Economic Performance*, Cambridge: Cambridge University Press.

Raffer, Kunibert (2001), 'Adopting international institutions to developmental needs', CSI Conference Paper, Innsbruck, November.

Raffer, Kunibert and Hans W. Singer (2001), *The Economic North-South Divide. Six Decades of Unequal Development*, Cheltenham, UK and Northampton, MA, USA: Edward Elgar.

Sen, Amartya (1999), *Development as Freedom*, Oxford: Oxford University Press.

Stiglitz, Joseph E. (2002), *Globalization and its Discontents*, London: Lane Penguin Books.

Tetzlaff, Rainer (1996), *Weltbank und Währungsfonds – Gestalter der Bretton-Woods-Ära. Kooperations- und Integrations-Regime in einer sich dynamisch entwickelnden Weltgesellschaft*, Opladen: Leske & Budrich.

UN ('UN Millennium Developmental Goals'): http://www.un.org/millenniumgoals/.

UN (website): http://www.un.org/english/.

UNDP (1990), *Human Development Report 1990. Concept and Measurement of Human Development*, New York: Oxford University Press (http://hdr.undp.org/reports/global/1990/en/).

UNDP (2000), *Human Development Report 2000. Human Rights and Human Development*, New York: Oxford University Press (http://hdr.undp.org/reports/global/2000/en/).

UNDP (2001), *Human Development Report 2001: Making New Technologies Work for Human Development*, New York: Oxford University press (http://hdr.undp.org/reports/global/2001/en/).

UNDP (2002), *Human Development Report 2002. Deepening Democracy in a Fragmented World*, New York: Oxford University Press (http://hdr.undp.org/reports/global/2003/en/).

UNDP (2003), *Human Development Report 2003. Millennium Development Goals: A Compact among Nations to End Human Poverty*, New York: Oxford University Press (see also http://www.undp.org/hdr2003/).

United Nations Development Programme (website): http://www.undp.org.

Williamson, Oliver E. (2000), 'The new institutional economics: taking stock, looking ahead', *Journal of Economic Literature*, **38** (3), 595–613.

World Bank (1980), *Poverty and Human Development*, New York: Oxford University Press.

World Bank (2001), *World Development Report 2000/2001: Attacking Poverty*, New York: Oxford University Press (http://www.worldbank.org/poverty/wdrpoverty/report/index.htm).

World Bank (CD-ROM): World Development Indicators 2001.

World Bank ('Understanding Poverty'): http://www.worldbank.org/poverty/mission/up1.htm.
World Bank (website): http://www.worldbank.org.
World Trade Organization (website): http://www.wto.org.
Ziegler, Jean (2003), *Die neuen Herrscher der Welt und ihre globalen Widersacher*, Munich: Bertelsmann.

DATA APPENDIX

Data Description and Sources

VEDS (variable of economic development, status): GDP per capita in purchasing power terms in 1998 (in 1990 international dollars); source: Maddison (2002), appendix C.

VEDC1 (variable 1 of economic development, change): average annual growth rate of GDP per capita (in 1990 international dollars), geometrical mean during the period 1975–98, per cent; source: Maddison (2002), appendix C, own calculation.

VEDC2 (variable 2 of economic development, change): standard deviation of GDP per capita growth (per cent, annually) during the period 1975–98; source: Maddison (2002), appendix C, own calculation.

VPDS (variable of political development, status): Freedom House Index (FHI) of Political and Civil Freedom (two variables yearly; a value of 1 is best, of 7 worst; given in steps of 0.5), arithmetical mean during the period 1993–8; source: http://www.freedomhouse.org/research/freeworld/FHSCORES.xls (Website of Freedom House), own calculation.

VPDC (variable of political development, change): relative change of FHI from 1972–7 to 1993–8 (arithmetical mean of the scores of Political and Civil Freedom of the years given), measured by the share of actual progress relative to the maximal possible progress (a value of 1 is best, of 7 worst); set to 1 if a country remains at a value of 1 (indicated by italics in the tables below); the value of FHI 1972–7 is set to 7 for Angola, Comoros, Cape Verde, Djibouti, Mozambique, Namibia, Seychelles and Vietnam and to 2.5 for Germany, owing to a lack of data; source: http://www.freedomhouse.org/research/freeworld/ FHSCORES.xls (Website of Freedom House), own calculation.

VSDS1 (variable 1 of social development, status): life expectancy at birth 1998 (in years); source: World Bank (CD-ROM), UNDP (2000).

VSDS2 (variable 2 of social development, status): adult illiteracy rate 1999 (per cent), for advanced countries (no actual data provided) set to 3 per cent in 1975 and to 1 per cent in 1999 (indicated by italics in the tables below); source: UNDP (2001).

VSDS3 (variable 3 of social development, status): women's development index in 1998/9, composed of the arithmetical mean of the normalized differences between women's life expectancy and adult illiteracy rate and the overall values of these variables (the value is taken relative to the minimum and maximum value of these differences in the sample); adult illiteracy rate for advanced countries (no actual data provided) set to 3 per cent in 1975 and to 1 per cent in 1999; source: World Bank (CD-ROM), UNDP (2000), UNDP (2001), own calculation.

VSDC1 (variable 1 of social development, change): absolute change in life expectancy at birth 1975–98 (in years); source: World Bank (CD-ROM), UNDP (2000), own calculation.

VSDC2 (variable 2 of social development, change): absolute change in adult illiteracy rate 1975–99 (per cent), for advanced countries (no actual data provided) set to 2 per cent (indicated by italics in the tables below); source: UNDP (2001), own calculation.

VSDC3 (variable 3 of social development, change): absolute change in the women's development index (VSDS3) from 1975 to 1999 (calculated as described above); source: World Bank (CD-ROM), UNDP (2000), UNDP (2001), own calculation.

Methodology

For cluster analysis the values of these variables were normalized (from 0 for the minimum value in the sample to 1 for the maximum value) and weighted: VEDS, VPDS and VPDC by one-sixth each, VEDC1 and VEDC2 by one-twelfth each, VSDS1, VSDS2, VSDS3, VSDC1, VSDC2 and VSDC3 by one eighteenth, so all status and change variables, whether composed or not, accounted for half of the measurement in each dimension of development, which are equally weighted by one third each. A total of 106 countries could be incorporated in the analysis – 16 from Western Europe, four so-called Western 'offshoots' (USA, Canada, Australia, New Zealand), 22 from Latin America, 28 from Asia and 36 from Africa – but no transformation countries, and only a few small countries.

Table 5A.1   Actual country data (before technical transformation)

	VEDS	VEDC1	VEDC2	VPDS	VPDC	VSDS1	VSDS2	VSDS3	VSDC1	VSDC2	VSDC3
Advanced countries 1 (AC1)											
Australia	20 390	1.96	5.007	1.0	1.000	78.8	1.0	0.774	6.2	2.0	−0.069
Austria	18 905	2.13	1.090	1.0	1.000	77.9	1.0	0.785	6.5	2.0	−0.074
Canada	20 559	1.59	2.530	1.0	1.000	78.7	1.0	0.753	5.3	2.0	−0.108
Chile	9 757	3.60	3.799	2.1	0.732	75.2	4.6	0.813	9.5	5.4	0.002
Korea	12 152	6.03	3.766	2.0	0.767	74.7	2.5	0.827	10.8	7.3	0.144
Denmark	22 123	2.13	1.850	1.0	1.000	76.1	1.0	0.731	2.1	2.0	−0.059
Spain	14 227	1.96	3.195	1.5	0.875	78.3	2.6	0.831	5.1	4.5	0.099
Finland	18 324	2.07	1.921	1.0	1.000	77.4	1.0	0.848	5.8	2.0	−0.077
Germany	17 799	1.71	1.391	1.5	0.667	77.6	1.0	0.785	6.2	2.0	−0.044
Greece	11 268	1.66	3.084	2.0	0.615	78.1	3.1	0.725	4.9	8.1	0.158
Ireland	18 183	4.04	1.918	1.1	0.750	76.4	1.0	0.753	4.7	2.0	0.004
Mauritius	9 850	4.03	3.534	1.5	0.615	71.1	16.2	0.822	7.0	13.2	0.242
Netherlands	20 224	1.82	1.900	1.0	1.000	78.0	1.0	0.753	3.6	2.0	−0.057
Norway	23 660	2.93	1.531	1.0	1.000	78.4	1.0	0.774	3.4	2.0	−0.042
New Zealand	14 779	0.69	1.958	1.0	1.000	77.4	1.0	0.753	5.3	2.0	−0.061
Portugal	12 929	2.87	2.038	1.0	1.000	75.5	8.6	0.801	6.2	13.9	0.064
Switzerland	21 367	0.94	1.839	1.0	1.000	78.8	1.0	0.806	4.1	2.0	−0.016
Sweden	18 685	1.21	1.806	1.0	1.000	79.6	1.0	0.731	4.6	2.0	−0.057
Trinidad and Tobago	12 254	1.29	2.850	1.5	0.545	74.1	6.6	0.684	7.5	7.1	0.041
Uruguay	8 315	1.88	6.266	1.7	0.821	74.2	2.4	0.910	4.9	3.8	0.066
USA	27 331	2.28	2.220	1.0	1.000	76.8	1.0	0.774	4.2	2.0	−0.115
Advanced countries 2 (AC2)											
Belgium	19 442	1.96	1.680	1.3	−0.050	78.2	1.0	0.795	6.3	2.0	−0.033
France	19 558	1.70	3.147	1.5	−0.017	78.4	1.0	0.880	5.2	2.0	−0.017
UK	18 714	2.01	2.262	1.5	−0.083	77.5	1.0	0.731	5.1	2.0	−0.083
Israel	15 152	1.76	17.266	2.0	0.333	78.6	4.3	0.617	6.6	6.6	0.026

Italy	17 759	2.20	1.971	1.5	0.000	78.4	1.7	0.798	5.8	3.0	0.013
Japan	20 410	2.58	4.967	1.6	-0.017	80.8	1.0	0.817	6.5	2.0	0.057

Well-developing countries (WC)

Argentina	9 219	0.54	2.083	2.6	0.385	73.2	3.3	0.868	5.0	3.0	0.040
Benin	1 257	1.14	10.856	2.1	0.800	53.6	62.3	0.359	7.6	23.5	-0.172
Bolivia	2 458	-0.10	4.489	2.4	0.650	62.0	15.6	0.527	13.3	20.9	0.049
Botswana	4 200	5.51	3.417	2.1	0.353	41.9	24.4	0.517	-13.2	23.5	-0.183
Brazil	5 459	1.16	5.153	3.2	0.389	67.5	15.5	0.923	6.5	12.7	0.245
Cape Verde	1 360	4.23	5.806	1.5	0.917	69.4	27.1	0.557	10.4	29.7	0.160
Ecuador	4 165	0.91	3.564	2.7	0.638	69.8	9.4	0.747	9.4	12.5	0.167
Honduras	2 035	1.13	4.896	2.8	0.500	65.7	26.6	0.797	9.4	15.8	0.138
Mali	783	1.03	3.636	2.7	0.702	51.2	61.8	0.432	11.6	28.7	-0.155
Mongolia	1 094	0.79	1.556	2.5	0.750	62.5	38.6	0.473	7.3	24.6	0.134
Namibia	3 796	0.39	6.494	2.5	0.750	44.9	19.2	0.444	-5.3	19.1	-0.068
Panama	5 705	1.34	6.871	2.5	0.727	73.9	8.6	0.741	5.9	9.4	0.080
Paraguay	3 160	1.55	5.284	3.5	0.390	69.9	7.2	0.695	3.6	9.8	0.073
Peru	3 666	-0.62	3.835	4.3	0.283	68.5	10.8	0.667	11.1	13.5	0.192
Philippines	2 268	0.49	1.953	2.8	0.550	69.0	5.2	0.685	9.9	8.3	0.057
South Africa	3 858	-0.44	9.874	1.7	0.774	53.9	15.4	0.696	-1.2	11.5	-0.070
Thailand	6 205	5.14	4.139	3.2	0.389	69.9	5.0	0.749	9.3	10.5	0.176

Developing countries 1 (DC1)

Algeria	2 689	0.28	0.278	6.1	0.000	69.3	34.5	0.404	13.0	34.7	0.094
Bahrain	4 620	0.72	4.656	6.3	-0.217	73.1	13.5	0.627	8.2	23.5	0.218
Cambodia	1 058	2.46	8.052	5.8	0.077	56.4	62.6	0.353	21.5	18.1	0.014
China	3 117	5.68	0.572	6.9	0.017	70.2	17.2	0.548	5.5	24.5	0.275
Cameroon	1 008	-0.19	4.584	5.9	-0.117	50.0	26.4	0.422	2.6	34.8	0.033
Cuba	2 164	-0.91	3.327	7.0	-0.017	75.8	3.6	0.719	3.6	5.5	0.052
Egypt	2 128	2.83	4.608	6.0	-0.117	66.9	46.3	0.401	13.6	18.4	0.079
Indonesia	3 070	3.15	3.166	6.0	-0.167	65.8	14.3	0.565	14.5	22.6	0.168
Iran	4 265	-1.37	4.412	6.4	-0.117	68.5	25.4	0.419	11.0	31.8	0.150

Table 5A.1 (*continued*)

	VEDS	VEDC1	VEDC2	VPDS	VPDC	VSDS1	VSDS2	VSDS3	VSDC1	VSDC2	VSDC3
Kenya	1 075	0.64	4.878	6.1	-0.233	51.3	19.5	0.423	-1.2	32.2	0.026
Laos	1 104	1.50	5.361	6.5	-0.150	53.1	54.0	0.291	10.8	25.0	-0.065
Lebanon	931	-1.25	2.576	5.7	-0.083	72.9	14.9	0.506	7.9	16.5	0.046
Mauritania	993	0.14	7.125	6.1	-0.033	51.1	58.8	0.434	6.4	13.1	-0.029
Myanmar	1 024	1.92	2.132	7.0	-0.167	56.0	15.9	0.630	5.3	11.2	0.208
Nigeria	1 232	-0.78	5.705	6.3	-0.200	51.5	38.9	0.317	7.1	35.2	-0.117
Oman	7 267	2.34	10.541	6.0	0.074	70.8	31.2	0.412	18.3	41.2	0.177
Rwanda	704	-0.59	4.157	6.6	-0.067	39.9	36.0	0.398	-4.9	30.5	-0.022
Saudi Arabia	8 225	-1.56	9.418	7.0	-0.167	71.3	24.8	0.401	14.5	31.8	0.162
Sudan	880	-0.15	2.374	7.0	-0.167	55.6	44.3	0.371	10.1	25.8	0.059
Swaziland	2 793	0.55	6.964	5.4	-0.133	47.0	21.7	0.552	-1.9	23.6	-0.090
Syria	5 765	0.15	6.027	7.0	-0.067	70.9	27.3	0.305	12.1	25.0	0.055
Tunisia	4 190	2.37	6.473	5.5	0.000	69.9	31.3	0.390	11.3	32.5	0.089
Vietnam	1 677	3.81	7.280	7.0	0.000	67.8	7.1	0.675	7.4	8.5	0.143
Developing countries 2 (DC2)											
Colombia	5 317	1.68	6.184	3.8	-0.267	70.9	8.8	0.859	7.9	10.0	0.174
Costa Rica	5 346	0.86	3.070	1.5	-0.083	76.2	4.7	0.787	6.3	5.2	0.078
Dominican Republic	3 163	1.78	5.610	3.1	-0.033	67.2	17.2	0.763	6.0	12.3	0.114
Guatemala	3 375	0.15	3.696	3.9	-0.150	64.5	32.7	0.656	9.5	18.1	0.177
India	1 746	2.94	3.015	3.3	-0.067	62.9	44.3	0.267	11.1	18.8	0.135
Jamaica	3 533	-0.37	3.383	2.4	-0.133	75.1	14.0	0.755	5.5	14.1	0.009
Kuwait	11 273	-2.05	8.074	4.9	-0.150	76.0	19.1	0.673	7.4	17.6	0.169
Malaysia	7 100	4.38	4.573	4.6	-0.267	72.2	13.6	0.655	7.8	21.2	0.197
Mexico	6 655	1.12	1.912	3.7	0.000	72.4	9.2	0.786	8.2	12.1	0.081
Morocco	2 693	1.69	4.600	4.9	0.000	67.2	52.9	0.409	12.6	22.6	0.012
Pakistan	1 935	3.01	3.859	4.3	0.000	59.6	56.0	0.156	7.3	19.8	-0.096
Qatar	7 304	-6.62	6.224	6.5	-0.183	69.3	19.6	0.672	5.0	16.9	0.180

El Salvador	2 717	0.32	3.189	2.8	−0.033	69.5	22.2	0.772	12.0	15.7	−0.012
Sri Lanka	3 349	3.34	3.250	4.0	−0.233	71.9	8.9	0.740	5.9	8.1	0.246
Turkey	6 552	2.13	6.266	4.7	−0.317	69.5	16.0	0.564	10.2	20.7	0.180
United Arab Emirates	13 857	−2.61	3.867	5.5	0.000	74.8	25.4	0.834	9.7	15.4	0.408
Venezuela	8 965	−0.67	4.298	2.7	−0.133	72.7	8.0	0.805	5.7	11.5	0.074
Non-developing countries (NC)											
Bangladesh	813	1.89	3.919	3.1	0.400	58.9	59.9	0.249	13.0	13.4	0.064
Central African Republic	653	−0.84	20.639	3.7	0.550	44.3	56.0	0.403	0.5	25.3	−0.128
Chad	471	−0.67	3.921	5.4	0.200	45.5	60.6	0.420	5.3	26.8	−0.107
Côte d'Ivoire	1 373	−1.17	6.685	5.3	0.104	47.8	55.5	0.323	0.8	24.9	−0.126
Comoros	522	−1.86	8.937	4.2	0.467	59.4	41.5	0.478	10.7	13.9	0.099
Congo-Brazzaville	2 239	−0.20	6.440	4.8	0.208	51.1	21.6	0.563	3.3	37.1	0.072
Djibouti	1 061	−2.85	4.602	5.6	0.233	44.0	37.7	0.387	1.8	27.4	0.035
Ghana	1 244	−0.05	7.165	3.6	0.490	56.6	30.9	0.422	5.4	32.7	0.033
Haiti	816	−1.02	2.635	4.8	0.255	52.4	52.2	0.741	2.6	21.6	0.162
Madagascar	690	−2.11	6.488	3.0	0.459	52.2	35.1	0.454	3.9	21.5	0.010
Mozambique	1 187	−0.73	5.199	3.6	0.567	39.8	57.7	0.269	−3.3	22.0	−0.146
Nepal	947	1.36	4.082	3.5	0.444	58.1	60.8	0.088	13.1	20.0	−0.046
Nicaragua	1 451	−3.31	3.503	3.4	0.294	68.1	32.1	0.780	11.5	8.9	0.087
Niger	532	−1.41	3.631	5.2	0.208	44.8	85.3	0.353	4.9	8.0	−0.201
Senegal	1 302	−0.30	14.549	4.2	0.289	52.9	64.5	0.476	9.8	17.5	−0.072
Tanzania	553	−0.33	2.408	5.1	0.180	51.1	26.4	0.399	3.1	30.1	0.084
Togo	644	−2.03	2.049	5.5	0.151	51.6	44.8	0.261	4.6	24.5	−0.088
Uganda	726	−0.33	2.617	4.3	0.450	43.2	35.0	0.316	−6.3	24.2	0.013
Yemen	2 298	0.81	9.419	5.5	0.250	60.1	55.9	0.160	15.1	29.2	−0.221
Zambia	674	−1.90	5.209	4.1	0.205	41.0	23.7	0.281	−7.5	23.4	−0.083
Zimbabwe	1 448	0.18	4.387	5.0	0.111	42.9	12.8	0.349	−10.0	23.1	−0.164
Special case											
Gambia, The	850	−0.83	11.591	6.4	−0.733	45.9	65.4	0.474	7.7	21.9	−0.103

Table 5A.2 shows, primarily, how much the variability in the sample is transformed from variability 'between' clusters into variability 'within' clusters, which is represented by columns (4) and (5); one can easily see that there are peaks of reduction and therefore especially 'efficient' solutions at the three- and five-cluster levels (the opposite is true especially at the eight- and two-cluster levels); for example, fusing at the three-cluster level the AC cluster and the DC cluster transforms 22.6 per cent of variability from 'between' to 'within' (which is 92.2 per cent of the remaining variability 'between'), while at the two-cluster level the integration of the special case, Gambia, not surprisingly transforms only 1.6 per cent.

Table 5A.2   Technical data of cluster fusion steps

(1)	(2)	(3)	(4)	(5)
12	0.0779	42.5	4.0	3.0
11	0.0810	44.2	3.8	3.0
10	0.0841	45.9	4.8	4.1
9	0.0881	48.1	7.0	6.5
8	0.0943	51.5	0.1	0.2
7	0.0944	51.5	8.1	8.6
6	0.1020	55.7	9.4	11.8
5	0.1117	60.9	20.7	32.3
4	0.1348	73.5	9.2	25.7
3	0.1473	80.3	22.6	92.2
2	0.1805	98.5	1.6	100.0
1	0.1833	100.0		

Notes: (1) number of clusters at the specific step of fusion; (2) total variable variability 'within' clusters of the specific step of fusion; (3) percentage of this variability within clusters relative to the overall variability in the sample (equal to the variability 'within' at the one-cluster level); (4) percentage of the variability transformed into variability within clusters by the specific step of cluster fusion, relative to the variability of the step of fusion started from; (5) the same percentage, but relative to the variability left before fusion.

6. The effects of IMF lending and freedom on the growth performance of developing countries

Sevinç Mihci and Hakan Mihci

INTRODUCTION

Neither the inquiry into the causes of the wealth of nations, nor the notion that institutions affect economic performance, is a new thing for economists. Towards the end of the eighteenth century, Adam Smith had already stated that the road to economic prosperity ought to be cleared of interventionist activities. From classical economists to the 'old institutionalists', many have written on the role institutions play in reducing poverty and raising welfare. For one, Douglass North (1990) has described the connection between institutions and economic performance. Debate over institutions and economic outcomes has witnessed considerable controversy as to which institutional regulations are most conducive to sustainable growth.

The past decade's renewed interest in growth has yielded a vast literature, theoretical as well as empirical, concerning the various potential determinants of growth, one which has produced no consensus, of course. In fact, institutions are particularly important for inducing economic agents to engage in productive activities that augment total output rather than simply redistributing it among activities. By 'productive activities', we mean activities that result in such an increase in output as to enhance consumption and/or investment. The stimulus for engaging productive activities, on the other hand, could originate in the better functioning of institutions. In this respect, international institutions play the role of defining the global rules of the game. This is particularly important for the developing world, where the (counter-) currents of globalization are more intense.

Alternatively speaking, institutions are supportive of overall welfare to the extent that individual/national efforts are channeled towards productive activities. The most effective institutions are those that also lead people and nations to be innovative in a long-run perspective, so that enduring economic growth is obtained. Therefore, when the unit of analysis is a developing country, growth research should consider institutions and also international ones.

In distinction from the previous studies in the field, this chapter considers the effects of the IMF, one of the leading international institutions in the world, by means of lending, on economic growth through the panel-data analysis of a sample of 32 developing countries over the period 1980–2001. In doing so, economic and political freedom indicators are also chosen as control variables. Hence the chapter is not just limited to discussing the theoretical aspects of the topic and surveying the literature, but is also an attempt at performing an empirical analysis.

Amongst all international institutions such as the World Bank, World Trade Organization, OECD and so on, the International Monetary Fund (IMF) has played the leading role in global financial affairs and, accordingly, in shaping the so-called 'New World Order'. Moreover the impact of the IMF on developing countries and emerging markets has intensified ever since the debt crisis of the early 1980s, and especially during the post-Cold War era, starting with the last decade of the twentieth century. The 44 states represented at the 1944 Bretton Woods conference having now grown to 182, the IMF is now a quasi-universal financial institution. So now it practically includes almost any national economy in the world. From, originally being the guardian of the adjustable peg exchange rate system of Bretton Woods as well as the financier of the temporary current account deficits of developed countries, the role of the IMF has now evolved to financier of development, and crisis manager for the developing world. Consequently economic growth has come to be a major target of the IMF.

Alongside international institutions, other institutional variables also play a prominent role vis-à-vis long-run economic success. In this context, various orders of freedom, such as economic, political or civil, are to be investigated, together with the different components of human, cultural and legal developments. The main purpose of this chapter is to test whether the IMF accomplishes its major goal of economic growth for developing countries. The method used especially to assess the effect of IMF actions on the economic growth of developing member countries has some peculiarities. Total IMF loans and credits to individual countries, not considered in the previous studies, are taken as a proxy for IMF actions. Then the impact of total outstanding IMF credits and loans on the GDP per capita level of developing countries that use IMF resources is estimated. The estimation equation also includes indexes of economic and political freedom as control variables.

The chapter is organized in the following way. The next section focuses on the impact of international institutions, and especially the IMF, on economic growth. While the changing role of the IMF is being emphasized, previous studies are also concisely surveyed. The third section reviews the theoretical and empirical relationships between various types of freedom and growth. The fourth section investigates, empirically, the relationship between IMF lending, freedom and economic growth. The final section is an elaboration of the chief findings of the study.

IMF AND ECONOMIC GROWTH

Amongst all other international institutions, the IMF has acquired an increasingly prominent role in the New World Order. The Fund was established in 1944 and conceived of as an institution that would maintain the Bretton Woods adjustable peg exchange rate system and as a financier of temporary balance-of-payments deficits in, especially advanced, countries (Bordo and James, 2000:4). That system collapsed in 1973. The new system had no need of the IMF and, the Fund now faced a major crisis of identity. To be more specific, IMF was criticized for its overconcern about balance of payments problems and its relative neglect of growth. Thus the IMF came to include, in economic programmes, policies to remove structural obstacles before growth and allocative efficiency (Khan and Sharma, 2001:20). Indeed, according to its Articles of Agreement, the IMF's goal also included 'the promotion and maintenance of high levels of employment and real income and ... the development of the productive resources of all members as primary objectives of economic policy'. Fulfilling this function, the IMF now transformed itself from a currency-regulation institution into an international organization involved in the national policies of the developing world, particularly after the onset of the debt crisis in the early 1980s. Further developments, such as the end of the Cold War era, the subsequent efforts of former socialist economies to revert to free-market capitalism, the growing income inequalities among nations with their roots in the new wave of globalization, together with the recent financial crises suffered by the emerging markets of Mexico and East Asia, reinforced the shift in the role of the IMF. The IMF thenceforth became the 'crisis manager' as well as 'development financier' for the developing countries (Barro and Lee, 2002:7; Boughton, 1997).

In the process of transformation, the importance of economic growth as a prime objective has been underlined and expressed by the former managing director of the Fund himself, in the following words:

> Our primary objective is growth. In my view, there is no longer any ambiguity about this. It is towards growth that our programs and their conditionality are aimed. It is with a view toward growth that we carry out our special responsibility of helping to correct balance of payments disequilibria and, more generally, to eliminate obstructive macroeconomic imbalances. (Camdessus, 1990:235)

Today, the Fund has 182 members that are eligible to take out loans. Part of the loans is taken in relation to the quotas of individual member countries. A member can draw up to 25 per cent of its quota without any policy negotiation. To draw on more than 25 per cent always requires an arrangement between the IMF, on the one hand, and the member country, on the other. As a part of the arrangement, the IMF compels the country in question to adopt specific policies in order to obtain the loan. That procedure is labelled 'conditionality'.

There are four main types of IMF arrangements: stand-by arrangements (SBA), the extended fund facility (EFF), the structural adjustment facility (SAF) and the enhanced structural adjustment facility (ESAF). The last two were introduced towards the end of the 1980s, in relation to the changing role of the IMF, in order to provide longer-term financing at subsidized interest rates for low-income countries.

The common components of a typical IMF arrangement include (a) securing sustainable external financing, (b) the adoption of measures to curb demand, and (c) the implementation of structural reforms. The first component determines the magnitude as well as the pace of the necessary adjustment effort. The terms and the amount of new foreign borrowing for a country experiencing balance of payments problems are determined at the start of the programme. The second component covers macroeconomic measures aiming at restoring and maintaining the equilibrium between aggregate expenditure and income in the recipient country. The measures in question typically include tight monetary policy (raising interest rates and reducing credit creation), fiscal austerity (cutting government expenditures and increasing taxes) and currency devaluations. The third component focuses on structural reforms. The latter comprise a wide range of policies, such as, trade liberalization, privatization, pension reform, financial sector reform, tax reform, banking sector restructuring, price liberalization, strengthening of social safety nets and labour market reform – all aiming at reducing government-oriented distortions and other institutional rigidities that are thought to prevent allocative efficiency and hinder economic growth.

Currently the IMF arrangements are being designed in close cooperation with the programmes of the World Bank and/or the regional banks. In consequence the conditionality over structural issues of the IMF programmes are now being linked with the concerns of other international financial institutions (Mussa and Savastano, 1999:23). On the other hand, criticism of IMF-supported programmes has being growing. The major underlying impulse behind such criticism is the manifest disjunction between the common components of a typical IMF programme and its goal of high-rate growth, as well as the ensuing goal of poverty reduction (Stewart and Fitzgerald, 2003). Raising interest rates, curbing government spending and a host of other demand-restricting policies seem to have pushed the objective of growth into second place. Accordingly the empirical evidence concerning the growth effect of IMF programmes and credits needs closer scrutiny.

Having said that, we think it is worth taking the time to summarize the various alternative methods that have been employed in assessing the growth effect of IMF programmes, together with the main results that have emerged.[1] Any research that attempts to measure the effectiveness of IMF programmes must perforce face the question of the counterfactual, that is, what would have happened in the absence of any such programme, and just what effects could be ascribed to the programme, as opposed to other factors.

As a matter of fact, there simply exists no satisfying way of dealing with this problem. The so-called 'before-and-after' approach tacitly assumes that other things remain constant, which they do not. The 'with–without' approach assumes the possibility of formulating a correct view as to what would have happened in the absence of an IMF programme. One way of doing that is to compare countries that have negotiated IMF programmes with countries that have not. But, then, finding countries that are similar in every other respect except having participated in a programme turns out to be a considerable challenge. To overcome this, attempts are to be made to allow for differences between countries that do and do not have programmes, in terms of economic conditions and how policies might change. This is what the 'generalized estimator evaluation' approach basically attempts, but the decision to participate in the programme itself creates significant differences in the policies pursued in which adjustment takes place, raising yet another empirical problem. The problem might be overcome by simulating the performance of an individual economy under different sets of policies. That, in turn, brings out the problem of 'simulation analysis': the specification of a model that describes the way in which individual economies function with some accuracy. But it is highly unlikely that a model would provide an accurate description of all countries that might turn to the IMF, for the simple fact that countries differ (Dicks-Mireaux et al., 2000). The 'case study' approach presents yet another alternative, but suffering, in turn, from problems of generalization.

There are other difficulties in assessing the effects of Fund programmes, associated with the time period over which effects are detected and the range of performance indicators that are analysed. Economic indicators might move in different directions over time and better performance in terms of one variable might be offset by worse performance in another. In short, the quest for methodological perfection seems to keep going on as long as the analysis of the effects of IMF programmes improves. Emphasis may now be given to empirical studies associated with the growth effect of Fund programmes using various methodologies.

While a number of pioneering studies found little connection, Goldstein and Montiel (1986) argued that IMF programmes had a significantly negative effect. Simulation tests by Khan and Knight (1982) also estimated that demand-management programmes similar to those supported by the IMF were bound to have negative short-run effects on growth, while suggesting in subsequent research that such effects could be further assessed by incorporating supply-side measures to protect investment (Khan and Knight, 1985). Conway (1994) finds significant divergence between short- and long-run effects of IMF programmes over economic growth and investment. Khan (1990) analyses 259 programmes in 69 countries for the whole period of 1973–88, where both one- and two-year comparisons are used. He concludes that, while growth rates decline in the programme year, once the time path of performance evaluation is extended beyond that, adverse growth effects are diminished. Also Killick (1995) finds a neutral relation with economic growth, though over a longer period the relation (statistical significance is limited) is positive.

While Hutchison (2001) discovers a significant negative effect on output growth over one to two years, Przeworski and Vreeland (2000) suggest that an enduring negative effect holds vis-à-vis growth. In contradistinction from Conway (1994), Przeworski and Vreeland (2000:402) argue that countries that emerge from IMF programmes do not grow faster than they did before or faster than those countries that never entered a programme. Indeed countries that never experienced IMF programmes grew the fastest. Similarly Johnson and Schaefer (1997) investigate the relationship between IMF loans and economic growth in less-developed countries from 1965 to 1995. It so turns out that, of the 89 loan recipients, 48 (54 per cent) were no better off in 1995, as measured by real per capita wealth, than before accepting the very first loan; 32 of the 48 were poorer; and 14 of the 32 had economies that were at least 15 per cent smaller than they had been before the first loan.

In a recent work, Barro and Lee (2002) provide instrumental variables for estimating the effects of IMF lending on economic performance. Instrumental estimates show that the size of IMF lending is insignificantly related to economic growth in the contemporaneous five-year period, but has a significantly negative effect in the subsequent five years.

On the other hand, Killick et al. (1995) examine the effects of IMF programmes in 16 countries over the period 1979–85, and they reach the conclusion that the Fund programmes led to an improvement in the growth rate. The challenging work of Dicks-Mireaux et al. (2000) deserves attention: a modified control-group methodology is used to measure the effect of IMF support on three key variables, including output growth. The sample comprises low-income countries' adjustment programmes supported by the IMF's enhanced structural adjustment facility (ESAF). Using this approach for only the ESAF, the sample reveals statistically significant beneficial effects of IMF support on output growth.

In summary, over the past two decades there have been a number of empirical studies attempting to analyse the effects of IMF programmes and loans on economic growth. The consensus seems to be that output is depressed in the short run as the demand-reducing components of the programmes dominate. In addition, several studies emphasize an insignificant or significantly negative effect of Fund programmes and loans on economic growth, although there are some exceptions.

Having reviewed the theoretical and empirical connections between IMF programmes/loans and economic performances of developing countries, we will, in the following section, focus on the role of institutions, and in particular economic and political freedom in the growth process.

FREEDOM AND ECONOMIC GROWTH

The last decade or so has witnessed the resurgence and proliferation of research on the principal determinants of economic growth. Beyond physical determinants, several countries of the world have promoted various types of freedom as a means of achieving long-run economic success. Economic, political and civil freedoms are concerned whenever economists refer to the 'institutions' of an economy, and the trend towards increased freedom suggests that 'proper' institutions are crucial determinants of, or prerequisites for, economic growth in particular, and development in general. The question is whether freedoms influence aggregate economic performance of a country indirectly, through an impact on investment, or directly, through an effect on total productivity, or both.

If freedoms mainly induce investment, they should affect economic growth indirectly via the investment channel. Besley (1995) presents three possible explanations for a positive relation between institutions and investment. First, ensured property rights as a part of economic freedom may protect the outcomes of investment from expropriation by economic agents such as the state or other individuals. Second, proper institutions ruling the financial markets could regulate contractual arrangements that are necessary to support investment. Third, economic and political freedom could facilitate transactions among economic agents, augmenting the gains from trade and, hence, increasing the potential return to investment.

An alternative channel through which institutions might influence economic growth is changes in the aggregate production function. Alternatively speaking, differences in level of economic and political freedom might cause alteration in productive efficiency across countries. The idea is that countries with abundant resources could nonetheless obtain a low welfare level due to the absence of economic freedom to carry out a system of efficient resource allocation. In this context, the argument that institutions affect total factor productivity could be tied to the level of technology specified as 'A' in the neoclassical growth model, hence, making the latter a function of institutions.

The institutions–growth relationship has been considered in several empirical studies of cross-country growth, but in such analyses a variety of institutional variables have been utilized without, however, closely scrutinizing the channels through which they affect economic growth. Barro (1991) finds that a different measure of political instability is negatively related to investment and economic growth. The existence of the same relation has later been confirmed by the empirical study conducted by Alesina et al. (1992). On the other hand, Vorhies and Glahe (1988) find a positive but statistically not-so-strong relation between political freedom and alternative measures of social development. Keefer and Knack (1995) use measures of property rights that are found to be positively associated with investment and growth. In their seminal work on growth empirics, Kormendi and Meguire (1985) attempt to test for an effect of civil liberties on economic performance and investment. They show evidence that civil liberties have a marginal effect on growth and a significant effect on investment for their sample of 47 countries over the period 1950–77. Similarly, and more recently, Levine and Renelt (1992) find that civil liberties play a role in explaining cross-country variation in investment.

On the other hand, Scully (1988) concentrates exclusively on the role of freedoms in economic development. For a sample of 115 economies over the years 1960–80, Scully presents strong evidence of a positive relationship between institutional variables and economic growth. For institutional variables, the author takes the level of economic freedom, civil liberties and political freedom. A decade later, Dawson (1998) studied the alternative channels through which institutions affect growth, and focused on the empirical relations between institutions, investment and economic growth by using panel data analysis. The main findings of the study indicate that institutions have a positive effect on growth; economic freedom influences growth through both a direct effect on total factor productivity and an indirect effect on investment, and political and civil liberties may stimulate investment.

In analysing cultural and institutional determinants of economic growth for 90 countries during the period 1968–87, Abrams and Lewis (1995) find that political, economic and individual freedoms statistically determine economic growth. Using a ranking of economic freedom constructed by Scully and Slottje (1991), Vanssay and Spindler (1994) have found a positive relationship between economic growth and the specific measure of economic freedom. In fact, Scully and Slottje (1991:137) had also pointed out the same positive association in their own study. De Haan and Siermann (1998) have applied the extreme-bound analysis using all variants of the Scully–Slottje index. The finding is that the connection between economic freedom and economic growth depends upon the specific measure that is used: for some variants of the Scully–Slottje index of economic freedom there appears to be a robust direct relationship, while for others no such relationship exists.

Torstensson (1994) also analyses the impact of economic freedom on growth performance, using data for the period of 1975–85 and covering 68 countries. Here the degree of state ownership does not seem to affect growth rates. Arbitrary seizure of property, however, affects growth negatively. Nelson and Singh (1998) use economic freedom as a control variable in their own model of the relationship between economic growth and political freedom. The study refers to the 1970–89 period and includes 67 developing countries. The conclusion is that economic freedom exercises a significantly positive effect on economic growth.

After analysing the robustness of the relationship between freedom and growth, De Haan and Sturm (2000) come to the conclusion that more economic freedom fosters economic growth, with the level of freedom not being related to growth. By decomposing the overall Gwartney index into subcategories, Carlsson and Lundström (2001) investigate what are the specific types of economic freedom measures that are important for growth. The results show that a number of economic freedom measures have a significant and sizable effect on growth. This does not, however, mean that increasing economic freedom in general increases growth, since some of the categories are insignificant, and also since some of the significant variables have a negative effect on growth.

As a result of the above, one could infer that the different types of freedom considered under the label of institutions seem to have a considerable impact on economic growth and that they should be investigated with care in the context of the 'engines' of growth.

MODELLING AND ESTIMATING THE RELATIONSHIPS BETWEEN IMF LENDING, FREEDOM AND ECONOMIC GROWTH

In this section, first the model used in the estimation process is presented and then estimation results are given.

Model Specification

On the basis of the influential works of Kormendi and Meguire (1985) and Levine and Renelt (1992), the basic theoretical framework used for the analysis of growth in this chapter relies upon the assumption that the explanatory variables are entered linearly into the growth regression. For the reason that the main aim of this chapter is to evaluate the effect of the amount of IMF credits and loans, rather than the effect of changes, or growth of credits and loans on growth indicators, the level of IMF credits and loans is taken as explanatory variable. Also, on the basis of the fact that the economic and political freedom variables in particular, as described in the following sections and the appendix, are not continuous variables and simply take on the discrete values from zero to seven, growth rates and logarithmic forms are not preferred in estimation models. In this context, since all explanatory variables are in the level form, we intentionally confine ourselves to analysing the impacts on per capita real income rather than on the rates of growth.[2] Alternatively speaking, we are assuming that the level of real per capita income is a linear function of the explanatory variables. Accordingly we estimate the following equation in order to test the effects on economic growth indicators of IMF credits and loans, together with other control variables:

$$GDPPC = \beta 0 + \beta 1 INVPC + \beta 2\ CRDPC + \beta 3\ EF + \beta 4\ PF + \beta 5\ DUM\ (90),$$

where *GDPPC* represents the economic growth indicator and is defined as GDP per capita in dollar terms.

INVPC refers to investment per capita in dollar terms. Instead of the capital–labour ratio as the determinant of GDP per capita, investment per capita is preferred, because of the difficulties involved in finding the necessary capital stock statistics for various countries. Additionally, if we consider the positive relation between saving rate and GDP per capita in the steady-state conditions of neoclassical growth models, the saving–investment relation makes investment per capita a preferable explanatory variable in the GDP per capita equation. However there can be bidirectional causality between GDP per capita and investment per capita; in other words, high GDP per capita may lead to more investment per capita. Therefore the GDP per capita equation is estimated with and without an investment per capita variable, in order to control the estimation problems likely to occur in the case of reverse causality between investment per capita and GDP per capita, besides the other purposes of separating the effect of all other explanatory variables on GDP per capita through the investment channel.

CRDPC corresponds to total IMF credits and loans per capita in special drawing rights (SDR) terms, as proxies of IMF action as an international institution. EF and PF refer, respectively, to economic and political freedom indexes. Finally, DUM (90) is the dummy variable for the period after 1990.

The data set for estimations is a panel of 32 countries and 22 years (1980–2001). The countries in question have been chosen from among the IMF member developing countries apropos the frequency of their involvement in IMF-supported adjustment programmes. Hence countries with most frequent engagement in adjustment programmes with the IMF are considered. These are the developing countries that use Fund resources repeatedly. Although there may have occurred selection biases due to leaving out of consideration certain countries that have taken IMF credits, we have nonetheless tried to include a sufficient number of cases to represent the whole. The preferred analysis period is 1980–2001, during which the role of the IMF was modified and an increased number of IMF-supported structural programmes were observed.

Estimation and Results

In the basic estimation equation, the dependent variable is GDP per capita and one of the exogenous variables is the IMF credits per capita. However one might well argue that IMF credits per capita is an endogenous variable. To be more exact, the amount of IMF credits per capita could be dependent on GDP per capita volume: when GDP per capita rises, IMF credits per capita may fall. To elucidate the direction of causality between GDP per capita and IMF credits per capita, a Granger causality test (Madalla, 1992:393–4) is run for the two variables. The result is that, in a Granger sense, GDP per capita does not cause IMF credits.[3] Therefore one finds inadequate evidence of IMF credits per capita being endogenous. Accordingly the preferred endogenous variable in all regressions is GDP per capita. Basically, panel data methods of pooled regressions and fixed-effect models are performed in all regressions. We have preferred to provide the results of both models to get thick modelling with more robust results. In other words, various possible model results are considered to see whether the significance, size and sign of the coefficients change or not under different modellings. Also sensitivity analysis is applied in order to separate the individual effects of variables. Various estimations are also run for different income groups of countries, in order to identify the income-level effect on the relationship between growth indicators and IMF credits variables and economic and political freedom variables.

Fixed-effects specification is mainly used to account for time-invariant unobservable heterogeneity that is potentially correlated with the dependent variable. Thus we also expect to get rid of omitted variable problems in the regression, capturing the idiosyncratic factors that might have affected GDP per capita. Table 6.1 presents the results of pooled regression for all years.

The first equation was estimated with full variables and data set with pooled OLS method. Regression results suggest that per capita investment,

Table 6.1 Pooled regressions, dependent variable: GDPPC[a]

Variable	1st equation		2nd equation		3rd equation		4th equation	
	Coefficient	t-ratio	Coefficient	t-ratio	Coefficient	t-ratio	Coefficient	t-ratio
Intercept	1832.350	0.77	1409.512	0.52	530.57	2.684**	1113.4	1.20
INVPC	2.567394	28.23**			2.63	12.38***	2.64	9.29**
CRDPC	-1.199869	-1.641*	-3.2596	-1.993**	-0.68	-1.68*	-0.72	-0.63
EF	17.94561	0.45	151.51	2.15**	-24.6	-1.160	64.94	0.92
PF	-5.621792	-0.49	-16.344	-1.2411	-1.45	-0.43	-12.76	-0.52
DUM(90)	116.2329	3.04**	140.58	1.673**	-7.15	-0.36	305.62	1.93*
AR(1)	0.992209	85.19***	0.980	50.66***	0.96	33.5***	0.95	35.64***
Adj. R²	0.9809		0.9508		0.9712		0.9600	
DWstat.	2.07		1.67		2.005		2.03	

Notes: [a] Standard errors and t-statistics of coefficients are computed using White's heteroscedasticity-consistent variance–covariance estimator because of the heteroscedasticity problem detected with LMh test; a single asterisk indicates statistical significance at the 10 per cent level; two asterisks indicate statistical significance at the 1 per cent level.

per capita credits and dummy variable for the period after 1990 are statistically significant explanatory variables. The sign of the coefficient for investment variable is positive as expected, and negative for credit variable. The signs indicate that there is a positive relation between investment per capita and GDP per capita and a negative impact of IMF credits on GDP per capita for the whole group of countries. The positive sign for the dummy variable suggests that, after 1990, other effects, most likely the end of the Cold War era, and the ensuing reorganization efforts of the world order not considered in our equation, have produced a positive effect on GDP per capita. The statistical insignificance of economic and political freedom variables as indicated by the regression results with low t-ratios means that such factors do not have any effect on GDP per capita for our group of countries and choice of the period. The AR (1) term is included in the equation because of the detected autocorrelation problem.[4] The AR (1) term turns out to be highly significant in the regression results.

In order to differentiate the effect of IMF credits, economic freedom and political freedom on investment and/or on productivity gains, we have estimated yet another equation without the investment variable. If the main channel through which IMF credits, economic freedom and political freedom affect growth is the volume of investment, then the coefficients of CRDPC, EF and PF would be expected to vary in a substantial way, whenever investment is excluded as an explanatory variable.[5] The results of this regression are given in Table 6.1 as the second equation. According to the regression results, besides the credit variable, economic freedom also becomes a statistically significant variable for the equation estimates. However the credit variable has a negative sign with a larger coefficient, in contrast to the positive sign of the coefficient of economic freedom variable.

When investment per capita is not included in the equation, the whole impact of explanatory variables on GDP per capita through investment and productivity channels becomes observable. In this context, the significance of the economic freedom variable in this equation with a positive coefficient can be interpreted as the positive effect of economic freedom on GDP per capita via the investment channel. Similarly the negative coefficient for credit per capita again shows that the overall effect of credit variable on economic growth indicator is negative via either productivity or investment channels. Additionally, since the sign and significance of credit variable does not change in the estimation results without investment variable, it can be concluded that likely bidirectional causality between investment per capita and GDP per capita does not create significant bias in the estimation results.

Finally the dummy variable representing the 1990s and the AR (1) term are, with positive coefficients, statistically significant terms in the results of the regression in contradistinction once again from the insignificance of political freedom index variable, indicating the non-existence of impact on investment through political freedom.

These results can be confirmed by estimating the investment equation with the same explanatory variables as in the GDP per capita equation. The coefficient of CRDPC is insignificant with a negative sign, whereas the economic freedom variable has a significant positive sign. The political freedom variable turns out, once again, to be an insignificant explanatory variable in the investment per capita equation. The results are consistent with the estimation results of GDP per capita equation without the investment term, indicating that economic freedom has a positive impact on investment per capita, while the negative impact of IMF credits on investment is rather negligible.[6]

The third and fourth regression estimates are performed through dividing countries according to their levels of income. The demarcation line of income level in grouping the countries is set to be where IMF credits per capita turn insignificant in the GDP per capita equation of the pooled regression. The demarcation line is $1400US per capita income. The result of the structural break test also indicates that there exists a structural break at that per capita income level.[7] Accordingly the third regression makes use of all variables, and the cross-section units are countries with average per capita income level of under $1400US (low-income countries) for the period between 1980 and 2001.[8] Regression results are not very different from those obtained in the first equation estimates. The only divergence is the low t-ratio; in other words, in the statistical insignificance of the dummy variable representing the 1990s. That might mean that the reorganization of the world order in the 1990s does not create much of a positive impact on the per capita income level of low-income countries.

The fourth regression is estimated with the same variables as in the third regression. But, the set of data belongs to countries having per capita income levels of over $1400US (middle-income countries).[9] As expected, for this group of countries, the basic difference in the regression results appears in the significance of the IMF credits variable, which emerges as statistically insignificant although it still carries a negative sign. The investment variable is still significant with a positive sign, while political and economic freedoms are insignificant as explanatory variables. In line with the findings above, one could argue that income levels of countries are crucial apropos the significant negative effect of IMF credits on growth indicators.

Besides the income level, other idiosyncratic differences among countries could have influenced growth indicators, as well as other variables that effect growth.[10] Hence we have also estimated fixed-effect models for our group of countries with the same variables used as in our previous estimation, to capture the variation in the intercept term, assuming that idiosyncratic factors are constant over time. The fixed-effect estimation results are given in Table 6.2.

The fixed-effect model regression with all countries and with full variables yields similar results and estimates with pooled regression with the same data and variables. Results of this first estimation under the fixed-effect model are given in the fifth equation (Table 6.2). Again investment per capita, IMF credits per capita and the dummy term for the 1990s are statistically significant explanatory variables for GDP per capita in the fixed model. While the investment and the dummy variables have positive coefficients, the IMF credit has once more a negative coefficient. Nonetheless the significance level of the credits variable has now declined to approximately the 10 per cent level. Overall the main difference is found in the significance of the economic freedom variable. In the fixed-effect model, the economic freedom index becomes the significant explanatory variable for GDP per capita for the 10 per cent level. This means that, by using the fixed-effect model in the estimation process, the explanatory power of the estimation increases and economic freedom also becomes a significant variable in explaining GDP per capita in the full variables model.

As a next step, the GDP per capita equation is estimated without including the investment per capita term by means of a fixed-effect model (sixth equation). According to the regression results, there is no difference in terms of significance and coefficient signs of variables. However the significance level and coefficient values of both IMF credit and economic freedom variables have increased. That means that both IMF credits and economic freedom have an effect on investment per capita. However the overall effect of IMF credits is still negative and, of economic freedom, positive, as evinced by the unchanged signs of coefficients. Besides, the significance level of the political freedom index increases, though still remaining insignificant.[11] The increased significance level with a negative sign may indicate the positive impact of political freedom on investment level since the level of political freedom increases for lower values of the index.[12]

In order to confirm the results obtained from the equation estimates without the investment term, an investment equation is estimated with all the explanatory variables in GDP per capita regression. CRDPC, EF and PF all turn out to be significant variables in the investment equation. Except for the EF variable, these variables have negative coefficients, confirming once more the negative effect of IMF credits and the positive effect of political freedom on investment per capita.[13]

The last step in our estimations is realized by dividing countries into two groups. The seventh equation is estimated for all of the variables with the group of countries having per capita incomes of under $1400US. Estimation results suggest some differences from previous estimations. While invest-

Table 6.2 Fixed effect model regressions, dependent variable: GDPPC[a]

Variable	5th equation		6th equation		7th equation		8th equation	
	Coefficient	t-ratio	Coefficient	t-ratio	Coefficient	t-ratio	Coefficient	t-ratio
INVPC	2.64	27.0**			2.6	9.7**	2.6	8.17**
CRDPC	−1.19	−1.60*	−3.52	−3.12**	−0.800	−1.460*	0.017	0.016
EF	56.28	1.63*	220.83	4.15**	10.00	0.56	126.7	1.830*
PF	−5.83	−0.48	−25.54	−1.4	−2.792	−0.69	−1.94	−0.2940
DUM(90)	32.31	3.46**	75.58	3.01**	−15.0	−0.74	97.71	4.7393**
AR(1)	0.834	32.21**	0.84	36.6**	0.852	19.34**	0.773	16.148**
Adj. R²	0.9816		0.9573		0.97593		0.9568	
DWstat.	1.9750		1.6066		1.9678		1.8565	

Notes: [a] Standard errors and t-statistics of coefficients are computed using White's heteroscedasticity-consistent variance–covariance estimator because of the heteroscedasticity problem detected with LMh test; a single asterisk indicates statistical significance at the 10 per cent level; two asterisks indicate statistical significance at the 1 per cent level; the constant terms representing the fixed effect are not stated.

ment per capita and IMF credits per capita are significant explanatory variables for GDP per capita, the economic freedom index and the dummy for the 1990s are no longer significant variables in the GDP per capita equation for the countries with GDP per capita of lower than $1400US. Once again, IMF credit per capita has a negative-sign coefficient besides the positive-sign coefficient of investment per capita and of economic freedom variable.[14] These results are similar to the pooled regression results (Table 6.1). When the same equation is estimated, excepting the investment term for the same group of countries, again the economic freedom and credits variables become significant with unchanged signs, indicating once more that economic freedom and IMF credits especially have an effect on GDP per capita via the investment channel in the case of low-income countries.[15]

The last estimation is realized with the cross section of countries having a per capita income level of more than $1400US. Estimation results of the eighth equation have some peculiarities. This is the first time that IMF credits per capita have a positive-signed coefficient in the GNP per capita equation estimates, though it is statistically insignificant. It means that IMF credits per capita does not have a negative influence on the GDP per capita level of middle-income countries. In line with the estimation results previously presented, other variables such as investment per capita, the economic freedom index and the dummy variable for the 1990s are, as expected, significant explanatory variables with positive coefficients, excepting political freedom. When the same estimation is repeated without including the investment term, credits again become a significant variable with a negative sign.[16] This shows that the overall impact of IMF credits on GDP per capita is negative, especially with the investment channel for the middle-income group of countries, while the effect on productivity is not certain.[17]

Review of Estimation Results

Summarizing now the overall results, the first point to note is that investment per capita is the significant explanatory variable for the GDP per capita equation in all cases. It has a positive coefficient in all the equations, indicating that there exists a positive relation between GDP per capita and investment per capita for the developing countries in the sample.

In most of the cases, IMF credits per capita variables turn out to have negative-signed coefficients for the GDP per capita equation estimates. That result is especially powerful in the case of low-income countries, owing to the positive coefficient of IMF credits variable in the eighth equation of GDP per capita for middle-income countries. Therefore the overall estimation results suggest that IMF credits have had a negative effect on GDP per capita in low-income countries. In addition to that, when the investment per capita variable is not included in the equations, IMF credit coefficients change slightly, to become significant with negative coefficients in all the specifications and for all country groups. This indicates that the overall effect of IMF credits on GDP per capita is negative especially via investment channel in all countries.

The conclusion on the impact of economic freedom on GDP per capita is that it has a positive effect overall in our sample of countries, although this result is not supported by the pooled regression, where the heterogeneity among countries originating from idiosyncratic differences is not considered. The effective channel of economic freedom on GDP per capita is the investment channel, as observed by the changing amount and significance level of the economic freedom coefficient in the equation estimates without the investment per capita term.

The political freedom variable never becomes significant in the equation estimates, thus indicating that political freedom is not a significant variable in explaining the GDP per capita levels of developing countries frequently using Fund credits and loans. The dummy variable representing the 1990s is a significant term in most of the GDP per capita estimation equations, with the exception of the low-income countries estimation. That could be taken to imply the ineffectiveness of the end of the Cold War era and the New World Order as implied by globalization movements on the per capita GDP level of low-income countries, in contradistinction from its positive influence on middle-income countries' growth performance.

CONCLUSION

In conjunction with the recent globalization movements, the role of the international organizations in the world arena has been re-examined and gained weight. Among others, the IMF stands out as one of the most prominent international organizations. Through stand-by arrangements and ensuing credits and loans, fostering economic growth in member countries is one of the main targets of IMF actions. This chapter has attempted to test whether the IMF has proved able of accomplishing its goal. In distinction from the preceding studies, the amount of IMF credits and loans is employed as a proxy for IMF actions.

Estimation results indicate that the volume of IMF credits does not have a positive impact on the GDP per capita level of developing countries resorting heavily to IMF funds. Despite some methodological differences, the results of the current study are similar to those of the preceding empirical works. Additionally, according to estimation results, the overall effect of IMF credits on GDP per capita is negative for every group of countries, although the negative effect is stronger in the case of low-income countries. The effective channel of credits is that of investment, while its effect through the productivity channel in middle-income countries is rather dubious.

In our view, the negative effect through the investment channel is the outcome of demand straining IMF-supported adjustment programmes conditional on IMF credit and loan allowances. The productivity effect may not be negative, even positive because of increasing efficiency in resource allocation resulting from adjustment policies. The changing coefficient signs and significance for credits variable in the middle-income countries equation estimates with and without investment term can highlight such a productivity effect.

The results obtained about the impacts of IMF credits and loans can be interpreted as short-run effects for the reason that only the contemporaneous values of regressors are included in estimation equations. To analyse long-run effect, lagged values of credits variable should be included in estimation equations. Analysing long-run effects can be an enlightening approach in terms of evaluating the impacts of IMF loans and credits. When attention is turned to the indexes of freedom, it is clear that economic freedom has unambiguous effects on the level of GDP per capita. The effect is more obvious in the case of middle-income countries, indicating that economic freedom grows more and more critical as income level is increased. It is possible that economic freedom levels of low-income countries are so low that changes in economic freedom do not even create a significant effect until a threshold is reached. In other words, improvements in economic freedom would become effective only above some threshold level. Hence it is evident that further research to investigate the relationship between economic freedom and growth for different income levels is needed.

Furthermore political freedom does not seem to have any impact on growth process in our sample of developing countries. That result is not consistent with previous studies. Inconsistency might originate in the variations in time periods and the panel of countries. The results should be interpreted while always keeping in mind that the panel of countries considered in this chapter consists of developing countries that attain Fund credits and loans on a repeated basis. Moreover results of the estimations suggest that the New World Order of the 1990s has created a positive impact in favour of the growth processes of middle-income countries, while not having had a significant impact on the low-income groups in the panel of countries.

Finally, as an international institution, the IMF does not seem to be playing a role in the improvement of the welfare levels of developing countries by means of providing loans and credits. Consequently one could argue that the IMF does not quite fulfil its fundamental goal as an international institution.

NOTES

1. For a more comprehensive summary of the literature and a more detailed critical analysis of the alternative methodologies, see Killick (1995) and Ul Haque and Khan (1998).
2. Specification criteria like AIC and adjusted R^2 all favoured the level of GDP per capita in contrast to the GDP per capita growth rate as dependent variable. While the adjusted R^2 is 0.98 in the level estimation, it is 0.14 in the rate of growth estimation.
3. The regression is:

$$CRDPC= -0.3945 + 1.24CRDPC(-1) - 0.31CRDPC(-2) - 0.0012GDPPC(-1) + 0.003GDPPC(-2)$$
$$\quad\quad\quad (-0.33)\quad (9.5)\quad\quad\quad\quad (-2.5)\quad\quad\quad\quad\quad (-0.49)\quad\quad\quad\quad\quad (1.07)$$

   with t-statistics in parentheses. According to the values of t-statistics, the lagged *GDPPC* variables are not significant. For detailed information on Granger causality tests, see Madalla (1992:393–4).
4. DW and LM test results of the regression without AR (1) term show that there is an autocorrelation problem in the estimation process.
5. However the high correlation among the explanatory variables *CRDPC, INVPC, EF* and *PF* may cause a multicollinearity problem in the estimation process. In order to detect the severity of multicollinearity in our data, the variance inflation factors for *CRDPC, EF* and *PF* are computed. Since the variance inflation factors (Madalla, 1992:274) are not greater than 10 (Neter et al., 1989:ch. 11), it is to be concluded that there exists no severe multicollinearity problem in the data.
6. The regression is:

$$INVPC= -58.75 - 0.645CRDPC + 65EF - 5.9PF+ \text{other variables}$$
$$\quad\quad\quad (-0.4)\quad (-0.98)\quad\quad\quad\quad (3.54)\quad (-1.38)\quad R^2= 0.92\quad DW=2.01$$

   with t-statistics in parentheses.
7. According to Chow-test result, F value is equal to 3.9; that is, greater than the critical level of 2.64.
8. Twenty countries within the whole group have per capita income levels of below $1400US. For the list of the low-income developing countries, see Appendix 2.
9. Twelve of the whole group of countries have per capita income level above $1400US. For the list of middle-income developing countries, see Appendix 2.
10. Also the F-test results support the heterogeneity among the group of countries. The F-value is equal to 36.03, and this value is large enough (the critical value for 5 per cent being equal to 1.46) to reject the null hypothesis of homogeneity.
11. Political freedom index becomes significant at the 15 per cent level.
12. For details, see Appendix 1.
13. The regression is:

$$INVPC= -1.16CRDPC + 6916EF - 10.4\ PF+ \text{other variables}$$
$$\quad\quad\quad (-3.89)\quad\quad\quad\quad (6.09)\quad (-2.02)$$

   The constant terms in the fixed effect model are not given; t-statistics are in parentheses; $R^2=0.92$, DW= 1.87.
14. Although the random-effect model is not preferred because of the time-invariance assumption of country-specific effects, random-effect model estimations do still provide significant negative-signed coefficients of the IMF credits variable for the group of countries with lower per capita incomes than $1400US. Also the random-effect model is not preferred for the simple reason that autocorrelation problems cannot be eliminated in any specification of random effect model estimations.
15. These results are verified by the investment per capita equation estimates with the same explanatory variables in the GDP per capita equation.

16. See note 14.
17. Although random-effect model estimation is not preferred because of the persistent autocorrelation problem, it suggests similar estimation results to the fixed-effect model. IMF credits do not have a positive effect on GDP per capita for, especially, low-income countries. The only significant variable in the GDP per capita equation is economic freedom.

REFERENCES

Abrams, B.A. and K.A. Lewis (1995), 'Cultural and institutional determinants of economic growth: a cross-section analysis', *Public Choice*, **83**, 273–89.

Alesina, A.; Ş. Özler, N. Roubini and P. Swagel (1992), 'Political instability and economic growth', NBER working paper, no. 4173.

Barro, R.J. (1991), 'Economic growth in a cross-section of countries', *Quarterly Journal of Economics*, **106**, 406–43.

Barro, R.J. and J. Lee (2002), 'IMF programs: who is chosen and what are the effects?', NBER working paper, no. 8951.

Besley, T. (1995), 'Property rights and investment incentives: theory and evidence from Ghana', *Journal of Political Economy*, October, 903–37.

Bordo, M.D. and H. James (2000), 'The International Monetary Fund: its present role in historical perspective', NBER paper series, no. 7724.

Boughton, J.M. (1997), 'From Suez to Tequila: the IMF as crisis manager', IMF working paper, No. 90.

Camdessus, M. (1990); 'Statement before the United Nations Economic and Social Council in Geneva', 11 July, IMF Survey, **19**(15), 235.

Carlsson, F. and S. Lundström (2001), 'Economic freedom and growth: decomposing the effects', Gotheburg University, working paper in economics, no. 33.

Conway, P. (1994), 'IMF lending programs: participation and impact', *Journal of Development Economics*, **45**, 365–91.

Dawson, J.W. (1998), 'Institutions, investment, and growth: new cross-country and panel data evidence', *Economic Inquiry*, **36**, 603–19.

De Haan, J. and C.L.J. Siermann (1998), 'Further evidence on the relationship between economic freedom and economic growth', *Public Choice*, **95**, 363–80.

De Haan, J. and J.E. Sturm, (2000), 'On the relationship between economic freedom and economic growth', *European Journal of Political Economy*, **16**, 215–41.

Dicks-Mireaux, L., M. Mecagni and S. Schadler (2000), 'Evaluating the effects of IMF lending to low-income countries', *Journal of Development Economics*, **61**, 495–526.

Freedom House (2002), 'Freedom in the World: 2000–2001', New York: Freedom House Publication; data retrieved from http:// www.freedomhouse.org.

Goldstein, M. and P. Montiel (1986), 'Evaluating fund stabilization programs with multicountry data: some methodological pitfalls', *IMF Staff Papers*, **33**, 304–44.

Gwartney, J. and R. Lawson, with W. Park and C. Shipton (2001), *Economic Freedom of the World: 2001 Annual Report*, Vancouver: The Fraser Institute 2001; data retrieved from http:// www.freetheworld.com.

Hutchison, M.M. (2001), 'A cure worse than the disease? Currency crises and output costs of IMF-supported stabilization programs', Economic Policy Research Unit, University of Copenhagen.

IMF (International Monetary Fund) *International Financial Statistics*; data retrieved from International Financial Statistics (IFS) CD-ROM.

Johnson, B. and B. Schaefer (1997), 'The International Monetary Fund: outdated, ineffective, and unnecessary', Heritage Foundation Backgrounder, no. 1113, 6 May.

Keefer, P. and S. Knack (1995), 'Institutions and economic performance: cross-country tests using alternative institutional measures', *Economics and Politics*, November, 207–27.

Khan, M.S. (1990), 'The macroeconomic effects of fund-supported adjustment programs', *IMF Staff Papers*, **37**, 195–231.

Khan, M.S. and M. Knight (1982), 'Some theoretical and empirical issues relating to economic stabilization in developing countries', *World Development*, **10**, 709–30.

Khan, M.S. and M. Knight (1985), 'Fund-supported programs and economic growth', IMF occasional papers, 41, International Monetary Fund, Washington, DC.

Khan, M.S. and S. Sharma (2001), 'IMF conditionality and country ownership of programs', IMF working paper, no. 142.

Killick, T. (1995), *IMF Programs in Developing Countries: Design and Impact*, London and New York: Routledge.

Killick, T., M. Malik and M. Manuel (1995), 'What can we know about the effects of IMF programmes?', *World Economy*, **15**, 575–97.

Kormendi, R.C. and P.G. Meguire (1985), 'Macroeconomic determinants of growth: cross-country evidence', *Journal of Monetary Economics*, **16**(2), 141–63.

Levine, R. and D. Renelt (1992), 'A sensitivity analysis of cross-country growth regressions', *American Economic Review*, **82**(4), 942–63.

Madalla, G.S. (1992), *Introduction to Econometrics*, New York: Macmillan.

Mussa, M. and M. Savastano (1999), 'The IMF approach to economic stabilization', IMF working paper, No. 104.

Nelson, M.A. and R.D. Singh (1998), 'Democracy, economic freedom, fiscal policy and growth in LDCs: a fresh look', *Economic Development and Cultural Change*, **46**, 677–96.

Neter, J., W. Wasserman and M.H. Kutner (1989), *Applied Linear Regression Models*, Homewood, IL:Richard D. Irwin.

North, D.C. (1990), *Institutions, Institutional Change and Economic Performance*, New York: Cambridge University Press.

Przeworski, A. and J.R. Vreeland (2000), 'The effect of IMF programs on economic growth', *Journal of Development Economics*, **62**, 385–421.

Scully, G.W. (1988), 'The institutional framework and economic development', *Journal of Political Economy*, **96**(3): 652–62.

Scully, G.W. and D.J. Slottje (1991), 'Ranking economic liberty across countries', *Public Choice*, **69**, 121–52.

Stewart, F. and V. Fitzgerald (2003), 'The IMF and the global economy: implications for developing countries', Queen Elizabeth House Working Paper Series, University of Oxford.

Torstensson, J. (1994), 'Property rights and economic growth: an empirical study', *Kyklos*, **47**(2): 231–47.

Ul Haque, N. and M.S. Khan (1998), 'Do IMF-supported programs work? A survey of the cross-country empirical evidence', IMF working paper, no. 169.

Vanssay, X. and Z.A. Spindler (1994), 'Freedom and growth: do constitutions matter?', *Public Choice*, **78**, 359–72.

Vorhies, F. and F. Glahe (1988), 'Political liberty and social development: an empirical investigation', *Public Choice*, **58**, 45–71.

APPENDICES

Appendix 1   Definitions and Data Sources

Gross domestic product per capita (GDPPC)
GDP in current prices is converted into dollar terms using market exchange rates. These values are divided by mid-year population figures to obtain GDPPC. Data are retrieved from International Financial Statistics (IFS) CD-ROM.

Investment per capita (INVPC)
Gross fixed capital formation values in national currency units are converted into dollar terms using market exchange rates and then divided by mid-year population figures. Data are retrieved from International Financial Statistics (IFS) CD-ROM.

IMF credits and loans per capita (CRDPC)
CRDPC corresponds to 'Total Fund Credits and Loans Outstanding', which relates to the use of Fund resources under GRA (General Resources Account), and to outstanding loans under SAF, ESAF and Trust Fund. Mid-year year population figures are used to obtain per capita values. Data are retrieved from International Financial Statistics (IFS) CD-ROM.

Economic freedom (EF)
In the chapter, the economic freedom index in Gwartney et al. (2001) is used. It is the most extensive measure available in terms of its coverage of countries, time and attributes of freedom. The Gwartney index is based on a number of quantifiable measures relating to the various dimensions of economic freedom. Seven subgroups of variables, relating to the size of government, the structure of the economy, freedom to trade, freedom to use alternative currencies, legal structure of private ownership and others, monetary policy and price stability, and freedom of exchange in capital markets, are all aggregated into one comprehensive index. Countries were given scores ranging from 1 to 10, where 10 indicate the highest level of economic freedom. The comprehensive index emphasizes the two fundamental goals of the government. The first is to provide an infrastructure for the operation of a market economy, which includes secure property rights, enforcement of contracts and stable monetary regimes, among other things. Secondly, the government should provide a few selected goods, which have characteristics that make them difficult for private business to provide; that is to say, public goods such as national defence, education, police and environmental protection. Consequently the definition of economic freedom in Gwartney et al.

(2001) is strict, based on a libertarian concept of freedom, and can be disputed. Without getting involved in such disputes, however, we assume that this index is a good measure of economic freedom.

Political freedom (PF)

The chapter uses the political rights index published by Freedom House (2002). Since its inception in the 1970s, Freedom House's 'Freedom in the World' survey has provided annual evaluation of political rights and civil liberties throughout the world. The survey attempts to judge all countries and territories by a single standard, emphasizing the importance of freedom and democracy. The survey evaluates a country's freedom by analysing its record in two areas: political rights and civil liberties. A country grants its citizens political rights when it permits them to form political parties that represent a significant range of voter choice and whose leaders can openly compete for and be elected to positions of power in government. The survey rates each country on a seven-point scale for political rights, 1 representing the most free and 7 the least free. Thus, the level of political freedom increases for lower values of the political rights index and vice versa.

Appendix 2   Developing Countries Included in Data Set

Middle-income developing countries: Argentina, Brazil, Costa Rica, Dominican Republic, Ecuador, Gabon, Jamaica, Mexico, Panama, Peru, Turkey, Uruguay.

Low-income developing countries: Bangladesh, Bolivia, Côte d'Ivoire, Egypt, Arab Republic, El Salvador, Honduras, Kenya, Madagascar, Malawi, Mali, Morocco, Nepal, Niger, Pakistan, Philippines, Senegal, Sierra Leone, Sri Lanka, Togo, Zambia.

PART II

Particular international institutions and poverty

7. WTO membership: what does it do for growth and poverty?

David Sapsford, V.N. Balasubramanyam and Stephan Pfaffenzeller

INTRODUCTION

Surprisingly little, if indeed anything, is known about the economic benefits that have accrued to countries as a result of their membership of the World Trade Organization (WTO hereafter), or indeed membership of its predecessor the General Agreement on Tariffs and Trade (GATT). This is especially surprising given the enthusiasm and vigour with which numerous countries, including Taiwan, have recently sought membership to either or both of these multilateral organizations. Our objective in this chapter is to shed some light upon the magnitude of the economic benefits that actual and aspiring member countries might reasonably expect to receive as a consequence of their membership of the WTO. In order to achieve this objective we examine the historical evidence relating to the experiences of a sample of countries as a consequence of their earlier decision to participate in the system of multilateral tariff reduction through their participation in the GATT. Although our theme is concerned with the role of international institutions in the alleviation of poverty, this chapter directs its attention solely to the influence which membership exerts on economic growth performance, on the grounds that, if there is one thing that the wealth of available evidence tells us, it is that an improvement in growth performance is typically, if not invariably, a necessary (but by no means sufficient) prerequisite for progress in alleviation of poverty. In short, the present chapter focuses on what may be thought of as the first link in the poverty alleviation chain.

The chapter is organized as follows. The next section sets the context for what follows by providing an overview of current thinking regarding the potential economic benefits of tariff reductions, while the third section explores a number of issues relating specifically to membership of the WTO. The fourth section describes the framework within which the potential economic benefits of reductions in tariff and non-tariff barriers may be evaluated, while the fifth section reports our findings and discusses their implications. A final section summarizes our main conclusions and suggests directions in which further research might proceed.

TARIFF REDUCTION: THE ECONOMIC CASE

The foundations of the economic theory of international trade were laid by Adam Smith (1723–90) in *The Wealth of Nations* (1776). Smith's analysis of division of labour is well known and to a large extent he saw the phenomenon of international trade as a logical extension of this process, with particular regions or countries (rather than particular individuals) specializing in the production of particular commodities. Smith's view is clearly demonstrated by the following quotation:

> It is the maxim of every prudent master of a family, never to attempt to make at home what it will cost him more to make than buy… What is prudence in the conduct of every private family, can scarce be folly in that of a great kingdom. If a foreign country can supply us with a commodity cheaper than we ourselves can make it, better buy of them with some part of the produce of our own industry, employed in a way in which we have some advantage. (1776:424)

Thus, according to Smith, countries do (and should) engage in trade with one another in order to acquire goods more cheaply than they could produce them domestically, paying for them with some proportion of the output that they produce domestically by specializing according to their own 'advantage'. Central to this view is the notion that relative prices determine trade patterns, with countries buying abroad when foreign prices are below domestic ones.

This widely cited quotation from Adam Smith captures with elegance and precision what remains to this day the central tenet of trade theory: namely that specialization provides countries with the opportunity to reap economic benefits in the form of increased consumption of goods and services (equated with increased economic welfare) for given resource endowments. However the case is usually demonstrated with respect to the two polar cases: autarky on the one hand and unfettered free trade on the other. The real world of international economic relations is, however, a very different place from the world inhabited by trade theorists, with few, if any, genuine cases of either autarky or totally unrestricted free trade existing in either the present or the past. In practice, and especially so in policy-making circles, the trade theorist's battle cry of 'free trade forever' has been modified to the somewhat diluted declaration that any move towards a 'freer' world trading system is to be welcomed in that it will result in potential consumption (welfare) gains to participating countries. Notwithstanding the fact that this scenario differs markedly from the comparison between autarky and totally free trade which lies at heart of the theorist's analysis, surprisingly little is actually known about the existence, let alone the magnitude, of potential benefits from moving closer towards the polar case of free trade.

Our purpose in this chapter is to explore the economic benefits that have accrued to countries as a result of their decision to seek to move further towards free trade by participating in the GATT/WTO system as a means of achieving reductions (if not the complete removal) of tariff and other non-tariff barriers. In other words, we seek to focus not on the potential benefits to countries of moving from the polar case of autarky to the other extreme of completely free trade (the case so beloved by trade theorists) but rather upon those economic benefits which arise in the more important practical case of a movement further along the line joining the polar cases, as the situation faced by a country when contemplating whether or not to apply for membership of the WTO.

For the purpose of the current chapter we confine our attention, in the interests of simplicity, to the consequences of membership for real output and its growth. Although this is clearly a restrictive view it is nonetheless useful in the sense that increased real output may be reasonably seen as providing a necessary, but by no means sufficient, condition for the achievement of other benefits, including poverty reduction.

WTO: CLUB RULES

John Kay, writing in the *Financial Times*, observed, 'Twenty years ago, few people could have told you that the initials GATT stand for the General Agreement on Tariffs and Trade. Today its successor, the World Trade Organisation, is front page news' (*Financial Times*, 8 October 2003).

It is unfortunate that the WTO should be front-page news mostly because of its image as a club of the rich countries dedicated to promoting their interests. Admittedly the organization has its faults; it has been less than successful in persuading the rich countries to lower if not eliminate subsidies to agriculture, provide increased market access to labour-intensive exports of developing countries and in general promote level playing fields in trade policy. But there is also much to commend the GATT and its successor, the WTO. The organization has been instrumental in lowering tariff protection, a major factor in the impressive growth in world trade. The Uruguay Round negotiations (1986–94), perhaps the most comprehensive of all the eight negotiating rounds since the establishment of the GATT in 1947, successfully reduced the weighted average tariffs of industrial countries from 6.4 per cent to 4 per cent. This compares with a weighted average tariff of 35 per cent

before the GATT was created. The Uruguay Round also integrated agricultural trade, trade-related intellectual property rights and textiles and clothing
into the WTO.

It can be argued, though, that it is difficult to establish a causal connection
between the tariff reductions and growth in trade or, more precisely, a relationship between membership of the WTO and trade prospects. Indeed it has
been argued by one analyst that countries outside the WTO appear to have
performed as well as the members of the organization in world trade (Rose,
2004). This sort of a conclusion based on econometric exercises with all their
attendant problems of data and methodology seems to miss the point. Members of the organization may or may not have fared any better in world trade
than non-members, but the difficult counterfactual is whether they would
have been worse off without membership. Much more to the point, it should
be recognized that the WTO is a club. Membership of the club confers certain
privileges on the members, but also duties. It is these privileges and duties
which enable members to cooperate with each other towards attaining a
common goal: an orderly, rules-based process of trade. It ought to be recognized that the WTO is not charged with the task of promoting free trade. As
Hoekman and Kostecki (1995:13) observe, 'nowhere is any mention made of
free trade as an ultimate goal'. Instead, the role of the GATT was (and is) to
facilitate the reduction of barriers to trade and ensure greater equality with
respect to conditions of market access for contracting parties.

Put this way, the overriding objective of the WTO is the promotion of
equity in commercial transactions for members of the club. This notion of
equity in trade relations is of significance to relatively small countries, such
as Taiwan, in the world economy. The four basic principles of the WTO are
designed to promote equity for members. The four principles are as follows:
non-discrimination, reciprocity, market access and fair competition (Hoekman
and Kostecki, 1995).

The principle of non-discrimination is enshrined in the most favoured
nation (MFN) and national treatment (NT) rules. The principle of MFN
requires that whatever privileges one member accords to another must be
accorded to all the members of the club. Thus, if a country offers a tariff
reduction on a specific product to a specific trading partner, the concession
should be accorded to all the members of the club. The principle of MFN
ensures non-discrimination between trading partners. It also ensures that
consumers have access to the lowest-cost producers. More importantly it
protects the interests of small countries, which in the absence of MFN may
be subject to discrimination by large countries with monopoly power in trade.

NT complements the MFN principle. It requires that imported goods, once
they have paid whatever border taxes apply and entered a country, should be
treated on a par with locally produced goods with regard to local taxes. NT

ensures that agreed upon tariff reductions are not offset by local taxes. It applies to both tax policies and non-tax policies; it ensures a degree of certainty regarding the policy environment and facilitates planning and organization of business.

Reciprocity is the chosen method for trade negotiations. Members exchange concessions on a quid pro quo basis. Reciprocity ensures gains from trade liberalization for a country, for there is the guarantee that others reciprocate one's concessions. In addition, it also enables members to sell trade liberalization to interest groups in their countries. They can point out that an import concession they have offered is matched by concessions on exports for their domestic industries. Further it also ensures that there are no free-riders, for concessions offered to a country have to be matched by its negotiating partners. It is also to be noted that reciprocal concessions are usually incremental and not absolute: one dollar of concessions offered by a country is matched by one dollar of additional market access by the other. Bhagwati and Irwin (1987) refer to this sort of a deal as 'first-difference reciprocity' as opposed to full reciprocity. First-difference reciprocity, which is a gradual process, may be politically much more palatable to members than full reciprocity.

The significant feature of the market access principle is that it ensures that, once tariff concessions are made, they are not nullified by non-tariff measures. Thus the WTO frowns upon non-tariff measures such as quotas. Article XI of the GATT prohibits quotas, with rare exceptions. And there are also rules governing subsidies. Once tariff rates are agreed upon they have to be bound, they cannot be increased without further negotiations. In the case where a country perceives that agreed upon market access is flouted by others, it may invoke the WTO dispute settlement procedures.

The other binding principle of the WTO is transparency (fair competition). Members must publish their trade regulations and inform the WTO of any changes, and trade policies of members are reviewed periodically by the WTO. Transparency again ensures stability of policy. These guiding principles of the WTO are designed to ensure equity and an orderly process of trade. These principles are especially relevant for small countries. Multilateral trade negotiations (MTN) provide them with advantages which bilateral treaties are unlikely to provide. Although they may continue to be at a disadvantage in negotiating with large countries, the rules and regulations of the club mitigate these advantages to an extent. MFN ensures non-discrimination, NT provides for stability of policies, market access shields them from non-tariff barriers to trade. Transparency and the dispute settlement machinery provide them with redress in case of injury.

As said earlier, the institution is far from perfect despite all its efforts to ensure level playing fields. For instance, decision making in the WTO is by consensus and not by majority voting, except when consensus cannot be reached. Then again, unlike the situation in the other international organizations, the WTO operates on the principle of one member, one vote. The problem, though, is that large countries may be able to impose their will on the smaller ones and force consensus. The organization may in effect be an oligarchy clothed in the garb of a democracy. This in fact is the major complaint of the developing countries. Even so, there are opportunities for economically weaker countries to form coalitions and hold their own on major issues of policy. The recent events in Cancún attest to the ability of countries to form coalitions and push their own point of view. In any case, consensus allows small countries to express a view on matters of import, which a system of majority voting may not do. In sum, small countries such as Taiwan have much to gain and little to lose from membership of the club.

ANALYTICAL FRAMEWORK

Trade liberalization, of which multilateral tariff reduction is one example, occurs in several forms. First, there can be unilateral liberalizations, where an individual country, for example, reduces the barriers which it has imposed against imported products. In practice such liberalizations frequently occur under the aegis of World Bank Structural Adjustment Loan programmes (see Greenaway and Morrissey, 1993). Second, there is the case of bilateral liberalization, where each of two countries agrees to offer the other some concession in exchange for concessions on their part. Third, as an extension of this, there is what might be called 'minilateral' liberalization, where a group of countries agree on a package of concessions applicable only to members of the group. Numerous such agreements exist in the form of Regional Integration Agreements, two notable examples being the European Union (EU) and the North American Free Trade Area (NAFTA). Lastly, there is the case of multilateral liberalization as offered by the WTO and its predecessor, the GATT. Although liberalizations of the second sort lie closest to the analytical heart of the trade theorist, it is those of the first sort that have been subjected to the greatest empirical scrutiny (for example, Krueger, 1978; Feder, 1983; Edwards, 1993; Greenaway and Sapsford, 1994a, 1994b). Nevertheless the techniques that have been developed in this literature can, with suitable modification, also be used to evaluate the economic consequences to countries participating in multilateral liberalization. It is to these methods that we now turn our attention.

The potential effects of trade liberalization are typically modelled within the framework of a single equation growth model, most commonly one of the so-called 'production function' variety. Within this sort of framework, liberalization is seen as influencing growth performance through either or both of two channels. The first such channel views exports as one of the arguments of the growth equation and assumes that a positive and statistically significant coefficient is attached to the export variable. Accordingly it is argued that trade liberalization raises exports, which in turn raise the growth rate. This is essentially the view adopted by Papageorgiou et al. (1991). The second channel recognizes the possibility that liberalization itself may have the potential to alter the coefficient of the export variable in the growth equation. Put simply, this second channel admits the possibility that liberalization may increase the elasticity of output with respect to exports. In other words, a given increase in exports may exert a greater growth-enhancing effect after liberalization than it did before liberalization. Econometrically this second channel of reasoning takes us into the realms of varying parameter models.

Exports and Economic Growth

Although originally developed as a method of modelling the export versus output growth relation, the model described below forms the analytical starting point for those previous studies that have sought to evaluate the significance and magnitude of the economic benefits (in the form of enhanced real output) arising from trade liberalization of which, as we have seen, tariff reduction is one form. According to this approach, real output is seen as being determined by an aggregate production function, the arguments of which include not only labour and capital inputs but also exports. A number of arguments for including exports in such an output equation may be found in the literature and these are well summarized by Salvatore and Hatcher (1991), who provide three reasons for the explicit introduction of exports into the production function. First, they argue that the neutrality of incentives associated with export orientation is likely to lead, *ceteris paribus*, to higher factor productivity because of the exploitation of economies of scale, better utilization of capacity and lower capital–output ratios. Second, they argue that exports are likely to alleviate potentially serious foreign exchange constraints (which themselves may constrain the country's ability to purchase imported raw materials and components) and can thereby provide greater access to international markets. Third, they argue that exports are likely to result in a higher rate of technological innovation and dynamic learning from abroad. In the usual notation the production function can be written as follows:

$$Y = f(L, K, X; t),$$

where

Y = real GDP,[1]
L = labour input,
K = capital stock,
X = real exports,
t = time trend, capturing technical progress.

Assuming that the above function is linear in logs, we can write the following expression:

$$y = \alpha + \beta l + \theta k + \psi x + \varphi t, \tag{7.1}$$

where lower-case letters denote logarithms and the parameters β, θ and ψ are the elasticities of output with respect to labour, capital and exports, respectively. The parameter φ captures the shifts in the production function which are brought about by (disembodied neutral) technical progress. In most studies, equation (7.1) is differenced prior to estimation to obtain the following equation describing the determinants of the *growth* rate of real GDP.

$$\dot{y} = \varphi + \beta \dot{l} + \theta \dot{k} + \psi \dot{x},$$

where a dot over a variable indicates its (proportional) rate of growth. In view of the well-known and formidable problems associated with attempts to measure the capital stock – especially in the context of LDCs – the usual practice in the previous literature has been to approximate the rate of growth of the capital stock by the share of investment in GDP (I/Y). Accordingly we may rewrite the preceding expression as follows:

$$\dot{y} = \varphi + \beta \dot{l} + \theta (I/Y) + \psi \dot{x}. \tag{7.2}$$

Trade Liberalization and Economic Growth

A number of theoretical arguments may be constructed to suggest the presence of a positive association between the growth performance of an economy and the degree of outward orientation, or openness, of its trade policy regime as this influences its exports. At the most basic level, the elementary trade theory (with all of its well-known assumptions) suggests that there may exist the potential to increase world output if resources are reallocated according to the principle of comparative advantage. Accordingly trade liberalization taking the form of a move closer towards free trade may be predicted to yield output gains through the achievement of an improved allocation of resources.

Viewing trade liberalization as a process aimed at 'getting (relative) prices right' (for example by reducing the level of tariffs on imported goods, and thereby moving internal relative prices more closely into line with the world price ratio) sees that such policies have the potential to promote the optimal allocation of resources within the economy (including allocation between the tradable and non-tradable goods sectors) and thereby to offer output gains from the redistribution of resources in response to the improved informational content of relative prices.

However, as already noted, the real world (especially the developing economies) may correspond only poorly to the 2×2×2 world of the trade theorist, a fact which has led some investigators to develop theoretical structures which might in some sense be seen as being more appropriate as a description of the situation actually faced by liberalizing economies. One such approach, which is two-sector in character, models the effects of exports upon output explicitly as the sum of an *externality* effect and a productivity differential effect (Feder, 1983; Ram, 1986; Falvey and Gemmell, 1989). This model subdivides the economy into two sectors: an export-oriented sector and a non-export-oriented or traditional sector. Within this framework, exports are seen as influencing output through two channels. First, there is what is called an 'externality' effect, which is allowed for by the inclusion of current exports in the production function of the non-export sector. Second, there is a so-called 'productivity differential' effect, according to which the marginal physical products of both capital and labour inputs are allowed to differ between the two sectors of the economy. Accordingly this model sees the potential for output gains from trade liberalization, with given endowments of factors of production, as arising from the reallocation of resources away from the low productivity traditional sector towards the expanding higher productivity outward-oriented sector. This approach has at least three attractions. First, it is seen by its proponents as capturing the essential features of what actually goes on during the process of liberalization, with the outward-oriented sectors of the economy (facing world competition and perhaps also benefiting from inputs of superior foreign know-how) achieving a positive factor productivity differential over the traditional sector, but with spillover mechanisms (such as learning by watching) of various sorts existing such that output in the traditional sector itself is positively related to that in the outward-oriented sector. Second, from the theoretical perspective, this approach (with its emphasis upon spillover/externality effects) is attractive because it fits centrally within the recent and rapidly expanding literature on so-called 'new' (or endogenous) growth theories. Third, the Feder approach allows us, in principle, to derive econometrically estimates of the magnitude of the separate externality and productivity differential effects (see Greenaway and Sapsford, 1994b, for some preliminary estimates).

Empirical Evidence

As already noted, previous empirical investigations have seen trade liberalization as influencing output growth through either or both of two possible routes; that is, by bringing about either an increase in the value of x (which is then filtered through the assumed constant value of ψ) and/or an increase in ψ, the elasticity of output with respect to exports.[2] Mention has already been made of the World Bank investigation undertaken by Papageorgiou et al. (1991) (PMC hereafter) who study the effects of trade liberalization upon the export versus growth relationship and of the fact that this study sees the potential growth-enhancing effect of trade liberalization as working through the former of these two routes.

PMC (1991) report the results of a large-scale investigation which covers 36 liberalization episodes in a sample of 19 countries between the 1950s and the 1980s. Using an informal methodology, which basically involved comparisons between average exports and growth during the three years before and after each liberalization episode, these authors concluded, quite unequivocally, that liberalization boosts both exports and growth. Notwithstanding the serious reservations raised regarding the methodological foundations of this study (see Collier, 1993; Greenaway, 1993) its results have been widely reported in some circles as conclusive proof of the efficacy of trade liberalization as a means of enhancing growth performance.

From the econometric perspective, the second possible route takes us into the realms of varying parameter models. In most previous studies, this issue has been handled by straightforward dummy variable analysis. One of the earliest applications of the dummy variable technique for evaluating the effects of trade liberalization was due to Krueger (1978). The particular variant of the approach adopted by Krueger was two-stage in character, being designed to shed light on the following two hypotheses: first, that more liberalized regimes result in higher rates of export growth and, second, that a more liberalized trade sector has a positive impact on aggregate growth. Krueger defined a liberalized regime as one that had reduced the degree of anti-export bias. In order to test the first of her two hypotheses, Krueger estimates a model which specifies the log of exports as a function of the log of the *exports' effective real exchange rate* (defined as the number of units of domestic currency received by an exporter per real dollar worth of exports) and a linear time trend. Intercept and slope dummies are added to this basic expression to allow both the intercept and the coefficient of the trend term to vary during periods of liberalization. The results obtained by Krueger indicated that for both traditional and non-traditional exports the intercept and (trend) slope dummy variables were both positively signed and significantly different from zero, thus confirming that a move towards a more liberalized regime has a positive effect on export growth. Krueger's second stage equation specifies the log of real GNP as a function of *only* the log of exports and the (trend) slope (but not the intercept) dummy variables employed in the first equation. This is clearly an extremely simplified approach in that it fails to control for the effects on real output of changes in either labour or capital inputs (see equation (7.1) above). In addition, the exclusion of the intercept dummies from the real GNP equation, plus the absence of a slope dummy for the *export term* is extremely restrictive, in that it does not allow the estimation procedure to pick up movement either in the intercept term (that is, an autonomous change in real GNP) or in the export coefficient which might be associated with liberalization. The fact that the dummy variables in this second equation failed to achieve significance led Krueger to conclude that liberalization influences growth via what she termed the *indirect* route (namely through generating higher export growth which itself results in more rapid GNP growth) rather than by exerting any *direct* influence in its own right by offering such dynamic advantages as increased capacity utilization and more efficient investment projects. In essence, she concluded that export performance which explains differences in growth performance with 'the fact that the regime itself is liberalised (or restricted) does not seem to have any additional independent influence' (ibid., 274).

In short, Krueger's results led her to conclude that the influence of liberalization upon output growth works via the first of the two channels described above; namely, by increasing exports as an argument of the output function. Stated differently, she concluded that trade regimes do not affect real output growth independently of exports. This conclusion has, however, been severely criticized in some quarters. In particular, various investigators have sought to challenge this explicitly by including in real output equations not only an export variable but also an additional variable which is designed to capture the character or orientation of the trade regime in operation at the time in question. With the export variable included to control for the effect of exports on real output, the trade regime variable should, in principle, allow one to test whether the regime itself exerts an independent influence upon real output. The difficulty, of course, with this approach is how precisely to measure trade orientation. This is no easy matter. One of the best known approaches was developed by Balassa (1985), who constructed as an index of trade policy the deviation of the actual volume of exports from the volume of exports predicted by what he saw as a simple structural model of trade. Assuming exports to be a linear function of only per capita income, population and the availability of mineral resources, Balassa interpreted positive residuals as reflecting *export promotion* policies and negative residuals as indicating *inward orientation*. Including this variable in a GDP growth equation, Balassa found its coefficient to be positive and significantly different from zero, a finding that was interpreted as indicating, contrary to Krueger's conclusion, that trade orientation does exert an (independent) influence on the rate of economic growth.[3]

As we have seen, Krueger's specification of the real output equation was rather restrictive in that it allowed neither for the possibility that liberalization brings about an intercept shift nor for the potentially important possibility that liberalization might influence the elasticity of real output with respect to exports. In two papers, Greenaway and Sapsford (1994a, 1994b) have estimated a less restrictive output equation which allows for both such possibilities. Including intercept dummies and slope dummies on the export variable (each of which is constructed to come into operation during periods of liberalization) in conventional real output equations (of the sort described in equations (7.1) and (7.2) above), these studies find evidence of significance for both the intercept and export slope dummies.[4]

More specifically, Greenaway and Sapsford (1994b) subject the PMC sample (or rather a subset thereof), to statistical scrutiny, using the above production function-based approach. The basic model set out in equation (7.2) above is augmented with slope and intercept dummies[5] specified to pick up what Krueger terms the direct effects of liberalization on growth and then estimated against data for 12 of the 19 countries in the PMC sample.[6] The PMC study documents some 36 trade liberalization episodes. The evidence reported by Greenaway and Sapsford (1994b) suggested that, in some two-thirds of all cases considered, liberalization appears to have had no discernible direct impact on the exports–growth relationship. In the remaining four cases, however, a diversity of experience is revealed.

Given the conviction with which the PMC results are reported, and the enthusiasm with which they have been embraced by the key lending agency, these results are a cause for concern. It could, of course, simply be the case that liberalization does not, typically, affect growth in a direct way. Another possibility is that the effect of liberalization on growth operates only via the indirect route of increasing exports. However the results obtained raise serious doubts about even the indirect channel, for they suggest that, when proper econometric steps are taken to overcome some of the problems inherent in earlier studies of the export–growth relation (namely the fact that exports are, via the usual national income accounting identity, themselves a component of income), there is little empirical evidence to indicate that export growth exerts a significant influence upon real output growth.[7] Yet another possibility is that liberalization does not have an impact on economic performance via a discrete break, but rather by initiating a transition from one parameter value to another. If this is so, conventional tests designed to locate the existence of a discrete break will generally fail to find one.

SOME EMERGING EVIDENCE: THE CASE OF TAIWAN'S WTO MEMBERSHIP

The discussion of the preceding section has highlighted a methodological framework within which the economic benefits of trade liberalization (narrowly defined in terms of possible enhancements to real national income and its growth) may be evaluated. In the present context, the particular form of trade liberalization in which we are interested is of the multilateral category arising from a country's decision to join GATT/WTO. In essence what the preceding section has suggested is that the analysis should proceed in two stages; first, it is necessary to examine the data in order to ascertain the extent to which membership appears to be associated with an increase in trade flows (typically, although not exclusively, in terms of exports); and second, a model of form (7.2) above needs to be investigated econometrically in order to provide an indication of the extent to which increased trade flows feed through into improved economic growth performance. As is clear from the discussion of the preceding section, the econometrics involved in this second analytical stage needs to go beyond the mere estimation of model (7.2) per se (as in the export-led growth literature) to allow for the possibility that trade liberalization may have other, more subtle, but nevertheless potentially important, effects that work through changes in one or more of the parameters of models like (7.2). In particular, we have mentioned some evidence to suggest that liberalizations can bring about a significant change in the elasticity of real output with respect to exports. Once this latter possibility is recognized we immediately see that studies, like that due to Rose (2003), which focus solely on the effects of WTO membership on trade flows and find no discernible effect, can lead to erroneous conclusions regarding the ineffectiveness of the WTO as they fail to admit the possibility that membership might result in a given level of exports effectively 'going further' in driving growth: perhaps because, as a consequence of membership, the structure of trade between member countries moves more closely into line with the actual pattern of comparative advantage.

It is also important to recognize that multilateral liberalization of the sort resulting from GATT and WTO membership are, by the very *modus operandi* of these bodies, not limited to the benefits that arise at and from the moment of joining. Once a country is an insider, it stands to gain further benefits from membership whenever new members are admitted and whenever a round of tariff reductions is successfully negotiated. For convenience we can refer to the benefits that accrue to a country when it joins the 'club' as first-order effects and those arising to the country once it is an insider from further expansion and/or the successful negotiation of a round of tariff reductions as second-order effects.

At the time of writing the only other study of which we are aware that seeks to provide an evaluation and assessment of the consequences of WTO membership is that due to Rose (2003), which utilizes the method of dynamic panel data analysis. However, as already noted, this study is of only limited use in the present context because it fails to look beyond the trade flow issue, with the consequence that it offers no insight whatsoever into the likely consequence(s) of membership for broader issues such as the course of real output movements, let alone economic welfare.

The WTO current membership list comprises 146 countries, some 112 of whom were previously members of the GATT. Especially interesting in the context of evolving international relations is the fact that, following China, Taiwan joined the WTO on 1 January 2002, as its 144th member.[8] The case of the likely benefits to accrue to Taiwan, as a new WTO member, has been analysed in some detail by Sapsford et al. (2003), on whose analysis the following discussion is based. Taiwan having been a member of the WTO for less than two years there is clearly insufficient statistical evidence currently available to allow one to undertake the sort of detailed econometric assessment indicated above. However the evidence that is available (Chou et al., 2003) does indicate the depth of the tariff reductions that were achieved by Taiwan during the run-up phase immediately prior to its accession in 2002. For example, these authors calculate that the bilateral negotiations between Taiwan and WTO members led to a reduction in the average nominal tariff rate from 20.6 per cent in 1987 to 8.25 per cent in 1998, while the corresponding figures for the average effective tariff rate showed a reduction from 7.02 per cent to 3.13 per cent over the same period.

Despite the limitations imposed upon us by available data it does seem reasonable to argue that at least some understanding of the potential benefits accruing to Taiwan and, more generally, other small developing economies contemplating seeking WTO membership can be gleaned from the experience of other Southeast Asian economies who joined the GATT/WTO 'club' in the less recent past. For the purpose of the current discussion we focus our attention on the following set of countries, where the dates in parentheses indicate their date of accession to the GATT: Hong Kong (1986), Indonesia (1950), Japan (1955), Korea (1967), Malaysia (1957), Philippines (1979) and Thailand (1982). While it is inherently hazardous to select a sample of representative economies it is nonetheless felt that, given both the nature of these economies and the timing of their accession to multilateral trade liberalization, their experiences will be of some relevance to those that will be experienced by Taiwan and others as recent or potential new members of the WTO.

Summary of Findings

In the interests of brevity we limit ourselves here to providing a brief summary of the findings that emerged from our analysis, which followed the multi-stage sequence described above. All data for this exercise were obtained from the World Bank's *World Development Indicators* database and cover the period 1960–2000. Copies of a Technical Appendix setting out our detailed results are available from the first named author on request. Our summary is conveniently set out under the following headings, which correspond to the individual stages of the analysis.

Trade flows

Time plots of exports for each of these seven countries reveal somewhat similar behaviour, with the export index increasing steadily over the last four decades of the twentieth century. While each country in this sample appears to have experienced a fall in exports in 1997, perhaps attributable to the so-called 'Southeast Asian financial crisis', it is relevant to note that in each case exports had shown evidence of strong recovery by 1999/2000. Of more relevance to the current discussion are a number of peaks in export which at least in some cases might perhaps not unreasonably be associated with accession (first-order effects). For instance the rate of growth of Hong-Kong's exports seems to have accelerated around the time of its accession to GATT in 1985. A similar acceleration in export growth is perhaps discernible in Thailand in 1984, some two years after its accession to GATT. In another case (the Philippines, who joined GATT in 1979) exports seemed to have increased around 1980, but apparently only to fall back to their previous trajectory within six years. While such observations can be little more than suggestive, the evidence does seem to indicate a diversity of behaviour, at least some of which might be associable with first-order (or joining) effects.

As regards second-order effects brought about by the successful conclusion of rounds of tariff reductions, the acceleration in the Philippines' exports after 1980 might possibly be, in part, associated with the successful conclusion of the Tokyo Round in 1979, in which some 102 countries participated and which resulted in an average one-third reduction in customs duties in the world's nine major industrial markets. These reductions were phased in over a period of eight years, involving harmonization. There is a hint of evidence of possible similar second-order experience in the case of Japan, although lasting only until 1983.

Exports and growth

As already noted, the weight of available evidence in the extensive export-led growth literature is far from overwhelmingly supportive of the hypothesis.

Despite their preliminary nature, the results that we obtained from fitting model (7.2) to data relating to the sample of countries were equally diverse. Perhaps the strongest empirical support for the export-led growth hypothesis is evident in the case of Japan. As is clear from the above discussion, such analyses are potentially complicated by the fact that accession and/or the successful completion of negotiation rounds has the potential to bring about structural changes in the parameters underlying the estimated model (7.2). Applying dummy variables to capture accession effects, as well as using both CUSUM and CUSUMSQ techniques in an attempt to let the data reveal the most likely break point, yield results that would seem to suggest that the Philippines experienced a structural break at around the time it joined the GATT which took the form of an autonomous upward shift in real output growth.

CONCLUDING REMARKS

In this chapter we have developed a framework within which the major economic benefit (in terms of real output) to Taiwan of its accession to the WTO may be evaluated. The limited time span of available data at the present time prevents us from applying the procedure directly to Taiwan's experience, but, by examining the experiences of a range of other Southeast Asian economies, we have been able to shed some light on the possible effects that might follow Taiwan's accession. In particular the analysis suggests that an increase in trade flows as a consequence of accession is neither a necessary nor a sufficient condition to reap benefits in the form of enhanced real incomes.

Two final comments are in order. First, if recent estimates obtained from computable general equilibrium models are to be believed (Chou et al., 2003), Taiwan can expect to experience a decline following its accession to the WTO in output in the *heavy industry* and the *services subsector* (including business and financial services) reflecting the evaluation of Taiwan's comparative advantage as currently lying in *non-heavy manufacturing industries*. To the extent that this structure of comparative advantage will persist into the future, this line of argument predicts opportunities for gainful trade in services, including financial services. However a word of caution is in order at this point because, if there is one thing which the experience of other Southeast Asian economies after joining the GATT tells us, it is that comparative advantage, contrary to its treatment in standard trade models, can and does change. In essence, therefore, the structure of comparative advantage, especially in a scenario of evolving multilateral tariff reductions, needs to be treated as endogenously determined. Second, in reality, even if the benefits in terms of improved real incomes turn out not to be large, this does not imply that membership of the 'club' is not of net benefit. As argued in the third section of this chapter, membership to such a club confers certain privileges on the members, but also duties. It is these privileges and duties which enable members to cooperate with each other towards attaining a common goal – an orderly rules-based process of trade offering certainty and transparency to each of its members.

NOTES

1. In order to avoid spurious correlation arising from the fact that exports are, by construction, one component of aggregate output, this particular variable, as the model's dependent variable, should strictly speaking be specified net of exports (Greenaway and Sapsford, 1994b). However many analysts have overlooked this requirement.
2. It is common in the literature to find expression (7.2) estimated in first-difference form. The parameter φ in (7.2) measures the effect of technical progress upon output and, being the coefficient of the time trend in the levels equation, it becomes the intercept in the differenced equation. Accordingly evidence indicating that liberalization is associated with a shift in the intercept term in an output growth equation (as revealed by a significant liberalization intercept dummy variable: for example Greenaway and Sapsford, 1994a, 1994b) may be interpreted as suggesting that liberalization exerts an influence by enhancing the beneficial effects of technical progress upon output growth.
3. See Edwards (1993:1386) for some reservations regarding Balassa's approach.
4. In these studies the sample of countries analysed comprise a subset of the 19 countries analysed in the PMC study. In all cases the dating of the liberalisation episodes is provided by the detailed policy accounts reported by PMC: see Greenaway and Sapsford (1994b: 159). It should be noted that, unlike Krueger (1978), who estimated her equations in levels form, Greenaway and Sapsford (1994a, 1994b) work in first difference form. Accordingly, the intercept dummy in the latter studies may be interpreted as capturing possible variations in the *trend term* in a levels formulation, of the sort adopted by Krueger.
5. The slope dummy was specified on the export term in order to capture any influence which liberalization might exert on ψ, the elasticity of output with respect to exports.
6. Data constraints prevented analysis of the remaining seven countries in the PMC sample.
7. The one country in the sample which presents the strongest evidence of the presence of an export growth coefficient which is significantly different from zero is New Zealand. However, in this case, the export–growth coefficient turns out to be negative.
8. Being followed by Armenia on 5 February 2003 and the Former Yugoslav Republic of Macedonia on 4 April 2003.

REFERENCES

Balassa, B. (1985), 'Exports, policy choices and economic growth in developing countries after the 1973 oil shock', *Journal of Development Economics*, **18** (2), 23–35.

Bhagwati, J.N and D. Irwin (1987), 'The return of the reciprocitarians; US trade policy today', *World Economy*, **10**, 109–30.

Chou, J., S. Wang, K. Chen and N. Kuo (2003), 'Taiwan's accession into the WTO and trade in services: a computable general equilibrium analysis', in T. Ito and A.

Krueger (eds), *Trade in Services in the Asia–Pacific Region*, London: University of Chicago Press, pp. 99–130.

Collier, P. (1993), 'Higgledy-piggledy liberalisation', *The World Economy*, **16**, pp. 503–12.

Edwards, S. (1993), 'Openness, trade liberalization, and growth in developing countries', *Journal of Economic Literature*, **31** (3), 1358–93.

Falvey, R. and N. Gemmell (1989), 'New evidence on government size and economic growth', mimeo, Australian National University, Canberra.

Feder, G. (1983) 'On exports and economic growth', *Journal of Development Economics*, **12**, 59–73.

Greenaway, D. (1993) 'Liberalising foreign trade through rose tinted glasses', *Economic Journal*, **103**, 208–22.

Greenaway, D. and O. Morrissey (1993), 'Structural adjustment and liberalisation: what have we learned?', *Kyklos*, **46**, 241–62.

Greenaway, D. and D. Sapsford (1994a), 'Exports, growth and liberalization: an evaluation', *Journal of Policy Modeling*, **16** (2), 165–86.

Greenaway, D. and D. Sapsford (1994b), 'What does liberalisation do for exports and growth?', *Weltwirtschaftliches Archiv*, **130** (1), 152–74.

Hoekman, B. and M. Kostecki (1995), *The Political Economy of the World Trading System; From GATT to WTO*, Oxford: Oxford University Press.

Krueger, A. (1978), *Foreign Trade Regimes and Economic Development: Liberalization Attempts and Consequences*, Cambridge, MA: Ballinger for NBER.

Papageorgiou, D., M. Michaely and A. Choksi (1991), *Liberalising Foreign Trade* (7 vols), London and New York: Oxford University Press.

Ram, R. (1986), 'Government size and economic growth: a new framework and some evidence from cross-section and time-series data', *American Economic Review*, **76**, 191–203.

Rose, A.K. (2004), 'Do we really know that the WTO increases trade?', *American Economic Review*, **94** (1), 98–114.

Salvatore, D. and T. Hatcher (1991), 'Inward oriented and outward oriented trade strategies', *Journal of Development Studies*, **27** (3), 7–25.

Sapsford, D., V.N. Balasubramanyam and S. Pfaffenzeller (2003), 'How might Taiwan benefit from WTO membership?', paper presented to Taipei Conference on Taiwan and the World Trade Organisation: New Agendas in the 21st Century, Shu Te University and Chung Hua Institution for Economic Research, 28 November.

Smith, A. (1776), *The Wealth of Nations*, London: Penguin, reprinted 1961.

8. Multilateral debt management and the poor

Kunibert Raffer

The 'mission statement' of the International Bank for Reconstruction and Development (IBRD) proclaims: 'Our dream is a world free of poverty.' The following line asserts, 'To fight poverty with passion and professionalism for lasting results' (IBRD, 2003a). The IMF's homepage lists 'Poverty Reduction' as a special 'Topic'. Masood Ahmed (IMF, 2003a:4), the parting Deputy Director of the Policy Development and Review Department, sees anti-poverty objectives as part of the IMF culture.

> Over the past three or four years there has been a much more direct focus on how the Fund can contribute to improving living standards of poor people, on how we can manage poverty and the social impact of policies that we recommend. Now most Fund mission chiefs working on low income countries think much more systematically about the impact on the poor of the policies and programs that a country is undertaking.

Judging by official declarations, a passionate anti-poverty focus has become part and parcel of multilateral debt management. This was not always so, nor are – according to many critics – strong declarations matched by appropriate on-the-ground policies. This chapter analyses the extent to which poverty reduction has actually been reflected in the policies of the Bretton Woods Institutions (BWIs). As a background, their attitudes towards poverty before 1982 are sketched.

POVERTY BEFORE 1982

Neither institution was created to fight poverty in Southern countries (SCs). The words 'and Development' were glued onto the original name, 'International Bank for Reconstruction' on the insistence of participating SCs (Raffer, 2003a; Raffer and Singer, 2001). The great risk of an impoverished Western Europe in the bipolar world made the USA reconsider the IBRD's ability to guarantee quick reconstruction and poverty reduction. The Marshall Plan, special programmes (Turkey, Greece) and a generous loan to Britain were deemed more appropriate to immunize Western Europe against communism. Relatively high IBRD interest rates were apparently one reason. Benefiting from the glued on 'Development', IBRD officials toured the South to drum up business (Caufield, 1998:56). Arguably one may say that the mandate for development includes poverty alleviation. One may ask whether the IBRD is better qualified to alleviate poverty in these countries, which are much poorer than Western Europe. Until McNamara became its President in 1968, the IBRD perceived itself as a 'bank' whose businesslike approach precluded financing social activities. It not only refused 'messing around with education and health' or a water treatment plant, but even forced Colombia not to accept a French loan for waterworks (ibid.:64), quite a contrast to its present PR image: 'The World Bank is not a "bank" in the common sense' (IBRD, 2003b).

The IMF was not designed as a development organization, but to enable (at first practically only industrialized) members of the Bretton Woods system with short-term balance of payments problems to stay within the agreed parity bands. Not all balance of payments problems were to be solved by drawings. Changing parities and the right to capital controls were foreseen: a membership right still enshrined in its Articles of Agreement. The demise of Bretton Woods left the IMF virtually without an agenda. It should have been dissolved. Its very few remaining tasks, such as the Compensatory Financing Facility, could easily have been transferred to another institution. The IMF cleverly used the debt crisis of 1982 to create itself another raison d'être, a perfect vindication of Parkinson's theory that bureaucracies, even if otherwise inefficient, are astonishingly good at surviving. Until the Cologne Summit entrusted both BWIs with HIPC II, which explicitly includes anti-poverty measures, the IMF had usually and rightly stated that this was not its mandate. Others should focus on it.

In its early years the IBRD was particularly strongly opposed to the principle of soft financing, demanding harder terms, nearer to the market. It rejected cheap money or more Marshall Plan-like terms advocated by the 'wild men at the UN', among them Sir Hans Singer, as harmful to development (Raffer and Singer, 1996:61; 2001:65). Such strong and principled concerns were immediately overcome once the IBRD, not the UN, was to administer the bulk of multilateral soft financing. IDA was established as its soft loan window for poor countries, not specifically aimed at the poor, though, shortly after (some argue because of) Castro's revolution. Pressure from within the UN – by the 'wild men' and some member countries – was another reason for the establishment of IDA.

McNamara was the first president focusing on poverty. Lending to poor countries, he argued, would not be sufficient. Loans should specifically aim at the poorest within SCs. McNamara had the merit of giving credibility to the idea that helping the poor is not wasting resources but makes economic sense. The basic needs approach (Streeten, 1993) became accepted development policy. Many aid administrations adopted poverty orientation.

The IBRD took up an idea put forward by the head of the International Labour Organization (ILO) team analysing poverty and employment policies in Kenya (Sir Hans Singer), although with a twist. The Kenya Report had argued that the incomes of the poorest must increase more rapidly than they would by growth and 'trickle down' alone. Redistribution from the increment of growth would mean adding to the incomes and assets of the poor without taking away from anyone else, an idea running counter to the ruling perception (Raffer and Singer 2001:75ff). A joint book published for the IBRD's Development Research Centre and the Institute of Development Studies, *Redistribution with Growth* (Chenery et al., 1974), suggested that a proportion of incremental income would be taxed and channelled into public services intended to raise the productivity of the poor. It even spoke of 'trickle-up' effects from greater incomes of the poor. The book's title became a widely used catchword at the IBRD. In a way the Bank's present official focus is a late homecoming: less radical than the 1970s, but arguably better marketed.

'On-the-ground results' of McNamara's efforts were less impressive. The IBRD admitted that it did not reach the poorest quintile (Lipton and Shakow, 1982). Independent sources paint a worse picture, criticizing the vague terms describing alleged positive effects of projects. Rather than providing verifiable data the Bank preferred speaking of people 'affected' by its activities. Christoffersen (1978:20), for example, formulates: 'benefits of 210 of these projects are expected to accrue predominantly to the rural poor', or 'They aim at affecting directly between 15 and 20 million rural families or some 90 to 120 million individuals' (ibid.). Reviewing IBRD publications, Tetzlaff (1980:438ff) called such figures a bluff, because the exact meaning of benefiting or affecting is nowhere explained. It is generally agreed that the Bank could not reach the really poor, which is no surprise given its structure, especially the costs and sizes of loans.

Rich (1994:198) reports a more recent meaning of 'affected': 'people living in project areas are either "beneficiaries" or, if their livelihoods and culture will be harmed or destroyed, "project-affected population"'. The IMF/ IBRD meeting in 1991 in Bangkok shows that one might be 'affected' without any project too. Rich (ibid.:1ff) describes how slums were razed and people forced to relocate to 'leaky army tents' to spare delegates discussing poverty the sight of poor people. Compensation was modest, according to Rich: per family less than the costs of one single night of one delegate in a hotel room. The Bank answered Rich's book with a public relations (PR) campaign telling success stories from the field. Despite repeated requests, the

Bank refused to provide verifiable details including project titles and loan numbers. For 64 per cent of allegedly successful projects no documentation whatsoever was released (Caufield, 1998:274).

'STRUCTRUAL ADJUSTMENT' AND NEOLIBERAL REFORMS

As late as 1982 the conclusions of a working group on poverty calling for measures to alleviate the effects of 'Structural Adjustment' on the poor were officially approved (Lipton and Shakow, 1982). But the tide had already turned totally. The term 'Structural Adjustment' is used with inverted commas, because the BWIs monopolized it to mean their own specific ideas, or whatever they were doing. While there was evident need for reform, or structural adjustment, in problem debtor countries, this does not mean that the specific set of BWI prescriptions promises success (cf. Raffer, 1994). Empirical outcome so far rather suggests the opposite.

Both BWIs insisted that carrying on 'Structural Adjustment' had positive impacts and was in the very interest of the poor. Special measures to protect them would be superfluous, if not harmful. Emphasizing human needs might obstruct needed reforms (Jolly, 1991:1811). The IBRD (1980:62) described the 'major drawback' of efficient food subsidies as being costly, often using up 'scarce foreign exchange or aid'. In other words, money that could be used to pay creditors was used up to feed the hungry. The going arguments are nicely summed up by the IMF's Tseng (1984): 'Structural Adjustment' costs are unavoidable and lower than the costs of non-adjustment; efficiency gains will more than make up for 'adjustment' costs; financial help by the BWIs decreases these costs further; bringing down inflation is of particular benefit to the poor likely to hold their assets in cash; successful economic reforms benefit everybody, including the poor; subsidies have to be abolished, as they are a huge part of public outlays, they discriminate against the rural poor, and create incentives for low wages industries, thus leading to rapid urbanization (and slums). To be on the safe side, Tseng adds that the IMF has no mandate regarding the poor anyway. Considering that the poor are the vast majority in low-income countries, critical minds might ask how proper and successful economic policies disregarding their economic situation could be possible.

Beckmann (1986) explains the IBRD's policy reversal by changed necessities of SCs: balance of payments equilibria reached by GDP and export growth benefit the rich as well as the poor; relying on market mechanisms does not mean less attention to the poor; planned actions are better than unplanned adjustment; sacrifices are necessary for a better future. The growth crisis made advances in poverty alleviation practically impossible. In line with his employer, the IBRD, Beckmann adds that many projects benefited the poor as well, even though the political climate of the 1980s is not conducive to helping the poor. To prove this he mentions that most IDA and IBRD funds went to poor countries and sectors, whose projects are supposed to benefit particularly the poor – which does not prove any benefit to the poor. However, as the Bank's policy is decided by its members and in consultation with borrowers, the IBRD itself has (the author asserts) limited room for manoeuvring. In plain English: while the Bank helped the poor by not specifically helping them it was not responsible for what it did, as it did not really decide anything.

Basically poverty reduction was seen as unnecessary and possibly harmful until UNICEF's *Adjustment with a Human Face* (Cornia et al., 1987), although the BWIs had been confronted with the effects of 'Structural Adjustment' on the poor already in 1984 (Helleiner et al., 1991). Pfeffermann (1988) qualified the proposed changes as a 'cri du cœur' rather than a serious guideline for economic policy in *Finance & Development*. Seeing the study's merits in raising governments' awareness of poverty, he called for practicable proposals instead of the study's ideas. In spite of his verdict reflecting the general mood at the BWIs, Pfeffermann himself had recommended targetting, a method advocated by the UNICEF study, in 1987. The 1988 World Development Report wrote about how to target effectively. Soon the BWIs officially accepted special programmes to help those affected by 'Structural Adjustment', arguing that these would make 'Structural Adjustment' more acceptable and thus more efficient, a point denied shortly before. Whatever the BWIs did, they always helped the poor. In practice, though, little was done. Stewart's (1991:1847) statement, 'while there was a big change in rhetoric, little action has so far followed', is still not incorrect. Arguments and publication titles changed, without essentially affecting policies, in spite of severe critique and even though it could not be proved empirically that the recipe worked.

According to the UNDP (1993:7) less than 7 per cent of bilateral DAC aid was spent on pro-poor human 'priority areas such as basic education, primary health care, rural water supplies, nutrition programmes and family planning services' in the early 1990s. A slightly better picture emerged for multilaterals allocating around 16 per cent on average to priority areas. The African Development Bank operating on the poorest continent had the smallest share (4 per cent). UNICEF spent 77.8 per cent on human priorities, IFAD 16.8 per cent, IBRD and IDA (lumped together by UNDP, 1994:74) 10.2 per cent. According to these figures IBRD and IDA did little for the poor.

On the other hand, negative effects on the poor can be proved. Strong public pressure forced the IBRD to assess the Bank's involvement in the Sardar Sarovar project in India, where people were resettled involuntarily. The Bank even ignored and distorted the advice of its own experts (Caufield,

1998:23) to be able to continue funding. The Morse Report was devastating, and finally the Bank was obliged to stop financing this project. The Morse Commission concluded 'that the abuses in Sardar Sarovar were not an isolated exception, particularly with respect to the mistreatment of thousands of forcibly resettled rural poor: "The problem besetting the Sardar Sarovar Projects are more the rule than the exception to resettlement operations supported by the Bank [= IBRD] in India."' (Rich, 1994:252; cf. also Raffer and Singer, 1996:52 and 208).

According to the IBRD's Cernea (1988), about 40 IBRD projects were supposed to 'cause the relocation of at least 600 000 people in 27 countries' during 1979–85. However 'the number of people needing to be resettled is *chronically underestimated*' (ibid.:45, emphasis in original). He conceded that forcefully resettled people often get a raw deal so that projects can be implemented more cheaply. If they get any compensation it is often inadequate, leading to impoverishment, particularly so in the case of dams. Cernea cites the destruction of productive assets, higher morbidity and mortality, ecological disaster and the destruction of social structures as effects of development projects with compulsory resettlement. Susan George (1988:158) reports that people resisting resettlement under Indonesia's huge IBRD-financed *transmigrasi* project were crushed by security forces.

It must be recalled that the IMF's first 'adjustment measures' were undertaken after 1973. The IBRD claimed the success of 'Structural Adjustment' in Africa with the famous statement, 'Recovery has begun', in 1989 (IBRD & UNDP, 1989:iii), but so far no overindebted Sub-Saharan country has reached economic sustainability. To economists this should come as no surprise. The IBRD's (1989:92) own Operations Evaluation Department (OED) stated in 1989: 'conditionalities should take into account the macroeconomic consequences of the policy prescriptions'. It called for an integrated analytical framework to understand better the links between programmes and their expected macroeconomic outcomes: 'Such a framework would also be useful for ex-post evaluations' (ibid.:6). Briefly, all the neoliberal policies forced upon debtor countries, allegedly to help the poor, had no theoretical basis. Since 'Structural Adjustment' was jointly controlled by the BWIs one must ask whether the IMF had a theoretical basis and, if so, why and how the Fund kept it secret from the Bank.

The Wapenhans Report (IBRD, 1992) mentioned grave shortcomings, such as project conditions conflicting with conditionality imposed by the BWIs, or insufficient attention to financial risks. Borrowers alleged that conditions liked by the Bank's management and board were included even 'where these may complicate projects so as to jeopardise successful implementation' (ibid.: iii). The question whether programmes with more than 100 conditions can be implemented answers itself anyway. While this says quite enough about the effectiveness of BWI-type troubleshooting, one should mention a very interesting finding from the econometric debate about whether 'Structural Adjustment' worked. The BWIs gave up long ago because of embarrassing results: often there was no statistically significant difference between programme and non-programme countries in spite of 'innovative' methods. One of the extremely few statistically significant results was published by Khan (1990), an IMF econometrician: significantly reduced growth in programme countries, a predicted reduction in the growth rate of at least 0.7 per cent of GDP each year a country had an IMF programme. According to the BWIs' own arguments this must mean catastrophic results for the poor.

When Williamson (1996) defined the Washington Consensus, the IBRD's chief economist, Stanley Fischer, wanted to include the social agenda far more explicitly than Williamson. Fischer's statement echoed IBRD declarations. When Husain (1994) expressed optimism that Africa's growth prospects would 'doubtlessly' increase if adjustment policies were not impeded, although poverty in Africa would not be overcome, he advocated increased investments in human capital and infrastructure to achieve growth, precisely those investments that had been cut by BWI programmes. User fees introduced under BWI pressure reduced access to health services and education for the poor. Social sectors were most severely affected by fiscal discipline to allow higher debt service payments. The Bank successfully avoided the 'major drawback' of social expenditures it had identified: using up scarce foreign exchange. Fischer's concerns had practically no real effects, as the IBRD's policies and neoliberal reforms forced upon debtors prove.

The IBRD was the engine promoting private pension schemes. In Chile, '40 percent of workers in the poorest income decile do not participate in the pension system' (IBRD, 2001:154). But 'Even a well-structured pension system will not initially reach the poor', which is surprising, as Chile had introduced its 'new' system in 1980. The Bank found that coverage was lowest among the poor. It pointed out that mandatory contributions to public systems might be difficult for them, failing to argue why monthly payments to private institutions should be any easier. The Bank argued that 'social assistance or social pensions should cover the poorest ... and those without family support'. Apparently the Bank suggests reintroducing yesteryear's solution, depending on family support in old age. People living on less than the famous daily buck might not be able to provide much support. By contrast, private pension funds owing their success to the BWIs have struck a bonanza. In Chile, commissions to administrators reached their peak in 1984 at 8.69 per cent of taxable salary. They were brought down to 2.96 per cent in 1997, still 18 per cent of a worker's total contribution (Kay, 2003:236). In Latin America, administrative costs may be over 4.5 per cent of wages or much higher than 20 per cent of contributions (Raffer, 2003b). Chile may

thus be regarded as an example of relatively moderate fees. Higher administrative costs than public pension schemes and regressive cost structures are
hardly promoting dreams of a world free of poverty. The regressivity of
private schemes was the reason why low-income workers are specifically
excluded from the superannuation-guarantee system in Australia or why Britain excludes many lower-paid workers from the system.

The *World Development Report* (IBRD, 2001:79) dedicated to the problem
of poverty stated: 'The general inadequacy, if not total absence, of health
insurance markets in most developing countries exposes both the poor and
the nonpoor to substantial financial risk and insecurity'. It fails to specify
how 'more than half the people' in SCs living on 'less than $700 a year'
(IBRD, 2003b), let alone the 1.2 billion living on less than one dollar a day,
could effectively use such markets.

THE HIPC INITIATIVES

While it was a huge and commendable step towards more efficient debt
management, HIPC I did not take the poor specifically into account. The
IBRD made a link between the Initiative and poverty reduction, but poverty
was visibly reflected neither in sustainability indicators nor in actual creditor
decisions. Limiting debt service may be seen as having pro-poor side-effects,
though. James Wolfenson's efforts to break the taboo of multilateral debt
reductions against fierce resistance from the IMF and from within the Bank
itself are to be commended. This did help the poorest countries.

It took many years before the Cologne Summit of 1999 officially and
explicitly recognized the negative effects of BWI debt management on poverty. Under unprecedented pressure from civil society – the international
Jubilee Movement presented over 17 million signatures collected worldwide
to the German Chancellor – the G7 admitted that HIPC I had failed and
decided to introduce HIPC II. For the first time, poverty reduction was
incorporated visibly. The Poverty Reduction and Growth Facility (PRGF) has
this aim in its name.

The old debate on 'ownership' continues: are programmes the country's
own or those of the BWIs? Apparently HIPC II is used to shift the blame for
failures onto the countries under the thumb of the BWIs: 'PRSPs [Poverty
Reduction Strategy Papers] have been produced by the country authorities,
and not by Bank and Fund staff' (IMF, 2000). Logically the country is to
blame, even though 'Greater ownership is the single most often cited, but
also the least tangible, change in moving to PRGF-supported programs.
There is no single element of program design or documentation that will
signal this change' (ibid.).

Important creditors controlling the BWIs soon accused debtors forced to cut pro-poor public expenditures in favour of higher debt service of neglecting their social sectors. Preparing the Genoa Summit, Italy (Presidenza, 2001:19) criticized:

> Health systems should protect people against the financial costs of illness. Yet, many low income countries have in place cost-recovery schemes that imply a regressive burden of user fee payments for health. ... The empirical evidence in the past decade shows that user fees can discourage in the poorest countries the recourse to formal health services, thereby negatively affecting health performances. Governments need to introduce better incentives, rather than deterrents, to facilitate people's access to health services.

User fees had been forced upon poor countries by the BWIs controlled by the G7, sometimes against debtor resistance, but with the support and applause of G7 countries. Suffice this to show that public expenditures did not reflect the priorities forcefully advocated by Fischer.

The IMF (2001) 'embraced a new anti-poverty focus' in 1999. The PRGF 'replaced' the Enhanced Structural Adjustment Facility, bringing 'with it a number of innovations designed to ensure that lending programs are pro-poor and in line with the country's own strategy for reducing poverty'. This is 'More than just a change in name'. When feeling less obliged to document its new poverty culture, the IMF (2003b) finds no difference: 'The Poverty Reduction and Growth Facility (PRGF), formerly known as the Enhanced Structural Adjustment Facility (ESAF) provides loans ... .' This contradiction recalls the contradictory statements claiming a pro-poor bias for totally different policies during the 1980s. The IMF (2001) tries to explain contradictions away. The 'PRGF explicitly makes poverty reduction a central goal, whereas under ESAF poverty reduction was an implicit by-product'. This would support the view that, bureaucratic and linguistic niceties apart, the two facilities are identical regarding outcome.

The PRGF has the positive feature of public participation, although practice still remains to confirm declarations of intent. This participation, and the recognition that resources have to be set aside for minimal social nets for the poorest, are welcome moves in the direction suggested by my model of international Chapter 9 insolvency for sovereign debtors that demands protection of the poor. When I proposed exempting resources to protect the poor, and civil society participation in 1987 (cf. Raffer and Singer, 2001:193ff) BWI employees were among the most fierce critics, stating assertively that this would be impossible.

UNCTAD (2002:14) found substantial contradictions between typical PRSPs and the 'voices of the poor'. These or the 'aspirations of the poor' result from extensive IBRD field research 'on the perceptions, expectations and experiences of the poor, covering 24 developing countries (including eight in Africa)' (ibid.:13). In particular, positions on agriculture, labour markets, macro-policies, income distribution and the private sector are largely incompatible with PRSPs: 'In these areas, policy preferences of IFIs and/or national governments rather than expectations and aspirations of the poor appear to have prevailed' (ibid.:15). While one may logically argue that denying people what they want may ultimately be best for them – many fairy tales illustrate this – such findings do not refute the hypothesis that 'consulting' the poor is but another exercise in lip service.

UNCTAD (2002) identified severe negative impacts on the poor. These included shifts in taxation from corporate, personal income and trade taxes to regressive consumption taxes, falling real incomes of unskilled workers (declines often exceeding 20 per cent) rising input prices for food crops accompanied by declining output and increasing fertilizer prices, the collapse of rural infrastructure such as rural roads, declining levels of rural credits, the transformation of rural property regimes taking away user rights from the poor, user fees in the sectors of education and health constituting an important impediment to access for the poor, the 'exorbitant costs of drugs' (ibid.:43) or the decline in public service institutions. BWI pressure to liberalize capital accounts has made increased stocks of international reserves necessary, 'one of the widely-used targets of poverty reduction strategies in Africa' (ibid.:31), although any IMF member has the right to capital controls pursuant to the IMF's constitution. Only current transactions are to continue. These are defined in Article XXX(d) as 'not for the purpose of transferring capital', including 'payments of *moderate* amount of amortization of loans or for depreciation of direct investments' or '*moderate* remittances for family living expenses' (emphasis added). This means that even restrictions on debt service are a membership right. Using these rights, which the BWIs force their clients not to do (the IMF in open breach of its own constitution) would not cost anything, unlike large reserves squirrelling resources away from poverty alleviation, transforming the IBRD's dream into a nightmare for the poor.

UNCTAD (2002) repeatedly quotes observations by IBRD sources that BWI reforms have sometimes hurt the poor, even that 'Agricultural market liberalization without the institutional framework ... could have serious consequences for poor people' (ibid.:39f, quoting IBRD, 2001:69). But the Bank always comes down on the side of continuing and consolidating reforms rather than in favour of creating the necessary preconditions for reforms to work without hurting the poor. The IBRD (2001:70) officially recognized that the regressive property of VAT hurts the poorest, but did nothing to protect them. Apparently the Bank knows what it is doing and that this diverges considerably from its officially posted goals and dreams.

UNCTAD (2002:21) concluded: 'country PRSPs have so far covered a broad spectrum of macroeconomic policies and structural reforms without assessing their likely impact on poverty', as ministers from HIPCs noted too. UNCTAD (ibid.:59) found that 'little attention has so far been given to social impact analysis', echoing other critics, and recalling the OED's conclusion about the usefulness of a theoretical framework for 'Structural Adjustment'. Again poverty is 'fought' without proper analysis but in excellent English and with new acronyms such as PSIA (Poverty and Social Impact Analysis) or an IMF PRSP Sourcebook. The Wapenhans Report already warned that 'the perception that the literary quality of the SAR [Staff Appraisal Report] is in itself a criterion of success' is wrong, that actually accruing returns, not wonderful English, matter and: 'that point should be driven home' (IBRD, 1992, Annex A, 8). The BWIs seem to have remained more successful with excellent English than with economic results.

PRSPs put so much strain on debtor countries' resources, and designing them takes so much time, that Intermediate PRSPs (I-PRSPs) had to be invented to allow the BWIs to continue disbursements. The 'approval culture' and 'the Bank's pervasive preoccupation with new lending' (IBRD 1992:iii) seem very much alive. One should therefore wonder whether 'poor design, poor management and poor implementation' (ibid.) are still alive too.

Trying to identify differences between the PRGF and past policies in Africa, UNCTAD (2002:57) concluded that the new poverty focus 'does not replace the development strategies implemented under structural adjustment programmes but complements them'. New conditionalities were added. The effects of largely relying on across-the-board user fees in the areas of education and health (ibid.:59) are problematic. In spite of years of HIPC II, pro-poor policies are still not properly implemented.

A sad illustration of what the BWIs' pro-poor focus means in practice is Malawi. The BWIs were accused of having forced Malawi to sell maize from its National Food Reserve to pay creditors. The IBRD encouraged the country 'to keep foreign exchange instead of storing grain' (Pettifor, 2002). In a BBC interview, Malawi's president said the government 'had been forced [to sell maize] in order to repay commercial loans taken out to buy surplus maize in previous years' (ibid.). The BWIs had insisted and Malawi had sold a substantial amount of maize. After harvest problems in 2002, famine struck. According to Action Aid, 7 million of a population of 11 million were severely short of food. Creditor interest was given priority over survival.

Confronted with this by the House of Commons' Treasury Select Committee (2002:11f, 18f), Horst Köhler insisted that this advice had been given by the IBRD and the EU Commission, so 'it is just plain wrong to accuse the Fund that it advised and made even a conditionality out of this'. Köhler suggested that MPs should ask the Bank and the EU:

I want to underline: this is an issue in the responsibility of the World Bank and the EU Commission. The IMF was part of this process of giving advice to the Malawi government and the IMF may also not have been attentive enough, but I just tell you that I am not accepting that the IMF is made the culprit for this case ... I have sent the President of Malawi a letter in which I made clear that he was involved with the World Bank and the EU Commission in this project; that the IMF was part of, say, the kind of international advice and the IMF may, again, not have been attentive enough how they exercised how to run this maize stock, but it was not the responsibility of the Fund to implement the advice.

Obviously, while being 'part of the kind of advice' that resulted in starving people, the IMF did not give this advice at all. In any case, the IMF is innocent. What is important to our argument, though, is that repayment was preferred over poor people's right to live.

Proposing its Sovereign Debt Resolution Mechanism (SDRM) the IMF did not mention any measure to protect the poor, although many poor live in eligible countries. The SDRM falls back behind HIPC II (cf. Raffer, 2002; Raffer, forthcoming). This hardly supports assertions of an anti-poverty focus.

IMMUNIZATION AGAINST ACCOUNTABILITY

An economically disquieting trend towards dodging accountability, already observed in the 1980s, has become more pronounced. The IBRD, whose projects can be checked more easily, has both changed its evaluation methods repeatedly and shifted towards financing projects without clear economic returns, meaning activities practically escaping economic scrutiny. The IBRD's Economic Rate of Return (ERR) was never a really hard economic concept, depending on costs and benefits measured by shadow prices or even incremental benefits thought (by the IBRD) to stem from projects. Particularly after the Wapenhans Report, the IBRD reinforced its strategy of immunization against accountability and blame.

As early as 1985–86, the IBRD (1989:15f; stress added) introduced a new methodology, a 'less mechanical and somewhat subjective judgement as to performance', characterized by '*subjectivity of assessments*, which *increased the weight given to evaluators' perceptions, some of which were difficult to explain fully*'. This somewhat subjective method reduced the share of unsatisfactory projects from 28 per cent according to the old method to 12 per cent with unsatisfactory or uncertain performance in 1987. 'Uncertain' was a euphemism, defined as: 'Project achieves few objectives, if any, and has no foreseeable worthwhile results' (ibid.:15). In spite of innovative change the share of satisfactory operations went on declining perceptibly. The Bank changed its method again in 1997. Soft criteria became more important, such as more emphasis on social impact, with–without project comparisons, qualitative observations and judgments on institutional development. In spite of claims to the contrary, no stringent rules for judgment can be found, even in material sent on request by the OED. In contrast to the first reform, this new method increased the share of satisfactory projects sustainably, 'a remarkable improvement' (IBRD, 1999:xiii).

Because pro-poor projects are by definition not expected to recover costs, but to have long-run benefits, which cannot be properly gauged in the short run, results can be substantially 'improved' and the rate of unsatisfactory projects 'reduced' by inexplicably positive assessments. Few or no hard economic data exist. The fact that the monetary equivalent of, say, primary education being extended to a larger share of the population, or of a more democratic system allegedly giving more voice to the poor cannot be objectively established may prove extremely 'helpful'. Evaluators enjoy enormous leeway in defining 'success'. This is likely to be compounded by financial unaccountability. The BWIs do not have to pay for their failures, but gain from them, extending new loans to repair damages done by prior loans. Even the gravest shortcomings have not triggered appropriate reactions by their shareholders. Without drastic changes the mechanisms that force the poor to pay for IFI inefficiency are likely to be further strengthened (Raffer, 1993). Focusing loans and credits from multilateral institutions on the social sector may be used as a means to hide BWI inefficiency, simply because the effects of these particular projects, necessary as they are, are largely beyond objective measurement on a monetary scale. Thus the danger of being challenged on the grounds of efficiency could virtually be overcome. It is to be feared that the likelihood of improvements in BWI management culture will decrease further.

Sectors where economic facts have a stronger impact, such as industry, have remained problematic. Fortunately industry became a sector with declining emphasis in the Bank. Projects less exposed to hard on-the-ground results, such as public sector management, could improve the percentages of satisfactory outcomes perceptibly. Adjustment loans continue to have higher average outcomes and sustainability than investment loans: one wonders why success is not visibly reflected by the performance of 'adjusting' economies.

Always enjoying the benefit that its activities cannot be evaluated as easily as a steel mill, the IMF has been less exposed. However the Bank's move generates positive externalities. The Fund, too, can use soft factors more easily to brighten otherwise gloomy results. The fact that evaluation was already very dependent on what the OED called subjectivity of assessment or perceptions 'difficult to explain fully', and that objective measures have further lost importance, should be cause for great concern. Reorienting activities to projects without clear economic returns, without income streams in foreign currency covering debt service, but with a lot of leeway to determine 'success' immunizes against blame. Institutional changes, such as reorganizing national legal systems, or supporting democratization, are examples. So are social sector activities to which defenders of human development would subscribe. An example is a local language school for Mexican indigenous children financed by the IBRD, no doubt a socially highly recommendable pro-poor project, serving human development priorities, which should be financed. But financing it with loans, particularly on normal IBRD terms, is simply not viable. Like institution building or fighting AIDS, this project cannot and should not earn foreign currency income directly. One can hardly expect poor indigenous Mexican children to pay sufficient school fees in US dollars. Nor does a now improved legal system release an immediate dollar stream; possibly it may not even generate many positive effects for the poor. Nevertheless these loans have to be repaid with interest in foreign currency. In countries with a crushing debt overhang new loans not earning their own debt service are bound to worsen the situation further. If undertaken on a larger scale they increase the debt burden dramatically. Particularly for countries unable to honour large parts of contractually due payments on time, this has highly negative economic consequences, especially so at the 'near-market' interest rates of international development banks. Projects really benefiting people living on one to two dollars a day cannot be financed this way.

Social agenda and urgently needed projects for the poor must be financed by grants unless recipient governments are sufficiently liquid, which is extremely unlikely in the case of most SCs. Highly concessional interest rates, where feasible, must be calibrated to allow debt service to be covered with relatively lower income streams generated by projects. Economic theory holds that the willingness to pay reveals true preferences. If poverty reduction is really as important as the BWIs and donors claim, they must finance it with grants, using an excellent opportunity to prove the honesty of their concern for the poor and values such as democracy.

Financing adjustment problems of net food importers due to the WTO agreements clearly illustrates the problem of destabilizing lending. When the agreements were about to be signed, OECD countries apparently perceived a need to assure SCs that relief measures against expected higher food prices would be financed. Once the agreement was signed and prices went up, no relief was granted. The WTO tried to help SCs, approaching the BWIs to discuss improved conditions of access to existing facilities, a softening of conditionality, new facilities for net food importers and ways in which the WTO could help the BWIs to be more forthcoming in these matters, but without success. The BWIs prevailed with their 'alternative', using existing BWI facilities. Economically this is not sensible. Consumption is financed by loans carrying interest. Even at IDA conditions this still means 0.75 per cent p.a. in hard currency which countries have to earn. In the case of Sub-Saharan African, for instance, a region paying only one-fifth or one-sixth of their contractually due payments at that time, even such soft credits increase the debt overhang, further accumulating arrears. New multilateral loans for consumption will certainly not alleviate debt problems, but will become part of unpayable debts that have to be reduced eventually. The HIPC initiatives prove this. They became necessary because multilaterals did not fund economically viable and thus self-liquidating projects and programmes.

Differing fundamentally from its self-description, opinion leaders have a critical perception of the Bank. In a worldwide, IBRD-commissioned opinion poll, 22 per cent of those interviewed said the IBRD did a 'good job' in reducing poverty, 28 answered a 'bad job' (PSRA, 2003:44). The Bank's efforts to build a climate for investment, growth and jobs got worse marks (ibid.). These were the IBRD's pro-poor policies of the 1980s. Under the heading, 'World Bank not to blame for rich/poor gap', one learns that the most common view was that the IBRD had no effect on this growing gap, while 'sizeable minorities' (in Kenya, 60 per cent) believed the IBRD had increased inequality (ibid.:28f). With more justification one could have written, 'IBRD unable to reduce poverty'.

CONCLUDING REMARKS

The divergence between declarations and activities shows forcefully that the BWIs are either unlikely to be really interested in fighting poverty or incapable of doing so. Both conclusions would not suggest that they should be allowed to go on with 'poverty alleviation'. Both institutions have repeatedly asserted that they have learned. Unfortunately the poor have been forced by the BWIs to pay their tuition. The suspicion cannot be dispelled that poverty seems to be another marketing device, a Parkinsonian survival strategy of institutions. If poverty reduction were indeed as dear a goal to the international community as various declarations, principles and targets state, this important issue must not be left to the BWIs.

REFERENCES

Beckmann, David (1986), 'Die Weltbank und die Armut in den 80er Jahren', *Finanzierung & Entwicklung*, **23**(3), 26ff.

Caufield, Catherine (1998), *Masters of Illusion, The World Bank and the Poverty of Nations*, London: Pan.

Cernea, Michael C. (1988), 'Involuntary resettlement and development', *Finance & Development*, **25**(3), 44ff.

Chenery, Hollis, Montele S. Ahluwalia, C.L.G. Bell, John H. Duloy and Richard
    Jolly (1974), *Redistribution with Growth*, Oxford: Oxford University Press.
Christoffersen, Leif E. (1978), 'The bank and rural poverty', *Finance & Develop-
    ment*, **15**(4), 18ff.
Cornia, G.A., R. Jolly and F. Stewart (eds) (1987), *Adjustment with a Human Face*, 2
    vols, Oxford: Oxford University Press.
George, Susan (1988), *A Fate Worse than Debt*, Harmondsworth: Penguin.
Helleiner, G.K., G.A. Cornia and R. Jolly (1991), 'IMF adjustment policies and the
    needs of children', *World Development*, **19**(12), 1823ff.
Husain, I. (1994), 'Anpassungsergebnisse in Afrika: Ausgewählte Fälle', *Finanzierung
    & Entwicklung*, **31**(2), 6ff.
IBRD (1980), *World Development Report 1980*, Washington, DC.
IBRD (1992), 'Effective implementation: key to development impact', Report of the
    World Bank's Portfolio Management Task Force, Washington, DC.
IBRD (2001), *World Development Report 2000/2001*, Washington, DC.
IBRD (2003a), 'Mission statement', downloaded via http://www.worldbank.org; 18
    August.
IBRD (2003b), 'What is the World Bank', downloaded via http://www.worldbank.org;
    18 August.
IBRD (OED) (1989), *Project Performance Results for 1987*, Washington, DC.
IBRD (OED) (1999), *1998 Annual Review of Development Effectiveness*, Washing-
    ton, DC.
IBRD & UNDP (1989), *Africa's Adjustment with Growth in the 1980s*, Washington,
    DC: IBRD.
IMF (2000), 'Key Features of IMF Poverty Reduction and Growth Facility (PRGF)
    supported programs', prepared by the Policy Development and Review Department,
    http://www.imf.org/external/np/prgf/2000/eng/key.htm#P31_2132; downloaded: 8
    September.
IMF (2001), 'IMF lending to poor countries – how does the PRGF differ from the
    ESAF?', http://www.imf.org/external/np/exr/ib/2001/043001.htm; downloaded 18
    August 2003.
IMF (2003a), 'Feature article: an interview with Masood Ahmad', Civil Society
    Newsletter (August).
IMF (2003b), 'IMF financial activites – update August 15, 2003', http://www.imf.org/
    external/np/tre/activity/2003/081503.htm; downloaded 18 August.
Jolly, Richard (1991), 'Adjustment with a human face: a UNICEF record and per-
    spective on the 1980s', *World Development*, **19**(12), 1807ff.
Kay, Stephen K. (2003), 'Testimony before the House Committee on Ways and
    Means Hearing on Social Security Reform, Lessons Learned in Other Countries',
    in Arno Tausch (ed.), *The Three Pillars of Wisdom? A Reader in Globalisation,
    World Bank Pension Models and Welfare Society*, Hauppauge (NY): Nova Science,
    pp. 235ff.
Khan, Moshin S. (1990), 'The macroeconomic effects of fund-supported adjustment
    programs', *IMF Staff Papers*, **37**(2), 195ff.
Lipton, M. and A. Shakow (1982), 'Die Weltbank und die Armut', *Finanzierung &
    Entwicklung*, **19**(2), 16ff.
Pettifor, Ann (2002), 'Debt is still the lynchpin: the case of Malawi', http://
    www.jubileeplus.org/opinion/debt040702.htm.
Pfeffermann, Guy (1988), 'Buchbesprechung', *Finanzierung & Entwicklung*, **25**(4),
    51.

Presidenza (del Consiglio dei Ministri, Ministero del Tesoro, del Bilancio e della Programmazione Economica) (2001), 'Beyond debt relief' (mimeo).

PSRA (2003), 'The global poll, multinational survey of opinion leaders 2002', prepared by Princeton Survey Research Associates for the World Bank, Washington, DC (mimeo).

Raffer, Kunibert (1993), 'International financial institutions and accountability: the need for drastic change', in S.M. Murshed and K. Raffer (eds), *Trade, Transfers and Development, Problems and Prospects for the Twenty First Century*, Aldershot, UK and Brookfield, US: Edward Elgar, pp. 151ff.

Raffer, Kunibert (1994), '"Structural Adjustment", Liberalisation and Poverty', *Journal für Entwicklungspolitik*, **X**(4), 431ff.

Raffer, Kunibert (2002), 'The final demise of unfair debtor discrimination? – Comments on Ms Krueger's Speeches', paper distributed by the G-24 Liaison Office to the IMF's Executive Directors representing Developing Countries (31 January); http://homepage.univie.ac.at/Kunibert.Raffer (también en español; aussi en français).

Raffer, Kunibert (2003a), 'Some proposals to adapt international institutions to developmental needs', in John-ren Chen (ed.), *The Role of International Institutions in Globalisation: The Challenges of Reform*, Cheltenham, UK and Northampton, MA, USA: Edward Elgar, pp. 81ff.

Raffer, Kunibert (2003b), 'Social expenditure, pension systems and neoliberalism', paper presented to the Conference on Privatization of Public Pension Systems: Forces, Experiences, Prospects, 19–21 June 2003, Vienna, Austria, http://homepage.univie.ac.at/Kunibert.Raffer.

Raffer, Kunibert (forthcoming), 'The IMF's SDRM – another form of simply disastrous rescheduling management?', forthcoming in Ch. Jochnick and F. Preston (eds), *Sovereign Debt at the Crossroads*, Oxford: Oxford University Press.

Raffer, Kunibert and H.W. Singer (1996), *The Foreign Aid Business: Economic Assistance and Development Co-operation*, Cheltenham, UK and Brookfield, USA: Edward Elgar (Paperback: 1997).

Raffer, Kunibert and H.W. Singer (2001), *The Economic North–South Divide: Six Decades of Unequal Development*, Cheltenham, UK and Northampton, MA, USA: Edward Elgar (Paperback: 2002).

Rich, Bruce (1994), *Mortgaging the Earth: The World Bank Environmental Impoverishment and the Crisis of Development*, London and Boston: Earthscan.

Stewart, Frances (1991), 'The many faces of adjustment', *World Development*, **19**(12), 1847ff.

Streeten, Paul (1993), 'From growth via basic needs, to human development: the individual in the process of development', in S.M. Murshed and K. Raffer (eds), *Trade, Transfers and Development, Problems and Prospects for the Twenty-first Century*, Aldershot, UK and Brookfield, US: Edward Elgar, pp. 16ff.

Tetzlaff, Rainer (1980), *Die Weltbank: Machtinstrument der USA oder Hilfe für die Entwicklungsländer?*, Munich/London: Weltforum.

Treasury Select Committee (2002), 'Treasury – uncorrected evidence', Thursday, 4 July, http://www.publications.parliament.uk/cmselect/cmtreasy/uc868-iii/uc86801.htm.

Tseng, Wanda (1984), 'Die Effekte der Anpassung', *Finanzierung & Entwicklung*, **21**(4), 2ff.

UNCTAD (2002), *Economic Development in Africa: From Adjustment to Poverty Reduction: What is New?*, Geneva: UN.

UNDP (1993), *Human Development Report 1993*, Oxford: Oxford University Press.

UNDP (1994), *Human Development Report 1994*, Oxford: Oxford University Press.
Williamson, John (1996), 'Lowest common denominator or neoliberal manifesto? The polemics of the Washington Consensus', in Richard M. Auty and John Toye (eds), *Challenging the Orthodoxies*, London/Basingstoke: Macmillan, pp. 13ff.

9. The role of international institutions and the government in development: the case of Croatia (poverty and inequality as a consequence of the transition path)

Mirjana Dragičević

INTRODUCTION

Transition from command to the market economy in Croatia started, as in all other CEE countries, with democratic elections which enabled the transformation of the one-party (communist) political system to a multi-party system. In spite of the war aggression in Croatia, government decided on adopting 'orthodox' market reforms under the guidance of the IMF and World Bank. The strategy of economic liberalization, privatization, deregulation and structural adjustment and 'conditionality' policies reflected the principles of the so-called 'Washington Consensus', which laid out policy priorities that were adopted in different combinations by many countries.

The economic and social consequences of the war, fast privatization and liberalization were increasing poverty and inequality. The objectives of this chapter are to analyse (a) the circumstances of the transition path in Croatia, (b) transition failures and causes of inequalities and poverty, (c) the role of government and international institutions in mapping the transition path, reduction of poverty and future development in Croatia.

TRANSITION IN CROATIA

The Heritage

Before the dissolution of former Yugoslavia, Croatia and Slovenia had been the most developed industrial republics, with a per capita GNP which was a third higher than the Yugoslav average. Unlike other countries in Central and

Eastern Europe, which had to operate behind the 'Iron Curtain' and had a command economy, Croatia, as a republic within the Yugoslav confederation (from the Constitution of 1974) was moving along a so-called 'mixed path'. This path was marked by self-management and social ownership, but also by the market as a factor of allocating goods and services. Even back in 1989, Croatia had the highest liberalization index (0.41) of all socialist CEE countries (EBRD, 2000).

Within such a model of development, Croatia enjoyed good economic and trade connections with Western Europe. About 50 per cent of production was export-oriented. The most prominent was the complex of metal processing, shipbuilding, part of the food industry, the construction industry and tourism, which earned an average of $5–6 billion a year. The education system was relatively advanced, especially in terms of technical education. The high degree of economic liberalization was reflected in the civilian sphere. Croatia was an open country with all the achievements of a civil society, which had been exposed to the influences of Western culture.

Owing to postwar economic emigration, Croatia had about a million emigrants in Western Europe who were a direct 'link' between Croatia and the Western economy and culture. According to everything that Croatia had stood for up to 1990, it might be assumed that it could have been a model for fast transition to a full market economy and a democratic society with low social costs.

The Circumstances of Transition

In 1990, the first multi-party elections were held in Croatia, and the party whose programme envisaged the transformation of Croatia into an independent state won by a large majority. Through a referendum held in 1991, 95 per cent of citizens of Croatia opted for independence and separation from Yugoslavia. In this way, Croatia, a small country with a population of 4.5 million, situated in the southeast of Europe, simultaneously initiated two historical processes: the development of a state and transition.

However the decision to create a state produced much more serious consequences for the Croatian economy and society than had been previously anticipated. Croatia was hit by a five-year war, which resulted in the disintegration of former Yugoslavia. During this period, the situation gave rise to the need to provide assistance for about one million displaced people and refugees, and was marked by huge direct destruction and indirect economic damage, particularly within the tourism sector.

By opting to create a sovereign state, Croatia entered transition with three key disadvantages:

1. the loss of the former Yugoslav market, which included 18 million people;
2. large costs caused by war damage and other consequences of war, amounting to about $50 billion. According to the estimates of the Croatian government, this was two and a half times the GDP of 2001;
3. the lack of a system of international assistance and support, such as Phare, characteristic of other CEE countries.

The First Stage of Transition: Causes of Rising Poverty and Inequality

Instead of exploiting the advantages of heritage, as was done by other transition countries, Croatia had to engage in a struggle to survive. A dramatic fall in production and the high demands of budgetary expenditure in the first years threw the economy into a widening budget deficit and increased money supply, which led to growing inflation.

In this way, in the period from 1990 to 1993, GDP fell by 40 per cent, and the high rate of inflation culminated in 1993 with a monthly growth in prices which ranged from 25 to 30 per cent (CRO STAT, 1999). In such conditions, Croatia was faced with a choice: to introduce a war economy and rationing or to opt for economic reforms directed towards a free market economy. Croatia opted for the latter.

At the beginning of 1993, the political and military pressures in the region declined. In October 1993, the government, supported by the IMF, launched a stabilization programme designed to stop hyperinflationary trends and to establish the foundations for future economic recovery. The programme of macroeconomic stabilization (1993) succeeded in fighting hyperinflation and in maintaining price stability, so that in 1994 the economy experienced an inflation rate of 3.0 per cent measured in terms of retail prices. This programme was implemented through a restrictive monetary and progressive fiscal policy. The stand-by arrangements with the IMF and agreements with the World Bank that followed the initial phase of the stabilization programme allowed for an improved position in international financial markets and for easier access to foreign financial resources, which were necessary for intensifying the processes of rebuilding and restructuring.

Although economic activity showed an initial recovery if seen through the rate of growth of GDP, which was 5.9 per cent in 1994 compared with 1991, when it was −21.1 per cent, the transition of the economic, as well as of the entire social, sphere, lagged behind considerably owing to the slow and conflicting moves of the ruling political elite. However 'for growth to be sustainable there has to be not just one macroeconomic intervention, but a deep, comprehensive program of institutional reforms' (Balcerowicz, 1995:87). Thus catching up has to be a very complex process, and only countries with appropriate development strategy and institutional features can successfully accomplish this task.

Nevertheless, the growth of foreign debt (IMF arrangements) during the first stage, and the softening of budget constraints, as well as tax evasion, led to the breaking down of non-budgetary restrictions.

The crucial issue of every transition is privatization as a process of transferring great wealth into private hands and of large opportunities for rent-seeking behaviour. The transition strategies that are implemented in individual countries are different from one another, some being fast, or a part of a 'big bang' shock therapy, and others gradual or incremental, so they bring along different models of privatisation (EBRD, 2000).[1] The choice of the fast privatisation model and the lack of transparency in its implementation allowed for the direct transfer of companies based on political affiliation and nepotism. The lack of public control and the sluggishness of the judicial system were characteristic of the first stage of transition, when the state had a rapid effect on the new ownership structure through the Privatization Fund.

This led to the emergence of conglomerates where ownership was not separated from management. The lack of management skills turned even profitable companies into losers whose assets were subsequently sold or plundered. Owners–insiders, protected by political power, opposed the introduction of competent and transparent management and the distribution of ownership rights. In non-transparent privatization, the activities of the new company owners, who were in most cases managers, were mostly geared to expenditure, and not to creating new value. The whole privatization process was also accompanied by the xenophobic fear of all the evil that competition, especially foreign competition, would bring. As a consequence, an institutional framework for promoting competitiveness was formed. Without effective competition policy, the existing monopolies remained exclusively in the hands of local owners.

A further consequence was an extremely low level of FDI in comparison with other transition countries. In the first ten years of transition, a total of about $4 billion entered Croatia, 80 per cent of which were portfolio investments. In the same period, FDI per capita inflow into Croatia amounted to $444, while in countries that were going through transition successfully, such as Hungary and the Czech Republic, the figure was $1627 and $967, respectively (EBRD, 2000).

In fact, the whole transition was being implemented with local resources, knowledge and capital, again apostrophized by the xenophobic thesis that Croatia could build its economy all by itself. The consequence of this was the concentration of economic power in the hands of privatization profit-seekers who were creating their 'business empires' assisted by the banking system, which was also controlled by the state. At the same time, tax evasion, an inefficient legal system, which was a source of legal insecurity, corruption and crime were all growing and social costs were multiplying. As a consequence, an increasing number of workers were laid off, which led to a growth in unemployment, which exceeded 23 per cent in 2001 and was the largest rate of unemployment among all CEE transition countries (CRO STAT, 2001). Rising and persistently high levels of unemployment have affected certain groups of workers disproportionally. Individuals with low education seem to have been affected the most by transition. The crucial problem is long-term unemployment (55 per cent of the unemployed).

The danger of poverty is connected with exclusion from the labour market. According to the first national research on poverty (World Bank, 2001b) 10 per cent of the population was below the national poverty line.[2] There are few dominant groups among the poor: elderly people, unemployed and uneducated people. The risk of poverty is especially high when the low degree of education comes together with unemployment. According to the data (World Bank, 2001b), 40 per cent of the poor come from families with pensions at a very low level and 50 per cent of the poor had a pension that was below the poverty line. The qualitative estimation of poverty (social estimation) demonstrates that poverty in Croatia has long-term characteristics. The main causes of such a situation are the poor economic performance that results in a higher job destruction than a job creation rate, early retirement prevailing and introduction of high labour taxes.

The subjective policy research is demonstrating that according to the high unemployment and the lowering of real wages, the evolution of subjective poverty is disturbing (Figure 9.1).

The high and growing early retirement as a consequence of the privatization process created a gap between the falling number of contributors to the pension system and the growing number of beneficiaries (Figure 9.2).

The consequences of this gap between employed and pension beneficiaries are lower payments to the transfer recipients. The governments raised the taxes and the labour costs grew too. The labour costs are at a level far higher than in Croatia's main competitors (Figure 9.3). At the same time, the level of payroll taxes and personal income taxes inhibits new employment growth.

At the same time, Croatia has the highest public sector of all CEE countries and especially EU countries, but the impact of public spending on poverty is lower than in other CEE economies. Expansion of social spending in Croatia (Figure 9.4) does not lower the poverty.

The gap between the rich and poor is wide and is wider in comparison to the countries with middle or low inequality (Figure 9.5).

UNDP (1999) data measured by the HD Index showed a growing social differentiation. Although 10 per cent of the population lived below the pov-

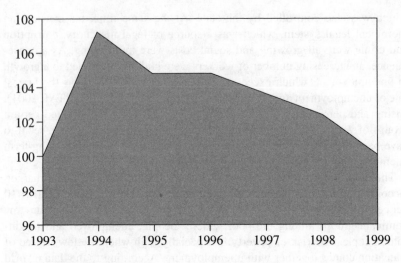

Source: World Bank (2001b).

Figure 9.1 The evolution of subjective poverty

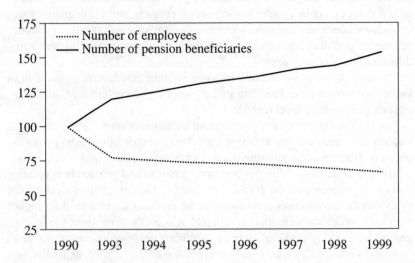

Source: CRO STAT (1999:154).

Figure 9.2 Employees and pension beneficiaries (1990 = 1000)

erty line, high unemployment and a decrease in the level of real wages were the reason for as many as 80 per cent of the population to consider themselves poor.

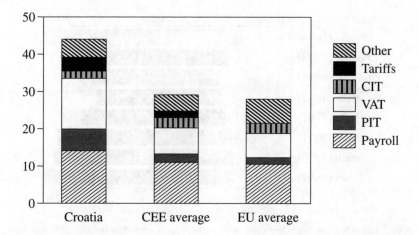

Note: Payroll = total social security contributions and other payroll taxes, VAT = value added tax, PIT = personal income tax, CIT = corporate income tax, tariffs = taxes on foreign trade, other = excises and property taxes.

Source: M. Keen et al. (2000).

Figure 9.3 Tax burden as % of GDP, by types of taxes, cumulative 1995–98

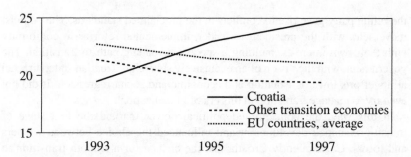

Source: CRO STAT (2000:201).

Figure 9.4 Social spending as % of GDP

In this situation, an emerging market found itself in a societal and governing vacuum. The market developed at the expense of the country's well-being, which was seriously shaken. This proved that putting the market before society, in a specific Croatian way, was to invite trouble and disappointment. Social costs multiplied primarily as a result of limited political competition and the concentration of political power, which meant that the xenophobic ideology of

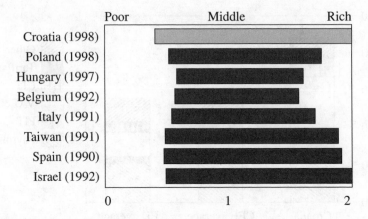

Note: Left side of the bar is tenth percentile to the median equivalent income, right side, 90th percentile; square root of family size is used to correct for economies of scale; data bottom coded at 1 per cent.

Source: Luxembourg Income Study Database (LIS, 1998), www.lissy.org, for Croatia, staff estimates based on Household Budget Survey.

Figure 9.5   The gap between the rich and the poor

the ruling party gave rise to conflicts in the proclaimed standards. The populist movement, with the president as leader, implemented reforms in conformity with their own interests, building a specific, Croatian, path to transition. The government, with the vision of an exclusively sovereign Croatian state, directed all its efforts towards isolation and economic and social regression. It did not even try to manage transition in this era of globalization.

In this way, the concentrated political power marked the first stage of transition, shaped development and influenced the choice between winners and losers. Consequently Croatia lost the chance for a smooth transition in the sectors which had a competitive advantage, and products for international exchange, even before the creation of the Croatian state. It missed the chance to restructure these sectors gradually and align them with the global network. Instead, most of them were destroyed through the political usurpation of the privatization model.

Croatia also missed the chance of partnership development, because ten years of transition had been implemented in conflict with the long-term interests of human development. This led to the social exclusion of the majority of the population, whose middle layer was depleted and discouraged. In short, the specific features of Croatia's acquired sovereignty and its transition in the first stage were as follows:

- the separation of Croatia from Yugoslavia, which caused the loss of a market of 18 million people;
- war and war destruction;
- IMF defined the macroeconomic stabilization programme and the government accepted it;
- fast, politically-mediated privatization;
- an increase in the number of refugees, unemployed and the growth of social poverty and inequality;
- an increase in ethnic discrimination;
- international blockades: there are no Phare or similar programmes in Croatia, and no FDI;
- the lack of an institutional infrastructure: a law on monopolies, a law on bankruptcy, and so on;
- incomplete implementation of reforms;
- the lack of long-term development strategy.

In the mid-1990s, primarily owing to the fact that Croatia had accepted the peaceful integration of parts of its territory, the international community made stronger pressure for Croatia to build a new institutional structure adjusted to EU standards. Consequently, at government level, this led to the formation of the Ministry of European Integration and the Agency for the Protection of Market Competition, as well as to the passing of the Law on Bankruptcy.

Although certain changes were made in the last four years of Croatian Democratic Union (the leading party) rule, these were still exclusively externally driven. Wherever possible, the functioning of new institutional forms was avoided, and obstructions were created to the implementation of new laws. Core structural reforms in the economy and society were not even conceptualized.

The dissatisfaction of the population was growing. Political apathy and disillusionment resulted from institutional weakness. The feeling of powerlessness to effect change and scepticism about the competency of politicians, together with suspicion of corruption, encouraged a willingness to contemplate a return to the security of the dominant public sector. New NGOs were set up and the seeds were gradually planted for a new institutional civil society network, which began to point to the need for change. These bodies worked on raising awareness of these issues.

Starting from 1996, the Croatian authorities began to accept declaratively the demands of the international community, but in reality it was noticed that the reforms were not carried out. This was primarily due to the fact that all the accepted recommendations were contrary to the then ruling view of life and the culture of state leadership. In other words, the externally imposed rules signified a restriction for the model of rule that was in place, so international organizations (IMF, WB and EU) began to control Croatia strictly and give it conditional support.

As a consequence, the system of government and rule, which had been formed at the beginning of the 1990s, entered a crisis. This fact also shows that ten years had been spent mostly in building a state, but not in developing democracy and a civil society, or in implementing economic and social reforms.[3]

In 1999, the economy achieved only 82 per cent of the GDP of 1990. Foreign debt amounted to $9.5 billion. The amount of investment was just a little higher than the level of depreciation. The gross rate of investment was 23 per cent of GDP, with an unfavourable structure for quick economic recovery. The share of the public expenditure in GDP amounted to 55 per cent (CRO STAT, 2001).

The Second Stage of Transition: Development without Poverty Reduction Strategy

In the first decade, without strategic leadership in the transition process, Croatia found itself in a kind of chaos, unable to identify its own development potentials, opportunities, limitations and the sequencing of the entire process. Croatia entered a new stage of development with the new multiparty elections in 2000, and with the victory of a party coalition with a dominantly social-democratic and liberal orientation. What had until then been the opposition now united into a coalition. It was supposed that it would begin to meet the expectations of the population who had voted for those politicians who offered a way out of the growing social misery and the increasing differentiation of society. The coalition also promised quick reforms in all areas of economic and social life.

Since not only the health of the economy was threatened but also the well-being of society, the new government was faced with substantial tasks and huge responsibility: finding a way out of the deep crisis and, at the same time, recovering from social damage; and determining their own opportunities and limitations, and formulating a vision of Croatia for the twenty-first century.

The heritage of the ten-year system geared primarily to the idea of building the state manifested itself in the direct dependence of state institutions on the ruling party, nepotism, crime and corruption. This was the 'price' Croatia had paid for the creation of its own state, while the building of civil society institutions and the transparent development of democratic institutions had been postponed. Consequently there was a strict need, first, to separate state institutions from the influence of a single autocratic party and restore people's trust in institutions under state authority. A reform of the judiciary and the inherited inefficient state apparatus was the focus of attention. In this way, it was only at the beginning of 2000 that the issues of transition, which had been characteristic of other CEE countries at the beginning of the 1990s, arose in Croatia,

Owing to a poor political image that Croatia had had in the world from 1990 to 2000, the democratic changes and the establishment of a new government alone changed in a positive way the view held of Croatia by institutional bodies of the world, particularly those of Europe. Interest in Croatia therefore increased and the level of assistance became stronger. With the support of EU institutions, and various regional and bilateral programmes, especially after the signing of the Treaty on Joining the EU and the Stability Pact, Croatia began with accelerated reforms and legislative changes. Currently, about 900 legal projects are under development. An extensive reform of the pension system, health-care system and labour legislation is also under way. The reform of the state administration has been developing much more slowly.

The objective position of the present government is determined by its high degree of cooperation with international and financial institutions and with the EU. The level of international support and financial aid is determined by the remaining political conditions (the Hague Tribunal, cooperation on the Balkans) and by the speed of execution of other structural reforms. Therefore the government accepted the quick delivery of services as determined by the international community, which at the internal level is in conflict with the interests of trade unions, local institutions and interest groups.

Since, on the other hand, space has not yet been made for a more significant economic development based on the propulsion of domestic enterprises and the inflow of international capital, the government cannot respond simultaneously to conflicting external and internal demands. In the short term it relies on neoliberal solutions through the privatization of state companies (telecommunications, oil, electric power supply, insurance) and the sale of state bonds (public debt). In such a way, through budget expenditure it generates growth (motorways and other public company projects), and funds social costs, which are the consequence of increasing unemployment. Croatia has therefore entered a dangerous area where public financial resources deriving from privatization are being drained and necessary structural reforms are not being carried out in due time. This presents a threat to the potential for medium-term and long-term growth and for the sustainable development of the country.

As a consequence, Croatia has arrived at a rather absurd stage of transition:

- the enterprise sector which has managed to survive, and which was privatized through a non-transparent privatization process, has mostly been restructured;

- the financial sector has been reformed and, within this, the banking system has been fully internationalized since domestic banks have been taken over by foreign ones (approximately 90 per cent of the sector);
- the human resources sector in the privatized companies which have survived has achieved enviable international corporate standards and culture;
- the sector of public physical infrastructure, thanks to previous and current investment, is currently the most advanced sector (telecommunications, roads, transport);
- the reform of the public sector, particularly in terms of human resources, has only just begun;
- the reform of the legal system in terms of harmonization with the EU is only just beginning;
- the number of unemployed persons is very high; unemployment rate: 23 per cent in 2002;
- the number of the supported population is higher than the working population;
- the poverty, the inequalities and social exclusion remain;
- the space for more significant economic and social development is still limited.

Since the decisions on selling the remaining state companies have already been made, it is expected that the entire economic sector will be privatized in the next few years, primarily through sales to foreign companies which, with a few successfully privatized domestic companies with a regional reach, will then be the key players in the Croatian economy.

In this way, a significant portion of the Croatian economy will be internationalized on the basis of inherited resources and competitive advantages through acquisitions and investment portfolios. As the public sector's expenditure has increased enormously over the last six years and the budget deficit has gradually risen out of control, this corporate structure is by no means capable of generating the kind of development which would cover the expected social costs of the remaining reforms of the public sector as well as public expenditure in general.

Currently there is a wide-ranging debate in Croatia about how to move on from here. Two contrasting concepts are emerging. One belongs to the government, advocating speedy reforms and internationalization with the support of the IMF,[4] WB and the EU, while the other comes from one part of the expert public. The latter promotes the view that Croatia should rely on its own strengths, slow down reforms, finance development through a neo-Keynesian policy, halt the 'sell-out' of the remaining non-privatized public companies to foreigners, and refuse to follow strictly the instructions and tutelage of the international community (Zdunić, 1995; Kulić, 1997).

Since the activity of NGOs, or institutions of a democratic and civil society, which criticize all the key development moves of the current authorities, is becoming stronger in Croatia, there is growing critical awareness among the public. Therefore there are increasing complaints that the government is an exponent of international capital and the IMF, seeking to perform reforms at all costs, particularly at the expense of high social costs, without respecting the sustainability of the system and without building a spirit of mutual concern and cooperation aimed at development.

Although the collective power of employers' associations, NGOs and trade unions is growing, there is a lack of local and partnership power to influence how development takes place. As a result, the IMF dominates and directs development through its banking logic, and the EU bodies are forcing Croatia to harmonize its standards in all areas.

Independent of various economic and political discussions, there is no doubt that the completion of transition in Croatia will be externally driven. The only question is the time needed for the remaining structural and institutional reforms, the financing of the social costs, and particularly the opening of the development process, based on the competitive advantages of Croatia, but, at the same time, by creating the conditions for gradual social inclusion. It is also crucial to build national awareness that the transitional adjustments to globalization are made for the benefit of Croatia's prosperity and economic identity.

In this context, Croatia is still awaiting a broad consensus from the government, entrepreneurs and the trade unions related to the speed and quality of the remaining structural and institutional reforms, bearing in mind the social costs that this involves. On the other hand, when speaking about the development of competitive advantages, apart from institutional reforms and in parallel with the removal of barriers to entry, Croatia needs radical decentralization into regions, because regions and local communities are the real space for the construction of competitiveness as a precondition for development in the era of globalization.

CONCLUSION

The transition process in Croatia was faced both by the war and by the absence of a strategic and holistic long-term approach to the transition development from the government side.

The support of the IMF in creation and implementation of the macroeconomic stabilization programme and the fast privatization was carried out in an institutional vacuum. A competition and regulatory framework was not established before the privatization. There was no awareness of sequencing: which tasks have to be done before other tasks. Partial market reforms resulted in growing poverty and inequality and, at the same time, engendered resistance, undermined the incentives of the people, and caused trust to decline. The processes of imposed change came partly from the outside (IMF, WB, EU) and predominantly from the internal government autocracy. The government started transition with fast privatization that was politically usurped. These processes were not socially justified. They generated rents for the elite.

The development was partially a matter of negotiation between a donor and the government, and mainly between interests of powerful elites inside the government. The failure to develop and establish the key institutional prediction to a market economy is the crucial factor contributing to the failures in the transition period.

In the second stage of transition, some efforts have been made in institutional building, but they were not a part of the government strategy: they were externally driven. And imposing change from the outside raises barriers to change. The whole transition period was faced by governments that were not open to participatory processes, to decentralization that responds to the needs of local community, and that were not responsible to the poor and socially excluded.

The transition path in Croatia proved that poverty and inequality is an outcome of economic, social and political processes that interact with each other in ways that can worsen the deprivation poor people face every day (World Bank, 2001a). To attack poverty requires not only the building and implementing of market reforms for growth, or making markets work for poor people and expanding poor people's assets and tackling structural inequalities. The economic growth has to be taken as an integral part of a broader development focus. The transformation of the society has to be the focus of development. Besides government, the business sector and trade unions, the strategy of the transformation of society must involve civil society, local community and citizens' participation.

This requires a strategic, democratic, holistic approach in designing the future society, not only the economy. The development strategy has to reinvent development of responsible and capable state and social institutions that empower poor people and that work for poor people. It has to involve the strategy to attack poverty that must be built on three pillars: opportunity, empowerment and security.

NOTES

1. Policy debates on economic liberalization also involved 'tactical choices' over sequencing and the pace of transition. What should come first: price liberalization, foreign trade and capital movements liberalization, banking and financial reforms or privatization? The speed and depth of the liberalization process raised larger and more controversial questions in CEE post-socialist transition countries. Gradualism or incrementalism was preferred by those not entirely confident of the correct mix of medicine required, given the weakness of the economies, the size of the task of restructuring, and the challenge of promoting fundamentally different economic behaviour in the East that had been common under state socialism. Some argued that small bites of reform and pain would be easier to swallow politically. Some analysts have argued that a gradual approach allowed for policy refinement and more effective choice among policy alternatives, insulating state agencies from particularistic claims, as well as providing benefits in building real support behind difficult options (Orenstein, 2001; Bartlett, 1997).
2. According to the international standard of poverty ($4.30 daily per person) the poverty rate was 4 per cent (World Bank, 2001b).
3. New democracy in Croatia according to Diamond (1999), who used the Freedom House Ratings and his own independent judgments, applied to Eurasian Post-state Socialist Cases in 1977, is categorized as non-liberal electoral democracy with rating 4.0 – the same level as Albania.
4. The IMF in the first and second stages of transition defined the economic development targets. Stand-by credits for Croatia in 2003 (US$146m.) were approved to carry forward the programme of fiscal consolidation and economic reforms.

BIBLIOGRAPHY

Balcerowicz, L. (1995), 'Socialism, capitalism, transformation', Central European University, Budapest.

Bartlett, David. L. (1997), *The Political Economy of Dual Transformations: Market Reform and Democratization in Hungary*, Ann Arbor, MI: University of Michigan Press.

Blanchard, O., Jean, Kenneth A. Froot and Jeffrey D. Sachs (1994), *The Transition in Eastern Europe. Volume 1: Country Studies*, Chicago, IL: University of Chicago Press.

CRO STAT (1999, 2000, 2001), *Statistical Yearbook*, Zagreb: Croatian Bureau of Statistics.

Diamond, L. (1999), *Developing Democracy: Towards Consolidation*, Baltimore, MD: Johns Hopkins University Press.

EBRD (1999), *Transition Report 1999*, London: European Bank for Reconstruction and Development.

EBRD (2000), *Transition Report 2000*, London: European Bank for Reconstruction and Development.

Giddens, A. (ed.) (2001), *The Global Third Way Debate*, Cambridge, UK: Polity Press.

Held, D. (ed.) (1993), *Prospects for Democracy: North, South, East, West*, Stanford: Stanford University Press.

IMF (1999), 'Republic of Croatia. Selected Issues and Statistical Appendix', December, 2000, IMF, Washington.

IMF (2000), *World Economic Outlook, October 2000. Focus on Transition Economies*, Washington: IMF.

Karatnycky, Adrian, Alexander Motyl and Amanda Schnetzer (eds) (2002), *Nations in Transition 2002: Civil Society, Democracy, and Markets in East Central Europe and the Newly Independent States*, New Brunswick, NY: Transaction Publishers/ Freedom House.

Keen M., T. Baunsgaard, J. King and O. Scherone (2000), 'Croatia: A Review of Tax Policy', *Fiscal Affairs Department*, IMF, Washington.

Klugman, J., J. Micklewright and G. Reymond (2002), 'Poverty in transition: social expenditures and working-age poor', Innocenti working paper no.91, UNICEF Innocenti Research Centre, Florence; available from http//www. unicef-icdc.org/ publications/pdf/iwp91.pdf.

Kulić, S. (1997), 'Žrtve zlouporabe moći svjetskih razmjera- poseban osvrt na poziciju Hrvatske' ('The victims of power usurpation on the world scale – the position of Croatia'), Ekonomski institut (Institute of Economics), Zagreb.

Laderchi, Ruggeri, C., R. Saith and F. Stewart (2003), 'Does it matter that we don't agree on the definition of poverty? A comparison of four approaches', Queen Elisabeth House working paper 107, Oxford.

Lavigne, M. (1999), *The Economics of Transition: From Socialist Economy to Market Economy*, 2nd edn, New York: St Martin's Press.

Luxembourg Income Study Database (1998), LIS org. for Croatia, *Household Budget Survey*, Luxembourg: LIS.

Ohmae, K. (1995), *The End of the Nation State: The Rise of Regional Economies*, New York: The Free Press.

Orenstein, M.A. (2001), *Out of the Red: Building Capitalism and Democracy in Post Communist Europe*, Ann Arbor: University of Michigan Press.

Roland, G. (2000), *Transition and Economics, Politics, Market and Firms*, Cambridge, MA: MIT Press.

Roland, G. (2002), 'The political economy of transition', *Journal of Economic Perspectives*, **16**(1): 29–50.

Sen, A. (1999), *Development as Freedom*, New York: Oxford University Press.

Stiglitz, J.E. (1998), 'Towards a new paradigm for development: strategies, policies, and processes', Prebisch lecture at UNCTAD, Geneva, Switzerland, 19 October; available from http://www.worldbank.org/html/extme/jssp101998.htm.

Stiglitz, J.E. (2002), *Globalization and Its Discontents*, New York: W.W. Norton.

UNDP (1999), *Human Development Report – Croatia, 1999*, Zagreb: UNDP Croatia and Institute of Economics.

Vasquez, I. (2002), 'Globalization and the poor', *The Independent Review*, **VII**(2), Fall, ISSN 1086–1653.

World Bank (1996), *World Development Report. From Plan to Market*, Washington: World Bank.

World Bank (1999), 'Croatia: a policy agenda for reform and growth', Washington: World Bank.

World Bank (2000a), *World Development Indicators*, Washington: World Bank.

World Bank (2000b), *Making Transition Work for Everyone. Poverty and Inequality in Europe and Central Asia*, Washington : World Bank.

World Bank (2001a), *World Development Report 2000–2001*, Washington: Oxford University Press.

World Bank (2001b), 'Croatia economic vulnerability and welfare study', World Bank Office in Croatia, Zagreb/Washington, World Bank Poverty Reduction and

Economic Management Unit Europe and Central Asia Region: available from http://www.worldbank.hr.

Zdunić, S. (1995), 'Strategija obnove proizvodnje i rasta' ('Strategy of production reconstruction and growth'), Ekonomski institut (Institute of Economics), Zagreb.

PART III

International institutions and regional issues

International institutions and regional issues

10. Institutions, integration and poverty in Eastern Europe and the former Soviet Union (EEFSU)

Syed M. Ahsan and Melania Nica

MOTIVATION

In this chapter, our goal is to discern and evaluate the process by which poverty may be reduced, and in particular isolate and interpret the role of economic growth, institutions (both domestic and international) and integration in that process. We carry out the above analysis in the context of the transition countries of Eastern Europe and former Soviet Union (EEFSU). Although we primarily conceive of institutions as the enabling framework that facilitates economic and non-economic exchanges à la New Institutional Economics (NIE), we also take international aspects of institutions into account. Among international institutions, one may think of international trade agreements or membership of global entities such as the World Trade Organization (WTO). Alternatively, in a regional (here European) context, one may examine the interactions with the European Union (EU). Since the end of the communist era, the EEFSU countries have launched an intensive transformation of their political and economic institutions, and the EU has been supporting these reforms; it is also providing direct assistance in the form of investment funds to the private sector. It is evident that these global/regional interactions may lead to advances in investment, trade and technology, and therefore constitute elements of the enabling framework cited above. Below we examine the effect of EBRD investments on growth and poverty.

The central tenet of new institutional economics is that institutions (political and economic ones) are generally incomplete in any setting and, hence, transactions are costlier than they ought to be in a full efficiency setting.[1] To North, institutions are the 'rules of the game', and he demands that 'institutions must not only provide low-cost enforcement of property rights, bankruptcy laws, but also provide incentives to encourage decentralised decision making and effective competitive markets' (1997:4). Among 'formal rules', he enumerates the polity, the judiciary and the laws of contract and property.

The formal rules are complemented by what is generally referred to as 'informal' ones. Different authors have identified routines, customs, traditions, culture and, above all, trust as among the fundamental aspects of 'societal embeddedness'.[2] These informal institutions are collectively called *social capital*, and have been popularized in the modern development literature (for example, see Coleman, 1988; Collier, 1998). While early citation of trust and its economic externalities have been found in the works of David Hume, Adam Smith and Antonio Genovese over two hundred years ago, Kenneth Arrow may have been the first modern economist to reflect on the possible role of social capital in helping agents allocate resources, and hence overcome the market inadequacies, although he did not coin the phrase.[3] He argued: 'Norms of social behaviour, including ethical and moral codes', may be interpreted as 'reactions of society to compensate for market failures' (1970:70). Arrow singled out the norm of *mutual trust* as one capable of serving the non-market allocative power alluded to above. He noted that, 'in the absence of trust, it would have been very costly to arrange for alternative sanctions and guarantees, and many opportunities for mutually beneficial co-operation would have to be foregone' (ibid:70).

Further note that the term 'governance' in modern policy discussions also originates in the NIE literature. It relates to institutions that a society must possess in order to monitor the 'plays of the game'. Williamson argues that transaction is the basic unit of analysis and regards governance as 'the means by which order is accomplished in relation to which potential conflict threatens to undo or upset opportunities to realise mutual gains' (1998:76). Conflicts in exchange may occur because of asset specificity of agents ('bilateral dependency') or wherever contractual hazards (such as succumbing to opportunism) may arise.

It is useful to clarify two important aspects of institutions. The NIE literature holds that institutions facilitate transactions both within and outside the market mechanism. Note that the formal institutions cited above are primarily responsible for allowing markets to function smoothly, while typically the informal one, namely social capital, is the catalyst for non-market transactions. Secondly, there is the claim that quality institutions are indispensable for facilitating both ex ante and ex post exchanges. Here again there may be a dichotomy of sorts; clear formal rules (such as on property rights) may suffice in drawing up ex ante contracts, but eventual sustainability of such contracting over time would require quality social capital and /or monitoring and governance institutions. Clearly some of the latter institutions (such as trust and norms) may not be formally coded in the laws of society and hence unenforceable by the polity. However human interaction may evolve in delivering an informal structure of governance carried out by a civil society structure. The latter would work so long as both parties in a conflict agree to abide by the verdict or face social sanctions, even when neither of which (the verdict or the consequent sanctions) may be part of the formal legal statutes of the land.

Ahsan (2003) has introduced the broader term of 'institutional capital' (IC), which denotes the totality of institutions as described above. In other words, IC is inclusive of all formal and informal institutions, and therefore embeds social capital. It also includes institutions of governance, which themselves may be formal as well as informal. Where relevant we will measure how the aggregate level of 'institutional capital' (IC) as well as its various components may affect economic growth or the poverty profile of the EEFSU region.

Within this broad theme, we also ask a further question, namely whether history (as specified by the concept of 'path dependence' by Douglass North, 1990) matters. Hence we would like to explore how the EEFSU countries differ in the design, delivery and endowment of institutions.[4] *In particular we will attempt to test a hypothesis, implicit in North's thesis (1990), that history matters; that is, the growth response to market reforms would depend on the legacy of formal as well as informal institutions inherited by the country in question prior to the socialist rule.*

Finally, we examine the interface between a broader concept, poverty and IC. Ever since Rawls rejected the old utilitarian basis of income (or commodities, for that matter) as the relevant welfare indicator, researchers and policy makers have called for a conceptualization of poverty going beyond the income/expenditure dimension. The idea of 'basic needs' had been a forerunner. A bolder vision emerged in the notion of capability: poverty must be seen as the deprivation of basic capabilities rather than merely as lowness of incomes (Sen, 1999:87). This approach attempts to measure how capable one is to enjoy the kind of life that one cherishes (including basic freedom). Over the decade of the 1990s, the capability concept led to innovations by the UNDP as it devised the 'human development index' in 1993, and the 'human poverty index' in 1997. Sen believes that this broadening of the concept enables one 'to enhance the understanding of the nature and causes of poverty and deprivation by shifting attention away from the *means* ... to *ends* that people have reason to pursue, and, correspondingly, to the *freedoms* to be able to satisfy these ends' (ibid.:90). Plausible components of the broader poverty index would include mortality, nutrition, risk/vulnerability, the lack of voice and political participation and the like. Below we develop a simple measure of non-income poverty (NIP) along the above lines, and analyse how the quality of institutions (vis-à-vis growth) may affect the evolution of NIP.[5]

The rest of the chapter proceeds as follows. In the next section we provide a brief outline of the recent literature on growth and poverty, and relate this to the transition context. We also explore the kind of testable hypotheses that one may derive from this review. The third section is devoted to an examination of the conceptual construction of institutional capital (IC) as an integral factor that allows economic (and other) exchanges to take place, thus alleviating market failure. We also examine the a priori scope of the level of IC among transition countries in explaining the observed difference in their performance over time and contemporaneously. In the fourth section we discuss measurement issues especially in light of data availability. The fifth section reviews the empirical findings, while the sixth concludes. The empirical results are described in Tables 10A.1 to 10A.9 in the appendix to the chapter.

GROWTH, POVERTY AND INSTITUTIONS

Measuring Poverty

There are many formal and informal notions of poverty and their relevant quantitative analogues. In order to focus attention on the very poor, we agree with Sen (1976) that *absolute* poverty is what matters. Freedom from hunger would require a minimum expenditure (or income), z, in order to provide for a socially minimal level of nourishment. The latter is a reasonable benchmark, and indeed this is the idea behind the notion of a poverty line. Head count poverty is simply given by $H = F(z)$, where z is the poverty line, and $F(y)$ denotes the cumulative density of income or consumption (y) as the case may be. If we use a discrete distribution function, H then becomes simply (q/n), where q is the number of persons with $y \leq z$, and n is the population size. Thus H denotes the fraction of population that is 'poor'. This logic has led the World Bank to popularize the metric of a 'dollar (or two) a day' per person as being a rough and ready poverty line. For the EEFSU region, however, the World Bank suggests using $4 (in 1993 international prices) as the appropriate headcount threshold, and we shall adopt the four dollars a day as the relevant headcount indicator in our empirical work to be described below. Indeed the acceptance of the headcount measure provides a foundation for the hypothesis that economic growth matters for poverty reduction.

There are of course other measures of absolute poverty. Foster, Greer and Thorbecke (FGT, 1984) introduced a very useful class of poverty indicators, often known as the P_α measure, or simply the FGT measures of poverty:

$$P_\alpha = \int_0^q [(z-y)/z]^\alpha \, dy, \tag{10.1}$$

or, in discrete terms,

$$P_\alpha = (1/n)\left[\sum_i^q (g_i/z)^\alpha\right], i = 1,2,...,q, \quad (10.2)$$

where $\alpha \geq 0$, g_i is the poverty gap ($g_i = [z - y_i]$, $i = 1,2,...,q$) of the ith household. The exponent α denotes the index of absolute inequality aversion. The FGT measures also satisfy the three Sen axioms (1976).[6]

Furthermore it turns out that the more popular measures discussed earlier in the literature obtain as special cases of the FGT measures of poverty. If $\alpha = 0$, then P_α becomes the headcount ratio:

$$P_0 = (1/n)\sum_i^q (g_i/z)^0 = q/n = H, i = 1,2,...,q. \quad (10.3a)$$

If $\alpha = 1$, P_a is the headcount times the average income shortfall (I), which is known as the *poverty gap* (PG) measure:

$$P_1 = (1/n)\sum_i^q (g_i/z)^1 = PG = HI. \quad (10.3b)$$

Similarly the *squared poverty gap* (SPG), the other well-known measure, is merely FGT with the inequality aversion set at 2:

$$P_2 = SPG = (1/n)\sum_i^q [(g_i/z)]^2, i = 1,2,...,q. \quad (10.3c)$$

Growth–Poverty Hypotheses

The received theory of how growth leads to poverty reduction is weak. It is plausible, indeed inevitable, that the growth process would bring about a change in the underlying income distribution. While Kuznets (1963) suggested otherwise, modern evidence indicates that growth may indeed exacerbate rather than abate inequality in its wake.[7] Of immediate relevance to the present discussion is the recent observation that greater equality due to continued growth in the already industrialized world (say, OECD) appears to have been reversed in the last 25 years or so. The growth process here operates, Aghion et al. (1999) argue, along trade liberalization, skill-based technical changes and organizational changes within the firm. The combined force of these diffusions has had an impact on growth such as to render the distribution of earnings inequitable, thus throwing doubt on the plausibility of the Kuznets process in modern contexts.

While development theories have been limited in scope, there has been a proliferation of empirical research on poverty and growth of late. The burgeoning literature dealing with the poverty elasticity of growth essentially started with Datt and Ravallion (1992), who showed that the change in poverty, ΔH, between two points in time can always be decomposed into a *growth component* and one measuring a change in the underlying distribution. This is merely definitional. The growth part is usually represented by a horizontal shift in the density function with an unchanged distribution, while the distributional change is described for the new level of mean (relative) income.

The poverty elasticity of growth highlighted in the empirical literature focuses on the first of these two components. In that context, Kakwani (1993) had analytically derived an elasticity for all poverty measures that satisfy the FGT class of functions. Since the growth component in the decomposition amounts to a distribution-neutral shift (in relative income), the interpretation of the poverty elasticity is simple. The elasticity figure merely yields the proportion of poor who would cross the set poverty line as the result of a 1 per cent increase in mean income.

However one cannot ignore distributional changes. Bourguignon (2003) has recently examined the issue on the presumption that income followed a log-normal distribution, which allows a greater degree of tractability. In effect he characterizes the Datt–Ravallion decomposition exactly:

$$(\Delta H / H) = (-)\varepsilon(DEV, IIQ) \cdot GRO + \beta(DEV, IIQ) \cdot CIQ. \qquad (10.4)$$

The notation is as follows. The right-hand side variables include the per capita GDP growth (GRO), the level of development (DEV, measured by the ratio of mean income to z, the poverty line), initial (IIQ) and the change in inequality (CIQ).[8] The ε-function is the famed (headcount) poverty elasticity, which, under the conditions of the Bourguignon model, rises with DEV and decreases in IIQ. The distributional change (measured by CIQ) is also accompanied by a coefficient (β), the poverty elasticity of a change in inequality. The latter itself is a non-linear function of DEV as well as IIQ.

The standard result from the (cross-section) analysis on the subject, typically ignoring the second term in the right-hand side of (2.4), suggests that economic growth is necessary, even though not sufficient, for income poverty to decline (Dollar and Kraay, 2002; Ravallion, 2001). Indeed these results suggest that the overall share of output going to the poor remains, on average, largely unchanged with growth. Clearly this process is consistent with a reduction in headcount poverty. However, given initial inequality, the share of the rich in any incremental output may well be many times greater than that going to the very poor.[9] Ravallion (2001) also finds that persistent (and rising) inequality may dampen the poverty elasticity of growth. On balance, however, Chen and Ravallion (2001) have described slow growth itself as a 'far more important reason for the low rate of aggregate poverty reduction than rising inequality within poor economies' (19).

Growth and Inequality

Modern growth literature has explored the implications of initial wealth inequality for growth. In a series of papers Alesina and Rodrik (1994), Perotti (1993, 1996), and Persson and Tabellini (1994) find that higher initial inequality hurts long-run growth, which Aghion et al. (1999) interpret as repudiating the first arm of the inverted Kuznets U. These authors argue that the likely explanation behind the result is that wealth inequality influences individual decisions in human and physical capital, especially in the context of capital market imperfections and moral hazard. Wealth inequality would thus seem to hamper poverty reduction indirectly, namely by slowing down growth. Although this literature does not describe economic cycles, related writings indicate that the poor typically fare disproportionately worse over economic fluctuations (for example, Rodrik, 2000).

Two predictions therefore emerge from the preceding analysis. First is that, given moral hazard and incomplete markets for physical and human capital, *initial (wealth) inequality would hurt growth, and thus indirectly (that is, via growth) retard income poverty reduction.* Secondly, insofar as the non-income poverty is directly related to the human capital outcomes (for example, in health and education), *wealth inequality would have a direct bearing on the behaviour of non-income poverty as well.*

Institutions, Integration and Growth

Earlier we noted that the entire set of institutional elements aimed at lowering transaction costs would be the conceptual framework of 'institutional capital' (IC) for our analysis. Insofar as countries (for example, in transition or developmental mode) suffer from weak institutions, elements such as extensive public control (for example, via state-owned enterprises, SOEs) and a cumbersome regulatory framework combine to lead to high transactions costs thwarting growth. A new literature has emerged on how institutions affect economic growth. Acemoglu et al. (2001) use the mortality rates of colonial settlers as an instrument for institutional quality and posit a causal effect between institutions and growth. Rodrik et al. (2002) have put forward an even stronger case in support of this hypothesis. The latter's empirical analysis finds the quality of institutions to be the primary determinant of long-run growth. Comparing three 'deep determinants', namely economic integration (say, the trade/GDP ratio), geography (as measured by the distance from the equator) and institutions ('rule of law'), they find that, 'once institutions are controlled for, integration has no direct effect on income, while geography has at best weak direct effects'. However they also find a 'wrong' sign for the integration indicator, whereas the 'measure of property rights and the rule of law always enters with the correct sign, and is statistically significant with t-statistics that are very large' (4). Campos and Coricelli (2000) discuss also the effect of institutions (rule of law and the quality of bureaucracy) on growth during transition and their results are consistent with Rodrik's. *This literature therefore suggests that IC would materially affect the growth profile of nations.*

Poverty and IC

It is rather intuitive that institutional quality would have a direct impact on poverty, both measured in terms of income/consumption and in its broader dimensions, especially via additional income accruing on account of advances in IC. It has been argued by many that the peer-monitoring model of micro lending pioneered by the Grameen Bank (GB) in Bangladesh and replicated pretty much worldwide succeeds because of the social capital (such as trust within the group, and between the group and the lender) that emerges in an NGO type of setting. The essential idea is that group lending allows the lenders to overcome informational asymmetries typical of any credit delivery mechanism. Moral hazard and adverse selection are the usual impediments to the functioning of the market in such a context. The principal devices by which the latter are minimized include peer monitoring and social sanctions within the group (and, possibly, the local community) working as safeguards against excessive risk taking, misuse of funds and default behaviour. The above devices work even when the borrower puts up no formal collateral (as in the case of GB).[10] In the micro credit context, the evolving social capital in the monitoring phase is believed to have contributed greatly to the success of projects, thereby leading to excellent repayment records. Consequently one observes significant income gains accruing to participants, and further benefits in health and education contributing to the alleviation of non-income poverty.[11] *An important hypothesis then emerges, namely that IC has an independent influence on poverty over and above its effect on growth, which we test in this chapter.*

Non-income Poverty (NIP)

We have already outlined the emergence of a broader conceptualization of poverty that puts a primary stress on non-commodities. The above review suggests several plausible hypotheses on the evolution of NIP. First is the role of income growth. Modern growth theory also suggests that the initial wealth distribution, which surely affects human capital as well as physical capital investment possibilities, plays a direct role in determining the level of broader poverty. Finally, the literature on institutions implies that the quality of economic, political and social institutions also allows a greater access to health, educational, and physical (including public utilities) infrastructure. Hence the levelling of the playing field has a direct bearing in shaping the non-income poverty outcome for a given level of output growth. Overall, therefore, we would expect NIP to respond to growth, initial inequality as well as IC.

The Implications for Transition Economies

The transition dynamics in the EEFSU region have many facets, and even a short review would entail a long detour. Nevertheless we offer a few salient aspects related to the present context. The transitional process, namely the withdrawal of the command system and the introduction of market and political liberalization, varied greatly among nations. While all suffered from the recession that followed immediately, the duration and severity differed perceptibly. In Eastern and Central Europe the contraction of output lasted for three to four years and ranged from 20 to 30 per cent, while in most CIS countries the output decline was both longer and deeper (Cornia and Popov, 2001:3). Hence one of the issues to explain here is how the negative growth affected absolute poverty among the EEFSU countries.

What about inequality?

While growth appears to be, *on average*, neutral with respect to inequality (à la Dollar–Kraay) at a global level, the EEFSU experience stands in sharp contrast. Inequality as measured by the Gini coefficient rose dramatically over the decade of the 1990s.[12] Modelling income distribution pre- and post-transition, Milanovic (1999) finds that falling share of wages in disposable income as well as increasing concentration of the emerging wage distribution have caused the Gini to go up. Indeed the former element alone (and given the large initial weight of wages in the functional distribution of income) contributed up to 75 per cent of the increase in Gini for many EEFSU countries. Thus, in line with the poverty decomposition analysis, one would expect that, controlling for other factors, countries with the larger increase in inequality would perform less well in fighting poverty.

What has been the role of institutions?

A key ingredient in the analysis of institutional change is that of *path dependence*, as proposed by Schotter (1981) and by North (1990). The latter states 'if the process by which we arrive at today's institutions is relevant and constrains future choices, then not only does history matter but persistent poor performance and long-run divergent pattern of development stem from a common source' (93). A clearly verifiable implication of this analysis is that economic performance between two countries would differ even if each were to decree similar formal institutions, but diverge in the quality of informal rules. This is so because the latter is necessary in order 'to provide a hospitable foundation for the establishment of formal rules' (North, 1997:16). Consequently one would be tempted to attribute the presumed slow adjustment to reforms in the FSU republics to the lack of quality informal institutions.

Some argue that the socialist state had contributed to the degradation of the civil society and its conventional value system, and replaced that with loyalty to the party hierarchy, thereby making it difficult to find the acceptance of the rule of law during the transition phase (Raiser, 2001). There are indications that even the role of the institution of the family was marginalized in Russia (in sharp contrast to the opposite tendencies in China; ibid.:226–7). Hence, depending on the country in question, one may face a total institutional collapse in the interim or, at least, some functional degree of *institutional discontinuity*. Campos and Coricelli (2002) state that 'there is enough evidence to argue that, in this first ten years ... there was rapid collapse of institutional structures followed by a vacuum in many countries, and the transition involved large social costs principally in terms of worsening income inequality, mortality and poverty rates'. Indeed one would expect that the Eastern European nations would have faced a milder degree of institutional collapse as they already had experienced, prior to the socialist rule, the market economy, and thus the associated informal institutions could reassert themselves relatively quickly. This then is the essence of the *path dependence hypothesis*, and indeed it is common knowledge that growth had been hampered less during transition in Eastern Europe vis-à-vis the FSU republics.

How consistent had the coordination of economic and political institutions been?

It is relevant to note that not all EEFSU countries have proceeded at the same pace with the process of transition. Kolodko (2000) had observed that the Czech Republic, Estonia, Hungary, Lithuania, Poland, Slovakia and Kyrgyzstan had been among those to embrace a vigorous transition process. In contrast, Russia and Ukraine and, to a lesser extent, Bulgaria and Romania moved only gradually, often taking steps in the face of fresh crises, hence reflecting a lack of overall strategy. Moreover the necessary electoral and political changes had been slow, piecemeal and indecisive in these cases. Such lapses have contributed to poor governance and a loss of credibility in the political leadership.

Did the early reformers suffer the least?

Often one belittles the cumulative value of gradual but perceptible changes that were undertaken mainly through economic reforms during the socialist reign. Given that these reforms were undertaken while the state had full authority (that is, governance by coercion), society had been able to develop appropriate behavioural (supply) response to these measures, and the results have been generally positive. Kolodko identifies Croatia, Estonia, Hungary, Poland and Slovenia as those benefiting the most from pre-liberalization reforms. Raiser examines the Polish situation closely, and highlights that the value added to gradual reforms undertaken over the years. One measure of this success is reflected in the fact that, by the time the transition began in 1989, the share of non-agricultural GDP in the private sector already stood at 35 per cent. Recall that agriculture had never been collectivized in Poland.

In sum, we believe that the three factors cited above differentiate winners from losers in the transition process. To reiterate, these are (a) the degree of institutional continuity, (b) the nature of interplay between economic and wider political reforms, and (c) the head start through reforms undertaken in the pre-transition era. Note that the above is very much an institutional story, one that fits the premise of the path dependence hypothesis most intimately. While it is difficult to estimate and isolate these elements econometrically, we believe this to be potentially a fruitful approach.

TESTABLE HYPOTHESES

Let us now collect all the hypotheses (not necessarily mutually exclusive) that emerged from the preceding discussion. Below we shall attempt an evaluation of these with the available data.

Explaining Growth

The empirical work described below attempts first to explain the growth behaviour. The growth process reviewed above suggests two hypotheses, namely (a) that higher initial inequality hurts growth (growth theory) and (b) that growth depends on IC (NIE, Rodrik et al., 2002). Thus we may write:

$$GRO = f(IC, IIQ), \quad f_1 > 0, f_2 < 0. \tag{10.5}$$

While the derivatives would have the a priori sign as noted above, we should add that, depending on how these are measured and calibrated, the sign pattern of the estimated coefficients would be determined accordingly. We shall review this in the data section below.

Explaining Poverty

We motivate our econometric specification of the poverty equation as follows. First recall the Bourguignon–Datt–Ravallion identity (equation 10.4 above):

$$(\Delta H/H) = (-)\varepsilon(DEV, IIQ) \cdot GRO + \beta(DEV, IIQ) \cdot CIQ. \qquad (10.6)$$

We now invoke the hypothesis explaining the change in inequality, which has an old Kuznetsian history as well as a modern growth connotation, as reviewed above:

$$CIQ = \varphi(GRO), \varphi' > 0. \qquad (10.7)$$

Combining (10.5), (10.6) and (10.7), we obtain:

$$(\Delta H/H) = (-)\varepsilon(DEV, IIQ) \cdot f(IC, IIQ) + \beta(DEV, IIQ) \cdot \varphi(GRO), \qquad (10.8a)$$

or

$$(\Delta H/H) = g(DEV, IIQ, IC, GRO), \quad g_1 < 0, g_2 > 0, g_3 < 0, g_4 < 0. \qquad (10.8b)$$

Thus, once we have utilized the growth–poverty identity described by (10.6), we only find a separate growth variable as associated with increased inequality. Again the postulated sign pattern follows from the current literature, as reviewed above. Faster growth, higher initial level of development and a higher quality of institutions all lead to faster poverty reduction, while high initial inequality is an impediment. The interpretation, however, is not always direct. For example, the IIQ variable would affect poverty in at least two ways (that is, even ignoring the second term on the right-hand side of 10.6): first, directly by lowering the absolute value of the poverty elasticity, and then by influencing growth (as in 10.5). Both these effects happen to reinforce each other. Similarly growth would affect poverty via the standard elasticity (even though we are not utilizing the analytical elasticity à la Bourguignon), but also possibly by changing the income distribution. Given (10.7), the stated sign, $g_4 < 0$ is suggestive of an implicit assumption that the latter effect is dominated by the elasticity effect. Our empirical specification (see Tables 10A.2 and 10A.3) is essentially a linear approximation of (10.8b).[13]

Explaining NIP

Earlier we have reasoned that initial inequality and poor institutions retard the fight against NIP. It is plausible that income growth would also have a positive effect on broader poverty, though one may be somewhat ambivalent as to its strength. Advances in NIP may occur even without commensurate income gains, presumably owing to better initial conditions (both at the level of institutional capital and in income and wealth distribution). We thus obtain

$$NIP = h(GRO, IC, IIQ), \quad h_1 > 0, h_2 > 0, h_3 < 0. \qquad (10.9)$$

Path dependence (North–Schotter) hypotheses
The review undertaken here is strongly supportive of the view that the overall quality of institutional capital surely depends on institutional continuity, a factor that we may measure by a zero–one dummy variable (DUM). In practice, we may fashion this dummy according to whether the country in question had an episode of market institutions prior to the imposition of communist rule following World War II.[14] Hence

$$IC = j(DUM). \qquad (10.10)$$

In view of the above, we may also restate growth behaviour itself; combining (10.5) and (10.10),

$$GRO = k(DUM, IIQ). \qquad (10.11)$$

DATA ISSUES

Operationalization of IC

Here we focus on conceptually identifying those elements that help lower transaction costs in exchanges among individuals (or groups, as appropriate). We also group the former into three convenient (though not mutually exclusive) categories: (a) those lowering the costs of communication and information, (b) those supporting market competition, and (c) those strengthening social capital.

Communication and information costs
The quality of the information regime (such as information–communication technology at the public's disposal) has a direct influence on the efficacy of exchanges. Possible indicators include the extent of the transport network, (especially rural, and around the main production and market centres), rural

energy supply and the telecommunication system (both wireless and conventional). The degree of computerization (for example, as measured by the number of diploma holders or the export value of software) is another element. Decentralization (administrative and fiscal) allows rural residents easier access to local public goods, and this may be viewed as lowering the communication costs more than in a unitary system of government.[15] The share of local government in national revenue may be taken as a rudimentary measure of decentralization. Unfortunately consistent data on the elements cited above are not available for the EEFSU countries, except for the last several years.

Market competitiveness

Quality of public expenditures in health, education and physical infrastructure, and the availability of credit are critical to helping markets for labour and for credit to perform better. At the same time, formal institutions such as the legal/regulatory framework, bureaucracy and the justice system (for example, independence, corruption and law enforcement) and bank supervision are just as significant. Again data on many of these are hard to assemble for a group of countries. The following elements, on which data are generally available, may therefore be taken to gauge the level of market competition instead.

Rule of law (ROL) While this factor is cited as one of six indicators of 'governance' by the World Bank Institute (WBI), we treat this as part of the formal institutions as spelled out in the second section above. The original WBI information was based on a survey of perceptions of the quality of governance carried out during 1997 and 1998, and has since been updated in 2001 (World Bank, 2001).

Corruption Control of corruption (COC) may be seen as helping markets to function (for example, in the process of bidding and allocation of public contracts, allocation of credit, public sector employment, career advancement and the like). Pervasive corruption typically stands in the way of private firms getting established and flourishing.

Social capital

This chapter highlights the role of informal institutions as strengthening or even supplanting the market mechanism. While, ideally, one would wish to have data on trust in society (among each other, among groups, and between individuals and branches of government and judiciary), the extent of networking and participation in voluntary and civil activities, this is not feasible at present.[16] While some authors (such as Inglehart et al., 1998) have compiled measures of social capital for a number of countries, this is most inadequate for the sample of countries in focus here. Thus, in the absence of direct observation on trust, variables such as micro credit availability, density of NGO and other voluntary agency activities, and wireless telephony (critical to rural group coordination and networking) may be valuable. Unfortunately even the latter variety of information is not available at the cross-section level.

We finally adopt two more of the 'governance' elements compiled by WBI as indicators of social capital in society. These are political stability/lack of violence (PLS), and voice and accountability (VOA). While the second of these would appear to reflect a strong civil society, social cohesion (and hence trust) may be associated with the lack of violence. Of course, both these components may also emerge primarily out of good governance and monitoring institutions. The point, however, remains that, without a vocal and active civil society, monitoring is usually poor.

To sum up the discussion on IC, let us note that many of the broad features we have discussed above are not available for the present analysis. For future reference, we nevertheless enumerate these in the form of a schema (Figure 10.1) in the appendix to the chapter. We are thus led to rely on available data and, in that context, we select four indicators derived by the WBI governance project cited above.[17] We have chosen (a) control of corruption and (b) the rule of law as measuring the quality of formal institutions, while (c) political stability/lack of violence, and (d) voice and accountability proxy for social capital indicators.[18] We construct an aggregate IC variable based on the data on the four selected WB indicators of the quality of institutions described above. Each individual country observation, under each category, was given a score between one (best) and four (poor) according to the quartile where the observation fell in the distribution. These ordinals were then added up to form an equally weighted aggregate measure ('weakness of institutions') of IC. The latter record may, by construction vary between four (for example, Estonia, Hungary and Poland) and 16 (Kyrgyz Republic). Given that these ordinals fall as the quality rises, the variable is itself labelled DIC ('decrease in institutional capital').[19] The above WB data may be contrasted with the Freedom House (FH) index of political and civil rights (as used by Rodrik, and Persson and Tabellini in related work). Indeed we develop an aggregate index (again, a weighted average) out of the three FH indices of political rights, civil liberties and the status of freedom, and call it PCF. This is done for two data points, 1973 and 2002, the difference being labelled DPCF, which measures the evolution of rights and liberties over the 30 year period.

The Role of International Institutions

The role of international institutions in the EEFSU countries has always been very important and significant. The financial loan and aid that the World Bank and IMF offered to the former communist countries in the Cold War period could be seen as a conduit through which the West hoped to gain a channel of influence. After 1990, the international institutions contributed not only financially but also by providing technical support in implementing political and economic reforms.[20] However it is hard to devise a measure of the extent to which the international institutions may have contributed to the rediscovery of *social capital* during the last 15 years. It is a fact that, early in the transition phase, underdeveloped capital markets (partly caused by poor social capital and inadequate domestic institutions) were a major bottleneck for domestic entrepreneurship. Consequently we consider that investments made possible by EBRD financing have a significant impact on growth and poverty. This may also be viewed as measuring the scope of integration in the present context. In the empirical studies that we perform, the financial influence is discussed in detail.

Thus, in order to measure the role of international institutions, we use the cumulative EBRD investment from 1990 to 2001 for the present sample. These have been normalized by population size (per hundred thousand), and the resulting figures are in units of hundred thousand dollars. This variable is labelled EINV. Initially efforts were also made to assess the significance of foreign direct investment and trade (as possible instruments for integration) for growth, but, owing to endogeneity problems, our results were inconclusive.

Operationalization of Non-income Poverty

Recall that here we would ideally measure the output of the economic game that has a bearing on broader poverty over and above the income/consumption aspects. In terms of the capability approach, we note that deeper aspects of voice and freedom are harder to quantify, but access to inputs and information would be consistent with the goal of maximizing the capabilities.[21] Consequently we focus on (a) female literacy (measured by gross secondary enrolment, SFE), health status of the very young, particularly (b) infant mortality (MIR) and (c) low birth weight (LBW), and (d) longevity (LFE). Literacy and child (or, maternal) health developments may result from deliberate public policy and formal rules of society (for example, compulsory attendance in school to a certain age or widely available public health facilities). Or these may derive from civil and public varieties of social capital (social support and networking) or a combination of both formal and informal institutions. In any event, it may be noted that the elements cited above indicate the outcome on the human capital side, and thus the physical capital accomplishment is undervalued in this construction. While it is not difficult to provide a conceptual measure of the latter (say, the interest rate differential between rural credit and the commercial sector lending rate), data availability is another matter.

Comparable Data

Even though the world is faced with the threat that poverty eradication is going to be a hard-fought battle for years if not decades to come, there is still little consensus about practical definitions which could yield comparable estimates from household survey data across countries. As a result, the attempt to gather information and data regarding the level of poverty among the EEFSU group is endangered by the risk of inconsistency in characterizing the poverty line adopted by different international organizations. In any event, the income poverty data that we use in this chapter are obtained from UNDP and a World Bank paper by Milanovic (1998), which describes the $4/day poverty line in the same way as UNDP's Human Development Reports (HDR). Therefore we were able to combine the data sets (that is, WB and HDR), as they are mutually consistent. We should note in principle that the relative prices (of non-tradables) can vary a great deal among countries, and hence the international measure need not adequately describe the underlying differences in poverty among countries. For the present group, though, such anomalies are unlikely to be serious.

While the present study covers the post-liberalization period (1988–2000/1), it is necessary to have observations at the pre-transition stage (say, as of 1987/8). The idea is to capture the 'longer-term' effects, there being the presumption of a lag over which the transition/liberalization process would settle in. However the latest year for which comparable data is available are 1999, and hence our longer-term poverty performance covers the change in headcount poverty between 1987 and 1999, for which we have only 15 countries. We also examine the immediate poverty increase during the transition, and this is captured by examining the poverty behaviour over the shorter span of 1987–95, which yields a sample of 18 countries.

The remaining data relate to GDP growth, inequality and broader poverty measures cited above. These are all taken from the latest World Development Indicators (2002), which applies a consistent methodology.

EMPIRICAL EVIDENCE

Here we briefly outline our empirical observations on the process of growth, inequality and the evolution of poverty based on the data set described above. However the data set is not without flaws. In many cases our explanatory variables are hard to measure and as a result we use proxies, especially for most of the institutional variables. Correlation charts may reveal how good, indeed, has been our choice of the proxies (Tables 10A.5 and 10A.6). However we do not believe that the correlation between the proxies and the other variables is high enough to create estimation and inference problems. While all regressions discussed here utilize the OLS procedures, the inference is based on F-tests which have been corrected for heteroscedasticity.[22] In this way the possibility of homoscedasticity in the error terms is removed and thus the inference is reliable. The results, however, must be interpreted taking into account characteristic problems of the data available in the area we are analysing: small number of observations and endogeneity (that is, the explanatory variables being correlated with the errors, which typically occur when omitted variables are included in the error term). Different approaches for correcting for these biases could be proposed (Instrumental Variable (IV) estimation or Generalized Method of Moments (GMM)), but we believe that our model is well specified and the bias does not influence our inference about the estimators in a significant way.

Growth

Focusing on annualized GDP growth rates over the reference period, 1990–2000, EEFSU average growth has been negative, indeed this is the only region to have this distinction. Ivaschenko (2003) noted the pace of deindustrialisation as a significant fact in the recent economic history of the region. World Development Indicators (WDI) data reveal that overall industrial decline had been at the annual rate of 6.6 per cent over the decade of the 1990s for the group of countries in focus here. Of these, notably Kazakhstan, Moldova and Ukraine recorded the worst industrial decline (average of 14 per cent annually) and these were indeed the countries where output decline was the steepest (annual average of 9.2 per cent). Agricultural losses, while less steep, were more uniformly distributed vis-à-vis the overall decline in GDP.

What can this body of data tell us about the growth process? Based on the results reported in Table 10A.1, both the Akaike and Schwartz information criteria suggest that regression (2) fits the data best, although (6) is very close behind. We find that a weakening of the institutional capital leads to a decrease in the growth rate. However the control of corruption (COC) rather than the aggregate DIC appears to be the key variable driving, not only regression (2), but also those just behind, namely (5) to (7). These indications are entirely consistent with the tenets of NIE and, even if preliminary, are an interesting vindication of our hypothesis (equation 10.5). We should empha-size that, while Dollar–Kraay (2002) found mild support for the role of 'rule of law', we find a rather robust coefficient for COC.

Does the initial level of inequality (IIQ) affect growth in the tradition of the evidence compiled, among other, by Alesina and Rodrik (1994)? Accord-ing to equation (2), the role of the initial (that is, 1988) level of inequality on the growth performance over the period 1990–99 is rather muted, though the sign is correct. Unfortunately, the COC (and indeed all IC components) are highly correlated with IIQ, and thus, unless we find a good proxy for one of these two variables, a more reliable estimation will remain elusive. Further note that, in the absence of wealth distribution, we have used income/ex-penditure data in measuring initial inequality. To what extent the income data would have tracked the initial wealth distribution for the EEFSU region remains unknown.

We also test for the role of international institutions as a proxy variable for integration, namely the relative size of the EBRD investment over the past decade (that is, the EINV variable) as seen in (4), (5) and (7). In regression (4) this variable is highly significant. Note that, in the sample of 18 countries, while EINV is not uncorrelated with other independent variables, the correla-tions are not significant.

In order to test equation (10.11) as spelled out above, we have created a dummy variable to distinguish the EEFSU countries according to whether they had market institutions (DUM = 1) pre-communism or not (DUM = 0). However, this too is highly correlated with IIQ (–0.63), thereby precluding a reliable test. Hence there again arises the necessity of a viable proxy.

Explaining the Rise in Inequality

As the sample EEFSU economies were very much in transition, causing great dislocation in the economic lives of citizens, the context matches, perhaps a bit too dramatically, the early modernization phase envisaged by Kuznets. Has the underlying growth contributed to the rampant rise in inequality? Estimating the above relationship we obtain:

$$CIQ = 0.036 - 0.33(GRO), \quad R^2 = 0.18 \quad \{F = 19.86, p = 0.026\} \quad (10.12)$$
$$(6.66) \quad (-2.46)$$

Contrary to the early phase of the Kuznets process, the relationship is nega-tive; growth seems to dampen the rise in inequality. To the extent that the quintile measure (the share of income accruing to the poorest quintile) used by Dollar–Kraay (2002) is related to the Gini, the authors find no systematic effect of growth on inequality.[23] Plausibly the dislocations due to the massive loss of jobs and high internal migration (frequently from urban to rural areas) may have caused too much turbulence to allow stable behaviour vis-à-vis the standard view of early industrialization. However we do have to keep in mind that the above is an incomplete specification, where growth alone explains a mere fraction of the total variability in the change in inequality.

Explaining Income Poverty

As discussed above, we focus here on the income poverty figures based on the international measure (four dollars a day). At this level significant poverty persists in all but a few cases (namely the Czech Republic, Hungary and Slovenia). While poverty rose dramatically soon after the start of liberalization, the high variability in the change in headcount poverty figures, especially over the longer time horizon (1987–99) is striking. The dramatically high poverty figures of 1999 for the Kyrgyz Republic (88 per cent), Moldova (82 per cent) and Kazakhstan (62 per cent) remain a matter of grave concern.

Poverty performance in early transition, 1987–95
Examining poverty data early in the transition phase reveals that the population living below four dollars a day increased from very low levels (mostly single digit) to a range where, in eight out of 18 countries, headcount poverty rose by over 50 per cent). Table 10A.2 reports the main results, where regressions (7), (2) and (5) are the leading ones.[24] In all these cases, growth of output is indeed the primary variable of interest. Alone it explains about 60 per cent of the variability in the independent variable (see equation 1). The leading regressions each have IIQ as a significant explanatory variable. GRO and IIQ together explain over 75 per cent of the variability in headcount poverty behaviour over the 1987–95 period. In regression (7), CIQ also features and is of borderline significance. Overall this regression fits the theory well, as described by equation (3).

Notwithstanding the importance of growth, the institutional quality is perhaps the single variable of most significance, as equation (3) in Table 10A.2 would suggest. On a direct comparison between (1) and (3), it is seen that the aggregate indicator of institutions, DIC, alone explains 70 per cent of the variability in poverty in the early transition phase. Econometrically, however, it is rather difficult to isolate effects of IC variables from those due to growth or indeed the level of initial inequality. Both the latter variables are correlated with DIC (Table 10A.5). One component of DIC, namely PLS, is not as highly correlated with growth (the coefficient being 0.5), but is still robustly correlated with IIQ (−0.64). This explains why PLS turns out to be statistically insignificant once we add IIQ in the set of regressors (compare equations 6 and 7 in Table 10A.2). Unfortunately, however, the data set at our disposal does not yield satisfactory proxies for the set of highly correlated variables (namely IIQ, DIC or its components).

Poverty over 1987–99

Looking at the longer horizon, note that regressions (3), (4) and (2a) in Table 10A.3 are, respectively, ranked first to third using the AIC indicator, while equations (1b) and (2) stand out in terms of the F-test.[25] All have GRO as an explanatory variable, and the estimated growth elasticity of poverty is significant except in (2a). It is of interest to note that the present result of the importance of growth, obtained largely in a regime of negative growth, is indeed consistent with the well-known results of Dollar and Kraay (2002) and Ravallion (2001). Using panel data (covering the last four decades) for 80 countries (developed and developing), Dollar–Kraay found that there was indeed a one-to-one relationship between annual per capita GDP growth and the income accruing to the poorest quintile, even though there was a fair amount of variation around the average relationship. Ravallion (2001) uses (dollar-a-day poverty) data for 47 developing countries (over the 1980s and 1990s), and discovers that his results echo those obtained by Dollar and Kraay (2002). Ravallion's growth coefficient of (–) 2.5 (t-value of 8.3) may be interpreted as suggesting that 'for every one percent increase in the mean, the proportion of the population living below $1/day … falls by an average of 2.5%' (Ravallion, 2001:9).

What is perhaps striking is that, for a sample of 15 countries, we get similar and almost as robust results for the EEFSU region. Quantitatively the coefficient for the four-dollar poverty is of the same order as that found by Ravallion and other authors of the same tradition. In our case, the poverty elasticity of growth is seen at −3.03 (t = −2.13), which is reduced slightly (−2.64, t = −1.89) when we add VOA, an IC variable in equation (4). The growth coefficient cited above suggests that were policy reforms successful in fully reversing the contraction of output witnessed over the period, population below the four-dollar poverty would have fallen from the average figure of 29 to 18.5 per cent. This would appear to be a dramatic decline indeed.[26] The above observation is also consistent with specific experiences of the few countries that were indeed able to register positive growth over this period.

Inequality and poverty

Previous research has shown that, even though growth and poverty reduction go hand in hand, the share of income going to the poor (however defined) remains largely independent of the growth rate of GDP. However, given initial inequality, this suggests that the rich (say the top quintile or so) must have gained proportionately more since the poor's share is about constant in any growth. The IIQ variable does yield the correct sign in our regressions, and is highly significant. Bourguignon's derivation suggests that the absolute value of the poverty elasticity of growth should be decreasing with higher initial inequality. Comparing regressions (1) and (1a), we do confirm this prediction. Empirically, Ravallion (2001) found that rising inequality also dampened the poverty elasticity of growth. Here we also detect support behind this prediction as the poverty elasticity falls in equation (4) vis-à-vis equation (3b). Hence Ravallion's suggestion that 'there is no sign that distributional changes help protect the poor during contractions' appears to be confirmed by the EEFSU data.

While in our data set, the initial inequality was about uniform (average Gini coefficient of 23.5, and s.d. of 1.63), unlike other regional data, inequality by the end of the 1990s had increased by an average of nine percentage points, reaching a figure of 32.4. Hence, with increased inequality, the poor's share of income must have declined commensurately. However, whenever we add the actual change in inequality (CIQ), results do not improve markedly. For example, when we go from equation (1a) to equation (1b), or from equation (3b) to equation (4), the statistical fit improves in each case, but the coefficient of the CIQ term fails to be significant. By contrast, whenever we replace IIQ with CIQ, the quality of fit suffers as the CIQ variable continues to remain statistically non-significant.[27] It would thus appear that, at least in this data set, the initial level of inequality is a more potent determinant of poverty outcome than is the actual change in inequality over the growth phase. This ambivalence is also reflected in the data. Looking at specific cases, we see that Russia, with the steepest rise in inequality, registers a large increase in the poverty rate. By contrast Estonia, having witnessed a sharp rise in inequality (worse than in Moldova or Ukraine), escapes much poverty thanks to its robust growth in the late 1990s. Hence the present episode of growth–CIQ interface would suggest that rising inequality might plausibly constrain growth (see equation (1) in Table 10A.1), and thus lead to a worsening of poverty, but has only a limited independent effect once the growth effect has been taken into account.

Institutions and poverty

Previous empirical studies generally failed to detect any discernible impact of institutions on poverty, or indeed of elements such as the openness of the economy, which may be viewed as growth-friendly. Dollar and Kraay (2001) find negligible correlation between changes in inequality and greater openness. It is of interest therefore to note that, in the present study, the *quality of institutions* does matter. A decline in institutional quality worsens the poverty outcome. Both VOA (regression 4) and DPCF, a measure based on the Freedom House indicators (regressions 3 and 2a), appear with statistically significant coefficients. Indeed comparing equations (1) and (2) it is evident that DPCF alone explains a larger share of poverty increase over the period 1987–99 than growth alone. Indeed the poverty elasticity of growth diminishes greatly as DPCF enters as a second variable (see equations 1 and 2a). However, as discussed earlier, we are handicapped by the lack of data which might allow the identification of valid proxies for several of the explanatory variables, particularly in the IC category.

The broad conclusion on the behaviour of income poverty must be that initial inequality and the quality of institutions largely drive poverty reduction. While growth materially affects the latter process, once the former variables are controlled for, GRO fails to remain highly significant on a consistent basis. This is remarkably different from the conclusion reached by authors such as Ravallion (2001), but entirely consistent with the ex ante predictions of the 'theory' of institutional capital.

Non-income Poverty

We focus on an aggregate indicator, NIP, which accords equal weight to four elements for which we have comparable data, namely life expectancy (LFE), infant mortality (MIR), female secondary enrolment (SFE), and the incidence of low birth-weight babies (LBW). On female enrolment, we note that there have been sizable advances in all countries. Judging by the incidence of low birth-weight babies (1992–8), we see that the Baltic countries boast the best record (at 4 per cent, which is well below the regional average of 7 per cent). Turning to infant mortality figures, again there has been a general reduction, although the regional average is rather high.

Analysing NIP, let us focus on the best fit in terms of the information criteria, namely regression (3). We find that neither GDP growth nor the rise in inequality (CIQ) is successful in the explanation (Table 10A.4).[28] While GRO by itself is highly significant, it does not explain a lot of the variability in NIP. By contrast, the institutional variable, DPCF, has about twice the explanatory power (compare equations 1 and 4). A focus on DPCF is interesting since it has the least correlation, followed by VOA, among all domestic IC variables vis-à-vis growth. However, given DPCF, as we add GRO, not only does the added coefficient become insignificant, but the resulting equation is dominated by one with DPCF alone on all goodness-of-fit criteria, shown in Table 10A.4 (see equations 4 and 5). As equation (3) demonstrates, the DIC components such as COC perhaps explain the behaviour of non-income poverty best in the present sample. The level of initial inequality is also highly significant, and it is fortuitous that IIQ has the least correlation with COC among all IC variables. Recall that our review of the literature on growth, inequality and institutions did yield a hypothesis that initial inequality would directly affect the NIP outcome. We thus find that *non-income poverty improves with better control of corruption, as well as with less unequal initial income distribution.* This is largely consistent with the finding on income poverty over 1987–99.

The relevance of institutional capital is quite evident; elements such as effective control of corruption, rule of law or public accountability do make for greater access to public resources (whether in health, education or infra-structure) for all citizens. Lower initial inequality also plays a similar role; it serves to complement the public resources that are available. Correspond-ingly, where public facilities are highly inadequate, personal wealth becomes indispensable, thus causing great disparities in access to physical and human capital.

A paper by Moser and Ichida (2001) analyses several aspects of non-income poverty for a sample of countries in sub-Saharan Africa (SSA). In particular they consider life expectancy, infant mortality and primary school enrolment, all of which are essentially included in our construction of NIP. They find that the positive effects of income growth on life expectancy, school enrolment and the decline in infant mortality are all robust, as con-firmed by OLS, GLS and 2SLS methods of estimation. They further infer that there is no evidence of reverse causality in their sample since they find that changes in the non-income poverty elements do not lead to significant gains in income. They also find that lower income inequality has an important role to play in the reduction of non-income poverty. These findings are largely consistent with those presented above. However, as we pointed out, the importance of income growth fades once institutional factors are brought to bear on the explanation, the latter feature being absent in the Moser–Ichida analysis.

To sum up the empirical evidence, we observe that the transition from the communist to hybrids of market economies has led to many challenges, mainly in the design and discovery of a hospitable institutional architecture. Some nations were better prepared, thanks to their earlier experience with the market, and especially those who were able to retain the vestiges of informal institutions commensurate with the market (and intuition about them) better than others. Hence the manner in which IC has been fashioned over the past decade or so provides the dominant explanation behind the growth process, and in its wake, the resulting poverty dynamics both in income (albeit indi-rectly, via growth) as well as in non-income dimensions. Indeed it is the latter effect that has been the most dramatic, overshadowing the standard explana-tion based on the prominence of growth or the rise in inequality over time.

CONCLUSION

The primary goals of this chapter have been to examine the EEFSU poverty and growth experience (1987–99/2000), for the sample of 18 countries, and attempt to discern the scope of the quality of institutions in affecting these. This was to be carried out in terms of an expanded model of poverty decomposition popularized by the work of Datt and Ravallion (1992) and Bourguignon (2003), where we had built in an integral role for institutional capital. Secondly, we wished to focus on some key indicators of non-income dimensions of poverty, and examine the differences in its behaviour among countries in terms of the underlying institutional capital, economic growth and distributional characteristics.

Our preliminary findings may be restated very briefly. The institutional variable appears to have a most emphatic role in explaining growth, while at the same time rising inequality may indeed dampen growth. Unlike other researchers on the topic, we do not find an overwhelming importance of growth in influencing *income poverty* reduction, especially over the longer horizon. Growth, however, is highly significant for the poverty early in the transition phase, that is, up to 1995. Initial inequality is another important variable in poverty reduction, in both income and non-income dimensions. When it comes to non-income poverty, however, economic growth does not at all figure in the explanation. The primary role is that of institutional capital, though an independent role of initial income inequality also appears to be robust.

In terms of the related literature, we note that there is little direct evidence on broader measures of IC, especially as they relate to the issues of poverty and inequality. There have, however, been attempts to address selected aspects of the phenomenon, chiefly democratization, rule of law and corruption, especially as they may affect economic growth. Closest perhaps to our interests is the finding by Dollar and Kraay (2002) that *rule of law* had a positive impact on growth. Rodrik et al. (2002) found that the rule of law explains income growth better than other 'deep' determinants such as geography or the scope of international integration (say, as measured by the trade/GDP ratio). We experimented with several indicators of the IC and found the corruption variable to yield more precise estimators in the EEFSU case. Somewhat further afield, Persson et al. (2000) examined the effects of the democracy type on the fiscal outcome (for example, size of the public sector and the nature of fiscal interventions). In terms of non-income poverty, ours appears to be the first effort to explain this behaviour empirically.

Data inadequacies afflict researchers in the type of analysis undertaken here, and especially so in the context of the transition countries. While we detected a most prominent role of institutional quality in determining growth and poverty, most indicators of IC we had access to happen to correlate highly with the initial level of inequality, another key variable in the analysis. It is therefore of utmost importance to discover additional data sources that may yield valid proxies so that adequate econometric analysis may be carried out. Different estimation methods could also be proposed in order to solve potential endogeneity concerns: for example, IV estimation or GMM. It would be important to isolate the relative domains of inequality and that of institutional quality in the explanation of growth. Likewise, for the overall strategy for poverty reduction, we need to identify the separate influences of growth, inequality and IC. Economic integration or the international aspect of institutions also has a potential role in poverty reduction and in generating faster growth, and here also data issues prevent a full analysis.

What can we infer on the direction of policy reform for poverty eradication? While growth does not consistently appear to have the designation of the primary determinant of poverty, income or non-income, as earlier studies (using broader data sets) have claimed, it nevertheless is a necessary goal. We also find evidence that rising inequality hurts growth. Polices must therefore promote distribution-friendly growth. The latter surely calls for a stable macro environment (low budgetary deficits and low monetary expansion).

Furthermore we find that EEFSU data empirically support the potential importance of the quality of institutions and the initial level of income inequality in both fostering growth and reducing poverty (income and non-income). Hence not only must we ensure that growth is distribution-friendly, there may well be scope for well-aimed and sustainable public transfer schemes (such as social insurance). Harnessing the information technology, and the design of efficient worker training incentives (for example, via the tax system) aimed at skill acquisition would also appear relevant.

Insofar as non-income poverty is concerned, policy interventions such as the promotion of self-employment (say, via group-based micro lending), which over and above direct income generation (and thus helping fight income poverty), are widely believed to permit group members to make more effective use of social capital. The latter externality is believed to lead to advances in non-income dimensions of poverty (such as health, sanitation, literacy and numeracy). Of course, deliberate NGO–civil society initiatives in these areas, with or without the contrivance of micro credit, may also speed up the broader poverty reduction goals in rural areas, and thus partly offset historical differences in initial conditions. Public authorities must therefore encourage free and unhindered initiatives by such organizations, which often appear efficient in the local provision of educational and health services that private markets *alone* are unable to allocate fully.

NOTES

1. Coase (1984) attributes the origin of the term 'new institutional economics' to Oliver Williamson.
2. See, among others, Arrow (1970), Matthews (1986), North (1997) and Williamson (1998).
3. See the papers by Bruni and Sugden (2000) and Quibria (2003).
4. The essential methodology behind the selection of countries is that comparable poverty data exist for the entire set. This is further discussed in the data section below.
5. More recently multilateral agencies have focused attention on measuring progress of nations vis-à-vis multidimensional attributes of poverty, hunger, education, health and the environment, known as the millennium development goals (MDGs).
6. These are *the focus axiom* (that is, poverty measure must be dependent only on the income/consumption of the poor), *the monotonicity axiom* (that is, poverty measure decreases as the incomes of the poor increase) and, lastly, *the weak transfer axiom* (that is, poverty measure declines whenever the income distribution of the poor improves). See Blackwood and Lynch (1994) for further elaboration.
7. Using both cross-section and time series data, Simon Kuznets (1963) had discovered an inverted U-shaped relationship between inequality and growth. At the early stages of growth, he reasoned, as urbanization and industrialization get under way, inequality rises with growth. However, as industrialization gathers pace, vigorous absorption of rural migrants in the urban sector helps reduce income inequality. However one may interpret Kuznets' hypothesis as merely suggesting an empirical regularity, without necessarily being associated with a *unique* causal process. Clearly the rationalization behind the Kuznets process, even if verifiably true over some time period, is surely of an ad hoc nature! Also note that Kuznets' inequality is over *all* sources of income (labour and capital).
8. Bourguignon actually measures inequality by the standard deviation (s.d.) of the logarithm of income, but switches to the Gini coefficient in empirical work for both the initial and the change levels. Evidently the Gini is an increasing function of s.d. However, in this chapter, we use Gini throughout.
9. To consider an illustration, let us posit that each rich (top decile) individual earns $16 000 income annually, while each poor person (in the bottom quintile), gets only $1000. Furthermore, being consistent with above figures, we take the top decile's initial share as 40 per cent, while the bottom quintile gets only 5 per cent. Then a 30 per cent growth over a ten-year period, distributed proportionately to all groups, implies that the incremental gain for the poor is a mere $300 each vis-à-vis $4800 (that is, 16 times greater) for each rich member of society. Of course, this assumes that income distribution had remained unaltered during the growth process.
10. See, for example, Besley and Coate (1995). Raiser (2001) also suggests that civil society institutions indeed help sustain and reinforce both moral and social norms. Morduch provides a brief but expedient review of the theory of peer monitoring credit mechanisms (1999).
11. There is a voluminous literature on related topics. Khandker (1998) and Pitt and Khandker (1998) are good examples of the empirical evidence that has been accumulated on the subject.
12. Ivaschenko (2003) analysed a panel data for 24 EEFSU countries covering the period 1989–98. His results indicate that variables that explain the rise in inequality include the Kuznets duo, namely (a) per capita real GDP, and (b) the same variable squared. In addition, plausibly he finds roles for (c) inflation, (d) deindustrialization, (e) privatization and (f) the aging of population.
13. Bourguignon has criticized the use of a naked 'growth' term as an independent variable in an equation explaining poverty. He would rather have the theoretical elasticity as a built-in multiplier in the manner of (10.6). Our defence is essentially that we are not merely testing for the 'identity check' behind (10.6). Our principal hypothesis is embodied in (10.5). Secondly, even within the decomposition methodology outlined above, it would be

presumptuous to impose a function as the logarithmic on a small sample size as we do (15 or 18 observations at this stage).

14. Doubtless there would be a large degree of correlation among the three elements of institutional bottlenecks during transition as cited in the second section. Thus, absent good and reliable instruments, it would be hard to examine independently all these.

15. Certainly, decentralization may also lead to better governance as well as the strengthening of the social capital (of the public variety). Such overlaps are unavoidable.

16. For specific country case studies, however, see Hjoellund et al. (2001) on Russia, and additional references cited therein.

17. Indeed two papers by Kaufmann et al. (1999a, 1999b) elaborate on the ideas and methodology behind the selection.

18. We have left out of consideration the two remaining WBI indicators, namely (e) regulatory effectiveness and (f) government effectiveness, for the simple reason that they appear a little too broad in scope.

19. The data files may be requested from the authors.

20. The *Economist* of 13 May 2004 reported that 'in the 1990s the central European and Baltic countries received, in all, about $18 billion in official finance from sources including the EU, the American government, the World Bank, the IMF and the United Nations Development Programme (UNDP)'.

21. See also Rodrik (2000).

22. The figures in parentheses underneath the estimated coefficients are the heteroscedasticity consistent t-values.

23. Dollar–Kraay point out that for log-normal distribution, the two measures of inequality cited above are closely related, though in a non-linear fashion.

24. While (7) comes first on information criteria, focusing on F-values equation (5) performs the best, followed by (2).

25. The Schwartz indicator however ranks equation (2a) (Table 10A.3) ahead of the pack, but indeed they are all very close together.

26. The dependent variable in the regression line we fitted was the change in the percentage of people below the poverty line over the period 1987–99. Thus the reversion of the contraction rate of 3.457 per cent throughout the entire decade would have caused poverty to decline by 10.5 percentage points. The growth impact would have been even stronger if we were to rely on equation (1b) (Table 10A.3). Note that the average $4 poverty rate stood at 29.1 per cent in 1999–2000.

27. This result is not reported in Table 10A.3, however.

28. The CIQ analysis is not actually reported in Table 10A.4.

REFERENCES

Acemoglu, D., S. Johnson and J. Robinson (2001), 'The colonial origins of comparative development: an empirical investigation', *American Economic Review*, **91**(5), 1369–1401.

Aghion, P., E. Caroli and C. Garcia-Penalosa (1999), 'Inequality and economic growth: the perspective of the new growth theories', *Journal of Economic Literature*, **37**, 1615–60.

Ahsan, S.M. (2003), 'Institutional capital and poverty: a transition perspective', in A. Shorrocks and R. van der Hoeven (eds), *Perspectives on Poverty and Growth*, Tokyo: United Nations University Press, pp. 41–92.

Alesina, A. and D. Rodrik, (1994), 'Distributive politics and economic growth', *Quarterly Journal of Economics*, **109**(2), 465–90.

Arrow, K.J. (1970), 'The organisation of economic activity: issues pertinent to the choice of market versus non-market allocation', in Robert H. Haveman and Julius Margolis (eds), *Public Expenditure and Policy Analysis*, Chicago: Markham.

Besley, T. and S. Coate, (1995), 'Group lending, repayment incentives, and social collateral', *Journal of Development Economics*, **46**, 1–18.

Blackwood, D.L. and R.G. Lynch (1994), 'The measurement of inequality and poverty: a policy maker's guide to the literature', *World Development*, **22**(4), 567–78.

Bourguignon, F. (2003), 'The growth elasticity of poverty reduction: explaining heterogeneity across countries and time periods', in T. Eicher and S. Turnovsky (eds), *Growth and Inequality*, Cambridge, MA: MIT Press.

Bruni, L. and R. Sugden (2000), 'Moral canals: trust and social capital in the work of Hume, Smith and Genovese', *Economics and Philosophy*, **16** (Spring), 21–45.

Campos N.F. and F. Coricelli (2000), 'Growth in transition: what we know, what we don't, and what we should', World Bank's Global Development Network: 'Explaining growth project', www. gdnet.org.

Campos N.F. and F. Coricelli (2002), 'Growth in transition: what we know, what we don't, and what we should', *Journal of Economic Literature*, **XL**, 793–836.

Chen, S. and M. Ravallion (2001), 'How did the world's poor fare in the 1990s?', *Review of Income and Wealth*, **47**(3), 283–300.

Coase, R. (1984), 'The new institutional economics', *Journal of Institutional and Theoretical Economics*, **140**, 229–31.

Coleman, J. (1988), 'Social capital in the creation of human capital', *American Journal of Sociology*, **94**, Supplement, S95–S120.

Collier, P. (1998), 'Social capital and poverty', *Social Capital Initiative, Working Paper* no. 4, World Bank.

Cornia, A. and V. Popov (eds) (2001), *Transition and Institutions*, Oxford: Oxford University Press.

Datt, G. and M. Ravallion (1992), 'Growth and redistribution components of changes in poverty measures: a decomposition with applications to Brazil and India in the 1980s', *Journal of Development Economics*, **38**(2), 275–95.

Dollar, D. and A. Kraay (2001), 'Trade, growth and poverty', paper presented at the WIDER Development Conference, Growth and Poverty, 25–6 May, Helsinki.

Dollar, D. and A. Kraay (2002), 'Growth is good for the poor', *Journal of Economic Growth*, **7**(3), 195–225.

Foster, J., J. Greer and E. Thorbecke (1984), 'A class of decomposable poverty measures', *Econometrica*, **52**, 761–6.

Hjoellund, L., G. Svendsen and M. Paldam (2001), 'Social capital in Russia and Denmark: a comparative study', paper presented at the IMAD Conference on Institutions in Transition, July, Otocec, Slovenia.

Inglehart, R., M. Basanez and A. Moreno (1998), *Human Values and Beliefs: A Cross-Cultural Sourcebook*, Ann Arbor, MI: University of Michigan Press.

Ivaschenko, O. (2003), 'Growth and inequality: evidence from the transitional economies in the 1990s', in T.S. Eicher and S.J. Turnovsky (eds), *Inequality and Growth*, Cambridge, MA: MIT Press.

Kakwani, N. (1993), 'Poverty and economic growth with application to Côte d'Ivoire', *Review of Income and Wealth*, **39**(2), 121–39.

Kaufmann, D., A. Kraay and P. Zoido-Lobaton (1999a), 'Governance matters', WB Policy Research Paper, no. 2196.

Kaufmann, D., A. Kraay and P. Zoido-Lobaton (1999b), 'Aggregating governance indicators', WB Policy Research Paper, no. 2195.

Khandker, S.R. (1998), *Fighting Poverty with Micro-credit: Experience in Bangladesh,* New York: Oxford University Press for the World Bank.

Kolodko, G.W. (2000), *From Shock to Therapy: The Political Economy of Postsocialist Transformation,* Oxford: Oxford University Press.

Kuznets, S. (1963), 'Quantitative aspects of the economic growth of nations: VIII. Distribution of income by size', *Economic Development and Cultural Change,* **12,** 1–80.

Matthews, R.C.O. (1986), 'The economics of institutions and the sources of growth', *Economic Journal,* **96,** December, 903–18.

Milanovic, B. (1998), 'Income, inequality and poverty during the transition from planned to market economy', World Bank, mimeo.

Milanovic, B. (1999), 'Explaining the increase in inequality during transition', *Economics of Transition,* **7**(2), 299–41.

Morduch, J. (1999), 'The microfinance promise', *Journal of Economic Literature,* **37,** 1569–1614.

Moser, G. and T. Ichida (2001), 'Economic growth and poverty reduction in sub-Saharan Africa', IMF Working Paper, WP-01-112, Washington, DC.

North, D. (1990), *Institutions, Institutional Change and Economic Performance,* Cambridge University Press.

North, D. (1997), 'The contribution of the new institutional economics to an understanding of the transition problem', *WIDER Annual Lectures 1,* Helsinki: UNU/WIDER.

Perotti, R. (1993), 'Political equilibrium, income distribution and growth', *Review of Economic Studies,* **60**(4), 755–76.

Perotti, R. (1996), 'Growth, income distribution and democracy: what the data say?', *Journal of Economic Growth,* **1**(2), 149–87.

Persson, T. and G.Tabellini (1994), 'Is inequality harmful for growth?', *American Economic Review,* **84**(3), 600–621.

Persson, T., G. Roland and G. Tabellini (2000), 'Comparative politics and public finance', *Journal of Political Economy,* **108,** 1121–61.

Pitt, M., and S.R. Khandker (1998), 'The impact of group-based credit programs on poor households in Bangladesh: does the gender participation matter?,' *Journal of Political Economy,* **106**(5), 958–96.

Quibria, M.G. (2003), 'The puzzle of social capital: a critical review', *Asian Development Review,* **20**(2), 19–39.

Raiser, M. (2001), 'Informal institutions, social capital, and economic transition: reflections on a neglected dimension', in A. Cornia and V. Popov (eds), *Transition and Institutions.*

Ravallion, M. (2001), 'Growth, inequality and poverty: looking beyond averages', *World Development,* **29**(11), 1803–15.

Rodrik, D. (2000), 'Institutions for high-quality growth: what they are and how to acquire them', *Studies in Comparative International Development,* **35**(3).

Rodrik, D., A. Subramanian and F. Trebbi (2002), 'Institutions rule: the primacy of institutions over geography and integration in economic development', NBER WP # W9305, November.

Schotter, A. (1981), *The Economic Theory of Social Institutions,* Cambridge: Cambridge University Press.

Sen, A.K. (1976), 'Poverty: an ordinal approach to measurement', *Econometrica,* **46,** 437–46.

Sen, A.K. (1999), *Development as Freedom,* New York: Knopf.

Williamson, O.E. (1998), 'The institutions of governance', *AER Papers and Proceedings*, **88**(2), 75–9.
World Bank (2001), *World Bank Institute*, Governance web site.
World Bank (2002), *2002 World Development Indicators*.

APPENDIX

List of Variables

CIQ   Annualized percentage change in *inequality* (Gini coefficient) over various periods: 1988–93 and 1988–98 as specified in Table 10A.7

COC   Control of corruption (World Bank Governance Project Data, 2000–2001), Table 10A.9

DIC   Composite indicator of the decline of institutional capital (equally weighted construction based on four indicators, COC, PLS, ROL and VOA (World Bank Governance Project Data, 2000–2001), Table 10A.9

DPCF   Composite indicator (a weighted average) of Freedom House data (1972–2002) made up of the actual difference between 1972 and 2002 of three elements, political rights, civil liberties and the status of freedom

DUM   Dummy (0, 1) depending on whether the country had an episode of the market economy prior to WWII (DUM = 1) or not (DUM = 0)

EINV   Cumulative EBRD investment for 1990–2001 normalized by population of the host country, Table 10A.7

IIQ   Initial inequality (Gini index) for 1988 (other) as specified in Table 10A.7

INC   Per capita income in USD for 1988 or as specified in Table 10A.7

GRO   Annualized GDP growth between 1990 and 2000, Table 10A.7

$GRO_{87/95}$ Annualized GDP growth between 1987 and 1995, Table 10A.7

LFE   Life expectancy at birth, Table 10A.8

LBW   The incidence of low birth weight babies (percentage of births), Table 10A.8

MIR   Infant mortality rate (per 1000 live births), Table 10A.8

NIP   Equally weighted aggregate of (LFE + SFE) – (LBW + MIR), Table 10A.8

PLS   Political stability (World Bank Governance Project Data, 2000–2001), Table 10A.9

ROL   Rule of Law (World Bank Governance Project Data, 2000–2001), Table 10A.9

SFE   Female gross secondary enrolment (%), Table 10A.8

VO   Voice and accountability (World Bank Governance Project Data, 2000–2001), Table 10A.9

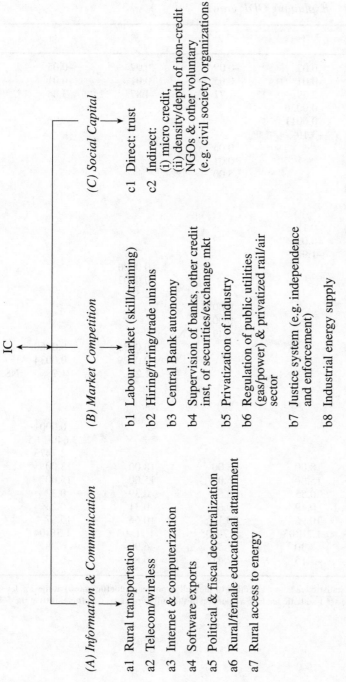

(A) *Information & Communication*

a1 Rural transportation

a2 Telecom/wireless

a3 Internet & computerization

a4 Software exports

a5 Political & fiscal decentralization

a6 Rural/female educational attainment

a7 Rural access to energy

(B) *Market Competition*

b1 Labour market (skill/training)

b2 Hiring/firing/trade unions

b3 Central Bank autonomy

b4 Supervision of banks, other credit inst, of securities/exchange mkt

b5 Privatization of industry

b6 Regulation of public utilities (gas/power) & privatized rail/air sector

b7 Justice system (e.g. independence and enforcement)

b8 Industrial energy supply

(C) *Social Capital*

c1 Direct: trust

c2 Indirect:
(i) micro credit,
(ii) density/depth of non-credit NGOs & other voluntary (e.g. civil society) organizations

IC

Note: (a) non-exhaustive, (b) overlap (no inconsistency, however) both within and between categories, (c) precise indicators to be chosen would depend on data availability.

Figure 10.1 Institutional capital schema

249

Table 10A.1 Explaining GDP growth

Ind. Variable	1		2		3		3a	
Constant	0.02		−0.09		−0.07		−0.05	
Std. error	0.01		0.05		0.01		0.01	
t-stat	2.39	**	−1.71	NS	−4.87	***	−3.85	***
DIC	−0.0036							
Std. error	0.0011							
t-stat	−3.19	***						
COC			0.05					
Std. error			0.01					
t-stat			5.00	***				
CIQ (88–98)								
Std. error								
t-stat								
CIQ (88–93)	−0.18							
Std. error	0.09							
t-stat	−1.90	*						
INC (1993)					0.0006			
Std. error					0.0002			
t-stat					2.36	*		
IIQ (1988)			0.0033					
Std. error			0.0022					
t-stat			1.49	NS				
DPCF					0.0035		0.0060	
Std. error					0.0029		0.0034	
t-stat					1.21	NS	1.78	NS
EINV								
Std. error								
t-stat								
INC (1988)							0.0001	
Std. error							3.640E-05	
t-stat							2.7473	**
No. of obs.	18.00		18.00		18.00		18.00	
d,f.	15.00		15.00		15.00		15.00	
R-squared	0.55		0.66		0.39		0.32	
Adj R-squared	0.49		0.61		0.31		0.23	
F-statistic	10.96		20.12		10.66		16.87	
p-value of F	1.2E-03		5.7E-05		1.3E-03		1.5E-04	
AIC	−7.30		−7.56		−6.99		−6.88	
Schwartz	−7.15		−7.41		−6.85		−6.73	

Note: *** t-statistic leads to a rejection of the null hypothesis (coefficient=0) at the 1% level of significance; ** t-statistic leads to a rejection of the null hypothesis (coefficient=0) at the 5%

4		5		6		7	
−0.05		0.01		−0.01		−0.01	
0.02		0.01		0.01		0.01	
−2.84	***	0.98	NS	−1.05	NS	−1.24	NS
		0.03		0.04		0.04	
		0.01		0.01		0.01	
		4.64	***	5.95	***	5.82	***
−0.52				−0.18		−0.23	
0.18				0.22		0.25	
−2.95	***			−0.81	NS	−0.91	NS
		−0.12					
		0.10					
		−1.27	NS				
0.0007							
0.0001							
6.24	***						
0.00005		0.00001				0.00002	
0.00001		0.00001				0.00001	
3.71	***	0.70	NS			1.77	*
18.00		18.00		18.00		18.00	
14.00		14.00		15.00		14.00	
0.59		0.66		0.64		0.66	
0.50		0.59		0.59		0.59	
16.53		12.51		18.95		12.80	
7.1E-05		3.0E-04		7.8E-05		2.7E-04	
−7.27		−7.47		−7.52		−7.46	
−7.08		−7.28		−7.37		−7.27	

level of significance; * t-statistic leads to a rejection of the null hypothesis (coefficient=0) at the 10% level of significance; NS = not significant.

Table 10A.2 Income poverty increase (change in poverty 95/87)

Ind. variable	1		2		3	
Constant	0.08		−0.97		−0.05	
Std. error	0.06		0.23		0.06	
t-stat	1.40	NS	−4.25	***	−0.88	NS
GRO(87/95)	−5.74		−4.59			
Std. error	0.93		0.60			
t-stat	−6.19	***	−7.60	***		
DIC					0.04	
Std. error					0.01	
t-stat					6.59	***
PLS						
Std. error						
t-stat						
IIQ			0.05			
Std. error			0.01			
t-stat			4.59	***		
CIQ (88–93)						
Std. error						
t-stat						
No. of obs.	18.00		18.00		18.00	
d.f.	16.00		15.00		16.00	
R-squared	0.61		0.78		0.70	
Adj R-squared	0.59		0.75		0.68	
F-statistic	38.28		49.91		43.44	
p-value of F	1.3E-05		2.3E-07		6.2E-06	
AIC	−3.58		−4.05		−3.84	
Schwartz	−3.48		−3.90		−3.74	

Note: Standard errors and F-statistics are heteroscedasticity corrected; *** t-statistic leads to a rejection of the null hypothesis (coefficient=0) at the 1% level of significance; ** t-statistic leads to a rejection of the null hypothesis (coefficient=0) at the 5% level of significance; * t-

4		5		6		7	
0.17		−0.69		0.12		−0.82	
0.06		0.25		0.07		0.37	
2.73	**	−2.72	**	1.83	*	−2.22	*
−4.25		−4.15		−3.73		−3.53	
1.03		0.94		1.02		0.99	
−4.15	***	−4.43	***	−3.67	***	−3.57	***
−0.18		−0.08		−0.15		−0.04	
0.06		0.07		0.06		0.07	
−2.72	**	−1.12	NS	−2.59	**	−0.56	NS
		0.04				0.04	
		0.01				0.02	
		3.46	***			2.60	**
				0.91		1.07	
				0.57		0.56	
				1.61	NS	1.91	NS
18.00		18.00		18.00		18.00	
15.00		14.00		14.00		13.00	
0.73		0.80		0.76		0.84	
0.70		0.76		0.71		0.79	
32.14		66.40		25.88		17.56	
3.8E-06		1.6E-08		5.7E-06		3.7E-05	
−3.83		−4.02		−3.85		−4.15	
−3.69		−3.82		−3.65		−3.91	

statistic leads to a rejection of the null hypothesis (coefficient=0) at the 10% level of significance; NS = not significant.

Table 10A.3   Income poverty increase (change in poverty 99/87)

Ind. variable	1		1a		1b		2		2a	
Constant	0.14		−1.23		−1.30		0.82		0.60	
Std. error	0.03		0.39		0.40		0.10		0.08	
t-stat	4.40	***	−3.16	***	−3.28	***	8.52	***	7.42	***
GRO	−5.72		−4.55		−3.88				−2.70	
Std. error	1.33		1.27		1.27				1.57	
t-stat	−4.31	***	−3.59	***	−3.05	**			−1.72	NS
VOA										
Std. error										
t-stat										
CIQ 88–98					2.31					
Std. error					1.37					
t-stat					1.69	NS				
IIQ			0.06		0.06					
Std. error			0.02		0.02					
t-stat			3.46	***	3.33	***				
DPCF							−0.13		−0.10	
Std. error							0.02		0.02	
t-stat							−7.49	***	−6.04	***
EINV										
Std. error										
t-stat										
GRO*INC(1988)										
Std. error										
t-stat										
No. of obs.	15.00		15.00		15.00		15.00		15.00	
d.f.	13.00		12.00		11.00		13.00		12.00	
R-squared	0.58		0.77		0.81		0.72		0.80	
Adj R-squared	0.55		0.73		0.75		0.70		0.76	
F-statistic	18.59		21.40		42.36		56.16		40.36	
p-value of F	8.4E-04		1.1E-04		2.5E-06		4.5E-06		4.7E-06	
AIC	−3.31		−3.78		−3.82		−3.73		−3.90	
Schwartz	−3.23		−3.64		−3.63		−3.63		−3.76	

Note: *** t-statistic leads to a rejection of the null hypothesis (coefficient=0) at the 1% level of significance; ** t-statistic leads to a rejection of the null hypothesis (coefficient=0) at the 5%

3		3a		3b		4		5	
−0.28		−0.44		−0.74		−0.80		0.05	
0.40		0.40		0.37		0.35		0.07	
−0.70	NS	−1.09		−1.99	*	−2.31	**	0.66	NS
−3.03		−3.24		−3.36		−2.64		−5.51	
1.43		1.38		1.43		1.40		2.19	
−2.13	*	−2.35	**	−2.34	**	−1.89	*	−2.52	**
				−0.12		−0.12			
				0.06		0.05			
				−2.14	*	−2.33	**		
						2.36		2.40	
						1.55		1.75	
						1.52	NS	1.37	NS
0.03		0.03		0.04		0.04			
0.01		0.01		0.02		0.01			
2.22	**	2.39	**	2.85	**	3.07	***		
−0.07		−0.07							
0.02		0.02							
−3.51	***	−3.70	***						
		0.00							
		0.00							
		1.34	NS						
								0.01	
								0.01	
								0.46	NS
15.00		15.00		15.00		15.00		15.00	
11.00		10.00		11.00		10.00		11.00	
0.83		0.83		0.81		0.85		0.85	
0.78		0.77		0.75		0.78		0.78	
35.20		28.62		22.41		24.60		24.60	
6.2E-06		1.9E-05		5.5E-05		3.7E-05		3.7E-05	
−3.94		−3.83		−3.82		−3.91		−3.16	
−3.75		−3.59		−3.63		−3.68		−2.97	

level of significance; * t-statistic leads to a rejection of the null hypothesis (coefficient=0) at the 10% level of significance; NS = not significant.

Table 10A.4   Explaining non-income poverty (NIP)

Ind. variable	1		2		3		4		5		6	
Constant	12.90		−16.56		126.53		−35.99		−23.61		−45.42	
Std. error	10.82		14.88		48.43		11.47		16.14		10.75	
t-stat	1.19	NS	−1.11	NS	2.61	**	−3.14	***	−1.46	NS	−4.22	***
GRO	559.66		296.37						254.72			
Std. error	192.45		152.16						179.58			
t-stat	2.91	***	1.95	*					1.42	NS		
DIC												
Std. error												
t-stat												
DPCF							10.59		8.68		7.33	
Std. error							3.23		3.66		3.59	
t-stat							3.28	***	2.37	**	2.04	*
VOA												
Std. error												
t-stat												
COC					41.65							
Std. error					9.32							
t-stat					4.47	***						
IIQ					−5.07							
Std. error					2.00							
t-stat					−2.53	**						
INC 88			0.26								0.23	
Std. error			0.09								0.09	
t-stat			2.87	**							2.59	**
EINV												
Std. error												
t-stat												
No. of obs.	18.00		18.00		18.00		18.00		18.00		18.00	
d.f.	16.00		15.00		15.00		16.00		15.00		15.00	
R-squared	0.18		0.37		0.67		0.30		0.33		0.45	
Adj R-squared	0.13		0.28		0.63		0.26		0.24		0.37	
F-statistic	8.46		10.92		26.07		10.76		9.89		18.87	
p-value of F	1.0E-02		1.2E-03		1.3E-05		4.7E-03		1.8E-03		8.0E-05	
AIC	7.57		7.42		6.75		7.41		7.48		7.29	
Schwartz	7.67		7.57		6.91		7.51		7.63		7.44	

Note: Standard errors and F-statistics are heteroscedasticity corrected; *** t-statistic leads to a rejection of the null hypothesis (coefficient=0) at the 1% level of significance; ** t-statistic leads to a rejection of the null hypothesis (coefficient=0) at the 5% level of significance; * t-

7		8		9		10		11		12		13	
−48.87		−4.17		−22.59		−25.07		42.64		38.34		37.27	
13.54		11.66		10.74		11.36		21.70		15.79		15.30	
−3.61	***	−0.36	NS	−2.10	*	−2.21	**	1.97	*	2.43	**	2.44	**
		105.50						−330.70					
		202.74						193.12					
		0.52	NS					−1.71	NS				
								−7.11		−5.66		−5.69	
								1.68		1.17		1.19	
								−4.24	***	−4.85	***	−4.80	***
7.72													
3.87													
1.99	*												
		31.36		26.37		27.17							
		9.77		8.69		9.15							
		3.21	***	3.04	***	2.97	**						
0.22				0.19		0.18		0.16		0.15		0.14	
0.09				0.07		0.08		0.04		0.04		0.05	
2.39	**			2.52	**	2.32	**	4.17	***	3.28	***	3.13	***
0.02						0.02						0.01	
0.02						0.02						0.01	
0.91	NS					1.16	NS					0.80	NS
18.00		18.00		18.00		18.00		18.00		18.00		18.00	
14.00		15.00		15.00		14.00		14.00		15.00		14.00	
0.45		0.47		0.56		0.57		0.66		0.68		0.63	
0.34		0.40		0.51		0.48		0.59		0.61		0.55	
13.39		12.46		22.11		25.03		37.40		19.97		32.80	
2.1E-04		6.5E-04		3.4E-05		6.9E-06		6.2E-05		2.5E-06		1.4E-06	
7.38		7.24		7.05		7.13		6.91		6.88		6.99	
7.58		7.40		7.20		7.34		7.11		7.04		7.19	

statistic leads to a rejection of the null hypothesis (coefficient=0) at the 10% level of significance; NS = not significant.

Table 10A.5   Correlation chart for 18 observations

	GRO(00)	GRO 95	DUM	INC 93	DPCF	IIQ	CIQ'93	CIQ'98	DH87–95
GRO(00/90)	1.00								
GRO(95/87)	0.92	1.00							
DUM	0.68	0.71	1.00						
INC 93	0.60	0.56	0.53	1.00					
DPCF	0.51	0.55	0.91	0.61	1.00				
IIQ	−0.35	−0.35	−0.63	−0.78	−0.71	1.00			
CIQ 88–93	−0.60	−0.49	−0.48	−0.20	−0.36	0.25	1.00		
CIQ 88–98	−0.43	−0.42	−0.27	−0.15	−0.16	0.25	0.42	1.00	
DH87–95	−0.77	−0.78	−0.73	−0.67	−0.62	0.66	0.62	0.41	1.00
VOA	0.54	0.58	0.91	0.60	0.95	−0.68	−0.31	−0.13	−0.62
PLS	0.64	0.50	0.76	0.59	0.73	−0.64	−0.48	−0.32	−0.69
ROL	0.68	0.65	0.92	0.64	0.89	−0.65	−0.50	−0.24	−0.73
COC	0.79	0.74	0.81	0.68	0.71	−0.62	−0.56	−0.40	−0.83
DIC	−0.70	−0.65	−0.91	−0.60	−0.87	0.68	0.55	0.31	0.84
LFE	0.67	0.78	0.84	0.60	0.75	−0.60	−0.52	−0.38	−0.81
LBW	0.25	0.23	0.07	0.08	0.17	0.05	−0.27	−0.39	0.04
MIR	−0.61	−0.60	−0.73	−0.79	−0.76	0.80	0.32	0.31	0.79
SFE	0.13	0.02	0.03	−0.02	−0.12	0.14	−0.07	0.01	−0.08
NIP	0.42	0.42	0.59	0.61	0.55	−0.66	−0.18	−0.09	−0.70
EINV	0.21	0.24	0.00	−0.13	−0.15	0.31	−0.32	0.16	−0.13
INC(88)	0.42	0.38	0.38	0.71	0.40	−0.48	−0.26	−0.18	−0.55
GRO*INC(88)	0.86	0.79	0.55	0.64	0.40	−0.29	−0.55	−0.37	−0.67

Table 10A.6   Correlation chart for 15 observations

	GRO(00)	GRO (95)	DUM	INC'93	DPCF	IIQ 88	CIQ'93	CIQ'98	DH–99
GRO(00/90)	1.00								
GRO(95/87)	0.92	1.00							
DUM	0.75	0.79	1.00						
INC 1993	0.60	0.58	0.42	1.00					
DPCF	0.66	0.71	0.94	0.48	1.00				
IIQ 88	−0.34	−0.39	−0.58	−0.70	−0.67	1.00			
CIQ 88–93	−0.63	−0.51	−0.67	−0.32	−0.74	0.44	1.00		
CIQ88–98	−0.43	−0.47	−0.42	−0.06	−0.36	0.16	0.46	1.00	
DH87–99	−0.77	−0.79	−0.84	−0.67	−0.85	0.67	0.60	0.50	1.00
VOA	0.67	0.73	0.92	0.46	0.90	−0.61	−0.64	−0.27	−0.80
PLS	0.84	0.71	0.81	0.55	0.78	−0.50	−0.76	−0.36	−0.71
ROL	0.75	0.72	0.90	0.56	0.86	−0.61	−0.73	−0.39	−0.82
COC	0.79	0.74	0.84	0.61	0.78	−0.57	−0.66	−0.39	−0.80
DIC	−0.74	−0.69	−0.89	−0.49	−0.89	0.61	0.73	0.38	0.80
LFE	0.67	0.78	0.85	0.58	0.84	−0.65	−0.60	−0.50	−0.83
LBW	0.23	0.21	−0.04	−0.01	0.03	0.19	−0.31	−0.47	−0.19
MIR	−0.60	−0.63	−0.74	−0.71	−0.78	0.74	0.48	0.24	0.85
SFE	0.40	0.26	0.22	0.30	0.15	−0.05	−0.11	−0.16	−0.42
NIP	0.38	0.40	0.58	0.55	0.57	−0.62	−0.23	0.01	−0.58
EINV	0.55	0.40	0.62	0.47	0.58	−0.46	−0.50	−0.08	−0.53
INC(88)	0.41	0.39	0.31	0.72	0.35	−0.44	−0.31	−0.19	−0.41
GRO*INC	0.86	0.79	0.60	0.70	0.52	−0.33	−0.57	−0.40	−0.65

VOA	PLS	ROL	COC	DIC	LFE	LBW	MIR	SFE	NIP	EINV	INC	G*INC
1.00												
0.73	1.00											
0.94	0.80	1.00										
0.79	0.79	0.92	1.00									
-0.89	-0.87	-0.94	-0.90	1.00								
0.80	0.62	0.86	0.85	-0.83	1.00							
0.00	0.01	-0.01	-0.09	0.05	-0.04	1.00						
-0.81	-0.67	-0.82	-0.86	0.85	-0.80	0.11	1.00					
-0.02	0.26	0.14	0.22	-0.12	0.03	-0.17	-0.01	1.00				
0.68	0.60	0.72	0.79	-0.76	0.71	-0.55	-0.88	0.22	1.00			
-0.11	-0.33	0.07	0.13	0.01	0.21	-0.18	0.05	0.07	0.06	1.00		
0.42	0.51	0.53	0.62	-0.48	0.58	-0.15	-0.56	0.22	0.57	0.08	1.00	
0.44	0.57	0.63	0.76	-0.56	0.67	0.14	-0.51	0.26	0.42	0.29	0.75	1.00

VOA	PLS	ROL	COC	DIC	LFE	LBW	MIR	SFE	NIP	EINV	INC	G*INC
1.00												
0.79	1.00											
0.94	0.91	1.00										
0.89	0.91	0.97	1.00									
-0.91	-0.94	-0.94	-0.91	1.00								
0.89	0.76	0.87	0.86	-0.84	1.00							
-0.22	-0.09	-0.15	-0.18	0.17	-0.12	1.00						
-0.85	-0.74	-0.85	-0.85	0.86	-0.86	0.27	1.00					
0.35	0.39	0.47	0.58	-0.38	0.25	-0.13	-0.48	1.00				
0.76	0.63	0.74	0.77	-0.75	0.72	-0.66	-0.89	0.51	1.00			
0.66	0.70	0.76	0.80	-0.66	0.56	-0.33	-0.61	0.61	0.66	1.00		
0.37	0.49	0.50	0.61	-0.43	0.58	-0.21	-0.56	0.37	0.55	0.64	1.00	
0.56	0.74	0.71	0.79	-0.60	0.68	0.13	-0.56	0.46	0.41	0.68	0.77	1.00

Table 10A.7   Data on Poverty, Inequality, Growth and EINV

Country	Inequality			Change in Inequality	
	1988 (other)	1993 (other)	1998 (other)	1988–1993	1988–1998
Belarus	22.8	28.4	21.7	0.0491	–0.0048
Bulgaria	23.3	34.3	26.4 1997	0.0944	0.0148
Czech Rep.	19.4	26.6	25.4 1996	0.0742	0.0387
Estonia	23	35.4 Jul–95	37.6	0.0770	0.0635
Hungary	21 1987	22.6	24.4	0.0127	0.0147
Kazakhstan	25.7	32.7	35.4 1996	0.0545	0.0472
Kyrgyz Rep.	26	55.3 Oct–93	34.6 1999	0.1878	0.0301
Latvia	22.5	31 1995	32.37	0.0540	0.0439
Lithuania	22.5	37.3 1994	32.4 1996	0.1096	0.0550
Moldova	24.1	36.5	40.6 1997	0.0858	0.0761
Poland	25.6 1987	28.4 Jun–93	31.6	0.0182	0.0213
Romania	23.3 1989	28.6 Mar–94	31.13	0.0455	0.0373
Russia	23.8	48 Jul–93	48.7	0.2034	0.1046
Slovakia	19.5	18.3	26.3	–0.0154	0.0317
Slovenia	21.5 1987	25.1	28.4	0.0279	0.0292
Turkmenistan	26.4	35.8	40.8	0.0712	0.0545
Ukraine	23.3	47.4 Jun–95	29 1999	0.1478	0.0222
Uzbekistan	28.2	33.3	44.65	0.0362	0.0583
Mean	23.44	33.61	32.86	0.07	0.04
st.dev	2.33	9.28	7.36	0.06	0.03

Source: 'Income, Inequality and Poverty during the Transition from Planned to Market Economy: Table 5.1, Table 5.2, Appendix 4', *EBRD Investments 1991–2002* (May 2003); EINV

| HC Poverty (%) | | | | | | |
| $4/day poverty in 1990 PPP | | | Mean inc. | EINV | GRO (%/annual) | |
1987–88	1993–95	1996–1999	1988(other)	1990–2001	2000/1990	1995/1987
1	22	N/A	71	16.19283	–0.01	–0.040
2	15	22	98.17	79.61157	–0.01	–0.011
0	0	0	130	87.49799	0.00	–0.009
1	37	18	81	304.45233	0.00	–0.042
1	4	0	94.92	129.95248	0.01	–0.015
5	65	62	61	52.45851	–0.03	–0.081
12	88	88	47	33.07856	–0.05	–0.067
1	22	28	78	127.71753	–0.03	–0.067
1	30	17	75	109.45926	–0.04	–0.042
4	66	82	61	41.88445	–0.10	–0.104
6	20	10	62	69.74935	0.04	0.019
6	59	23	25	99.30790	–0.02	–0.027
2	50	53	72	32.63260	–0.04	–0.056
0	0	8	130.17	177.77914	0.00	–0.021
0	0	0	400.67	295.83047	0.02	–0.005
12	61	N/A	47	35.53292	–0.06	–0.083
2	63	25				
			65	25.28940	–0.08	–0.088
24	63	N/A	28	942.80222	–0.02	–0.032
					–0.42	–0.771
4.44	36.94	29.07	91.88	155.06	–0.02333	–0.04283
6.13	27.94	28.84	84.83	219.95		

was computed as (EBRD finance 1000 EUR/population 1000) *Human Development Report 2002*; WDI 2002.

Table 10A.8 Non-income poverty (NIP) indicators

Country	Life expectancy at birth, total (years)	Low-birthweight babies (% of births)	Infant mortality rate, (per 1000 live births)	School enrolment, secondary, female (% gross)	NIP
Belarus	68.11	5.50	11.30	86.02	**13.52**
Bulgaria	71.55	7.20	13.33	85.91	**−12.91**
Czech Republic	74.82	5.50	4.10	84.00	**55.67**
Estonia	70.60	4.00	8.40	106.07	**63.38**
Hungary	71.25	7.90	9.20	98.65	**9.83**
Kazakhstan	65.47	9.00	21.13	86.51	**−79.11**
Kyrgyz Republic	67.30	4.90	23.07	87.56	**−39.75**
Latvia	70.38	4.00	9.90	86.24	**40.22**
Lithuania	72.62	4.40	8.60	90.31	**47.73**
Moldova	67.76	4.80	18.40	81.89	**−18.52**
Poland	73.28	8.20	8.60	96.11	**9.59**
Romania	69.86	9.60	18.70	80.56	**−73.62**
Russia	65.34	5.30	16.20	88.77	**−10.04**
Slovakia	73.05	6.40	8.30	86.49	**24.00**
Slovenia	75.26	5.40	4.57	100.13	**67.24**
Turkmenistan	66.34	5.20	27.27	111.70	**−47.16**
Ukraine	68.29	8.00	12.80	96.16	**−14.67**
Uzbekistan	69.74	5.50	21.53	88.66	**−35.41**
Average	70.06	6.16	13.63	91.21	**0.00**
Weight equalizer	1.00	11.38	5.14	0.77	

Table 10A.9 Institutional capital indicators (DIC)

	Voice and accountability	Political stability	Rule of law	Control of corruption	DIC
Belarus	-1.04	0.04	-0.81	-0.06	12.00
Bulgaria	0.59	0.37	0.02	-0.16	6.00
Czech Republic	1.04	0.74	0.64	0.31	4.00
Estonia	1.19	0.75	0.76	0.65	4.00
Hungary	0.94	0.73	0.78	0.73	4.00
Kazakhstan	-0.80	0.29	-0.60	-0.83	12.00
Kyrgyz Republic	-0.57	-0.32	-0.72	-0.85	16.00
Latvia	0.81	0.50	0.36	-0.03	4.00
Lithuania	1.00	0.29	0.29	0.20	6.00
Moldova	0.12	-0.29	-0.42	-0.83	13.00
Poland	1.21	0.69	0.55	0.43	4.00
Romania	0.50	-0.08	-0.02	-0.51	12.00
Russia	-0.35	-0.41	-0.87	-1.01	15.00
Slovakia	0.99	0.62	0.36	0.23	4.00
Slovenia	1.07	0.87	0.89	1.09	4.00
Turkmenistan	-1.42	0.11	-1.02	-1.12	15.00
Ukraine	-0.31	-0.59	-0.63	-0.90	14.00
Uzbekistan	-1.18	-1.17	-0.71	-0.66	15.00
Min.	-1.42	-1.17	-1.02	-1.12	
1st quartile	-0.51115163	-0.233354435	-0.691334588	-0.829879012	
Median	0.55	0.29	0.00	-0.11	
3rd quartile	0.998913072	0.671618807	0.503610379	0.285766279	
Max.	1.21	0.87	0.89	1.09	

Note: DIC reflects the sum of ordinal ranks assigned to each country based on which quartile it belongs to.

Source: World Bank, Governance Matters II: Updated Indicators for 2000–2001.

11. Privatization and poverty: the case of Russia

Alois Wenig

INTRODUCTION

The classical Soviet-type command economy was in a severe crisis in the whole eastern hemisphere by the mid-1980s. The communist leaders had again and again promised to catch up with the standard of living in Western countries, but, instead of the economic gap between the East and the West being closed, the differences became increasingly large. The people in the communist countries had lost all hope that their economies would ever overcome the notorious shortages of consumption goods, the inefficiencies of the public administration, the omnipresent corruption and the lack of political and economic freedom. In the Soviet Union and its satellite states even the members of the communist parties agreed that drastic changes, in particular economic reforms, were inevitable if they were to avoid a total collapse of their societies.

Earlier endeavours to restructure the centrally planned economies in the East had failed. In Czechoslovakia, for example, a military invasion led by the Soviet Union in 1968 abruptly ended the attempt to implement market elements in a system of strict central planning and to try a more democratic political life instead of the strict dictatorship of the communist leaders. Only Hungary and Yugoslavia had managed to combine market elements with their otherwise also state-run economies. However, when Mikhail Gorbachev came into office as president of the Soviet Union, the situation changed. He proclaimed a political thaw and an economic reconstruction (glasnost and perestroika), a programme which finally led to a breakdown of the Soviet Union. In 1989, the country split up in its main part – Russia – and a collection of more or less independent neighbouring states.

The political changes which then took place in Russia are well known. The country became a presidential democracy and made a dramatic shift from central planning to a market economy with private ownership of capital. This process began in 1992 and was completed by the end of 1994. This chapter describes the process of economic reconstruction in Russia and analyses its social consequences.

MASS PRIVATIZATION IN THE RUSSIAN FEDERATION FROM 1992 TO 1994

In June 1992, the Russian parliament passed a law according to which a vast majority of Russian firms were put up for privatization. A state committee (SKS) was established to organize and monitor the transformation. The law offered three options. Two-thirds of the employees' votes of a firm were necessary to select one of the three alternatives. If none of the options was able to reach this qualified majority then option one applied.

Option 1

In this scheme 25 per cent of the shares of a company were given to its employees free of charge. Another 10 per cent were sold to the employees of the company with a discount of 30 per cent below face value. The payment for these shares could be stretched over a period of three years. The management received 5 per cent of the shares as a free gift; 29 per cent of the shares were sold in public auctions to which everyone was admitted as a bidder; and 31 per cent remained in the hands of the state to be sold later to strategic investors.

Every employee also received a certain number of 'vouchers'. Instead of cash these vouchers could be used as a means of payment either in share auctions (of whatever company) or in direct share sales. The vouchers themselves were transferable and could thus be traded against cash.

Option 2

This option clearly preferred ownership control by the employees of a company, who could buy 51 per cent of the shares of 'their' firm at a discount of 30 per cent below face value. Half of these shares could be paid for with vouchers, the other half had to be paid for in cash within a period of three months; 29 per cent of the shares were offered in public auctions, while the state reserved a stake of 20 per cent for financial or strategic investors or, alternatively, for future auctions.

Option 3

In this option a group of employees of the firm (including the management) could make an offer for a stake of 20 per cent of the shares to be sold at face value. The buyers of these shares had the obligation to invest another 200 minimum wages per person, thus increasing both the liquidity position of the firm and the number of their shares. The buyers who took up the obligation to invest additional funds were granted the privilege of reorganizing and managing the firm. As in option 2, all employees could, in addition, buy another 20 per cent of the shares at a price 30 per cent below face value and a fraction of 29 per cent was sold in public auctions. Finally, the state kept 31 per cent of the shares, to be brought to the market in the near future.

For small firms with fewer than 200 employees or a capital stock of not more than one million rubles in face value (on 1 January 1992) a simplified scheme applied. All shares were sold in public auctions against vouchers or cash. In the case of large firms in which the employees had the choice between the three options described above the decision of the workers had to be made by 1 October 1992. In many cases no qualified majority for options 2 or 3 could be reached, so that the bulk of the large firms was privatized in the form of option 1.

The common basic idea behind these different schemes of privatization is obvious: the Russian parliament wanted the economy to be turned over to the workers, a principle very much in line with the old communist claim that the workers should exercise control over the means of production. An arrangement similar to what Russia wanted to achieve with the privatization of its economy had been realized in Yugoslavia under Tito where the workers owned – at least nominally – their own companies. In Russia, however, the workers should become the 'real' owners of the firms' assets with all the property rights of a 'capitalist'.

Parallel to the privatization process price controls were lifted. The firms were free to make their own decisions on the quantities and qualities of their products, on their investments and on exports and imports. In other words, Russia became a market economy. By the end of 1994, most firms were privatized, and the transition from central planning to decentralized market coordination was completed.

For political reasons the speed of the transition was considered critical in Russia at the beginning of the 1990s because it was feared that slow reforms would soon be blocked by conservative forces. Most Western advisors, too, favoured 'shock therapy' because they considered a rapid transition under all circumstances superior to a long and painful preservation of the old and rotten institutional framework. Opposition came only from members of the discredited Communist Party who were caught in their traditional Marxist and Leninist views of the right way to happiness.

THE STRUCTURE OF OWNERSHIP DURING AND AFTER THE PROCESS OF PRIVATIZATION

Immediately after the beginning of mass privatization in Russia the managers kept only a relatively small portion of the shares of their companies. In most cases their stake was not more than the 5 per cent of the shares which option 1 reserved for the business leaders. By the end of the decade, however, the assets of the Russian economy, in particular those of large corporations, were highly concentrated in the hands of a relatively small number of individuals, now known as Russia's 'oligarchs'. No official statistics exist on the distribution of ownership in Russia today, but putting the casual evidence together (scattered over many different sources, such as Russian and international newspapers, business magazines, TV and radio reports, official documents of the Russian parliament and publications of banks) gives the impression that modern Russia is a country in which at least the key assets are controlled by a small number of people. In an article published in the *Stanford Law Review* in 2000, Black, Kraakman and Tarassova list the leading business tycoons at the end of the previous decade.[1] The results of their findings are shown in Table 11.1.

In the original table more details about the tycoons and their holdings are listed. This is of course only a small part of the whole spectrum of influential businessmen holding important companies in Russia. It is interesting to note that many of them are tied to media companies which they also use as instruments of propaganda for their own purposes, a phenomenon which is also not unknown in Western countries.

In their article, Black et al. argue that most of the property amassed by the individuals listed in Table 11.1 is the result of illicit activities. No evidence, however, is given in the whole paper that – except maybe for individual cases – the acquisition of the assets occurred in an illegal way, given the institutional and legal conditions which applied in Russia during the process of privatization. The authors take the Western law of corporate governance as the yardstick for their judgment, thus confusing moral and legal considerations. From a moral point of view the actions taken by the Russian tycoons during the process of mass privatization may in general be questionable. Owing to the absence of an appropriate regulatory framework the Russian tycoons and many other people who became rich in this period of transition cannot, in general, be accused of having systematically committed crimes or minor offences. What happened in the years after 1992 is comparable to what is likely to happen at all times of revolution: there are people who are clever enough to take advantage of the legal vacuum that exists in between the old and the new regimes.

*Table 11.1	Important holdings of business tycoons in Russia at the end of the 1990s*

Person	Principal Companies	Ties to Media Outlets
Vagit Alekperov	Lukoil	Izvestia newspaper
Boris Beresovsky	Sibneft, Aeroflot, Avtovazbank Obyedinenni Bank	ORT, TV-6, NSN-radio Several newspapers and magazines
Viktor Chernomyrdin	Gasprom	
Mikhail Fridman	Alfa Group holding, Alfa Bank Tyumen Oil, Alfa Cement Various real estate companies Construction companies	Alpha TV, ORT-TV (with Berezovsky)
Vladimir Gusinski	Media Most holdings Most Bank	*Novaya gazeta*, other newspapers and magazines, NTV, TNT television
Mikhail Khodorkovsky	Rosprom holdings, Yukos Oil, various manufacturing and retail companies, copper and chemical industries, timber companies	*Moscow Times* *St Petersburg Times* *Literaturnaya Gazeta* Other newspapers

THE CAUSES OF THE UNEQUAL DISTRIBUTION OF WEALTH IN RUSSIA

There are many reasons why a relatively small number of people now own most of the Russian business assets. First, Russian managers were not poor to begin with. As early as 1989, still in the era of Gorbachev, the Russian government had lifted the restrictions on foreign currency operations. Firms were then free to conduct their foreign trade as long as they could pay for their imports with the proceeds they received in foreign currency from their exports. Under this regime the managers of Russian corporations started their own personal subsidiaries abroad, which were then used to carry out the foreign trade of their firms in Russia. Preferred locations of these 'branches' were the island of Cyprus or the state of Delaware in the United States. Of course, this arrangement was a gateway to self dealing. The firm abroad received the goods for export at a low price from the Russian firm and resold it at world market prices. In the case of imports the Russian firm was charged a price above the world market price at which the foreign company had purchased the commodity. Russian managers who had access to the world markets could in this way earn substantial profits. At the beginning of the privatization process many managers of firms in Russia were therefore not penniless. For obvious reasons they had also quite an incentive to keep control of their company. For both their internal benefits as managers and for the profits they could reap with foreign trade operations it was essential to remain in power.

On the other hand, the interest of Russian workers in the shares or vouchers they received in the course of mass privatization was very limited. The dollar value of the vouchers on the free market may in 1992 have been the equivalent of the price of a bicycle. Were the shares one could buy for the vouchers worth a bicycle? Most workers had not the slightest idea what the fair price of a share could be, let alone how to handle the tricky task of buying and selling the shares later on the stock market. The general tendency of the workers was to get rid of the vouchers and the shares as soon as possible, and to use the proceeds from this sale to purchase consumption goods. The enormous supply of vouchers and shares in the initial phase of the transition process led to a sharp decline in their prices. They were traded much below the actual value they represented. Furthermore, since the market for vouchers and stocks was underdeveloped in Russia in the early 1990s insider trading – then not illegal – allowed an unpredictable price manipulation of the listed shares. For the bulk of the shares which were not yet listed, and for the vouchers, the firms opened an internal market on which these papers could be traded. Normally the only buyers in these markets were the managers of the firm, while the employees sold at any price. For relatively small dollar amounts the managers could in this way substantially increase their stakes in the corporations. The shares of corporations whose market value today is 30 or 40 dollars could in the early 1990s be purchased for a few cents.

Although many employees sold their vouchers and shares very early, the remaining stake of the employees in their firm could still be large enough to play an important role in shareholder meetings. To avoid opposition from the workers in these meetings the management offered the employees the administration of their shares in investment funds which were then under the control of the management. Together with their own shares the managers could in this way often exercise complete control of the company.

Another source for increasing the stake in a firm were the shares which were still in the hands of the state. In the period of transition the financial situation of public households in Russia was fragile. Tax rates for both individuals and firms were low, but even under these conditions taxpayers were reluctant to meet their obligations. Not to pay taxes was a national sport, and the Russian internal revenue service was notoriously understaffed and not very efficient. In order to limit the rapid increase of national debt the state tried to raise funds by selling shares. Managers of Russian firms well connected to the ministries were the 'natural' buyers of the shares of 'their' company. Given the situation at that time, the prices of the new shares could not be high, and it is also not unlikely that in this case corruption helped to make deals that were mutually beneficial to public administrators and managers.

The law of corporate governance is underdeveloped in Russia. This is true today and was even more so in the early 1990s. Self dealing of managers was not an offence and thus widespread. Nothing is better suited for looting a company than the ability of the managers of a firm to cast deals with their own company. The practice of asset stripping by means of foreign trade through a personally owned company abroad has already been described. But there are numerous other methods of achieving this goal. The managers can, for example, split a corporation up into several parts. Continuous trading of the new companies among each other allows a reallocation of the assets in such a way that one company bleeds to death. In bankruptcy proceedings this company can then be purchased for a symbolic dollar. In the next step another part of the conglomerate can be driven out of business, in this way being earmarked for a takeover by the management. This continues until the whole conglomerate is owned by the managers.

Morally even more questionable is a strategy which forces the employees of a company to sell off the assets they own. After privatization quite a number of Russian firms stopped paying wages to their workers, so that the employees had to finance their consumption by realizing their reserves. Since the signal from their firm was rather discouraging, they preferred to sell the shares they owned, so putting downward pressure on the prices. Again the managers were the only buyers of the shares, which they obtained at a large discount.

In the cases described so far, the managers or the persons with whom they were financially connected paid with their own funds for the increase in the stakes of their firms. Credit inside Russia was in short supply in the years from 1992 to 1994, so that cash – preferably in US dollars – was essential to these transactions. Some businessmen in Russia, however, did manage to finance their empire of corporations on the basis of loaned money. The prominent tycoon Vladimir Gusinski, for example, centred his Most Holdings conglomerate around his major creditor, Most Bank, a financial institution which paid a rate of interest for deposits much above market rates. The deposits were used to finance the numerous acquisitions of firms in the Most Holdings empire.

Gusinki's empire building failed. The bank went broke because Most Holdings could not meet its obligations vis-à-vis Most Bank from the steadily increasing loan portfolio. The holding company was not profitable enough to earn more than an average interest rate. After the collapse of his bank, Gusinski left Russia in order to avoid an indictment for fraud and for the violation of banking rules. Today many people consider him a crook, but the facts also allow for another interpretation. He may have started honest, played with debt and finally lost. One would expect stories like this to crop up at times of revolutionary change.

Other tycoons who built big conglomerates on the basis of loaned money were luckier than Gusinski. The most successful businessman in Russia is probably oil magnate Mikhail Khodorkovsky. He put his Yukos Oil conglomerate together with money borrowed from abroad. In 1997, he used his already substantial stake in Yukos as collateral for a loan to buy the majority of the shares. Although the productivity of the oil company was (and still is) much below the level of Western oil producers Yukos was profitable enough to serve the loans until 1998. In that year of financial turmoil in Russia, Khodorkovsky, too, was in stormy waters and he had to surrender 30 per cent of his stake in his oil company to Western lenders. But in April 2003, Yukos was again strong enough to unveil a deal in which the company acquired its competitor Sibneft for 13 billion dollars, a transaction which created the world's sixth-largest publicly traded oil and gas producer. The new company will be the first Russian heavyweight in the international energy arena.[2] In Khodorkovsky's case, the sky-rocketing oil prices helped overcome all financial troubles in the end. However, on his way to becoming a global player, he also stripped cash from subsidiaries of Yukos to make the parent company strong enough to survive. An investigation by the Russian Securities Commission into these transactions, however, went nowhere. The deals were probably not 'illegal enough' and they were likely to have political support from the top because the Russian government could not countenance the collapse of this important oil producer.

Certainly, by Western standards of both ethical business conduct and corporate law, many of today's Russian business leaders are shady characters. Given the landslide changes in the institutional framework of the Russian economy in the past decade, however, no one who wanted to enjoy success in business life could be strictly law-abiding. This was impossible because the laws were permanently changing and often contradicting each other. And it was also impossible to live up to Western standards because the communist legacy of corruption and favouritism could not be abolished overnight. The mere introduction of private ownership of capital together with the coordination of individual activities by markets could not be expected to quickly change the moral basis of the whole society.

Individuals who were clever and lucky and those who were willing to take enormous risks could become rich or even very rich in the process of privatization. Others who did not seize or realize the economic opportunities in the years after 1992 remained poor. And there are very unfortunate individuals who were in the end definitely much worse off compared to the times of communism. As a result, mass privatization created a very uneven distribution of wealth in Russian society.

MACROECONOMIC CONSEQUENCES OF PRIVATIZATION

The supporters of the shock therapy approach have argued that every outcome in the distribution of wealth was superior to the alternative of no privatization at all. In the long run (this has been the hope of economists) there will be forces to even out the differences.[3] On the other hand, it has to be admitted that, in the process of mass privatization, not only had the idea of turning the productive assets of Russia over to the hands of the labourers failed, but at the beginning of privatization the standard of living of the Russian population dropped substantially. The lower strata of Russian society were driven into poverty. For every visitor to Russia this became obvious after a few days in the country. But the poverty also shows up in the statistics published by Goskomstat, the Russian statistical office, and by other sources such as the International Labour Office (ILO).

In Table 11.2 we show major macroeconomic indicators which describe the development of the Russian economy in the decade after the beginning of privatization in 1992. The figures make it clear how desolate the economic situation in Russia became in the time following the first steps of the privatization programme. With the exception of the year 1997, in which GDP rose slightly, Russia had negative growth rates between –3.4 per cent in 1996 and –12.7 per cent in 1994. Industrial production even shrank by 20.9 per cent in 1994, and on average by around 10 per cent in the years after 1992. Correspondingly unemployment rose from relatively low levels to 13.3 per cent in 1998 and then dropped again by a few points from period to period. By Russian pre-privatization standards, unemployment in the country is still high today. And, given the little unemployment compensation from which

Table 11.2 Growth rates of major macroeconomic indicators for the Russian economy, 1993–2001

Indicator	1993	1994	1995	1996	1997	1998	1999	2000	2001
GDP	-8.7	-12.7	-4.1	-3.4	0.9	-4.9	5.4	9.0	5.0
Industrial production	-14.1	-20.9	-3.3	-4.0	1.9	-5.2	8.1	11.9	4.9
Agricultural production	-4.4	-12.0	-8.0	-5.1	1.5	-13.2	4.1	7.7	6.8
Gross investment	-11.6	-24.0	-10.0	-18.0	-5.0	-12.0	5.3	17.4	8.7
Retail sales (in real terms)	1.1	-0.2	-7.0	-0.4	3.6	-3.4	-7.7	8.7	9.1
Nominal wages	906	278	120	48	20	11	45	46	47
Consumer prices	874	308	198	48	15	28	86	21	17
Rate of unemployment	6.0	7.7	9.0	9.9	9.9	13.3	12.2	9.8	8.9

Source: Gomkostat (2002a, 2002b).

273

people must make a living, even a low unemployment rate causes a severe social problem. In addition, soaring rates of inflation (almost 1000 per cent in 1993) had wiped out the real value of savings, so that Russians also had no recourse to the (small) reserves they had accumulated before 1992.

The data for the first half of 2002 are similar to those of 2001. For 2003, only preliminary data exist. They indicate that the Russian economy experienced a substantial recovery after 2002. Gross domestic product, industrial production, agricultural production and gross investment are given in real terms. The rate of unemployment is the ratio of unemployed persons to the whole labour force (not the growth rate of unemployment, as Table 11.2 might suggest). The rate of inflation (growth rate of consumer prices) is measured by the Russian consumer price index (CPI).

Since the initial standard of living was not high before privatization, the dramatic decline in production and real income drove large segments of Russian society into poverty. It is a miracle that, under such conditions, social stability did not collapse completely, although crime rates in large cities rose and corruption (already high under communism) became omnipresent. The hopes for a higher standard of living which most Russians had in the early 1990s turned into pessimism. The proverbial Russian fatalism that characterized the communist era again dampened the general mood and paralysed the economic potential of the country. Fortunately, today, the mood has again changed, this time for the better.

THE CAUSES OF THE DECLINE IN PRODUCTIVITY AND THE EARLY FAILURES OF THE MARKET SYSTEM

The time immediately after the beginning of mass privatization in 1992 had been a period of vehement and merciless struggle for property rights. The Russian parliament had wanted business leaders to become the agents of the workers by giving the labour force the role of shareholders. For almost a century the management had been the labourers' principals. The 'philosophy' behind the new doctrine was that the people should be the real rulers of the country. But the Russian principals – managers and party leaders alike – did not want to give up their privileged positions. In the end they have managed to stay in power while the labour force is back in the position of the management's agents. The party leaders survived in the bureaucracy, and the managers are in their old positions, now really owning the assets which they previously administered 'on behalf of the people'.

For the average Russian the question of ownership of business assets had always been of minor importance. He knew instinctively that a small minority stake in a company does not provide much influence on the firm's business activities anyway. For the average Russian the key question in the process of privatization was its impact on the standard of living. After it became clear that, in this respect, no improvement could be expected in the near future, the whole process of privatization became very unpopular. On the other hand, only a few communist hardliners wanted to return to the old institutional regime, so that the society seemed to be stuck in a deadlock.

Why did the new (and old) masters of the Russian economic universe not roll up their shirt-sleeves and give their companies a big kick forward, thus pushing the Russian economy out of the recession? One might expect that increasing the value of his business assets would always be the optimal strategy for a manager who owns a big part of the firm he leads. That this did not happen on a large scale immediately after privatization was completed in 1994 has had several causes.

First, we have already pointed out that increasing a firm's productivity may not be in the interests of the management as long as it does not yet control a majority stake. Running a firm down may be a superior strategy if one can buy it cheaply in bankruptcy proceedings. Taking over a flourishing company may in many cases have even been out of the reach of the managers because they could not get enough credit for a management buyout. Since the struggle for majority stakes in the Russian firms continued long after 1994, the strategy of sabotaging all steps to improve productivity hampered the development of Russia until very recently.

In the public opinion, it has sometimes been argued that incompetence of managers had been another main reason for the decline of the Russian economy. Although this may apply in a few cases, it is certainly not true for the business elite in general. On the contrary, most Russian managers played the game well – to their own advantage.

Another factor responsible for the low productivity of the Russian economy and for the decline in total production after privatization is the market structure inherited from the old regime. This is hardly mentioned in the literature, although the lack of competition and the attempt of many firms to preserve their monopolies led to the kind of inefficient managerial behaviour described in the antitrust literature. Under central planning the whole industrial sector was split up into branches, each under the control of a planning agency (normally a ministry). This agency decided on the spectrum of products, the quantities, the technology applied, the volume of investments and on all other important aspects of the economic activity of the sector. The fact that all industries were in this way organized as monopolies was, under central planning, seen as an advantage since the whole branch could be organized along the lines of an optimal division of labour. Under market conditions, of course, the monopolies would behave differently. They would reduce output, increase prices and boost X-inefficiency, together with the cost of production.

Only competition can keep these developments in check, but implementing competitive market structures is time consuming and requires an antitrust policy, which is still in its early stages.

The most important reason for the decline in Russian GDP and in the productivity of its economy is a political one. No one in Russia could, after 1992, take it for granted that the property rights he or she had acquired were guaranteed in the future. Uncertainty about the institutional development induced cautious managers to loot their firms and put their assets aside somewhere abroad. To many businessmen, investing in Russia meant exposure of their wealth to the enormous risk of a total loss, either by actions taken by the government or by the volatility of the markets in the years after privatization. Potential investors, therefore, preferred to store their assets in safe havens and to wait until the smoke of the revolutionary guns had dispersed.

CONCLUSIONS

In the aftermath of privatization in Russia the population did not earn the dividend it had desperately hoped for. The standard of living of most Russians dropped. Many were pushed down into severe poverty. The shock of the dramatic institutional change led to a dramatic decline in productivity, to high rates of inflation, to a sharp drop in GDP and national income per person, and to a flight of Russian capital to safe tax havens. But the managerial elite of Russia (most of them former high-ranking members of the Communist Party) survived the economic and social changes. Former business leaders are now the owners of the company they had led in the years before privatization. Some control vast empires. Compared to other industrial nations, inequality in the distribution of both income and wealth is probably as great as nowhere else. In a few years some Russians have managed to get themselves onto the list of the 50 wealthiest people in the world.

Was privatization a failure, given these results? The old regime could not survive. This can be taken for granted because the dissatisfaction with life under socialism had grown to a level which cried out for substantial changes. The majority of Russians believed that the communist system was unable to give them an economic perspective. Even the members of the Communist Party asked for reforms which pointed in the direction of decentralization and privatization. No one was able to predict that this change meant purgatory for a whole decade.

Could and should the changes have been more cautious? Would a piecemeal engineering approach to the institutional reconstruction have been more promising because it would have avoided the enormous costs of adjustment? It is, indeed, true that the U-turn in Russian society has brought about uncertainty and poverty for many. On the other hand, the recent big increases in Russian GDP, the visible changes to a higher standard of living in the past two years, and the return of Russian capital into the country, now beginning, show that the institutional revolution towards a market economy is beginning to bear fruit. Small changes for a long period of time had implied the risk of total failure of the transition process because they would have been accompanied by a permanent political struggle over the 'right' direction to take. Only the shock therapy made it clear to everybody in Russia that there was no way back, so that people must look into the future rather than remaining stuck in half-hearted reforms.

NOTES

1. Black et al. (2000:1748–9). In their table the authors use the expression 'kleptocrat' rather than 'business tycoon'. We prefer 'tycoon' because the word 'kleptocrat' is associated with a negative connotation which we consider an inappropriate value judgment in the context of our analysis. Russians, however, do tend to use the name 'kleptocrat' for their nouveau rich business elite.
2. See *The Wall Street Journal Europe*, Friday/Saturday/Sunday, 16–18 May 2003, **XXI**(73), 1.
3. See, for example, the paper by Joseph E. Stiglitz: 'Distribution of wealth among individuals', *Econometrica*, **37**(3), July 1969, 382–97.

BIBLIOGRAPHY

Black, Bernard, Reinier Kraakman and Anna Tarassova (2000), 'Russian privatization and corporate governance: what went wrong?', *Standford Law Review*, **52**, 1731–1808.
Brüggemann, M. (2003), 'Kreml greift hart gegen Oligarchen durch', *Handelsblatt*, 22 July, **138**, 5.
The Economist (1999), 'The great pretenders', 21 August, p. 61.
Gomkostat (2002a), *Social'no-economiceskoe polozenie Rossii. 2001 goda*, Moscow.
Gomkostat (2002b), *Social'no economiceskoe polozenenie Rossii. Janvar–mart 2002 goda*, Moscow.
Koslov, Michail (2000), 'Wirtschaftstransformation und Reform des Finanzsektors in der russischen Föderation', unpublished disseration, Halle.
Muraviev, A. and L. Savulkin (1998), 'Korporativnoe upravlenie mi ego vlijanie no povedenie predprijatij', *Voprosy Ekonomiki*, **7**, 110–19.
Nickell, S.J. (1996), 'Competition and corporate performance', *Journal of Political Economy*, **104**(4), 724–46.
Stiglitz, J.E. (1969), 'Distribution of wealth among individuals', *Econometrica*, **37**(3), 382–97.
The Wall Street Journal Europe (2003), Friday/ Saturday/Sunday, 16–18 May, **XXI**(73), p. 1.

12. The 1997/98 economic crisis in Southeast Asia: policy responses and the role of the IMF

Teofilo C. Daquila

INTRODUCTION

What began as a currency crisis in Thailand resulted in a banking crisis and eventually generated a contagion effect to neighbouring countries including Indonesia, Malaysia, the Philippines and Singapore.[1] However it was not contagion from Thailand that made the countries vulnerable to a financial crisis but the home-grown economic problems, which included a growing current account deficit, excessive short-term foreign borrowings, a banking sector weighed down by speculative property loans and corrupt government and business practices.[2] The disturbances, however, were not limited to the Southeast Asian region, but some economies in the Asian region also felt the pinch, including South Korea, Hong Kong, Taiwan and Japan. Wade (1998) and Adelman and Yeldan (2000) also spoke about the global impact of the crisis.

This chapter discusses the economic policies which were immediately adopted by the respective governments of Thailand, Indonesia, Malaysia, Singapore and the Philippines. These include international financial assistance, demand-management policies (fiscal, monetary and exchange rate policies), supply-side policies, capital controls and financial restructuring. We also examine the role of the international financial institutions in the crisis, particularly the IMF.

INTERNATIONAL FINANCIAL ASSISTANCE

Thailand and Indonesia had availed themselves of the international financial assistance organized by the IMF and the World Bank. In August 1997, the Thai government accepted an international financial package which consisted of a medium-term loan of US$17.2 billion with contributions from other countries to shore up Thai's foreign exchange reserves.[3] It also obtained

US$1billion trade assistance from the Asian Development Bank (ADB) to help Thai exporters. This came in the form of an ADB-guaranteed export-financing facility involving nine or ten commercial banks from the USA, Japan and the EU.

On 8 October 1997, Indonesia sought IMF assistance and, on 5 November 1997, the IMF announced a US$43 billion financial package for Indonesia. This package consisted of a combined loan of US$18billion from the IMF, the World Bank and the ADB, US$20 billion from bilateral donor countries and US$5 billion from Indonesia's own reserves.[4] The bilateral donor countries include Singapore, Malaysia, Japan and Australia, which had offered an additional US$11 billion financial rescue package to Jakarta since these countries trade heavily with Indonesia and have long-term investments that they understandably want protected.[5]

Malaysia succumbed to the crisis with only a little foreign debt exposure and this had enabled the country to muddle through without an IMF-sponsored rescue package.[6] Moreover Prime Minister Mahathir did not want to follow a 'high-interest rate and reduced-spending' strategy imposed by the IMF. While high interest rates would lead to exchange rate stability in the short run, they would certainly be detrimental to banking and industries in the medium to long run. Certainly the Malaysian government had shown a stronger preference for a 'low interest rate and increased spending policy' as it could generate a less severe impact on the larger proportion of its population.

The Philippines, which was supposed to exit from over three decades of economic stewardship by the IMF, was given an extension to do so provided that the government passed a new oil deregulation law and boosted government revenues. It entered into a precautionary arrangement which had less stringent conditions than the full-fledged standby arrangement that Indonesia and Thailand entered into with the IMF.[7] The IMF agreed to extend a US$1.3 billion aid package to the Philippines and effectively put an end to the planned graduation from the IMF programme in the meantime.[8] Singapore has been blessed with a healthy financial position, so that it did not need to resort to IMF funding. Singapore is in a position to lend a helping hand instead, as illustrated by its assistance to Indonesia, Thailand and Malaysia.

DEMAND-MANAGEMENT POLICIES

Fiscal and Monetary Policies

During the early phase of the crisis, Thailand and then Indonesia, after some time, followed some expenditure-reducing policies through restrictive fiscal and monetary policies, following the IMF's prescribed policies. The Thai and

Indonesian governments undertook austerity measures and reduced the expansion of domestic credit. Singapore, Malaysia and the Philippines also adopted IMF-like austerity measures in some areas, particularly on current government operations. Singapore, however, has continued to increase its expenditure on areas which would increase its productivity, including investments on infrastructure and education.

The problem with the IMF's restrictive measures is that, given an economic slowdown, any further tight fiscal and/or monetary policies will certainly aggravate the recessionary conditions faced by Southeast Asian economies. In the case of Singapore, it had remained committed to implementing infrastructure development projects to counteract the slowing down of its economy. In Malaysia, monetary policy had become expansionist, with a massive injection of domestic liquidity which resulted in lower interest rates. Benchmark interest rates fell from 11 per cent to 8 per cent on 7 September 1998. Moreover statutory reserve requirements were reduced from 14.5 per cent in March 1989 to 4 per cent in September 1998.

Exchange Rate Policies

It was argued that the hedge funds had contributed significantly to the massive exchange rate changes as they specialize in high-risk financial instruments which involve currency and stock movements. During the 1992–7 period, the number of hedge funds expanded more than three times, to around 1500 funds. These hedge funds had managed assets of more than US$200 billion, including the large investments of some giant international banks.[9] However some of these banks incurred huge losses from these investments in hedge funds. For example, Citigroup's Salomon Smith Barney unit lost US$1.33 billion in trading during the third quarter of 1998. Another example is the UBS Warburg Dillon Read unit which lost money in 1998, and the near collapse of the hedge fund LTCM cost the bank 790 million francs. Bank America lost about US$573 million on loans to D.E. Shaw & Co., a hedge fund and securities firm.

As the baht, rupiah, ringgit, peso and Singapore dollar faced mounting attacks during the initial phase of the crisis, the respective central banks in Southeast Asia defended their currencies by intervening in the foreign exchange market; that is, selling US dollars in exchange for domestic currencies. The Bank of Thailand (BOT), indeed, had wasted a large proportion of its foreign exchange reserves in order to defend the baht, but to no avail. In an interview during the World Economic Forum at Davos in 1999, Senior Minister Lee Kuan Yew noted that the Thai mistake was not that they did not know that hedge funds were attacking their currency, but that they tried to defend it, with the result that their reserves were depleted by US$23 billion.[10] This was indeed a very costly mistake which was made more serious by the BOT's (through the Financial Institutional Development Fund) extension of financial support to the beleaguered financial institutions in the amount of 1.1 trillion bath (US$29 billion). In the case of South Korea, its former central bank governor admitted that the Bank of Korea wasted up to US$26 billion between late 1996 and February 1997 in a futile attempt to defend the won.[11] In the case of the Philippines, when speculation against the peso became heavy in July 1997, the authorities used almost one billion US dollars of reserves within a few days, without any positive results.[12] In the case of Malaysia, Bank Negara Malaysia sold close to US$1.5 billion to prop up the ringgit when it came under heavy speculative attack in mid-May 1997.[13]

Faced with tremendous attacks on their currencies, and given the limited amount of international reserves, the first reform introduced by Thailand and Indonesia was the adoption of a flexible exchange rate system. The Thai baht and the Indonesian rupiah were floated on 2 July 1997 and 13 August 1997, respectively. The Thai bath/US$ rate moved immediately from 25 to 30 and rose drastically to 55 by January 1998.[14] It subsequently moderated, to 45, by February 1998. The Indonesian exchange rate reached Rp15 000 per dollar in late January 1998 from Rp2658 per dollar immediately before the August 1997 devaluation.[15] The Malaysian ringgit, the Philippine peso and the Singapore dollar also experienced significant weakening, but of different magnitudes. However, despite deep currency devaluations, the region's exports continued to be very weak during the 1997/8 period. This indicates that devaluation by itself is no guarantee for an export-led recovery. The main problem faced by Southeast Asian manufacturers was the lack of trade finance as most banks had held back from extending loans because of fear of losing money.

SUPPLY-SIDE POLICIES

Short-run policies include those which the government can directly influence, such as cuts in both labour and non-labour costs including office and industrial rents, utility charges, statutory charges and port tariffs. In Southeast Asia, Singapore has relied heavily on the use of supply-side policies, as it is a very open economy which limits the effectiveness of demand-management policies. Aimed at reducing the costs of doing business in Singapore, these policies consisted of a S$10.5 billion cost-cutting measure.[16] This package consisted of a 10 per cent rebate in corporate taxes, property tax rebates, cuts in industrial land rentals of up to 40 per cent, lower transport charges through cuts in customs and excise duties for cars and petrols, and lower utility and telecommunication rates.

A large component of the production costs is labour cost. Thus the Singapore government has depended on wage guidelines including wage cuts, restraint in wage increases and even cuts in the contribution rates to the CPF, a compulsory savings scheme in Singapore in which employers and employees each contribute 20 per cent of the employees' salary to this fund. As part of cost-cutting measures, these contribution rates have been reduced. Moreover the government cut the annual variable component bonus for civil servants in 1998 to three-quarters of a month, down from the two months given in the previous year. High-salary officers and civil servants also received wage cuts of 1 to 5 per cent. Even ministerial pay was cut by 10 per cent.

Long-run policies include training and retraining programmes for workers and more research and development activities for innovations and improvement in technology aimed at improving productivity. In Singapore, there are more than 600 000 workers with secondary education or lower. It is therefore extremely important that these workers upgrade their skills and learn new tasks to be more productive and to be more employable in the future. There are also other schemes such as the job redesign programmes implemented by the Singapore Productivity and Standards Board which involves changing both job content and arrangement to encourage workers to become more productive.

CAPITAL CONTROLS

Malaysia was also hit by the crisis, as manifested in the loss of investors' confidence, significant capital outflows, depletion of foreign exchange reserves, a severe impact on the stock markets and marked depreciations of the ringgit. With Anwar Ibrahim as finance minister, Malaysia followed IMF-like policies including tight monetary and fiscal policies (essentially a combination of high-interest rate and reduced government spending policy) together with financial reforms. However, with the sacking of Anwar Ibrahim in August 1998, Prime Minister Mahathir rejected the IMF-like policies. Instead, as Malaysia's finance manager, Dr Mahathir had rescued the Malaysian economy through a combination of easier fiscal and monetary policies (higher government spending and lower interest rates, respectively) and imposition of capital controls.

Dr Mahathir argued strongly that the speculators were mainly responsible for the crisis and suggested that international monetary authorities led by the IMF should be able to impose measures that would contain the flows of international financial capital, particularly short-term. While Malaysia continued to experience massive pressures on its ringgit and while no concrete measures were taken to curtail short-term capital movements, Malaysia unilaterally imposed currency and capital controls on 1 September 1998. The controls, which cover external accounts, authorized deposit institutions, trade settlement and currency held by travellers, were expected to contain the speculation on the ringgit and to minimize the impact of the short-term capital flows on the domestic economy.[17] The ringgit was also fixed to the US dollar at RM3.80. Malaysia was not the first, or only, country in the world that imposed capital controls. As at 1997, the IMF reported that 128 countries had regulated their international financial transactions in some ways.[18]

These controls were largely aimed at the substantial offshore ringgit market in Singapore which constrained the ability of Malaysia's authorities to lower domestic interest rates. Consequently all offshore ringgit had to be brought on shore by the end of September 1999. Moreover the government restricted capital outflows by imposing a one-year holding period for repatriation of portfolio capital inflows. As Singapore's economy has been too closely linked with that of Malaysia, the Singapore government decided to stop trading on its Central Limit Order Book (CLOB) over-the-counter market, which was dominated by Malaysian stocks. This act resulted in a temporary freezing of over US$10 billion worth of Malaysian assets held in Singapore.

The imposition of capital controls is indeed costly and ineffective, arising from administrative problems and rampant evasion. However it was argued that short-term effects would be favourable to Malaysia. In fact, Malaysia reported that its current account balance had improved and that its foreign exchange reserves had increased in 1998. With capital controls, the Malaysian government was able to inject domestic liquidity into the economy aimed at boosting domestic demand, particularly domestic investment, and this has allowed the economy to pick up. In May 1999, the former IMF managing director Michel Camdessus noted Malaysia's ability to recover from the crisis through its adoption of a 'soft system of control' together with structural reforms.[19] Thus, as Tomioka stated, 'Malaysia subsequently proved that the negative opinions [about its capital controls] were not necessarily prophetic, as the economy has shown a relatively healthy recovery.'[20] As Haggard stated, capital controls (in Malaysia) were carefully crafted to reassure foreign direct investors and, by mid-2001, they had been dismantled.[21]

FINANCIAL RESTRUCTURING

The first set of policies involves comprehensive measures and restructuring in the banking sector, including the closure of insolvent banks and finance companies, as well as recapitalization and mergers of weak but viable financial institutions. In Indonesia, 16 banks were closed in November 1997 and four state banks were merged into a single institution. The government established the Indonesian Banking Restructuring Agency (IBRA) to supervise and manage the restructuring of banks in poor financial condition and to manage the assets acquired during the restructuring process. Immediately IBRA acquired 54 banks which accounted for 40 per cent of the banking assets. In August 1998, it further took over seven major banks, and the activities of seven other banks were frozen. It was estimated that the restructuring of the banking system will require the huge amount of over 400 trillion rupiahs, which is equivalent to more than half of the country's GDP.[22] In 2003, many of the institutions and arrangements put in place following the 1997 financial crisis came to an end: the IBRA will close, Indonesia will graduate from the IMF programme and the government will benefit from its final year of Paris Club rescheduling of official debt.[23] However one of the controversies regarding IBRA was that it created a 'stick and carrot' approach for dealing with the debt of bank owners: owners deemed cooperative in settling their debts to the government would be discharged from any further obligation, and the remaining shareholders would have 90 days to make payment or face legal action.[24] Despite criticism of IBRA's poor performance in pursuing debtors and former bank owners, it has broadly met its budgetary targets.[25]

In Thailand, the Financial Institution Development Fund (FIDF) was created to repair the banking system, including the screening of the rehabilitation plans submitted by the 58 suspended financial companies in order to determine their status. This led to the closure of 56 financial companies. In the first half of 1998, it was reported that borrowings by FIDF to finance its bail-out of weaker financial institutions had reached over 700 billion baht in May 1998. To lessen its dependence on the costly repurchase securities market, the Thai government passed a new law in May 1998 which enabled it to issue government bonds of up to 500 billion baht to pay for the debt of the FIDF.[26] Moreover, with seed money of 1 billion baht, the Thai government established the Asset Management Corporation to manage the disposal of the assets which belonged to the closed finance companies.

In Malaysia, the Asset Management Company (AMC) known as Danaharta was established to repair the banking sector. It intended to acquire 18 banks under Phase I (weaker banks that required recapitalization by Danamodal). By the end of December 1998, Danaharta had signed agreements with 13 banks and expected to acquire the remaining banks by the first quarter of 1999.[27] A significant step undertaken by the Malaysian government was the merger of 58 financial institutions into six large banking groups which were expected to provide competition with foreign banks.[28]

THE ROLE OF THE IMF

Did the IMF fulfil its Role during the 1997/98 Crisis?

Whether the IMF has prescribed the correct policies or not has received a lot of attention and debate. Based on its practice of extending loans with conditionalities, the IMF had imposed its orthodox policies of restrictive fiscal and monetary policies (cutbacks in government spending and high interest rates), financial restructuring including closures of companies and financial institutions deemed insolvent, and privatization, among others. However it was perceived by many that the policies set by the IMF were 'highly controversial' and 'dead wrong', because, despite these policies the crisis-hit Asian economies continued to deteriorate, including the failure of the high interest rates to attract capital inflows and prevent capital outflows, and the resultant rising level of debt service obligations.[29] Jeffrey Sachs, one of the well-known critics, argued that 'the region does not need wanton budget cutting, credit tightening and emergency bank closures. It needs stable or even expansionary monetary and fiscal policies to counterbalance the decline in foreign loans'.[30] Even then the World Bank's chief economist, Joseph Stiglitz, critically stated that 'One ought to focus on things that caused the crisis, not on things that make it more difficult to deal with.'[31] Also IMF's own policy division director Jack Boorman admitted that 'mistakes were probably made when [the IMF] recommended the 16 bank closures without giving investors adequate guarantees' and 'that the policy regarding depositor guarantees now appears to have been ill-advised'.[32] On another occasion, Hubert Neiss, IMF's former top representative to Asia, added that 'Had we known the depth of the recession, we would not have recommended such a tightening of fiscal policy, instead of a loosening of policy.'[33]

Expansionist, instead of restrictive, policies should have been implemented immediately to counteract the contractionary impact of the crisis. As Corden put it, 'The IMF is not straightforwardly right or wrong. It is probably now mostly right with its prescriptions and conditions for the countries affected by the Asian financial and currency crisis. But it went off the rails at the beginning in 1997, though it has gone gradually back on again, being flexible.'[34] However there has been a chorus of disapproval as regards the role of the IMF; that is, whether the IMF has ameliorated or exacerbated the crisis situation. As a consequence, it has been suggested that there is a fundamental need to strengthen the international financial architecture, including reform of the IMF. Among the proposals to reform the IMF, the French suggested boosting the role of a 24-member IMF advisory group that includes ten representatives from emerging markets and giving them a louder voice in IMF decisions. It has been perceived that IMF policies reflect too much the views of the United States. However the French proposal was opposed by the USA.[35] The British proposed to merge parts of the Fund with the World Bank and the former US Secretary of State George Shultz proposed to scrap the IMF.

On the other hand, there are others who view that the IMF should continue to exist and what is needed is to provide it with additional resources to provide temporary assistance to afflicted economies. As Corden further declared, 'The IMF is needed, desperately needed, in situations like the Asian crisis, that there is no need to establish a new organisation, and that it would be foolish – as some US rightwingers propose – to abolish it.'[36] Corden further argued that the IMF should be provided with adequate resources to cope with major crises and that these resources should not be used primarily to rescue international banks and other financial institutions – nor the owners and managers of domestic institutions in crisis countries – but to provide temporary relief to allow for necessary adjustments without major recessions or adverse effects on the mass of the population, and especially the poorest.[37]

Should there be a Bailout Mechanism by the IMF and who actually Benefits from this Bailout?

It has been argued that no firm or company should be shielded from bankruptcy by the IMF, nor should there be any official bailout, nor should foreign lenders be bailed out, knowing that 'it was misguided allocation of credit that got Asian countries into difficulty'.[38] It has also been suggested that this bailout mechanism has actually benefited, not the poor population, but a rather limited number of people, including investors and lenders, at the expense of the larger majority of the population. In the Mexican case, it was the bailout that punished 100 million people and, in the Thai case, the rescue package, rather than benefiting the 60 million people, may end up in the hands of politically connected speculators who will bail out their money-losing ventures.[39] Johnson also stated that the IMF's money which went to Thailand, Indonesia and South Korea did not go to the people of those countries as it went to the foreign banks that made too many shaky and imprudent loans to Thai, Indonesian and South Korean banks and businesses in the first place.[40] Thus, Corden proposed that, in the restructuring of the financial architecture, both the creditors and investors should also be made accountable and share the consequences should a crisis occur.[41]

Has Globalization been Too Fast?

It was argued that globalization of financial markets has taken place at a much more rapid pace than the globalization of commodities and labour because of the tremendous developments in the information and communications technologies that have made financial transactions easier, faster and cheaper. However the only constraints on financial transactions are national regulations which have been liberalized at a fast pace. As Tobin stated, 'most observers, West and East, public and private, in governments and international institutions, in banks and businesses, in big countries and small, now agree that financial globalisation went too far too fast'.[42] He further stated:

> As these [national regulations] have been liberalised in country after country, international financial flows have flooded national securities markets and inundated banking systems all over the world. These flows could be the vehicles by which savings in the advanced capitalist democracies are channelled into productive capital investments in the developing countries of Asia, Africa, and Latin America. Or they could be causes of currency crises, recessions and depressions, unemployment and deprivation in those countries. Or both.[43]

The Asian crisis showed that the ill-planned liberalization of capital flows could lead to financial instabilities. As Jeffrey Sachs argued, 'It was financial market reform that allowed Thai and South Korean banks to tap into short-term international loans in the early 1990s, thereby bringing together these banks with excited young investors who were happy to be in Bangkok and Seoul for the first time.'[44]

When countries free their capital accounts, they become more susceptible to crisis because of the weaknesses in the domestic financial system arising from the lack of adequate and stringent supervision and regulation of financial institutions. As pointed out by Ha-Joon Chang, the Korean crisis is a crisis from underregulation rather than from overregulation.[45] In Thailand's case, Olarn Chaipravat, the president of Siam Commercial Bank, admitted that Thailand committed mistakes involving its financial and foreign exchange market regulations, such as the Bank of Thailand's lax regulations, which allowed the inexperienced local commercial banks to conduct foreign exchange transactions directly with offshore banks, and the lax finance and banking regulations in supervising the offshore baht-denominated debt market.[46]

Is the East Asian Economic Model still Relevant?

The IMF's 'free market, minimal government intervention, and market-friendly approach' framework has been generally accepted as a useful model to explain the East Asian 'economic miracle' during the pre-crisis period. It has also been known as the East Asian Economic Model (EAEM) which is characterized by high dependence on the external economy through foreign direct investment (FDI) and trade, with the government acting to mobilize these resources. Because of its success in East Asia, it has been lauded by the IMF and has even made it as a model for other developing countries. However the 1997/8 crisis has exposed the dangers of being highly dependent on foreign investment and exports, and institutional problems like crony capitalism in which the allocation of funds has been based on political connections.

Southeast Asia and even Northeast Asian economies, particularly the badly hit economies of Thailand, Indonesia, Malaysia and South Korea, are still feeling the impact of the 1997/8 crisis so that the EAEM is seen as no longer relevant during the post-crisis period. It has even been said that this model is 'defunct' and that the time has come for an 'end of the EAEM'.[47] In Southeast Asia, Thailand and Malaysia have re-examined the validity of this model. In Thailand's case, PM Thaksin has considered an alternative two-track model in which the role of FDI is lessened and SMEs are given more emphasis to stimulate economic growth. Under the leadership of Mahathir, and presumably even under his successor Badawi, the Malaysia economy will be leaning more towards the domestic economy. Malaysia's domestic orientation is due to its new 'Look East' policy arising from the successful economic recovery of South Korea following its 'self-reliant' model which emphasizes the agribusiness sector as an engine of growth.

In the case of the Philippines, the previous and current administrations have been supportive of the IMF/WB policies and reforms. However there has been so much resistance coming from various groups since, in spite of the reforms, the Philippines has had a disapppointing economic growth performance. According to the 1996 World Bank report, the Philippines has not been able to sustain the required growth long enough to reduce the poverty incidence to the levels of neighbouring Southeast Asian countries. In fact, the Philippines has been excluded from the 1993 study by the World Bank because of its lacklustre performance. Despite the skilled and educated labour force and abundant natural resources, the Philippines has lagged behind other countries in Asia. It seems that the EAEM does not really work for the Philippines.

In the case of Indonesia, there has been much dissatisfaction with the intervention by the IMF and the World Bank. As legislator Syamsul Balda stated: 'We have been working with the IMF for years, and it has caused us a lot of disadvantages and few benefits.'[48] In consequence, in the spirit of increasing nationalism, there were calls by some legislators in the National Assembly to cut Indonesia's ties with the IMF, arguing that its policy prescriptions are not suitable for Indonesia. There was also a coalition of economists who reportedly stated that Indonesia's economic growth would return to the pre-crisis level if only Indonesia would part from the IMF immediately.[49] Leading a concerted campaign to free Indonesia from foreign control, Indonesia's own National Development Planning Minister Kwik Kian

Gie, former coordinating minister for economy and finance, had criticized Jakarta's dependence on the IMF.

As for Singapore, the EAEM is still very relevant. Singapore has continued to depend on FDI and trade as these are Singapore's main engines of growth, given a small economy and lack of natural resources. As a free trader and a vocal champion of global free trade, Singapore has placed its highest priority on and support for a strong rule-based multilateral trading system embodied in the WTO. Singapore has also supported regional initiatives such as ASEAN, APEC and ASEM, which Singapore believes are all complementary to the WTO process. However the Singapore government has recently forged bilateral Free Trade Agreements (FTAs) with New Zealand, Japan, EFTA, Australia and the United States and currently has negotiations with Mexico, Canada, South Korea and India. The Singapore government has always emphasized that her FTAs are intended to complement both multilateral and regional initiatives, and not to replace them.

Because of the questions raised against the continued relevance of the EAEM in the developing world, the World Bank launched a new book, *Can East Asia Compete? Innovation for Global Markets*, which provides an optimistic scenario for East Asia's future. The book argues that East Asia can regain its competitive advantage (a) through innovations with research and development, financial and business services, and information and communication technology as the three engines, and (b) through opening up East Asian markets. The question now is whether East Asia will buy the World Bank model.

CONCLUSION

Southeast Asian governments responded differently to the crisis including use of financial assistance, demand-management policies, supply-side policies, capital controls, financial restructuring, privatization and other measures. Those differences are logical considering the following factors. The first factor is in terms of the willingness of the political leadership to subscribe to the IMF and its conditionalities, including implementation of restrictive fiscal and monetary policies, in exchange for its financial rescue package. Thailand followed the IMF's prescription and was rewarded for its efforts with a US$17 billion package. Indonesia, on the other hand, brought up the idea of setting up a currency board system but was unsuccessful and had to succumb to IMF's wishes. Malaysia, on the other hand, strongly resisted the IMF's rule and money, as Dr Mahathir does not want to follow a high-interest rate and reduced spending strategy imposed by the IMF. Malaysia therefore followed an expansionary fiscal and monetary policy as such a policy would help the Malaysian economy to recover.

The second factor is in terms of the relative effectiveness of expansionary demand management, as in the case of Malaysia, and supply-side policies as in the case of Singapore. In the case of a very open economy like Singapore, demand management policies would be less effective, and so Singapore has relied more on supply-side measures. Short-run measures include wage cuts, cuts in Central Provident Fund (CPF) contribution rates and cuts in non-wage costs. Long-run measures include training and retraining programmes.

The third factor is in terms of the lack of concrete measures to control the outflows of short-term capital which prompted the Malaysian government to impose capital and currency controls. Other considerations which could explain the differences in policy responses by Southeast Asian governments include (a) the extent and nature of the crisis (for example, Malaysia's relatively smaller foreign debt versus Indonesia's huge foreign debt); (b) the pervasiveness and severity of the impact of the crisis (for example, Singapore's banking and financial sector being less affected than that sector in Thailand and Indonesia); (c) the governments' priorities, in terms of achieving either a move towards internal balance (less severe impact on unemployment) or a move towards external balance (trade surplus) or both.

In East Asia, there have been 80–100 crises over the past quarter-century.[50] Crises have become more frequent and more severe, indicating a fundamental weakness in global economic arrangements. In the case of the 1997/8 economic crisis, the impact was so severe that even the ADB characterized the economic hardship during the crisis as similar to that suffered during the Great Depression.[51] The severity of the crisis, the speed of its transmission and the weak international response have all contributed to wide-ranging deliberations on the governance of international finance. To prevent future crisis, there has been a clamour to improve the global financial architecture, and to manage crisis more effectively should it occur. These proposals include (a) controlling capital flows, (b) improving regulatory standards, (c) rethinking exchange rate regimes, (d) creating an international lender of last resort, and (e) bailing in the private sector, that is, making the private sector accountable to the govenment should the latter be unable to pay their obligations in times of crisis.[52]

NOTES

1. The crisis even spread outside the region, hitting Asia's third largest economy, South Korea in November 1997 with the Korean won falling sharply, by 10 per cent per day, the limit of its trading band. Moreover several major firms became insolvent and, by mid-December, smaller companies collapsed at the rate of 50 per day. Korea's short-term interest rates increased to 30 per cent and above. For more discussion, see Dean (1998: 267–83). For excellent discussion on the nature of the Korean crisis, see Chang (1998: 1555–61).
2. Anna Schwartz (1998).

3. Key elements of the financial package included financial restructuring measures (including closure of insolvent financial institutions); fiscal adjustment measures equivalent to some 3 per cent of GDP to bring the fiscal balance back into surplus and contribute to shrinking the current account deficit; and control of domestic credit. For full discussion, see Lane and Schulze-Ghattas (1999:2).
4. Djiwandono (2000:56).
5. Rosenberger (1998: 244).
6. Athukorala (1998: 281–9).
7. Djiwandono (2000:52).
8. Sicat (1998:292).
9. Bloomberg News (1999:47).
10. Chua Lee Hong (1999:3).
11. AFP (1999:15).
12. Sicat (1998:292).
13. Athukorala (1998:282).
14. Warr (1999:645).
15. Fane (1999:662).
16. Zuraidah (1998:1).
17. Zainal (1999:5).
18. *The Straits Times* (1998:37).
19. *Business Times*, 18 May 1999, p. 9.
20. Tomioka (2001:47–65).
21. Haggard (2001:71–98).
22. Hadi Soesastro, 'The Indonesian Economy under Habibie', Paper presented at the 1999 Regional Outlook Forum, organised by ISEAS, Singapore, January (1999:14).
23. Waslin (2003:5).
24. Ibid.:17.
25. Ibid.:18.
26. Sussangkarn (1999:3).
27. Zainal (1999:10).
28. Shanmugam (1999:11).
29. For more discussion, see Dean (1998:267–8).
30. Sachs (1997) as cited in Robison and Rosser (1998:1594).
31. *The International Herald Tribune*, 16 January1998, p. 11.
32. Ravi (1999:1).
33. Tang (1999:93).
34. Corden (1998:2).
35. *The Straits Times* (1998b:42).
36. Corden (1998:61).
37. Ibid.
38. See Dean (1998:268).
39. Anna Schwartz (1998).
40. Johnson (1998:653–61).
41. Corden (1998:61).
42. Tobin (2000:1102).
43. Ibid.:1101.
44. Sachs (1997) as cited in Robison and Rosser (1998:1594).
45. See Chang (1998:1555–61).
46. *The Nation* (1998:B1).
47. Yang (2002:28).
48. *The Straits Times* (2002:A6).
49. Centre for Strategic and International Studies, opinion and editorial, 'IMF' (2003).
50. Lindgren et al. (1996:20), as cited in Joseph Stiglitz (2000:1075).
51. See Asian Development Bank (1999:21).
52. For a complete discussion, see Asian Development Bank (1999:38–45).

REFERENCES

Adelman, Irma and Eric Yeldan (2000), 'The minimal conditions for a financial crisis', a multiregional intertemporal CGE model of the Asian crisis', *World Development*, **2** (6), 1087–100.

AFP (1999), 'Seoul wasted forex reserves in bid to halt meltdown', *The Straits Times*, 26 Jan., p. 15.

Asian Development Bank (1999), *Asian Development Outlook*, New York: Oxford University Press, pp. 21, 38–45.

Athukorala, Prema-chandra (1998), 'Swimming against the tide: crisis management in Malaysia', *ASEAN Economic Bulletin*, **15** (3), 281–9.

Bloomberg News (1999), 'Banking giants beat hasty retreat after hedge fund losses', *The Straits Times*, 27 Jan., p. 47.

Centre for Strategic and International Studies (2003), 'IMF', 7 Mar. (CSIS website: www.csis.or.id/imf1.htm, accessed on 20 Sept. 2003).

Chang, Ha-Joon (1998), 'Korea: the misunderstood crisis', *World Development*, **26** (8): pp. 1555–61.

Chua, Lee Hong (1999), 'Europe can differentiate now, says SM', *The Straits Times*, 3 Feb., p. 3.

Corden, Max (1998), 'The Asian crisis: is there a way out?', public lecture delivered in Singapore as a Distinguished Fellow in International Economics and Finance, ISEAS, Singapore, p. 2.

Dean, James (1998), 'Asia's financial crisis in historical perspective', *Journal of the Asia Pacific Economy*, **3** (3), 267–83.

Djiwandono, Soedradjad (2000), 'Bank Indonesia and the recent crisis', *Bulletin of Indonesian Economic Studies*, **36** (1), 56.

Fane, George (1999), 'Indonesian economic policies and performance', *The World Economy*, **22** (5), 662.

Hadi, Soesastro (1999), 'The Indonesian Economy under Habibie', paper presented at the 1999 Regional Outlook Forum, organized by ISEAS, Singapore, p. 14.

Haggard, Stephen (2001), 'Politics, institutions and globalisation: the aftermath of the Asian financial crisis', *American Asian Review*, **19** (2), 71–98.

Johnson, Chalmers (1998), 'Economic crisis in East Asia: the clash of capitalisms', *Cambridge Journal of Economics*, **22**, 653–61.

Lane, Timothy and Marianne Schulze-Ghattas (1999), 'IMF-supported programs in Indonesia, Korea and Thailand: a preliminary assessment', occasional paper no. 178, International Monetary Fund, Washington, DC.

Lindgren, C., G. Garcia and M.Saal (1996), *Banking Soundness and Macroeconomic Policy*, Washington, DC: International Monetary Fund, p. 20; as cited in Joseph Stiglitz (2000), 'Capital market liberalisation, economic growth, and instability', *World Development*, **28** (6), 1075.

Ravi, B. (1999), 'We badly misgauged Asian crisis', *The Straits Times*, 20 Jan., p. 1.

Rosenberger, Leif Roderick (1998), 'Southeast Asia's currency crisis: a diagnosis and prescription', *Contemporary Southeast Asia*, **19** (3), 244.

Sachs, Jeffrey (1997), 'IMF orthodoxy isn't what Southeast Asia needs', *International Herald Tribune*, 4 November, p. 8; as cited in Richard Robison and Andrew Rosser (1998), 'Contesting reform: Indonesia's new order and the IMF', *World Development*, **26** (8), 1594.

Schwartz, Anna (1998), 'International financial crises: myths and realities', *The Cato Journal*, **17** (3) (http://www.cato.org/pubs/journal/cj17n3-3.html).

Shanmugam, M. (1999), 'Merger by decree', *Malaysian Business*, 16 Oct., p. 11.

Sicat, Gerardo (1998), 'The Philippine economy in the Asian Crisis', *ASEAN Economic Bulletin*, **15** (3), 292.

Sussangkarn, Chalongphob (1999), 'Thailand: toward economic solvency', paper presented at the 1999 Regional Outlook Forum, organized by the Institute of Southeast Asian Studies (ISEAS), Singapore, p. 3.

Tang, Edward (1999), 'IMF to review bail-out conditions', *The Straits Times*, 29 Jan., p. 93.

The International Herald Tribune (1998), 16 Jan., p. 11, as cited in James Dean, 'Asia's Financial Crisis', p. 268.

The Nation (1998), 'Learning from Thailand's mistakes', 17 Nov., p. B1.

The Straits Times (1998a), 'Malaysia's real problem', 7 Oct., p. 37.

The Straits Times (1998b), 'Camdessus supports plan', 8 Oct., p. 42.

The Straits Times (2002), 'Mega pressured to cut IMF ties', 9 Aug., p. A6.

Tobin, James (2000), 'Financial globalisation', *World Development*, **28** (6), 1102.

Tomioka, Noriyuki (2001), 'Causes of the Asian crisis, Asian-style capitalism and transparency', *Asia–Pacific Review*, **8** (2), 47–65.

Wade, Robert (1998), 'The Asian debt-and-development crisis of 1997–?: causes and consequences', *World Development*, **26** (8), 1535–53.

Warr, Peter (1999), 'What happened to Thailand?', *The World Economy*, **22** (5), p. 645.

Waslin, Mike (2003), 'Survey of recent developments', *Bulletin of Indonesian Economic Studies*, **39** (1), 5.

Yang, Razali Kassim (2002), 'Will East Asia buy World Bank's economic model?', *The Straits Times*, 12 Oct., p. 28.

Zainal, Aznam Yusof (1999), 'Malaysian economic outlook: moving towards a slow recovery', paper presented at the 1999 Regional Outlook Forum, organized by ISEAS, Singapore, p. 5.

Zuraidah, Ibrahim (1998), 'Government decides on $10.5 billion cut', *The Straits Times*, 25 Nov., p. 1.

13. Development crisis in Sub-Saharan Africa: globalization, adjustment and the roles of international institutions

Kwan S. Kim

INTRODUCTION

If there is any developing region whose living standards are as poor today as they were some 30 years ago, it is Sub-Saharan Africa (SSA). In 2001, the SSA region was made up of 46 black republics with different historical heritage and economic characteristics and had a total population of some 630 million. Sub-Saharan Africa's average per capita GDP measured in purchasing power parity US dollars, including South Africa, was $1831 as compared to per capita income of $7050 for Latin America and the Caribbean, $3850 for all developing nations that include SSA, and $26 989 for the industrialized world (UNDP, 2003).

The grouping of countries for this region, as initially devised by the World Bank (1979), is based on geographical location and per capita GDP. Nonetheless the region must not be considered as a homogeneous and monolithic economic unit: the population size of these countries varies from that of Nigeria (80 million) to the Seychelles (100 000), while per capita GNP in 1997 ranged from Nigeria's $440 to South Africa's $3370. The region also includes three oil-exporting countries, Nigeria, Angola and Gabon, whose patterns of economic development can be distinguished from those of the rest of the continent. Despite some discernible variations exhibited by a small group of countries,[1] the region as a whole has faced commonly similar development problems. The continent has the largest incidence of poverty on this planet. In 1990, the region's share of the world's poor was 30 per cent and projected to rise to 40 per cent by 2000.[2]

Economic performance in the Sub-Saharan region since the first global oil shock in the early 1970s has been dismal, giving little cause for cheer. While a few countries, such as Botswana, Cameroon, Gambia and Mauritius, have better weathered the development crisis that has afflicted the region as a whole, the rest of the continent has experienced more than three decades of economic stagnation and decline. A recent World Bank (1989/99) projected figure of 3.8 per cent average annual growth rate in real per capita GDP over the period 1998–2007 pointed to some hopeful signs of economic recovery in Africa. Yet, given the high population growth rate of close to 3 per cent per annum, this translates into less than 1 per cent annual growth in per capita income.[3] Moreover the region's respectable growth in the mid-1990s did not reduce the actual numbers of the poor in the continent. The World Bank estimates that at least an annual growth rate of 4.7 per cent will be needed to achieve a reduction in the absolute size of the continent's poverty.[4]

This chapter provides an overview of policy issues pertaining to the development crisis in SSA.[5] It starts by examining the origin, scope and nature of the crisis in SSA (next section), looking in particular at the causes of the crisis from a recent historical perspective (third section). While there are competing and complementary explanations for the African crisis, special attention is given to the external factors in the global economy (fourth section). African economies are primitive and fragile compared with other regions of the developing world. They are also highly vulnerable to external shocks. Global economic and geopolitical forces have thus played a critical role in determining the patterns of development in the region. The chapter concludes with discussion of the elements of development strategy that would be required for the sheer survival or economic recovery in the context of the contemporary global economy.

THE DEVELOPMENT CRISIS: NATURE AND DIMENSIONS

Post-independence, Sub-Saharan Africa had experienced a modest economic growth until the early 1970s, when the first global oil shock hit the continent (Table 13.1). This period, for about a decade and half after independence, witnessed inflows of concessionary foreign capital as well as relatively favourable terms of trade for African exports, which were helped by booming economic growth in the industrialized world. Many African countries were able to improve their industrial infrastructures as well as health, educational and other social services.

As oil prices quadrupled in 1973, virtually all energy-dependent African countries were severely affected. With the soaring trade deficits that resulted in the beginning of the accumulation of external debt, a process of deindustrialization followed. Without leaving an adequate period for structural adjustment from the first shock, the second oil shock ensued in the late 1970s. It delivered another devastating blow to African economies. Moreover the two oil shocks were followed by declining trends in African export prices.

Table 13.1   Growth rates of real per capita GDP, 1966–98

	1966–73	1974–90	1991–97	1998	2000–01
World	2.9	1.1	0.8	0.3	0.2
Sub-Saharan Africa	2	–0.9	–0.2	–0.5	0.7
Industrialized world	3.8	2	1.4	1.1	0.6
Asian NIEs	7.9	6.7	5.6	–3	4.5
South & other Asia	2.9	4.3	6.9	1	2.5
Latin America & the Caribbean	3.9	0.3	1.5	1	–1.1
Middle East & N. Africa	5.8	–2	0.6	–0.5	—
E. Europe & Central Asia	5	2.1	–4.7	0	2.4

Source: World Bank, *World Development Report*, various years.

In the seven years from 1985 to 1992, Africa's terms of trade fell by an annual average of 3.85 per cent, which was the largest decline in the developing world. Mengisteab (1996: Table 3.4) and Yansane (1996:19) point out that, during the 1980s, the sharpest declines were in coffee and cocoa prices. Cocoa prices were already at a 15-year low by 1980. These products are major export products on whose revenue some 15 African countries depend to meet their capital goods imports. For raw material-exporting countries, the declines in export prices resulted largely from the simultaneous development in the industrialized world of synthetic substitutes for primary products.

The decade of the 1980s was a period of hostile global environment for Africa in other aspects. The industrialized West began to resort to increasingly protectionist trade policies as the globalized oil shocks induced recessions in their own economies. African nations soon faced rising OECD trade barriers. More stringent conditions were imposed on loans from the multilateral financial institutions. Rising protectionism in the 1980s reflected a surge in the West of the counterrevolution for economic liberalization, an ideology that called for free trade but no aid and market reforms in Africa.

These African plights have been compounded by the continent's poorly endowed human and physical capital base.[6] Low productivity, high costs of investment and excessive interference of inept governments in many African nations have turned away Western investors from the continent. The result of falling export prices, protectionism in the West and dissipating private resource inflows is that most African countries have perennial trade deficits that have to be financed by external debts incurred by their governments. Since the early 1970s, Africa's external debts have been rising faster than the region's economic growth (Table 13.2).

Table 13.2   External debt indicators: Sub-Saharan Africa versus developing nations

Debt shares (%)	1980	1990	1999
Debt stocks/exports			
Sub-Saharan Africa	68.5	209.6	225.1
All developing nations	88.3	162.5	136.6
Debt stocks / GNP			
Sub-Saharan Africa	23.5	63.0	75.8
All developing nations	20.3	34.2	41.5
Debt service/exports			
Sub-Saharan Africa	7.2	12.9	14.8
All developing nations	13.5	18.3	18.7
Concessionary debt/debt stocks			
Sub-Saharan Africa	26.9	33.1	39.1
All developing nations	18.2	21.5	18.6

Source: World Bank, *Global Development Finance*, 2000.

The economic stagnation throughout the 1980s and the early 1990s culminated in steadily declining living standards. As shown by Table 13.1, between 1996 and 1973, Sub-Saharan Africa's per capita real income grew by an average rate of 2.0 per cent per year; it continued to slide downward thereafter. The declining living standards have been accompanied by political crises and ethnic conflicts in a number of African countries. As African governments failed to shelter their citizens from a deepening economic crisis, they began to lose their political legitimacy. It is well to note that African governments are generally perceived as self-serving predatory institutions, partial in the distribution of meagre resources among different ethnic groups, religious entities and social classes within the nation. In the midst of the economic downturn, political crises and social conflicts intensified throughout the region, which posed a major threat to nation building as well as a stumbling block to prospects for foreign investment.

The conclusion of the Cold War in the late 1980s further isolated Africa from the global economic system. As the United States emerged as a hegemonic power in the global economy, a new global economic order began to be established. Global economic integration, trade liberalization, freer mobility of capital and production facilities across borders have become the hallmark of the new global order. Freed from the political need in the Cold War era to help the developing world, the industrialized West began to manifest a growing lack of interest in African development and has been disengaging itself from Africa.[7] During the Cold War era, African countries, like other developing nations, were able to derive many economic concessions from the West and the East. They often derived the benefits from playing off the two superpowers against each other. Western Europe's trade and capital, which traditionally were directed to Africa, were diverted to Eastern Europe, and official foreign aid to Africa from the United States as well as from multilateral donor agencies diminished with the enforcement of a global liberal economic regime.

Sub-Saharan Africa is now perhaps the most marginalized developing region. In 1990, the share of Africa in total world output and exports was no more than 1.5 per cent and 0.7 per cent, respectively,[8] whereas the African share in the world population was close to 7.5 per cent. That is so marginal that in the map comparing the GNP of countries, the entire Sub-Saharan African region, excluding South Africa,[9] comes about equal to Belgium in size (Figure 13.1).

As for the gravity of SSA's deepening crisis, Africa has now become the only continent in which poverty is rising. As shown in Table 13.1, the decline in real per capita income persisted in Africa during most of the period from 1974 to 1998. At a further disaggregated level, Table 13.3 shows growth performance of the group of 42 poor nations for which data are available. The selected countries were identified by the UN as 'least developed' in terms of very low per capita GDP and fragile human and physical assets. Sub-Saharan African nations account for the lion's share of the group of 49 least developed countries (LDCs) that include 12 non-African nations: Bangladesh, Bhutan, Cambodia, Haiti, Laos, Nepal, Yemen and five small island republics in the Pacific Ocean. The table shows that extreme poverty, as measured by per capita income, has been deepening and persistent in Africa. The poverty incidence in Africa has not only been most widespread but has also been rising faster compared to other regions.

Recent UN estimates also show that the self-sufficiency rate in cereals for the region as a whole fell from a high of 97 per cent in 1969–71 to 86 per cent in 1988–90.[10] Daily calorie intake is at only 92 per cent of requirement, compared with 109 per cent in all developing countries.[11] Malnutrition, starvation and disease are more widespread today in Africa than they were a generation ago. According to the same UN report, the crisis either will become worse or at least continue for a long time. In the absence of a major effort to boost indigenous food and livestock production drastically, some 300 million people, which is about one-third of the continent's population, will suffer the scourge of chronic malnutrition by 2010. The continent, already

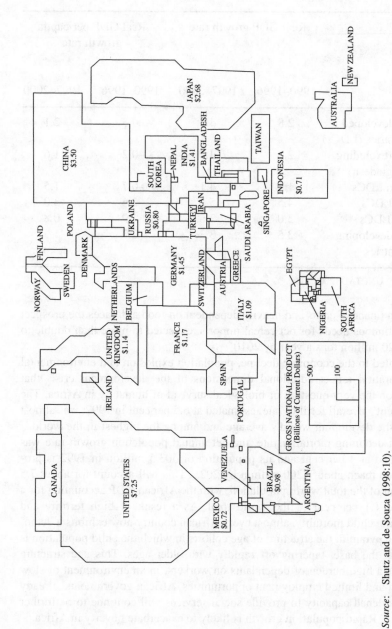

The cartogram displays country names with Gross National Product values (in billions of Current Dollars):

CANADA

UNITED STATES $7.25

IRELAND

UNITED KINGDOM $1.14

NORWAY

SWEDEN

FINLAND

DENMARK

NETHERLANDS

BELGIUM

FRANCE $1.17

SPAIN

PORTUGAL

GERMANY $1.45

SWITZERLAND

AUSTRIA

ITALY $1.09

GREECE

POLAND

UKRAINE

RUSSIA $0.80

TURKEY

IRAN

SAUDI ARABIA

CHINA $3.50

SOUTH KOREA

NEPAL

INDIA $1.41

BANGLADESH

THAILAND

JAPAN $2.68

TAIWAN

SINGAPORE

INDONESIA $0.71

AUSTRALIA

NEW ZEALAND

MEXICO $0.72

VENEZUELA

BRAZIL $0.98

ARGENTINA

EGYPT

NIGERIA

SOUTH AFRICA

GROSS NATIONAL PRODUCT
(Billions of Current Dollars)
500
100

Source: Shutz and de Souza (1998:10).

Figure 13.1 Gross national product cartogram

Table 13.3　　*Least developed countries' real GDP and per capita GDP growth rates, 1990–2000 (annual average growth rate, percentage)*

	Real GDP growth rate		Real GDP per capita growth rate	
	1990–1996	1997–2000	1990–1996	1997–2000
Least developed countries (LDCs)	2.8	4.5	0.3	2.1
LDCs (excluding Bangladesh)	2.0	4.2	–0.2	1.6
African LDCs	1.5	4.1	–0.7	1.5
Asian LDCs	4.5	5.0	2.6	3.0
Island LDCs	3.0	3.6	1.9	0.8
Other developing countries	3.5	3.3	2.3	1.9

Source:　UNCTAD (2002:3).

deep in financial crisis and heavily dependent on food aid, faces the prospect of continuous needs for net cereal imports, expected to more than double to some 20 million tons a year by 2010.

Related to the economic decline, population explosion and environmental deterioration reflect additional dimensions of the development crisis that touch on the very question of biological survival of humanity in Africa. The continent's overall fertility rate, estimated at 6.5 per cent in 1992, was almost twice the developing world's average and among the highest in the world.[12] With a declining mortality rate, the net annual population growth rate was estimated at 3 per cent and its population of 503.5 million in 1992 is projected to reach about 1200 million by 2025. This will account for about 7.5 per cent of the total world population, with the African GDP accounting for a meagre 1.1 per cent of the world total. As a result of high fertility and declining child mortality, almost every African country now exhibits a demographic pyramid: the structure of age cohorts in which the child population is large at the base, tapering off rapidly with older ages. This age structure implies a high burden of dependants on workers. In an environment of slow growth and limited employment opportunities, African governments' already overburdened capacity to provide social services will continue to be further stressed. Rapid population growth is likely to exacerbate poverty in Africa.

Rising poverty, coupled with rapid growth of population (particularly of the rural poor), periodic droughts and the communal nature of Africa's land tenure systems all together have contributed to severe environmental degradation. Deforestation in Africa takes place at an annual rate of 0.9 per cent of the total forested area.[13] It has adversely affected the production of such cash crops as coffee and cocoa by making the land too dry. Portable water and firewood have become scarce in many areas, severely lowering the already woeful standards of living. Poor and insufficient farming and grazing lands have become serious problems, especially in the countries of the Sahara and the Horn of Africa.[14]

With growing poverty and malnutrition, Africa is facing a health care crisis. For example, the AIDS epidemic is very serious in Africa, especially in the central African region. The epidemic is beyond the control of the resource-strapped states of the region. Even curable infectious diseases, such as malaria, continue to kill millions of people throughout the continent.[15] As shown in Table 13.4, Sub-Saharan Africa's human development indicators in every aspect of measurement have been grim and substantially below those of other developing nations.

Although the long-term indicators such as life expectancy, child mortality and adult literacy show some improvements over the years, other social and economic indicators seem to have stagnated or declined. One further disturb-

Table 13.4   Sub-Saharan Africa's human development indicators

	All developing countries	Sub-Saharan Africa
GDP per capita in ppp US$ (2001)	3859	1831
Undernourished population as % of the total (1998–2000)	18	33
Percentage of population with access to improved water source (2000)	78	57
Infant mortality per 1000 births (2001)	62	107
Annual population growth rate, % (2001)	1.8	2.8
Projected population growth rate, % (2001–5)	1.4	2.1
All school enrolment as % of the school age population	60	44
Life expectancy at birth (2001)	64.4	46.5
Total fertility rate per woman (2000)	2.9	5.4

Source: UNDP, *Human Development Report 2003*.

ing picture that emerges from this dismal landscape is unjust distribution of social services. In most African countries, access to educational, health and social services has been far better for the richer groups in society, where the needs are less.[16] Underclass Africans, relatively more numerous in market-oriented African countries, remain deprived of access to sanitation, clean water, basic health care and education.

Finally the confluence of these intricately intertwined economic, political, social and environmental problems has culminated in a deep-seated general crisis. Prolonged crisis can trigger more civil wars and the breakdown of state governance. The effects of civil wars and violence in Africa have already produced the largest number of refugees. By the end of 1993, there were close to six million refugees from the African continent, which accounted for 35.8 per cent of the total number of world refugees.[17]

THE NEOLIBERAL RESPONSE TO THE CRISIS BY INTERNATIONAL INSTITUTIONS

Africa's economic crisis, which has gradually intensified since the early 1970s, presented a difficult challenge to the development community. As the crisis worsened, the lender countries as well as other multilateral donor institutions perceived urgent need for changes in policy measures to reverse the declining trends and to place African economies on a path of sustainable growth. In the early 1980s, the policy response to the African crisis emerged in the form of structural adjustment programmes (SAPs). SAPs were formulated and supported by the two Bretton Woods institutions of the International Monetary Fund (IMF) and the World Bank (WB). Both institutions have played a critical role in determining the pattern of African development. The World Bank, although it has not deviated from the original conceptual framework for macroeconomic reforms, began to focus in later years on microeconomic institution building to enhance Africa's capacity for sustainable development.

The thrust of SAPs for Africa is liberalization of the economy through disengagement of the state from economic activity. It is based on the conventional economic theory that an optimal allocation of resources can only be obtained in a competitive, free market where prices reflect relative scarcities of the resources. To 'get the prices right', it is necessary to minimize the role of the state in economic affairs. Much of the African crisis has been seen as related to the pervasive intervention of the self-serving African state.

It is worth noting that many African nations, including Nigeria, Tanzania, Guinea and most post-independence socialist regimes (Ethiopia, Congo-Brazzaville, Angola, Mozambique, Somalia) showed a great deal of reluctance and reservation in accepting the IMF's conditionality. These states were suffering hard economic times and had little choice but to accept the IMF loans as they feared a loss of international credibility. As Mengisteab (1996) notes, SAPs typically consist of two segments: the first deals with macroeconomic stabilization measures, which are under the IMF governance, and the second with structural adjustment measures under the World Bank governance. Stabilization policies are intended to restore macroeconomic stability and the required adjustment period is conceived to be short-term. Structural adjustment aims at a longer-term, sustained growth through improved resource allocation and more efficient management at both the microeconomic and macroeconomic levels. In the case of Africa, an agreement on stabilization measures must be made with the IMF before a country enters into any structural adjustment programme. Aid donors and commercial banks have often insisted that the receiving country conclude an agreement with the IMF and/or the World Bank as a precondition for economic support.

The IMF and the World Bank have governed the economies of some 30 African countries. Many African governments, given the dire need for capital, have little choice but to embark on market reform measures, as dictated by these multilateral agencies. Although several countries have experienced some gains in economic growth, those adjustment polices cannot by and large be judged as successful in attaining such goals as sustainable economic growth and reducing poverty in the continent. On the contrary, the austerity requirements of SAPs appear to have further exacerbated the already severe human misery in Africa. The development crisis that engulfed the continent has worsened. At the aggregate level, for instance, Africa's GNP fell by an average of 2.2 per cent per year in the 1980s. In those African countries with IMF-World Bank programmes, spending on health fell by 50 per cent and on education by 25 per cent during the 1980s. Throughout Africa the health systems have been collapsing for lack of medicines, and educational institutions are suffering from a debilitating lack of libraries, laboratory and other facilities.

Even in the countries that are believed to have made progress in the process of adjustment, the growth rates have been very low. The World Bank itself acknowledges that, after a decade of implementing structural adjustment programmes, not many African countries have succeeded in finding a sound macroeconomic policy.[18] For instance, Ghana, which the Bank considers as the showcase of IMF–World Bank intervention, is now slated for its bleak economic prospects: it is projected that the average poor in Ghana will not cross the poverty line for another 50 years.

In retrospect, many of the adverse consequences of SAPs are attributable to the fundamental flaws with its strategy. The IMF makes loans to troubled countries, but insists that the governments cut their expenditures, which leads to reduction of social spending and benefits for workers and the poor, and should sell their assets to foreign investors. The purpose of these programmes is to make a country attractive to foreign investors and to encourage cheaper exports. The result has generally turned out to be raising profits for multinational corporations while increasing poverty and unemployment for Africa's working people. In this context, some African critics view SAPs as an international device inadvertently supporting an indigenous capitalist class against the national interest of poverty-stricken masses of the population (Mkandawire, 1992).

The neoliberal solution for Africa stands at odds with African reality concerning poverty. SAPs are in essence designed to promote economic growth by enhancing economic efficiency via the market system and redistribution of income is left to the market system. In reality, however, it has been shown that progressive redistribution of income rarely works spontaneously in a market economy. This is particularly the case for Africa where poverty is largely a phenomenon of the subsistence peasantry, which is the dominant mode of production in agriculture. Most of the poor (about 60 per cent of the total population) in Africa depend on subsistence agriculture for a living, whereas many SAPs have been intended to deal with economic activities operating within the formal market system. For example, a typical IMF package includes price decontrols, devaluation and export promotion. The benefits of this package have essentially been confined to a small number of export-oriented, cash-crop producers.[19]

Furthermore, the pervasive poverty in Africa is caused, not so much by low productivity of the economy, as by other social forces that generate fundamental imbalances in resource use. Often it is an ineffective and corrupt system of governance that results in a lopsided distribution of resources to a small self-serving elite. For instance, politics inhibits progress in land reform; Africa's rural poor are remote from the capital cities and do not affect the political elite in cities and, as a result, have not been a target population for concern. The rural poor have limited access to credit, land and extension services; lack of both genuine political commitment and strong public sector support for rural producers is another major factor exacerbating rural poverty. In this context, structural adjustment policies, which tend to focus on macroeconomic financial problems, have failed to benefit the rural poor and are blamed for exacerbating poverty. As citizens of developing countries began to protest angrily against SAP policies, riots frequently broke out after the IMF ordered price subsidies to be lifted on goods such as bread and gasoline. Towards the end of the 1980s, political momentum of the SAP also grew in more prosperous developing countries. As the IMF's intervention during the Asian financial crisis in 1997 and 1998 made the economic contraction there much worse, the structural adjustment issues blew up in the IMF's face.

Meanwhile the worldwide Jubilee movement began to gain increasingly winning support for the idea of debt cancellation for the poorest countries.

The failure of SAPs was officially recognized at an international conference on African economic recovery in Khartoum in March 1988. The Khartoum declaration sharply criticized the austerity programmes and their dehumanizing impacts on Africans. In response to the severe criticism of SAPs, the Fund launched a modest, modified debt relief programme through its Enhanced Structural Adjustment Facility (ESAF), also known as the Poverty Reduction and Growth Facility, in exchange for the least developed group of countries' agreeing to more closely supervised structural adjustment. Political momentum against the IMF, nonetheless, was ratcheted up when the US Congressional Meltzer Commission, a bipartisan advisory commission on the IMF reform, made two basic recommendations. First, the IMF (along with the World Bank) should use its existing resources to cancel all debts owed to these institutions by the poorest countries; second, the IMF should get out of the business of long-term lending –the kind of development loans to which structural adjustment conditions are normally attached.

In summary, SAP and ESAF have not proved effective in arresting the declining economic trends in Africa. More importantly, they have been short on concrete measures to alleviate poverty, which is the most urgent issue in Africa, as its widespread hunger is prone to escalate into famine, political violence and armed conflicts.[20] The failure of the structural adjustment programmes by global agencies was documented in a recent report by UNCTAD, which surveyed the results of the ESAF-supported structural adjustment programmes in the developing world (Table 13.5).

Focusing on 20 ESAF recipient countries for which data were available, Table 13.5 compares economic performance and poverty trends for three years before the year of the adoption of the programme with two subsequent three-year periods after the adoption. For this 'least developed' group consisting predominantly of Sub-Saharan economies, it is striking that the decline in per capita real income by 1.4 per cent three years before the programme persisted in the second three-year period after the programme. In a similar vein, the average living standards as measured by per capita private consumption in 1985 PPP dollars declined from $493.2 in the three years before the programme to $486.7 in the first three years after and to $477.6 in the subsequent three years. More strikingly, there is no evidence to indicate that poverty incidence has been reduced as the proportion of the total population below the one or two dollars-a-day poverty line rose slightly after the adoption of the structural adjustment programmes. The results of the UNCTAD study tells us that the Fund's ESAF anti-poverty programmes have failed to generate any discernible impacts on poverty incidence in these poor countries. Although the share of exports has increased in a number of traditional

*Table 13.5   Economic performance of the LDCs, before and after the
adoption of* SAP/ESAF *programmes*

Average annual real growth rate (%)	3 years before	1st 3 years after	2nd 3 years after
GDP per capita	−1.4	0.5	−1.4
Exports of goods and services	0.1	6.1	3.4
Gross capital formation	0.8	2.1	−2.6
Average per capita private consumption (1985 PPP$)	0.1	−0.1	−2.4
Average annual ratio (as % of GDP)			
Exports of goods and services	19.6	19.2	18.8
Gross capital formation	16.1	18.7	18.3
Gross domestic savings	0.7	2.5	1.1
Genuine domestic savings	−5.6	−4.1	−5.9
Average poverty incidence (% of population)			
Living on less than $1 a day (1985 PPP$)	51.3	52	53.3
Living on less than $2 a day (1985 PPP$)	83.1	83.7	84.1
Average per capita private consumption (1985 PPP$)	493.2	486.7	477.6

Source: UNCTAD Secretariat (2002) report based; World Bank, *World Development Indicators*, 2001.

export sectors, the ESAF strategy has been unable to catalyse foreign capital inflow, or to promote economy-wide structural change towards more dynamic export sectors.

Confronted by a renewed public protest against the structural adjustment policies in the wake of the Fund's admitted policy failure during the 1997–8 crisis, in September 1999 the World Bank and the IMF approved the Poverty Reduction Strategy Papers (PRSP), which outlines a national programme for poverty reduction. The PRSP provides the foundation for lending programmes with the IMF and the World Bank and for debt relief for Heavily Indebted Poor Countries (HIPCs). All HIPC countries are required to produce a PRSP as a basis for concessionary lending. They must have a PRSP before they can seek new programme support from the IMF or Bank. The Bank and Fund Boards must approve a country's PRSP before a lending programme is agreed.[21]

The basic principles underlying the poverty reduction strategies include recognition of the multidimensional nature of poverty, long-term perspectives for poverty reduction, multilateral and non-governmental participation as developmental partners, and national management of poverty strategies that involve broad-based participation by civil society and private sectors in all operational steps.

To allow for increased discretion in policy towards individual nations, the IMF agreed to engage in the process of streamlining its loan conditionality. Although the number of conditions applied by the IMF may be reduced, critics continue to argue that prior policy commitments by major donor institutions in the area of governance and conditionality will actually increase. There is indeed little evidence to date that policy autonomy for borrowing countries has been enhanced or that the IMF conditionality is strictly limited to macroeconomic issues. The PRSPs that have been produced by recipient countries have not differed much from previous adjustment programmes as far as the core economic strategies are concerned. They have not essentially departed from the Washington Consensus in the choice of policies.

GLOBAL INTEGRATION AND DEEPENING CRISIS

A related flaw with the SAP solution is the contestable premise that attributes the African crisis primarily to the factors internal to the domestic economy. With hindsight, Africa's problems can be seen as much or perhaps more importantly attributable to the factors external to the domestic economy. In fact, the economic situation deteriorated as African countries, under the prodding of international donor agencies, intensified efforts to integrate their economies with the global system beginning in the early 1980s. The main elements of policies for global integration consist of the opening of the economy and disengagement of the state from economic activities. Most African countries have been undertaking domestic market reforms and liberalization of foreign trade and investment.

The conventional theory tells us that the economies with integrated regimes grow faster, resulting in greater poverty reduction at the same time. The recent empirical studies nonetheless repudiate this relationship (Rodriguez and Rodrik, 1999). The impact of globalization on growth and development is shown to vary significantly across developing countries and regions. Interestingly, in the short run, rapid globalization has been associated with a rising incidence of poverty (UNCTAD, 2002:115–17). Poverty has been increasing unambiguously in those economies that have adopted an extensively open trade regime and in those that have continued with an extensively closed trade regime. The positive effects of economic liberalization on poverty are found to depend more significantly on complementary policy measures (World Bank, 2001:ch.2). Winters (1999:59) concludes: 'Overall the fairest assessment of the evidence is that, despite the clear plausibility of such a link, open trade alone has not yet been unambiguously and universally linked to subsequent economic growth', although he adds that 'it certainly has not been identified as a hindrance'.

In the context of Sub-Saharan Africa, available evidence does not show that global integration in Africa has produced significantly positive results. Many African nations have faced particular difficulties in adjusting to globalization, especially in financial areas. A recent article in the *Economist*[22] states that in Africa 'the combination of malfunctioning domestic finance, weak regulation and erratic economic policy is perfectly designed to get the worst out of financial openness. In countries where those failures are severe and cannot be corrected, an incautious opening of the economy to foreign capital is likely to do much more harm than good'. The annual GDP loss from banking and currency crises spawned by the debt crises in Africa during the 1990s averaged 0.7 per cent of GDP (although the dollar figures of other benefits from financial openness have not been included in the calculations).

Several factors explain why the integration strategy that has been implemented to derive maximum benefits from international markets has paradoxically reinforced marginalization of many African economies from the global system. It is important to note that Africa has been as open to global markets as any other developing regions have been. Mengistead (1996:Table 3.2) notes that the share of the total trade in GDP for Africa in 1990 was 46 per cent, compared to 42 per cent for all developing countries. The problem with the strategy for openness and export promotion is that African exports are primary commodities produced with marginal participation of the peasantry and often at the expense of the internal food needs. Apart from the volatile market problems inherent in primary products in international markets, African exports are simply not competitive with more mechanized, government-subsidized European or American farm products.

Most African nations since 1960 have ended up with worsened terms of trade for their primary goods exports, falling foreign investments and crippling external debt burdens that stood at US$313 billion for the region in 1994. Taking the poorest, primary goods-exporting 15 countries in Africa, Sapsford (2001) calculated trends in their terms of trade for two distinct subperiods distinguished by fundamental structural changes which occurred in each country in the 1960–93 period. As shown in Table 13.6, most of these poor countries experienced deteriorating trends in their primary goods export prices relative to manufactured goods import prices. Only three of 28 reported cases over the two subperiods in his study showed any positive trend in barter terms of trade movements. Other estimates by the World Bank similarly indicated that Africa's terms of trade plummeted by about 15 per cent between 1987 and 1991, compared with a 1 per cent decline for all

Table 13.6   Trends in the barter terms of trade of the least developed
            African nations, 1960–93*

Country	Period 1	Annual average % change	Period 2	Annual average % change
Burkina Faso	1960–1968	0.00	1969–1991	–3.12
Burundi	1965–1993	–7.99	—	—
Chad	1960–1972	12.50	1973–1993	1.77
Dem. Republic of the Congo	1960–1984	–9.18	1985–1993	–6.18
Ethiopia	1960–1974	0.00	1975–1993	10.38
Guinea-Bissau	1965–1977	–10.72	1978–1993	0.00
Madagascar	1960–1991	–1.98	—	—
Malawi	1960–1973	21.95	1974–1993	–2.86
Mali	1960–1981	0.00	1982–1993	–1.47
Niger	1960–1986	–6.17	1987–1993	–0.72
Rwanda	1960–1974	0.00	1975–1993	12.30
Sierra Leone	1960–1977	–2.60	1978–1993	–3.28
Sudan	1960–1987	–2.44	1988–1993	–5.77
Tanzania	1960–1973	0	1974–1993	–4.15
Zambia	1960–1979	–21.1	1980–1993	–7.5

Note: * Net barter terms of trade: primary export goods prices relative to imported manufactured goods prices.

Sources: UNCTAD report (2002) and Sapsford (2001).

developing countries, and continued to fall by an average of 2.87 per cent annually between 1991 and 1994.[23]

The declining price trend must be seen as offsetting any positive gains from trade on economic growth. Nevertheless, a recent report (Hussaín et al., 2000) argues that the terms of trade are positively and closely related to real GDP growth for Africa. More specifically, the deterioration in the terms of trade of 29 non-oil-exporting African countries reduced Africa's annual growth rate by an average of 0.84 percentage points over the period 1970–90. In terms of other macroeconomic measures, the falling prices eroded, on average, 42 per cent of the growth effect of the increase in exports and 34 per cent of the growth effect of capital inflows in Africa. Studying Africa's vulnerability to global markets, Lewis (1986:480) calculated that the impact of OECD import growth and Africa's barter terms of trade together accounted for over

80 per cent of the variations in the growth rates of African economies between 1960 and 1990. As a result, Africa's debt burden continued to increase, sapping the regional economy's capacity to import and invest.

The debt crisis of Africa is another story. Table 13.2 showed the trends in the Sub-Saharan region's various external debt indicators over the period 1980–99. It is striking that in all measures consisting of the ratios of the total debt to exports, the total debt to GNP, debt service to exports and concessionary capital inflows to the total debt, the Sub-Saharan region persistently maintained a higher level compared to other developing regions. Moreover, unlike other regions that maintained a stable pattern of the debt burden, the African economies registered a sharp growth in dependency on external debts over the period. The share of external debts in both the country's exports and GNP more than tripled over the period 1970s, 1980s and 1990s. Rapid growth of the debt burden has occurred in spite of increased concessionary grants and debt forgiveness given to the African region. The global energy crises during the 1970s proved to be the genesis of Africa's crippling debt crisis in the 1980s. While the oil crises-led recessions in the West and its protectionist policies hit African economies severely, the oil shocks resulted in a massive inflow of petrodollars into the Eurocurrency market, and infusions of loans to African countries followed. Encouraged by favourable interest rates and despite growing trade deficits, Africa's borrowing continued unabated to keep up with the increased level of government services required for maintenance of domestic tranquillity.

African countries' plights began to surface when African export prices continued to decline and the debtors were forced to reschedule their loans at higher interest rates towards the mid-1980s. African governments had to scale back government services and cut back on social services. With high debt services and little capital investment from the West, net capital flows changed direction and began flowing out of Africa to the West.[24]

The economic situation in Africa further deteriorated in the post-Cold War era as trade liberalization unfolded on a global scale. There was erosion in the favourable trade arrangements between Third World nations and their market partners. During the Cold War era, African and other developing countries were able to exert some influence on the international system. The European Economic Community–African, Caribbean and Pacific (EEC/ACP) agreements and the generalized system of preferences of the GATT were some concessions of the Cold War era from which African states derived benefits. In the wake of the collapse of the Berlin Wall in 1989, Africa was seen as politically less useful from the perspective of the West, and the importance of Eastern Europe superseded Western interest in Africa. The continent became more isolated from the industrialized world. Along with large reductions in official aid to Africa, access to foreign markets and private capital that was available to Africa in the preceding two decades drastically diminished. For example, foreign direct investments in Sub-Saharan Africa as a ratio of the total foreign investments in developing countries fell markedly throughout the early 1990s.[25]

In addition, Africa is the only region of the world which is expected to be adversely affected by the new General Agreement on Tariffs and Trade (GATT)'s Uruguay Round, at least in the short run (Yeats, 1995). The agreement has diminished African export revenues as the existing tariff preferences for Africa have continued to be eroded under multilateral trade liberalization. At the same time, African countries that specialize in primary products exports will lose their export competitiveness in global markets. Moreover imports from Europe and the USA whose agricultural products are subsidized by their governments can displace Africa's domestic production of food. In effect, the rich countries' agricultural subsidies can work directly against their efforts to combat poverty in impoverished Africa. By driving down international farm prices, Western subsidies drive out African growers from their farms. For instance, in the case of cotton, the USA has a major influence on the global market because a large proportion of US production – more than 50 per cent – is exported under a heavy government subsidy. Some 95 per cent of the world's farmers live in the developing world, with many of them seeking their way out of poverty through fair trading in global markets.[26] Many African countries were expected additionally to experience reductions in textile exports, given the failure to bring the Multi-Fiber Agree-

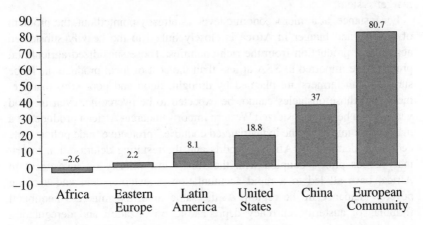

Source: UN Department of Public Information. *Africa Recovery*, **8**(3), December 1993–March 1994, 9.

Figure 13.2   Revenue effects of the new GATT, by region (projections to 2002)

ment under the GATT discipline. Recent OECD calculations, as shown in Figure 13.2, indicated that net annual losses for Africa would reach $2.6 billion in the period up to 2002. In contrast, the industrialized countries would reap $135 billion or 64 per cent of total annual gains in world income from the new GATT (Goldin et al., 1993).

CONCLUDING REMARKS: ELEMENTS OF THE CHALLENGE AND ROLES OF INTERNATIONAL INSTITUTIONS

Sub-Saharan Africa today faces the daunting challenge of economic development. Over the past three decades and a half, Sub-Saharan African countries have been impoverished by a combination of factors internal and external to their national economies. Whereas the continent's development crisis has been caused as much or perhaps more by the internal factors related largely to poor governance by often corrupt African governments, the focus of this chapter is on the external factors. This chapter makes a point that, in relation to other regions of the developing world, Africa has been more adversely affected by the changing global environment since the early 1970s. The adverse economic conditions the continent has been confronted by have often been beyond its control. Many of the adverse impacts, particularly on small, open African economies, can be seen as endemic in the nature of the global market system.

For instance, at a microeconomic level, as already pointed out, the problem of poverty and hunger in Africa is closely linked to the heavily subsidized agricultural production from the rich countries. Those subsidized agricultural products are imported to SSA at less than the cost of local production. To be sure, African farmers are plagued by drought, flood and poor crop management, and those obstacles cannot be expected to be overcome, even in good years, when heavily subsidized Western imports undercut African produce. At a macroeconomic level, the industrialized countries' protective trade policies, the decline in demand for African exports and the resulting deterioration in primary goods prices, coupled with the West's low priority on investment in Africa, have all led to a rapid accumulation of external debt and a rising poverty incidence in the region. At the same time, the mindless neoliberal formulas of austerity, currency depreciation, privatization and deregulation which have been imposed on the indebted countries exacerbated the process of marginalizing the continent and impoverishing Africa's working population (Mengisteab, 1996; Mkandawire, 1991, 1992; Hope, Sr.1997; Onimode, 1988).

Since the external factors inhibiting African development are closely interwoven with the internal factors contributing to the continent's poverty, it is worth dwelling on the scope and nature of such linkage here. Clearly the new reality facing Africans today is that they must take charge of their own fate against the backdrop of the post-Cold War global order. In the new age, much of the global economy has returned to pre-Depression capitalism, a Darwinian economic system that rewards rich and punishes poor nations. While neoliberal economists see global integration as the key to rapid growth in the developing world, we also see how these emerging markets of East Asia, Russia and Brazil have become mercilessly vulnerable to global market forces. For most SSA countries, their years-long accumulated debt burdens have turned into an inhibiting factor diminishing the possibilities of economic revitalization. Recent decades have thus witnessed a rising tide of discontent concerning globalization in the developing world.

Despite the discontent, neoliberal global integration continues as the driving paradigm within the international development policy establishment. Moreover, from the perspective of profit-seeking multinational investors, the SSA continent is now seen as economically unimportant. Politically, the West regards Africa as irrelevant in the post-Cold War era. This attitude is exhibited by the West's diminishing enthusiasm in responding to economic distress in Sub-Saharan Africa. Prospects of securing new resources from outside sources for the region – official and private – seem more remote today than a decade ago.

What must and can be done for the continent? This takes us far beyond the scope of this chapter. It suffices here to refer to a few elements of development strategy that need to be taken into account in overcoming the crisis (Yansane, 1996; Chug, 1997). First of all, countries in SSA need to consider the modalities of economic restructuring that are pragmatic, eclectic between the market and the state and incremental in transition. Restructuring efforts cannot be based on an all-or-nothing choice between the market's 'invisible hand' and the state's 'grip of the fist'. The market model, while it may have improved performance in many areas of economic activity, has in the past intensified poverty, starvation and inequality by lowering wages and social incomes of the underclass (Hussain et al., 2000). Such a model is ill-suited to deal with African poverty. The strategy for the alleviation of poverty must include changes in social structure, specifically, the empowerment of working poor and women.[27] The masses of underclass Africans must have access to opportunities for education and productive resources so that they can seek their own solutions. Under a recessional environment over the past several decades, provisions of basic education, training, health care and even food security have been neglected in SSA.

Doubts must also be raised as to whether neoliberal reforms can lend themselves to a deep-seated structural transformation, which calls for concrete policy measures in moving into high-value technology sectors (Adei,

1996), diversifying from monoculture and reducing export dependence and foreign concentration in industry (Stein, 1995; Kim, 1995).[28] These are economic activities essential to the future survival of Sub-Saharan Africa that cannot be resolved by private sector initiatives alone and should involve the actions of the state.

Apropos of the role of the state, it is worth emphasizing that governance has to be recognized as a critical component in African development. If good governance is understood in the sense that the fundamental role of the state is to serve the people, and not to control the people, there is cause for grave concern about the governance of African states (Maxfield and Schneider, 1997). Economic collapses in Sub-Saharan Africa have too often been accompanied by the crises of governance, as evidenced by ethnic, clan and religious conflicts, rising crime and violence, human rights abuses and widespread rent-seeking activities. Self-serving authoritarian regimes cannot induce sustainable development of a competitive private sector that can lead future growth. In African reality, state reforms seem imperative in order to build sustainable democratic institutions: in particular, an institutional infrastructure that promotes integration among different ethnic and social groups. Only a reformed African state could safeguard any success in economic reforms as well as the safety nets for the working poor and the underprivileged.

As regards external relations, this chapter has questioned the relationship between trade and development in the context of contemporary Africa. The point has been made that a simplistic trade liberalization is unlikely to promote sustainable development in Africa.[29] Contrary to the received theory, the sheer abundance of low-cost labour by itself will not ensure a comparative advantage in Africa's primary goods exports. Few African economies have currently the necessary capital and technical infrastructure to engage their labour resources productively. There is thus no denying the economic imperative that African economies must ultimately keep engaged with wider global markets. The tenuous linkage of Africa's regional economy to the global economy can nonetheless work as a limiting factor for economic development, at least until the time when African economies are adequately equipped for export competitiveness in global markets. In this context, international institutions must play more proactive roles in helping these marginalized countries to develop a globally competitive export sector.

An important point raised in the chapter is that problems of many African nations are long-term structural in nature. The short-term IMF-type stabilization policies have often in the past failed in assuring long-run sustainable growth as they tended to overlook their consequences for African countries' structural change required to warrant a sustainable growth path.

There are a few immediate actions that international institutions can engage in. First, while they help poor countries to improve their investment climates and to learn to take advantage of opportunities in a changing economic environment, they must at the same time call upon rich countries to open their markets to exports from those countries. For this, international institutions must see to it that rich nations bring down their trade barriers and eliminate their large agricultural subsidies which undercut poor country exports. The industrialized world's agricultural subsidies currently amount to $350 billion a year, which is roughly seven times what rich countries spend on development aid. These subsidies not only hurt the working poor in developing countries but also result in higher taxes and higher prices for consumers in rich countries. As affirmed at the Grand Baie African Ministerial Conference of the WTO in June 2003,[30] agriculture is of vital importance to Sub-Saharan Africa and holds the key to lifting millions of Africans out of poverty. Global institutions must support African nations in their efforts to remedy the adverse consequences of rich nations' farm subsidy policies for subsistent peasants in Africa. As regards the global market access to non-agricultural products, future multilateral trade negotiations must also take into account the vulnerabilities of African industries, specifically in such sectors as textiles, clothing, leather and food processing. Provision of a preferential tariff structure remains critically important for Sub-Saharan nations to be able to continue their industrialization processes.

The second urgent task is to help reduce their debt burden. Reductions of external debt for these marginalized countries, especially the highly indebted poorest nations in Africa, are the first step in enabling them to participate in globalization and to share the benefits it could bring. For many African nations, debt services alone have far exceeded net capital inflows. For instance, in 1997, Africa had a negative trade balance, with its export revenue declining by 17 per cent over the previous year. Net resource flows to the continent fell by nearly 40 per cent, from $4.5 billion in 1997 to $3 billion in 1998. The cost of debt servicing for Africa, on the other hand, rose to $35 billion in 1998, which accounted for more than 30 per cent of the region's exports.[31] Debt relief is certainly a precondition for those countries to be able to improve their investment climate and social services to reduce poverty. Thus the least the international institutions could do is to make it easier for the industrialized West to forgive or reschedule the continent's external debt. The debt reduction initiative alone may not significantly affect Africa's burden, but will be an important step needed to keep up Africa's structural reforms to encourage private investment and to promote growth.[32] Moreover, also from the lender's perspective, the debt relief for Africa can be seen as more than a moral imperative.[33] There are compelling reasons in the long run for the international community to help Africa. It will be in everyone's interest to see a stable and steadily developing Africa participating in an interdependent global system.

In this context, the debt reduction initiative launched in 1996 by the IMF and World Bank for the Highly Indebted Poor Countries (HIPCs) has proved a step in the right direction.[34] The main objective of the initiative is to reduce the debt burdens of the HIPCs to sustainable levels at which the debts can be managed. The amount allocated for the debt relief, however, still appears too modest to be of much consequence in effecting poverty reduction and social policies for poor countries.[35]

Third, even if the poor countries were relieved from all of the external debt burdens, substantial increases in concessionary external assistance would be necessary, particularly to address problems in education and health. Over the decade of the 1990s, international economic aid to Africa fell by a third, from $17billion at the start of the decade to $12billion. Since sizable private sector foreign investments in those countries are unlikely for the foreseeable future, a viable option for the industrialized world would be to help create space for non-governmental organizations' (NGOs) activities. The recent past witnessed an increased involvement in African development of civil society organizations, including NGOs or other multilateral donor institutions. NGOs could play a more proactive, instrumental role in facilitating the building of democratic institutions and human capital infrastructure at the grass-roots level.

Finally, another urgent agenda for international institutions to help Africa would be promotion of region-based economic cooperation among neighbouring states. Africa's problems cannot simply be resolved by freer global trade and more foreign ownership. Africa needs control of its own vital resources for long-term structural transformation of the primary commodity economy. At present, interregional trade among African nations accounts for less than 1 per cent of global trade. The future challenge for Africa, with its immense energy, mineral and agricultural resources, is to work together for more internal trade and to build a unified regional stance in dealing with other global trade blocs. Effective regional cooperation could result in a robust, regionally integrated economy relatively more secure from uncertain global markets but capable of exploiting the advantage that the pooling of national markets and resources makes possible.[36] It could make the African region play in the world marketplace with collective clout and vigour and would be a stepping stone leading to a wider global-scale integration.

It is well to note that international security and peace cannot be assured unless global economic integration is managed with greater justice. The task for African recovery is enormous and daunting, but not impossible. The history of economic development is not unkind in this respect. Some 40 years ago, newly industrialized countries in East Asia were in no better economic condition than today's African economies are. African development must not be written off as a lost cause.

NOTES

1. In a recent World Bank report (1998/99), seven African countries (Botswana, Gabon, Mauritius, Mayotte, Reunion, Seychelles and South Africa) are listed as belonging to the upper middle income group (defined for per capita income range of $3126–$9633). Except for South Africa, the rest consist of small countries (Gabon and Botswana) and island republics.
2. UNDP (1991), *Human Development Report 1991*, New York: Oxford University Press. p. 23.
3. World Bank (2003) estimates SSA's per capita GDP annual growth rate for 2000–2001 at 0.6 per cent.
4. World Bank, Human Resources and Poverty Division, Africa Region, 'Status Report on Poverty in Sub-Saharan Africa, 1994', Washington, DC.
5. An important objective this chapter seeks is to raise the level of consciousness among policy makers, scholars and students concerning the current development crisis in SSA.
6. No attempt is made in this chapter to assess the relative weight of internal factors versus external conditions in causing the African crisis. In addition to the difficulty of obtaining necessary data, this involves conceptual and ideological problems in defining the operational meaning of 'external' and 'internal'.
7. For example, trade between the USA and Africa in recent years has been insignificant. Despite its population of 800 million in1997, Africa accounted for only 1 per cent of US trade. Africa exported $16.4 billion to the USA in the same year, of which 70 per cent consisted of oil sales from two countries, Nigeria and Angola.
8. IMF, *World & Economic Outlook*, Washington, DC, October 1993, p. 125.
9. South Africa accounts for about 40 per cent of the region's total GDP.
10. United Nations (1993–4:8). The self-sufficiency rate for all developing countries in 1988–90 was 91 per cent.
11. UNDP, *Human Development Report* (Oxford University Press, 1994).
12. Ibid.
13. Ibid.
14. There have been chronic conflicts between nomads and sedentary peasants (particularly in East Africa) over access to and control of land. Land degradation was a key factor contributing to increased frequency of conflicts.
15. According to recent World Health Organization estimates, there are up to 500 million cases of malaria, with fatalities ranging between 1.5 and 3 million people annually. About 90 per cent of these cases occur in Africa.
16. See World Bank, 'The Many Faces of Poverty', available at http://www.worldbank.org/aftdr/findings/english/find35.htl.
17. US Committee for Refugees, *World Refugee Survey*, Washington, DC: USCR,1994, p. 40.
18. United Nations (1993–4:18). Direct foreign investment in Africa is so paltry that it is not even measured in the latest World Bank study.
19. In this regard, a World Bank (1995) survey shows that, between 1985 and 1992, the proportion of the Sub-Saharan African population living below the poverty line rose by 1.5 per cent.
20. Towards the late 1980s there was a shift in the World Bank SAPs to pay greater attention to human resource problems and public institutional reforms in Africa.
21. As of the end of 2002, 28 least developed countries completed a full Poverty Reduction Strategy document, with another 45 countries delivering an interim document for approval. The IMF and the Bank have renamed their lending facilities for poor countries. The IMF's Enhanced Structural Adjustment Facility (ESAF) was renamed as the Poverty Reduction and Growth Facility (PRGF). The interest rate and repayment conditions remain the same. The Bank created Poverty Reduction Support Credit (PRSC) as a lending instrument designed to support implementation of the PRSPs.
22. *Economist*, 'A Survey of Global Finance', 3–9 May 2003, p. 8.
23. World Bank, *World Development Report 1994*.

24. The severity of the external debt can best be illustrated in the case of Sudan, where 94 per cent of its citizens live below the poverty level. During the mid-1990s, famine-stricken Sudan was receiving about $26 million a year in international development funds while paying out $60 million a year to service its debt to the IMF, its main creditor.
25. World Bank, *Financial Flows and the Developing Countries*, Washington, DC, 1994; and *Global Economic Prospects and the Developing Countries*, Washington, DC: 1995, 1996.
26. Acccording to the WTO statistics, the developing countries' share of world agricultural exports dropped from 40 per cent in 1961 to 35 per cent in 2002.
27. For a discussion on gender bias as a cause of poverty in Africa, see Kasliwal (1995:chs 3–4).
28. For a comprehensive analysis on this issue, see Stein (1995) and Kim (1993).
29. For the importance of some degree of self-determination in African development, see Yansane (1996).
30. www.sarpn.org.za/documents.
31. *Financial Times*, 'Africans off target in war on poverty', 10 May 1999.
32. According to the Resource Guide prepared by the Catholic Task Force on Africa (http://afin.cua.edu/in.html), the first international Jubilee campaign leveraged $34 billion in debt cancellation for 34 most impoverished nations – mostly in Africa – by the end of 2002. Most of the cancelled debts were spent on health care and education, resulting in tripling of school enrolment in Uganda, vaccinating half a million children against epidemic diseases in Mozambique and providing resources to fight AIDS in Mali, Senegal and Cameroon.
33. In this context, the Pope and the Council of Bishops called for a debt relief jubilee for Africa to coincide with the year 2000.
34. The author is grateful for helpful comments of a referee on HIPCs debt reduction.
35. According to IMF data (as of March 2004), debt reduction packages have been approved for 27 countries, 23 of them in Africa. The total debt service relief in net present value terms amounted to US$31billion.
36. For a study on the promising case of integration in Southern Africa, see Kim (1988b); and for a case of failed integration in East Africa, see Kim et al. (1979). Arguments favouring regional integration for Africa are discussed in Mengisteab (1996).

BIBLIOGRAPHY

Adei, Stephen (1996), 'National capacity building and long-term development: the role of technical cooperation in Africa', in A.G. Yansane (ed.), *Prospects for Recovery and Sustainable Development in Africa*, Westport, CT: Greenwood Press, pp. 51–63.

Chug, Michael (1997), 'Sub-Saharan Africa: underdevelopment's last stand', in Barbara Starlings (ed.), *Global Change, Regional Response*, Cambridge: Cambridge University Press, pp. 309–45.

Goldin, I., O. Knudsen and D. van de Mensbrugghe (1993), *Trade Liberalization: Global Economic Implications*, Paris and Washington, DC: OECD and World Bank.

Hope, Sr., Kempe Ronald (1997), *African Political Economy: Contemporary Issues in Development*, New York: M.E. Sharpe.

Hussaín, M.N., K. Miambo and T. Oshíkoya (2000), 'Global financial crisis: an African perspective', *African Development Review*, September, 1–24.

Kasliwal, Pari (1995), *Development Economics*, Los Angeles: Southwestern College Publishing.

Killick, Tony (1995), 'Structural adjustment and poverty alleviation: an interpretative essay', *Development and Change*, **26**(2), 305–31.

Kim, Kwan S. (1988a), 'Continuing crisis in Sub-Saharan Africa', in Lee A. Tavis (ed.), *Rekindling Development – Multinational Firms and World Debt*, Notre Dame, IN: University of Notre Dame Press, pp. 103–17.

Kim, Kwan S. (1988b), 'Issues and perspectives in Tanzanian industrial development: with special reference to the role of SADCC', in M. Hodd (ed.), *Tanzania after Nyerere*, London: Francis Pinter Publishers, pp. 92–102.

Kim, Kwan S. (1993), 'An alternative strategy for equity with growth – case of Mexico', *Hitotsubashi Journal of Economics*, **34**(2), 47–68.

Kim, Kwan S. (1995), 'The Korean miracle (1962–80) revisited: myths and realities in strategies and development', in H. Stein (ed.), *Asian Industrialization and Africa – Studies in Policy Alternatives to Structural Adjustment*, New York: St. Martin's Press, pp. 87–143.

Kim, Kwan S. (1997), 'Income distribution and poverty: an interregional comparison', *World Development*, **25**(11), 1909–24.

Kim, Kwan S., Michael Shultheis and Robert Mabelel (eds) (1979), *Papers on the Political Economy of Tanzania – Studies in the Economics of African Series*, London and Nairobi: Heinemann Educational Books.

Lewis, Stephen (1986), 'Africa's' trade and world economy', in R.J. Berger and J.S. Whitaker (eds), *Strategies for African Development*, Berkeley, CA: University of California Press.

Maitra, Priyatosh (1996), *The Globalization of Capitalism in Third World Countries*, Westport, CT: Praeger.

Maxfield, Sylvia and Ben Ross Schneider (eds) (1997), *Business and the State in Developing Countries*, Ithaca and London: Cornell University Press.

Mengisteab, Kidane (1996), *Globalization and Autocentricity in Africa's Development in the 21st Century*, Trenton, NJ: Africa World Press.

Mkandawire, Thandika (1991), 'Crisis and adjustment in Sub-Saharan Africa', in Dahram Ghai (ed.), *IMF and the South*, London: Zed Books, pp. 80–94.

Mkandawire, Thandika (1992), 'The political economy of development with a democratic face', in Giovanni Andrea Cornia, Rolph van der Hoeven and Thandika Mkandawire (eds), *Africa's Recovery in the 1990s*, New York: St Martin's Press.

Onimode, Bade (1988), A *Political Economy of the African Crisis*, London: Zed Books.

Rodriguez, F. and D. Rodrik (1999), 'Trade policy and economic growth: a sceptic's guide to the cross-national evidence', NBER Working Paper 7081, National Bureau of Economic Research, Cambridge, MA.

Sapsford, D.(2001), 'The terms of trade of the world's poorest countries', mimeo, background note prepared for the Least developed Countries Report, 2002, pp. 142–3.

Schutz, Frederic P. and Anthony R. de Souza (1998), *The World Economy: Resources, Location, Trade and Development*, Upper Saddle River, NJ: Prentice-Hall.

Stein, Howard (ed.) (1995), *Asian Industrialization and Africa – Studies in Policy Alternatives to Structural Adjustment*, New York: St Martin's Press.

United Nations Department of Public Information (1993–4), *Africa Recovery*, **8**(3), December 1993–March 1994, 9.

UNCTAD (2002), *The Least Developed Countries Report 2002 – Escaping the poverty trap*, New York and Geneva: United Nations.

UNDP (2003), *Human Development Report 2003*, New York and Oxford: Oxford University Press.

UNECA (1988), *African Alternative Framework to Structural Adjustment Programmes for Socio-Economic Recovery and Transformation*, Addis Ababa: UNECA.

Winters, L. Alan (1999), 'Trade, trade policy and poverty: what are the links?', Background paper for World Development Report 2000/2001, Washington,DC.

World Bank (1979), 'The global framework', Staff Working Paper 355, September.

World Bank (1994–96 and 1998/99), *Global Economic Prospects and the Developing Countries*, Washington, DC.

World Bank (1995), *Trends in Developing Economies – Extracts:Vol. 3. Sub-Saharan Africa*, Washington, DC.

World Bank (2000), *Entering the 21st Century*, Washington, DC.

World Bank (2000/2001), *Attacking Poverty: World Development Report 2000/2001*, Washington, DC.

World Bank (2003), *Sustainable Development in a Dynamic World: World Development Report 2003*, Washington, DC.

World Bank (2004), *Making Services Work for Poor People: World Development Report 2004*, Washington, DC.

Yansane, Aguibou Y. (1996), 'Are alternative development strategies suitable for Africa to remedy its deepening crisis?', in A.Y. Yansane (ed.), *Prospects for Recovery and Sustainable Development in Africa*, Westport, CT: Greenwood Press, pp. 3–33.

Yeats, Alexander J. (1995), 'What are OECD trade preferences worth to Sub-Saharan Africa?', *African Studies Review*, **38**(1), 81–101.

Index